Employment Law

Going Beyond Compliance to Engagement and Empowerment

Rosemarie Feuerbach Twomey
Fairleigh Dickinson University

McGraw-Hill
Irwin

Boston   Burr Ridge, IL   Dubuque, IA   New York   San Francisco   St. Louis
Bangkok   Bogotá   Caracas   Kuala Lumpur   Lisbon   London   Madrid   Mexico City
Milan   Montreal   New Delhi   Santiago   Seoul   Singapore   Sydney   Taipei   Toronto

 **McGraw-Hill Irwin**

EMPLOYMENT LAW: GOING BEYOND COMPLIANCE TO ENGAGEMENT
AND EMPOWERMENT
Published by McGraw-Hill/Irwin, a business unit of The McGraw-Hill Companies, Inc., 1221
Avenue of the Americas, New York, NY, 10020. Copyright © 2010 by The McGraw-Hill
Companies, Inc. All rights reserved. No part of this publication may be reproduced or
distributed in any form or by any means, or stored in a database or retrieval system, without
the prior written consent of The McGraw-Hill Companies, Inc., including, but not limited to,
in any network or other electronic storage or transmission, or broadcast for distance learning.

Some ancillaries, including electronic and print components, may not be available to customers
outside the United States.

This book is printed on acid-free paper.

1 2 3 4 5 6 7 8 9 0 DOC/DOC 0 9

ISBN   978-0-07-302697-8
MHID   0-07-302697-2

Vice president and editor-in-chief: *Brent Gordon*
Publisher: *Paul Ducham*
Sponsoring editor: *Dana L. Woo*
Developmental editor: *Megan Richter*
Executive marketing manager: *Rhonda Seelinger*
Project manager: *Kathryn D. Mikulic*
Lead production supervisor: *Michael R. McCormick*
Design coordinator: *Joanne Mennemeier*
Media project manager: *Suresh Babu, Hurix Systems Pvt. Ltd.*
Cover design: *Mike Twomey, GraphicStorm.com*
Typeface: *10/12 Times New Roman*
Compositor: *Aptara®, Inc.*
Printer: *R. R. Donnelley*

Library of Congress Cataloging-in-Publication Data

Twomey, Rosemarie Feuerbach.
    Employment law : going beyond compliance to engagement and empowerment / Rosemarie
Feuerbach Twomey.
       p. cm.
    Includes index.
    ISBN-13: 978-0-07-302697-8 (alk. paper)
    ISBN-10: 0-07-302697-2 (alk. paper)
    1. Labor laws and legislation—United States. 2. Industrial relations—United States. I. Title.
KF3319.T96 2010
344.7301—dc22

                                                                                        2008044833

I dedicate this book to Dan.
Without his unwavering love, support, and
encouragement, this book would not have
been written.

About the Author

Rosemarie Twomey is a professor of legal studies in business at the Silberman College of Business, Fairleigh Dickinson University (FDU), in Madison, New Jersey. She received her JD from West Virginia University College of Law and practiced law in Morgantown, West Virginia, for 10 years before pursuing a full-time academic career.

She was a charter member of the Center for Human Resource Management Studies (CHRMS) of FDU. The objectives of CHRMS include (1) being an innovator and leader in partnering with business and (2) being a leader in integrating research and practice. More recently Professor Twomey helped establish the Institute for Sustainable Enterprise (ISE) at FDU as the superordinate organization of CHRMS. She was involved in founding a two-day professional development workshop, the Action Research Practitioner Series, at the annual Academy of Management Meeting that ran from 1995 through 2005.

Her research interests include employment law and global business, and her articles have been published in a variety of academic journals including the *International Journal of Organizational Analysis,* the *Employee Rights and Employment Policy Journal,* the *Journal of Global Competitiveness,* and the *North East Journal of Legal Studies.* Her articles have included "The Family and Medical Leave Act of 1992: A Longitudinal Study of Male and Female Perceptions," "Global Responses to the Employment Needs of the Disabled," and "Examining the Prima Facie Case in Mental Disabilities Discrimination Cases."

At FDU she was responsible for organizing and managing a campuswide, 17-event diversity theme semester. She initiated and managed a series of HR law roundtables, bringing together HR practitioners and lawyers from both the plaintiff–employee bar and the defendant–employer bar to discuss employment-related issues. She served on the university grievance committee, the college and departmental personnel review committees, and the university academic senate. For several years she was chair of the campus diversity council.

Professor Twomey teaches in the executive MBA and regular MBA programs at FDU. Among the courses she teaches are Legal Aspects of Workforce Management; Social, Political, and Legal Environment of Business; Society, the Legal System, and Ethics; and Field Study of Business, Culture, and Global Sustainability.

She is married to Daniel F. Twomey, professor of management, also at FDU. Together they initiated an innovative study-abroad business course for undergraduates that involves a two-week trip to Costa Rica, and they have taught this course for several years. They have four children with successful careers in education, journalism, law, and business in Connecticut, New York, and New Jersey—Mike, Teresa, Matt, and Luke.

Preface

Writing this textbook was the natural result of the author's teaching a course titled Legal Aspects of Workforce Management and her association and active membership in the Center for Human Resource Management Studies at Fairleigh Dickinson University over the past 18 years. As a result, the textbook incorporates management ideas and theories into each chapter, predominantly through the "Management Perspective" sections.

THE CHESS ANALOGY

Effective management of people in an organizational setting involves knowledge of the "rules of the game" and an appreciation of strategy. The best chess players value all of the pieces for the unique roles they play in any winning strategy. So, too, do the best human resource managers understand the laws that apply to the employer-employee relationship and, within that context, enable all employees to realize their full potential as they contribute to the goals of the organization.

Central Ideas

The book focuses on the laws that have the greatest impact on the behavioral relationships between employers and employees—in particular the common law governing the employment relationship, which has dramatically changed the application of the employment at will doctrine, and the many statutory requirements of fair employment practices that promote equal opportunity for all employees.

Organization and Key Objectives

The introductory chapters describe the framework and origin of employment laws, followed by the several ways that legal disputes are resolved. A separate chapter is devoted to mediation—a method that has a long history in other types of disputes, such as domestic relationships, and has only in recent years been embraced by the EEOC and applied more frequently in employment disputes.

Fair employment practices encompass the demands of federal and state statutes that carve out "protected classes" of people against whom employers may not discriminate. These laws are described in the remaining chapters and are presented chronologically, reflecting their development and evolution under federal law.

Within each chapter, and for each statute, Congress's reasons for adopting the law are given, and the key principles and requirements of the law are described and analyzed. Excerpts of cases are presented to further explain the principles and to illustrate how the courts apply these principles in actual situations. At the conclusion of each case, questions for discussion are provided.

Although the book is designed for an American audience with a focus on U.S. law, each chapter has a "Global Perspective" section that provides a snapshot of what is happening in other countries as they address societal concerns such as discrimination and other employment issues. Readers' appreciation of the laws governing employment can be enhanced by exposure to the nuanced treatment of workers in different political and cultural climates.

Each chapter concludes with a summary and a set of questions, some of which have extensive factual content. These questions provide a platform for class discussion about the numerous circumstances that give rise to legal disputes in the employment relationship. Instructors are encouraged to have students consider and use the "Management Perspective" sections to explore and comment on the behavior of the managers involved in the facts of each case. By consistently referring to such ideas and suggestions, students can strengthen their own competencies as they strive to become more effective managers.

Premise

This book is premised on three beliefs of the author. (1) Managers can gain a meaningful understanding of the laws that apply to the employer–employee relationship and the implications of those laws for how business is conducted. (2) To a great extent, compliance with employment laws is best accomplished by following effective management practices that include fair treatment of workers. (3) Understanding, appreciating, and following the spirit of employment laws—and not being unreasonably constrained or paralyzed by the letter of those laws—will contribute significantly to the strategic goals of any organization.

The law is sometimes seen as an impediment to efficient management—something not directly related to organizational goals. However, the objectives of the laws, particularly the laws governing the employment relationship, go hand in hand with the purposes of almost any organization. Managing people at work in ways that promote loyalty, motivation, creativity, and retention is not antithetical to the laws, but rather is synergistic with the spirit of those laws.

PEDAGOGY

Excerpted Cases

Excerpts of cases are presented to explain each chapter's principles and to illustrate how courts apply these principles in actual situations. Questions for discussion are provided to test readers' understanding of the principles and to encourage inquiry about how the facts led to the filing of a legal action against the employer and what behavior on the part of managers and supervisors might have averted the problem.

Management Perspective Boxes

Each "Management Perspective" box incorporates management ideas and theories to enrich the topic coverage within the chapter.

Global Perspective Boxes

"Global Perspective" boxes raise awareness and appreciation of the sociological and historical context of employment law, as well as promoting better understanding of different cultures in a shrinking commercial world.

Key Terms

Terminology critical to readers' learning is printed in bold type within the text and is defined in the margin at each term's first occurrence.

End-of-Chapter Questions

Several questions at the end of each chapter are available for classroom and individual use to strengthen the competencies needed by effective managers.

SUPPLEMENTS

Online Learning Center

- Can be accessed at www.mhhe.com/twomeyle.
- Includes an instructor's manual with answers to the end-of-chapter questions.
- Includes PowerPoint sets of instructional slides for each chapter.
- Includes test bank files for instructor use.
- Gives students access to chapter quizzes, created by John Tiede of Missouri Southern State University, to test progressive knowledge.

Acknowledgments

The author greatly appreciates the significant effort made by the reviewers of the drafts of this textbook. Their insight, experience, and suggestions were critical to the completion of the work:

Susan Boyd
University of Tulsa

Debra Burke
Western Carolina University

Teri Elkins Longacre
University of Houston

Michelle Grunsted
University of Oklahoma–Normal

Dan Krcma
Northcentral Technical College

Laurie MacDonald
Warren National University

Sal B. Marchionna
Triton College

James Morgan
California State University–Chico

Dr. John Poirier
Bryant University

Anne W. Schacherl
Madison Area Technical College

James Schindler
Columbia Southern University

James Sisk
Gaston College

John Tiede
Missouri Southern State University

The author also wants to thank Robert Richlan, J.D., the FDU attorney–librarian, who was always there when she needed him. Also, the author thanks the students who, over the past few years, have given freely of their time to help with various phases of this book.

Most of Chapter 4 was written by Teresa Marie Twomey, who, through her experience as a lawyer and expertise as a mediator, provided invaluable information and insights. Her review of other aspects of the book is equally appreciated.

Special thanks go to Sponsoring Editor Dana Woo (past, Kelly Lowery) and Development Editor Megan Richter (past, Kirsten Guidero), who have been diligent in providing me with guidance and information, and patient with me throughout the process. It has been a delight to work with them.

Thanks also to Andy Winston, who was my first contact at McGraw-Hill and who encouraged me in the earliest stages of the formation of this textbook.

Special thanks to Mike Twomey (GraphicStorm.com) for his generous and timely contribution in designing the cover of the book and to Drew Harris for his enthusiastic support and for coming up with the perfect title.

Contents in Brief

Preface   v

Acknowledgments   viii

PART ONE
Introduction   1

  1   Overview   2

PART TWO
Basic Legal Concepts and Forums   29

  2   Litigation   30

  3   Alternative Dispute Resolution:
Arbitration   51

  4   Alternative Dispute Resolution:
Mediation   68

PART THREE
**Employment Law and the
Common Law   89**

  5   Employment at Will   90

  6   Privacy Rights, Restrictive
Covenants, and Intellectual
Property   136

PART FOUR
**Reaching for Equal Opportunity Based
on Sex and Race   161**

  7   Civil Rights Act of 1964
(Title VII)   162

  8   Race and Color Discrimination   182

  9   The Civil Rights Act of 1991,
the Glass Ceiling Act, and the
Pregnancy Discrimination Act   205

  10   Sex Discrimination, the Equal
Pay Act, and the Civil Rights
Act   225

PART FIVE
**Reaching for Equal Opportunity Based
on Religion, National Origin, Age,
and Disability   255**

  11   Religious Discrimination   256

  12   National Origin Discrimination and
Immigration Issues   282

  13   Age Discrimination   306

  14   Disability Discrimination   334

PART SIX
**Employment Benefits and Family
Leave Law   353**

  15   The Family and Medical Leave
Act, Workers' Compensation, and
the ADA   354

Index   369

Contents

Preface   v

Acknowledgments   viii

PART ONE
INTRODUCTION   1

Chapter 1
Overview   2

Introduction   2
Judy's Art Studio   4
Laws That Impact Judy's Art Studio   4
The Major Laws Governing Human
Resource Management   7
Statutory Laws in General   9
Federal Statutory Laws   10
State Statutory Laws   13
Case Law   14
Constitutional Law   15
Administrative Law   17
Executive Orders   17
Potential Human Resource Problems in a
Changing Environment   19

PART TWO
BASIC LEGAL CONCEPTS
AND FORUMS   29

Chapter 2
Litigation   30

Introduction   30
Litigation of Employment
Discrimination Claims   30
Characteristics of Litigation   31
Adversarial Nature   31
Formality   32
Discovery   32
Public Nature   36
Trial by Jury   36
Appellate Review   36

EEOC Litigation   40
EEOC Procedures for Initiating a
Discrimination Case   43

Chapter 3
Alternative Dispute Resolution:
Arbitration   51

Introduction   51
The Rise of Alternatives to Litigation   52
Arbitration   52
Characteristics of Arbitration   53
The Federal Arbitration Act   56
Related Issues Involving Arbitration   58
The American Arbitration Association   60

Chapter 4
Alternative Dispute Resolution:
Mediation   68

Introduction   68
Mediation versus Arbitration   69
Types of Mediation   69
Ordinary Mediation   69
Transformative Mediation   69
Evaluative Mediation   70
Shadow Mediation   70
Benefits of Mediation   70
Drawbacks of Mediation   71
An Example of a Successful
Mediation Program   72
Mediation "Surprises"   72
Mediation and the National Labor Relations
Board (NLRB)   73
Mediation and the Equal Employment
Opportunity Commission (EEOC)   74
Statistics on EEOC Mediation   75
Internal Mediation Programs   75
Developing Internal Mediation Programs   75
Employer Considerations Regarding
Mediation   76
Mediation Outcomes and Appeals   79
How Mediation Fits in the Legal Framework   81

PART THREE
EMPLOYMENT LAW AND THE COMMON LAW   89

Chapter 5
Employment at Will   90

Introduction   90
When Does the Employment at Will Doctrine Come into Play?   93
Erosion of the Employment at Will Doctrine   94
Exceptions to the Employment at Will Doctrine   94
   The Public Policy Exception   95
   Breach of Implied Contract   98
   The Implied Covenant of Good Faith and Fair Dealing   101
   Violation of Statutory Law   109
Common Law Tort Violations   110
   Abusive (Wrongful) Discharge   111
   Intentional Infliction of Emotional Distress   111
   Negligent Infliction of Emotional Distress   114
   Fraud   116
   Defamation   118
   Self-Compelled Defamation   120
   Intentional Interference with Contractual Relations   122
The Model Employment Termination Act   125
What about Bullying?   128

Chapter 6
Privacy Rights, Restrictive Covenants, and Intellectual Property   136

Introduction   136
Employee Privacy Rights   137
   Public Sector versus Private Sector   137
   E-Mail   138
   Internet   139
   Camera Phones   139
Dilemma for Managers   140
HIPAA: Federal Legislation on Privacy Rights   142
Restrictive Covenants   147
   U.S. Policy against Restraint of Trade   147

Ownership of Intellectual Property   149
   Work for Hire: Independent Contractor   150
   Work for Hire: Employee   150

PART FOUR
REACHING FOR EQUAL OPPORTUNITY BASED ON SEX AND RACE   161

Chapter 7
Civil Rights Act of 1964 (Title VII)   162

Introduction   162
Legislative History and the Role of the Courts   163
Disparate Treatment and Disparate Impact Cases   163
   Defenses for Disparate Treatment Cases   164
   Defenses for Disparate Impact Cases   164
Affirmative Action   170
   Reverse Discrimination   170
   Public Sector: Constitution and Executive Order 11246   170
   Private Sector: Affirmative Action and the Civil Rights Act   174
   Retaliation for Exercising Rights under the Civil Rights Act   174
   The Civil Rights Act of 1866: Retaliation   175

Chapter 8
Race and Color Discrimination   182

Introduction   182
   Statistics   182
Defining Race and Color   184
   The Meaning of Race   184
EEOC Facts about Race and Color Discrimination   186
   Race-Related Characteristics and Conditions   186
   Disparate Treatment and Harassment in a Race Discrimination Case   191
Disparate Impact and Race Discrimination   194
Affirmative Action: Race Discrimination   197
   The Federal Sector   198

Chapter 9
The Civil Rights Act of 1991, the Glass Ceiling Act, and the Pregnancy Discrimination Act 205

Introduction 205
The Civil Rights Act of 1991 205
  The Civil Rights Act of 1991 and Mixed Motive Cases 206
  The Civil Rights Act of 1991 and Disparate Impact Cases 206
  How the Civil Rights Act of 1991 Changes the Disparate Impact Case 210
  The Civil Rights Act of 1991 and Expatriate Employees 212
  The Civil Rights Act of 1991: Expanded Remedies and the Right to Jury Trial 213
  The Civil Rights Act of 1991: The Glass Ceiling Act 213
The Pregnancy Discrimination Act of 1978 216
  Statistics on Pregnancy Discrimination Charges: EEOC 216
  The EEOC Takes Pregnancy Discrimination Seriously 218

Chapter 10
Sex Discrimination, the Equal Pay Act, and the Civil Rights Act 225

Introduction 225
Unintended Consequences 226
The Equal Pay Act of 1963 226
  Continuing Wage Gap 227
  EPA Remedies 227
  The EPA and the Civil Rights Act 227
Comparable Worth Theory 230
The Civil Rights Act of 1964 233
  Disparate Treatment and Disparate Impact Cases 233
  The Prima Facie Case 234
Sexual Harassment 238
  Quid Pro Quo Harassment 238
  Hostile Environment Harassment 239

  Same-Sex Harassment, Discrimination Based on Sexual Orientation, and Discrimination Based on Gender Identity 246
The Employment Nondiscrimination Act (ENDA): Proposed Legislation 249

PART FIVE
REACHING FOR EQUAL OPPORTUNITY BASED ON RELIGION, NATIONAL ORIGIN, AGE, AND DISABILITY 255

Chapter 11
Religious Discrimination 256

Introduction 256
What Constitutes an Employee's Religion or Belief? 257
What Constitutes Reasonable Accommodation for Religion? 258
The Workplace Religious Freedom Act 265
  Opponents' Position on WRFA 265
The Ministerial Exception 266
Public Sector Religious Discrimination 269

Chapter 12
National Origin Discrimination and Immigration Issues 282

Introduction 282
The Governing Statutes for National Origin Issues 283
Employers Must Determine Whether an Alien is Authorized to Work in the United States 284
  Defining Terms 284
  EEOC Guidance Regarding Documentation Considered Sufficient to Establish Authorization to Work 287
  Specialized Visas 288
  Developing Issues on Visas 288
National Origin Discrimination: Civil Rights Act (Title VII) 289
  The Meaning of "National Origin" 290
  English-Only Rules 291

*The Distinction between Citizenship and National
Origin Discrimination   293*
   Extraterritorial Application of Title VII   294
Rights of Unauthorized Aliens under
Discrimination Laws   297
   EEOC Guidelines   297

Chapter 13
Age Discrimination   306

Introduction   306
Statistics on the U.S. Aging
Population   307
Issues That Arise under the ADEA   308
The Bona Fide Occupational Qualification
and Other Exceptions or Defenses under the
ADEA   316
   Defenses under the ADEA   317
Remedies Available under the ADEA   321
The Older Workers Benefit Protection
Act of 1990 (OWBPA): An Amendment to
the ADEA   325

Chapter 14
Disability Discrimination   334

Introduction   334
Congressional Purpose   334
What Is a Disability under the ADA?   335
   Definition of "Person with a Disability"   336
   *Definition of a "Qualified" Individual with a
   Disability   336*

Essential Functions of the Job   336
Reasonable Accommodation   337
The Undue Hardship Defense   337
*The Three-Pronged Test to Enforce
Disability Rights   337*
*Employer's Decision Based on the
Disability   338*

PART SIX
EMPLOYMENT BENEFITS AND
FAMILY LEAVE LAW   353

Chapter 15
The Family and Medical Leave Act,
Workers' Compensation, and the
ADA   354

Introduction   354
The Family and Medical Leave Act of
1993   354
   Major Provisions of the FMLA   355
   FMLA 2008 Update   356
The FMLA, State Leave Laws, Workers'
Compensation, and the ADA   359
   Workers' Compensation   359
   The Americans with Disabilities Act   360

Index   369

Introduction

1. Overview

Chapter **One**

Overview

Here at New Lanark were neat rows of workers' homes with *two* rooms in every house; here were streets with the garbage neatly piled up awaiting disposal instead of being strewn in filthy disarray.... No worker was punished, and save for a few adult incorrigibles who had to be expelled for chronic drunkenness or some such vice, discipline seemed to be wielded by benignity rather than fear. The door of the factory manager stood open and anyone could (and did) present his objections to any rule or regulation. Everyone could inspect the book which contained the detailed report of his deportment ... And for the business-minded gentlemen ... there was the irrefutable fact that New Lanark was profitable, marvelously profitable.

The Worldly Philosophers, describing an 18th-century water-powered cotton mill in Scotland[1]

INTRODUCTION

The executives of the 18th-century company New Lanark Mills, just described, believed that treating employees with respect and an understanding of their needs was beneficial to both the employees and the company itself. There have always been employers that followed this philosophy, but unfortunately many have not. If the Lanark way had been widely followed over the years, there would likely be fewer laws today restricting employers' treatment of employees.

How an employer treats its employees is critical not only for the employees, but also for the success of the business. In addition, companies are increasingly evaluated by investors on the basis of social capital and what is often referred to as the "triple bottom line"—attention to people, planet, and profits. A recent four-year, multicountry study of CEOs examined the role and importance of corporate reputations and concluded, among other things, that "Among social responsibility initiatives, the treatment of employees will be the most important in the future."[2]

As a result of many abuses of employees over the years, companies in the United States now face a long and growing list of restrictions on management treatment of employees. Beginning in the 1930s Congress and various state legislatures enacted a multitude of statutes protecting employees. In addition to laws passed by legislators (*statutes*), courts have modified long-standing legal principles in employment-related cases, and in so doing have expanded employee rights, particularly in cases involving possible wrongful discharge. Therefore, employers are being challenged by both new statutory laws and new applications of *common law*—that is, the law found in judges' opinions. Common law employment cases involve charges of negligence, defamation, intentional infliction of emotional distress, and other forms of wrongdoing. Public policy is changing to recognize that employees are entitled to fair treatment from their employers whether they are in the public or private sector, in or out of a protected class, and in a union or nonunion setting. The role of the human resource manager has been made more demanding by the many laws governing employers and the concomitant increase in the number of lawsuits and threats of high damage awards.

In addition to the explosion of employment laws, other factors affect managers, such as the growing public awareness that ethical behavior is sorely lacking in many businesses, as evidenced by high-profile cases in the news such as Enron, Tyco, WorldCom, and others. Ethical questions and other societal concerns, such as exploitation of workers at home and abroad, have prompted the creation of new business paradigms and new ways of analyzing the value of corporations and other business enterprises by constructing "social responsibility" barometers. Throughout this book, we will explore these and other management ideas within the context of human resource management.

This book is founded on two premises: (1) Managers can understand in a meaningful way not only which laws apply to their businesses but also the ramifications of those laws to their businesses; and (2) adherence to laws need not be detrimental to an organization and in fact can be accomplished by following effective management practices. Such practices can facilitate the success of any organization's strategic plan while keeping the organization within the confines of human resource law.

To illustrate the impact of employment laws, consider the following scenario, which gives rise to several legal concerns.

Judy's Art Studio

Judy, a recent MBA graduate, opened an art studio. She and her husband owned a building that could be converted into a place to work on projects, space to store artwork, and a shop where the work could be sold.

Judy was the sole proprietor of the business. She purchased all the materials needed by the craftspeople and decided exactly what each person would produce, how much they were to produce, how the work was to be done, and in what time period. For their efforts, the artists were paid according to their time spent at the workshop, but this came to less than the minimum wage. Their products were sold in the shop; and when an item sold, Judy paid the artist for the piece and kept a commission for herself.

Judy considered the artists "independent contractors." She did not pay workers' compensation or unemployment premiums for them and did not withhold funds for income taxes. The artists were interviewed for the jobs in the art studio, and Judy had turned away several Spanish immigrants who lived in the same town in which the studio was located.

Judy also hired people for regular duties in the studio, such as cleaning and maintaining the building, bookkeeping, managing the artists, performing general clerical work, managing the shop, and keeping track of supplies and inventory. Judy considered these workers to be employees of the business. They were paid more than the minimum wage and enjoyed benefits such as health insurance and workers' compensation. Money was deducted from their paychecks for income taxes and Social Security.

Laws That Impact Judy's Art Studio

In an employer–employee situation many laws come into play, including wage and hour laws (minimum wage, overtime, child labor); workers' compensation laws; unemployment insurance laws; Social Security laws; laws prohibiting discrimination on the basis of race, creed, color, national origin, and sex; and disability discrimination laws. Similar laws exist at both the federal and state levels. Several legal issues are of concern in Judy's case; some of them are listed here.

1. Employee or Independent Contractor?

Judy is running a risk in treating her artists as independent contractors. Whether an arrangement is an employee–employer situation or an independent contractor situation is determined by law, not by the parties. The greater the employer's control, the more likely the worker is an employee rather than an independent contractor.

The Employer's Supplemental Tax Guide of the IRS[3] has the following to say about determining employee or independent contractor status:

> An employer must generally withhold federal income taxes, withhold and pay Social Security and Medicare taxes, and pay unemployment tax on wages paid to an employee. An employer does not generally have to withhold or pay any taxes on payments to independent contractors.
>
> In any employee–independent contractor determination, evidence of the degree of control and the degree of independence must be considered.

Behavioral control. . . . All of the following are examples of types of instructions about how to do work.

- When and where to do the work.
- What tools or equipment to use.
- Which workers to hire or to assist with the work.
- Where to purchase supplies and services.
- What work must be performed by a specified individual.
- What order or sequence to follow.

. . .

Financial control. Facts that show whether the business has a right to control the business aspects of the worker's job include:

. . .

The extent of the worker's investment. An independent contractor often has a significant investment in the facilities he or she uses in performing services for someone else. However, a significant investment is not necessary for independent contractor status.

. . .

How the business pays the worker. An employee is generally guaranteed a regular wage amount for an hourly, weekly, or other period of time. This usually indicates that a worker is an employee, even when the wage or salary is supplemented by a commission. An independent contractor is usually paid by a flat fee for the job. However, it is common in some professions, such as law, to pay independent contractors hourly.

The factors just listed are considered as a whole by judges. No single factor is determinative. According to law, it is likely that the artisans in Judy's studio would be considered employees. If Judy wishes to have the artists qualify as independent contractors, she should allow them to decide what they will create, how much they will create, when and how they will create it, and so on. Under such an arrangement, the individuals would be responsible for their own Social Security payments, their own unemployment insurance, their own medical and liability insurance, and so forth. Remember that the courts are not persuaded by a company's labeling of a worker as an independent contractor; rather, they analyze cases individually and consider many factors in making the determination.

The consequences of mislabeling workers as independent contractors in violation of the law could be severe for a small company like Judy's. At a minimum, back employment taxes with interest and penalties would be assessed against the company.

2. Antidiscrimination Laws

Depending on how many employees Judy hires, she may be required to comply with certain laws at the federal and state levels. To determine whether any of these laws apply, it is necessary to read the statutes. For example, the Civil Rights Act of 1964 prohibiting discrimination on the basis of race, creed, color, national origin, and sex applies to employers who have 15 or more employees.[*] If Judy sets up business in New Jersey, the New Jersey Law against Discrimination applies to all employers.[**]

If the law considers the artists to be employees, Judy's actions in turning away Spanish immigrants who applied for artist positions could be found to be illegally discriminatory, and the studio could be liable for violation of the Civil Rights Act if the total number of employees is 15 or more. If she has fewer than 15 employees, Judy must consider whether a similar state law applies to her business. For example, if the studio were located in New Jersey, that state's Law against Discrimination would apply.

To decide whether Judy has violated any antidiscrimination laws, several factors are significant. For example, what were Judy's criteria for hiring artists, and how consistently did she apply them to applicants? How did the Spanish candidates measure up to those qualifications? Were the qualifications necessary for the performance of the job? Was there any evidence that Judy had discriminatory motives, such as comments indicating a stereotypical attitude toward that class of applicants ("I don't think those people would understand what I want, and it would be too hard to train them")?

3. The Legal Nature of the Business and the Law of "Agency"

To the extent that the artists or other employees act or make decisions on behalf of the business, they are acting as *agents* of the business. For example, if one of the artists caused an auto accident during an errand to purchase supplies, the studio might be held liable for damages to anyone injured in that accident. The law considers actions occurring in the *course of employment*—that is, in furtherance of company business—to be in essence the acts of the principal (Judy/the business). Under the common law principles of agency, a principal (the *master*) will be held *vicariously liable* for the actions of someone acting on his behalf (the agent or "servant"). Because Judy is the sole owner of the business, her personal assets are at risk in a situation like this. If Judy were running the business as a

---

[*] *Employer* is defined in the Civil Rights Act as follows[4]:

For the purposes of this subchapter—

. . .

(b) The term "employer" means a person engaged in an industry affecting commerce who has 15 or more employees for each working day in each of 20 or more calendar weeks in the current or preceding calendar year, and any agent of such a person, but such term does not include (1) the United States, a corporation wholly owned by the Government of the United States, an Indian tribe, or any department or agency of the District of Columbia . . . or (2) a bona fide private membership club (other than a labor organization) . . .

[**] *Employer* is defined in the New Jersey Law against Discrimination as follows[5]:

(a) "Employer" includes any individual, partnership, association, corporation, business trust, legal representative, or any organized group of persons acting directly or indirectly in the interest of an employer in its relations to employees.

(b) "Industry" refers to any trade, business, industry, or branch thereof, or group of industries, in which individuals are employed.

partnership with others, their personal assets would also be at risk. This would not be the case if Judy set up the business as a limited liability company or as a corporation.

For similar reasons, agents acting within the scope of their authority have the power to bind the principal (Judy/the business) in contract. A contract of sale between an agent of the business and a customer is binding on the business. Therefore, if the shop's salesclerk wrongfully sells a work of art for less than its value, Judy is bound to that price for that customer.

The business's internal parties, of course, can make whatever rules or agreements they wish regarding matters among themselves.

4. Intellectual Property Law

The product involved in Judy's business is artwork that can be the subject of copyright law. Who holds copyright protection in the goods: Judy or the artists? For example, if a painting produced by one of Judy's artists were to be purchased and used in a commercial calendar, who would be entitled to the royalties? This is a matter of negotiation and contract agreement between Judy and the artists.

THE MAJOR LAWS GOVERNING HUMAN RESOURCE MANAGEMENT

Managers need not know about all the laws that have an impact on employment relationships. Not all laws apply to any single firm. What is important is that managers recognize which laws apply to their organization, what the primary objectives of those laws are, and how those laws affect the company and its goals.

FIGURE 1.1A
Sources of Federal Law

Federal Law Source	Examples
U.S. Constitution	First Amendment: the government cannot deprive people of their right to freedom of speech, religion, and the like.
Statutory law	Civil Rights Act of 1964: Employers cannot discriminate on the basis of race, creed, religion, national origin, or sex.
Administrative law	Department of Labor (regulations); Equal Employment Opportunity Commission (EEOC guidelines).
Executive orders	President Johnson's Executive Order 11246 of 1965, which prohibited discrimination on the basis of race, creed, color, or national origin by the government, by federal contractors, or by recipients of federal funds.
Case law	Federal court opinions.

FIGURE 1.1B
The Five Major
Sources of U.S. Law

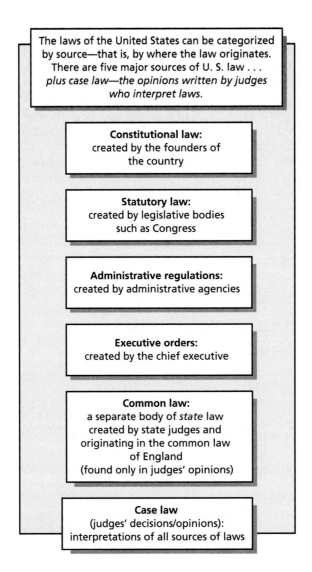

The laws of the United States can be categorized by source—that is, by where the law originates. There are five major sources of U. S. law . . . *plus case law—the opinions written by judges who interpret laws.*

Constitutional law:
created by the founders of the country

Statutory law:
created by legislative bodies such as Congress

Administrative regulations:
created by administrative agencies

Executive orders:
created by the chief executive

Common law:
a separate body of *state* law created by state judges and originating in the common law of England (found only in judges' opinions)

Case law
(judges' decisions/opinions): interpretations of all sources of laws

U.S. laws can be categorized according to their source. Hence we have the following:

1. *Constitutional* law set forth originally by the founding fathers and amended periodically by the designated process.
2. *Statutory* law enacted by legislative bodies (at the federal level by Congress, comprised of the Senate and the House of Representatives).
3. *Administrative* law created by government agencies such as the Department of Labor, the Occupational Safety and Health Administration, and so on.

FIGURE 1.2
Sources of State Law

State Law Source	Examples
State constitution	Many similarities to U.S. Constitution.
Statutory law	New Jersey Law against Discrimination: Employers cannot discriminate on the basis of race, creed, color, national origin, ancestry, age, marital status, sex, handicap, or sexual orientation.
Administrative law	Many similarities to federal agencies.
Executive orders	Governors' orders on various matters.
Case law	State court opinions.
Common law	"Law" created by judges and not found in the other sources of law, such as contracts, torts, and agency: Employment at will doctrine. Wrongful discharge. Defamation. Intentional infliction of emotional distress. Negligent hire. Negligent retention.

4. *Executive orders* created by the president or a state governor.
5. *Case* law.
6. *Common* law, which is a discrete body of law separate from all the previous sources, originating from judge-made laws adopted from England and retained within the jurisdiction of the courts.

   Common law is almost entirely state (as opposed to federal) law. The doctrine of *employment at will* (discussed in depth in a later chapter) is an example of common law, as is the law of **torts.**

   The following synopsis of laws relating to human resource management will give managers a reference point from which they can pursue further information about the laws affecting their organizations. These laws will be discussed in more depth in later chapters of this book.

torts
Civil wrongs, not associated with contract law, that result in injury to others, and for which the courts provide a remedy by requiring the wrongdoer to compensate the injured party.

Statutory Laws in General

Managers are advised to determine whether a particular law is a federal or state law and whether it applies to their organization. This can be determined by reading the specific language of each statute that defines *employer* for that law and that also states which organizations are exempt from its provisions. This information is normally found in the early paragraphs of a statute under the heading "Definitions." Frequently the definition of *employer* will state, among other things, the number of workers an organization must employ to be bound by the provisions of a statute.

FIGURE 1.3
Major Federal
Statutes Applicable
to Human Resource
Management*

Law	Public Sector (Government Is Employer)	Private Sector
National Labor Relations Act, 1935	X	X
Fair Labor Standards Act, 1938 (FLSA)	X	X
Equal Pay Act, 1963 (EPA)	X	X
Civil Rights Act, 1964, Title VII (CRA)	X	X
Age Discrimination in Employment Act, 1967 (ADEA)	X	X
Employee Retirement and Income Security Act, 1974 (ERISA)	O	X
Rehabilitation Act, 1973	X	O**
Immigration Reform and Control Act, 1986 (IRCA)	X	X
Worker Adjustment and Retraining Notification Act, 1986 (WARN or "Plant Closing Act")	O	X
Polygraph Protection Act, 1988	O	X
Americans with Disabilities Act, 1991 (ADA)	O	X
Civil Rights Act, 1991	X	X
Family and Medical Leave Act, 1993 (FMLA)	X	X
Uniformed Services Employment and Reemployment Rights Act of 1994 (USERRA)	X	X

Key: X = The law is applicable.   O = The law is not applicable.
* Federal law is applicable to private organizations that "affect interstate commerce" and meet the definition of *employer* in the respective statute.
** This law applies, however, to private companies that contract with the federal government (for more than a specified amount) or receive federal funding (as defined in the law).

Federal Statutory Laws

The U.S. Congress was given limited constitutional authority to enact laws regulating private businesses. However, its power has grown extensively over the years so that today people commonly accept that Congress can pass laws governing the private sector whenever a business entity engages in activities that affect interstate commerce—a requirement that is broadly interpreted—or any time such a law promotes well-recognized federal purposes, such as enforcement of fundamental constitutional rights.

The early labor laws, such as the *Fair Labor Standards Act (FLSA)* that guarantees minimum wages and overtime pay, and the *National Labor Relations Act (NLRA)*[6] that provides employees with leverage in bargaining with employers over terms and conditions of work, broke ground for the many employee rights statutes that followed. Today union employees enjoy the

collective bargaining agreements
The results of negotiations between unions and management over the terms and conditions of employment.

benefits of comprehensive **collective bargaining agreements,** which provide legal protection in virtually every facet of employment. Current issues arising under the FLSA include how to calculate overtime pay for employees who work at home under flexible work arrangements and whether recently discharged employees who are subsequently rehired on a consulting basis are independent contractors or are in fact employees. As we noted in the discussion of Judy's art studio, if they are employees and not independent contractors, the employer must provide certain federally mandated benefits.

A second wave of federal laws recognizing employee rights began with the enactment of the *Civil Rights Act of 1964.* That statute and its progeny—*Title VII,* the *Pregnancy Discrimination Act,* and the *Age Discrimination Act,* among others—have given certain protected classes (people of a particular race, creed, color, sex, national origin, or age) the right to challenge employers' actions on the basis of illegal discriminatory motives. Today's employers are usually aware of the need to abide by equal employment guidelines for selection criteria and to be conscious of the number of minorities they employ as well as the composition of the labor market from which their employees are drawn. The Civil Rights Act and its amendments are more fully explored later in this book.

The *Rehabilitation Act of 1973* protects the rights of the handicapped and applies to three types of employers: federal agencies; employers who contract with the federal government for $10,000 or more; and employers who receive federal financial assistance. In 1990 Congress passed the *Americans with Disabilities Act,* which prohibits all private sector employers that employ 15 or more employees from discriminating against disabled people. It was estimated when this law was passed that 43 million Americans could be categorized as disabled under statutory definitions.

The *Civil Rights Act of 1991,* an amendment to the Civil Rights Act of 1964, was passed specifically to reverse the effects of several U.S. Supreme Court decisions that had made it difficult for employees to win discrimination cases. Among the major provisions of this 1991 act are the following:

disparate impact cases
Cases in which unlawful discrimination may be found to exist even in the absence of a finding of intent, such as when there is statistical evidence that the percentage of an employer's minority workers is less than the percentage of qualified minorities in the relevant labor market—the population from which the employer draws its employees. The *Griggs v. Duke Power* case is an example of a disparate impact case.

- Plaintiff–employees can now pursue additional remedies, such as punitive damages, for intentional discrimination and unlawful racial and sexual harassment.
- The terms *business necessity* and *job related* were modified to place a greater burden on defendant–employers than that which the Supreme Court had required.
- Changes were made in the burden of proof required in **disparate impact cases.**
- Prior to the enactment of the 1991 act, an employee had to demonstrate that an employer's practice caused a disparate impact on a protected class; but under the 1991 act, if a plaintiff can demonstrate that the elements of an employer's decision-making process cannot be separated, the plaintiff can challenge the employer's entire system as "one employment practice." Therefore, employers must be prepared to defend their entire selection and promotion process, and they are advised to be keenly aware of the minority representation in their workforce as it compares to the minority percentage in the relevant labor market.

The *Family and Medical Leave Act (FMLA)* was passed in 1993 because of a perceived lack of employment policies accommodating working parents. Among other things, it was believed that the antidiscrimination provisions of the Civil Rights Act did not adequately address the dilemma faced by working mothers, to whom the primary care of children usually falls. The FMLA requires employers to grant leaves to employees (both men and women) for the birth or adoption of a child or for the care of a child, spouse, or parent who has a serious health condition. The Family and Medical Leave Act is more fully described in Chapter 15.

Amendments in 1991 to the *Immigration Reform and Control Act of 1986* encouraged an increase in the number of immigrants in the workforce. Problems posed by this increase include additional paperwork and reporting requirements, as well as concern over the act's antidiscrimination provisions protecting legal aliens.

Other federal legislation of concern to human resource practitioners includes the *Employee Polygraph Protection Act of 1988* and the *Worker Adjustment and Retraining Notification Act of 1988* (WARN). The polygraph law prohibits the use by private employers of lie detector tests either for preemployment screening or as a basis for discharging, disciplining, or failing to promote an employee. Among other things, WARN requires that private employers of 100 or more workers give employees a 60-day notice of a mass layoff or plant closing.

Case for Discussion 1-1

This case is an example of how the U.S. Supreme Court analyzes and interprets statutory laws. In *NU-LOOK Design, Inc. v. Commissioner of Internal Revenue,* the Court focused on two federal laws: the Federal Insurance Contributions Act (FICA) and the Federal Unemployment Tax Act (FUTA).

NU-LOOK DESIGN, INC. V. COMMISSIONER OF INTERNAL REVENUE, 543 U.S. 821, 125 S.CT. 60 (2004)[7]

Facts

Ronald A. Stark was the president and sole shareholder of Nu-Look Design, Inc. This home improvement company offered services such as carpentry, siding installation, and general residential home construction services to the public. Stark managed the company, performed necessary bookkeeping, and hired and supervised workers. The corporation did not withhold or pay FICA (Federal Insurance Contributions Act) or FUTA (Federal Unemployment Tax Act) taxes on Stark's income and did not give him a salary or pay him wages. Instead money was distributed to Stark as his needs required. The net income of the company for the years 1996, 1997, and 1998 was reported to the IRS. On June 8, 2001, the IRS issued to Nu-Look a Notice of Determination Concerning

Worker Classification under Section 7436, classifying Stark as an employee for purposes of federal employment taxes and stating that such taxes could be assessed for calendar years 1996, 1997, and 1998. Nu-Look filed for redetermination in the U.S. Tax Court. The Tax Court held that Stark was an employee and that Nu-Look was not entitled to relief. Stark appealed the Tax Court decision.

Issue on Appeal

**subchapter "S"
corporation**
A type of organization with limited liability (similar to corporations) that is taxed as if it were a partnership; therefore, the profits of the company are not taxed, and owners have limited personal liability.

Whether an officer and sole shareholder of a **subchapter "S" corporation** who manages the company, hires workers, and performs bookkeeping and other financial work for the company should be classified as an employee for FUTA and FICA tax purposes.

Decision

Yes. "Both the FICA and the FUTA impose taxes on employers based on the wages paid to individuals in their employ. 'Wages,' as defined by both Acts, include, with certain exceptions not applicable here, 'all remuneration for employment. . . .' Employment is 'any service of whatever nature, performed . . . by an employee for the person employing him. . . .' Employee is defined by the FICA as (1) any officer of a corporation; or (2) any individual who, under the usual common law rules applicable in determining the employer–employee relationship, has the status of an employee. Under the FUTA, the term employee, with certain exceptions not relevant here, has the same meaning as Sec. 3121(d) of the FICA."

Questions for Discussion

1. Why might Stark have believed that he should not be classified as an employee?
2. Based on your reading of this case, do you believe the meaning of the word *employee* differs from one law to another?
3. How would you describe the types of law involved in this case?

State Statutory Laws

When Congress enacts a major federal law, states often pass laws that are similar in content. For example, most states passed their own versions of the federal Civil Rights Act—a major antidiscrimination statute enacted in 1964. Although states often take their cues from federal legislation, they sometimes are the initiators and enact legislation before Congress considers similar bills. For example, at least 41 states had passed laws restricting or banning the use of polygraph tests in the workplace before Congress passed the Polygraph Protection Act; and at least 14 states had enacted parental leave statutes applicable to private industry before Congress passed the federal Family and

Medical Leave Act in January 1993, mandating unpaid leave for employees who request it upon birth or adoption of a child, or serious illness of self, spouse, or parents[8].

Today some states are considering various forms of unjust dismissal statutes restricting the right of employers to fire employees "at will." The at will doctrine is explored later in this chapter and in greater depth in Chapter 5.

Montana is the only state, to date, that has passed a statute limiting the effects of the employment at will principle. It is interesting to note that Montana's law does not require "just cause" for dismissal but rather limits the amount an employee can collect after a successful unjust dismissal charge. Additionally, the law requires employers to submit the issue to arbitration. A model Employee Termination Act has been approved by the National Conference of Commissioners on Uniform State Laws (an advisory body) to guide states that may be considering passage of such a statute. The model act prohibits dismissal of an employee without good cause; and like Montana's law, it limits damages and encourages arbitration of disputes rather than court review.

Some states have enacted statutes specifically designed to regulate drug and alcohol testing in the workplace. Most restrict testing of employees to instances where there is probable cause to believe that an employee is a user and that the employee's job performance is being affected. On the other hand, random drug testing is generally upheld when the employee is in a "safety-sensitive" position. The *Hennessey* case cited later in this chapter illustrates such a situation.

Case Law

After statutory laws are passed by legislators, it is up to the courts to interpret and apply those statutes to cases that come before them. Although legislators are careful to word laws as precisely as they can, it is not possible to predict all the circumstances a law may impact. Ambiguities and gaps in the laws must be dealt with by judges. The judges are bound by the clear meaning of a law; but when there is doubt, they must look beyond the language of a statute to try to understand what the legislators intended. The decisions of judges, especially those at the appellate level, become as binding as the express language of a law itself. In the U.S. legal system, the concept of *precedent* rules; that is, the logic and reasoning of prior decisions must be followed. Thus the refinements in the meaning of statutes constitute law created by judges, otherwise known as *case law*. This is true in both the federal and state systems of law.

There is a distinct difference between *case law* and *common law*. Essentially *case law* encompasses all the decisions made by judges in both the federal and state systems and contains interpretation and application of all categories of law, including *common law*. *Common law* (state law), found only in case law, includes *only* the discrete body of law that had its origins in England in the form of English common law (created by judges over time). The English common law was adopted by each state when it joined the United States. Unless and until common law is superseded by statute or another category of law, it remains in effect as common law. Areas of employment that remain under common law include keeping the workplace safe, not harming people or the property of others, contracting for services, and so on. To the extent that laws are passed by legislators, agencies, or others with the power to do so, changing, eliminating, or overriding common law principles, the newly created laws supersede common law. The common law regarding safety in the workplace, for example, has been modified by the federal Occupational Safety and Health Act.

To repeat this important point: *Case law* is all the opinions written by judges, and it covers all categories of law (constitutional, statutory, administrative, common, and executive orders). *Common law* can be found only in judges' opinions (case law), but it is the subset of case law that is not found in any other categories of law.

Constitutional Law

Constitutional law restricts the practices of government, not the practices of private industry. Therefore, private employers cannot violate the constitutional rights of their employees, except in unusual circumstances explained here.

Although constitutional law is not generally a concern of private employers in the area of employee rights, some legal arguments link constitutional law to private employers' actions. Such a nexus between constitutional law and private employers' actions was explored in a New Jersey case decided in July 1992. In *Hennessey v. Coastal Eagle Point Oil Company*[9], a discharged employee challenged the validity of the company's drug testing program by arguing that the constitutional safeguard against unreasonable search and seizure, as well as the *state's* constitutional right of privacy, established a clear mandate of public policy that the employer violated by random urinalysis testing of employees when there was no individualized suspicion of drug use.

A lower court agreed with the plaintiff's argument, but this decision was reversed on appeal. The New Jersey Supreme Court held in favor of the defendant company, balancing the company's interest in a safe workplace against the plaintiff's privacy rights.

In a *public policy* argument, a party relies on an established right or principle that has been violated. Although the right or principle is grounded in law (such as the Constitution), that law might not afford a legal remedy to the party who has been harmed. The plaintiff in *Hennessey,* for example, relied on the constitutional guarantee against unreasonable search and seizure and the state's constitutional right to privacy as the basis for his public policy claim. Note that the plaintiff's attorneys did not claim that the employer had violated the Constitution. Rather, they claimed that the defendant company's action was contrary to public policy as established by the Constitution's language. The court held in favor of the employer–defendant, pointing out that Hennessey's job was one in which a mistake (possibly caused by ingestion of drugs) could have catastrophic consequences; therefore, the invasion of privacy was justified. The reasoning of this decision, however, leaves open the possibility that an employee in a less safety-sensitive position might succeed in making a public policy argument similar to Hennessey's—even though the argument is grounded in constitutional law and the defendant is a private entity.

The notable exception to the premise that constitutional law applies only to government action is known as the *public function* doctrine. The U.S. Supreme Court has applied constitutional restrictions to private entities that perform acts of a public nature. For example, a private shopping center could violate the constitutionally guaranteed free speech rights of union picketers if it seeks to prohibit picketing at the shopping center. The rationale would be that the shopping center is so public an area that it is comparable to publicly owned land. Also, the closer the relationship between a private entity and the government, the greater the possibility that its activities can come under constitutional scrutiny. The public function doctrine was, however, significantly restricted by the U.S. Supreme Court in the *Hudgens v. NLRB* case in 1976.

Common Law and the Erosion of the Employment at Will Doctrine

common law
Judge-made law that is not found in statutes, agency regulations, or constitutional law. It is found only in the written opinions of judges as they decide cases involving certain types of legal issues, including agency, contract, and tort law.

As noted previously, **common law** refers to the body of law that is created by judges and is found only in judges' decisions. It is predominantly state law. In essence, it is the law that was adopted from English common law by the various states when they became annexed to the United States. For that reason, common law follows a different trajectory from state to state. In deciding the cases before them that involve common law, judges modify the law to reflect changes in society. In the employment relationship, the common law topics of agency, contracts, and torts are at the heart of many of today's lawsuits.

A subject of increasing litigation is the doctrine of employment at will—a common law principle with a long history in this country. Under the employment at will doctrine, either party can terminate an employment relationship for any reason or for no reason at all. Many workers are hired for a particular job at a specified wage, but there is no indication of how long the employee is expected to work; this is known as a *contract for an indefinite term*. In the absence of any law to the contrary, an employer may therefore dismiss an employee even when there is no just cause to do so. Many lawsuits involving charges of wrongful dismissal are premised on legal arguments grounded in common law; in other words, the plaintiff–employee bases his or her claim not on statutory violations or constitutional grounds, but on recent judicial trends that are modifying the common law in favor of employees. The doctrine of employment at will is the subject of Chapter 5, but its major premises are given here.

In recent years courts have held employers liable in at will situations when (1) a dismissal was found to have been contrary to public policy as argued in *Hennessey,* (2) the employer breached an implied contract promise or an implied covenant of good faith and fair dealing, or (3) the employer violated established tort principles. Courts in a majority of states have held that job security promises may constitute legally binding contracts even when this was not the intent of the company. Also, the common law equitable principle of **promissory estoppel** could be argued by employees in such a situation.

Note, however, that when termination decisions are based on sound business reasons, courts often recognize management's discretion and uphold the rights of employers.

In addition to the contract and public policy arguments, employees have asserted novel claims involving tort law. Employees have sued their employers for damages stemming from charges of fraud, intentional infliction of emotional distress, defamation, invasion of privacy, intentional interference with contractual relations, negligent hiring, and other tort theories. A successful tort action can be especially costly to an employer because the plaintiff may be awarded punitive damages—an option not available under contract law and only sometimes permitted under statutory law.

Managers are advised to ascertain the status of the doctrine of employment at will in the courts of their respective states, and anticipate its effect on their management practices. Chapter 5 more fully discusses the common law doctrine of employment at will and its numerous exceptions.

Administrative Law

Administrative law consists of the rules and regulations that emanate from the government's administrative agencies, such as the Equal Employment Opportunity Commission and the Department of Labor. At the national level these "laws" are found in the Code of Federal Regulations (CFR). Each day proposed and newly enacted regulations are published in *The Federal Register,* a daily publication originating in Washington, DC. Eventually the regulations are codified in the Code of Federal Regulations.

Executive Orders

Executive orders are laws created by the executive head of government: the president at the national level and governors at the state level. Their powers are limited by the federal and state constitutions, and their rulings (executive orders) cannot extend beyond their jurisdictions. Hence the president can issue orders that affect federal government agencies, entities that receive federal funding, and entities that contract with the federal government; but he or she cannot otherwise impose obligations on businesses in the private sector. Proposed and newly created federal executive orders can be found in *The Federal Register.* The orders are eventually codified in the Code of Federal Regulations.

promissory estoppel
A promisor cannot deny the benefits of a promise that he has made if a promisee has detrimentally relied on that promise. This theory is used when the promise is not supported by the elements of contract—for example, when no consideration is given in exchange for the promise. Promissory estoppel for a job security promise would be composed of the following facts that the plaintiff–employee must prove: (1) The employer made a promise of job security to the employee; (2) the employee reasonably relied on the promise; (3) the employer defaulted on the promise; (4) the employee was detrimentally affected (perhaps she quit her previous job and incurred substantial expenses and inconvenience in moving to a new location in reliance on the promise).

The role of the human resource manager has changed over the years, as has been noted by David Ulrich, a leading executive educator and author of several books about human resource management. As a featured speaker at the 2005 Society for Human Resource Management (SHRM) Annual Conference, he encouraged human resource professionals to transform themselves to increase their companies' value. His remarks were based on an 18-year global study of more than 29,000 HR professionals and line managers. Excerpts of his speech, focusing on the emerging role of the HR manager, follow[10]:

HR organizations are currently being split in two. Part of HR work deals with the administrative and necessary processes for organizations to operate. People have to be hired, trained, relocated, paid, and given benefits. Many of these tasks are standard, routine transactions that can be done more efficiently. And they are being increasingly done through service centers, e-HR, and outsourcing. The criterion for these administrative tasks is efficiency: doing more with less, thus reducing costs that add value to investors and customers. But HR is also about transformation not just transaction. . . . We have found that the transformation of HR does not end by putting in a new HRIS system or by forming centers of expertise. It requires a complete overhaul of the HR organization to assure that HR will be governed in a way to deliver on strategy.

***

. . . We have collected data for about 18 years from nearly 30,000 people on what makes a competent HR professional. We have collected this data in waves and across nearly all continents. We now can say with some assurance what HR professionals must know and do not only to be seen as competent by those who rate them, but also to contribute financial value to their firm. And the competencies are

- Strategic capability: HR professionals must help a company deliver strategy.
- Personal credibility: HR professionals must gain the trust of those they serve.
- HR mastery: HR professionals must become experts in their chosen domain.
- Business literacy: HR professionals must be able to communicate in business terms.
- HR systems: HR professionals need to learn to use technology.

***

A major reason I am choosing to stay in the HR profession is that we are the soul of our organizations. We continue to help the helpless and offer insight to those in need. We are about business and competitiveness and winning. But HR value is more than numbers; it is building the value of responding to a set of universal needs.

***

The universal needs for meaning, hope, learning, and relationships go beyond work, but work is the place where these relationships are played out in what Kenny Moore calls a universal language. Meaning comes as we articulate values and set visions; hope comes through our goals and strategies; growth comes via education, training, and job experience; and relationships come through mentoring, teams, and work design.

I am proud to be in HR because we offer meaning, hope, growth, and relationships to those we serve. Ultimately, we create organizations we are proud of, not just for the business value, but for their personal values.

Let us not lose sight of this remarkably important and enduring source of energy that unifies all of us in this noble HR profession. We create value for each individual who crosses our path or who is touched by our efforts. And as a result of our work, their lives are a bit richer and more abundant.

POTENTIAL HUMAN RESOURCE PROBLEMS IN A CHANGING ENVIRONMENT

Organizations have entered an era characterized by widespread global competition and technological advances affecting every aspect of business. As managers respond to the challenges posed by societal changes, they must be aware of the legal implications of their actions in an increasingly litigious environment. A major issue for managers is how to create a more productive workforce in a rapidly changing world while staying within the letter and spirit of a complex array of laws. In the following discussion, new and existing laws are applied to problems that human resource managers are likely to face. The problems are based on certain assumptions, and recommended strategies are presented.

A. *Assumptions*

The number of qualified entry-level applicants will decrease. Qualified applicants will be able to be selective. Employees who are not satisfied with their present positions will find it easy to leave for employment elsewhere.

Potential Management Problem

Employers will be tempted to offer more to qualified applicants and employees than they can deliver and thereby risk breach of contract claims by dissatisfied employees.

Recommended Strategy

1. Managers are cautioned not to make promises that cannot be kept. Statements made orally or in writing can be used against an organization by an employee claiming breach of implied contract promise or breach of an implied covenant of good faith and fair dealing.

2. When promises are made, abide by them. For example, if a company provides programs to help or reward workers, such as grievance procedures, training programs, or improvement periods, failure to follow through with such benefits can violate the law. If the policy of an employer is to

provide a period of close supervision for employees whose work is less than satisfactory, the employer should make a reasonable effort to do so before taking any disciplinary action or discharging the employee. Otherwise, a poorly performing employee could argue that termination violated the promise of help implicit in the policy. Without evidence of the promised assistance, an employer could lose such a case in spite of the employment at will principle.

B. *Assumptions*

Technological changes will multiply, with the following effects:

1. There will be rapid obsolescence of certain positions, necessitating either layoffs or retraining of desirable employees.
2. Incompetent employees with little potential for successful retraining will have to be identified and transferred, demoted, or terminated.
3. Ease of information storage and retrieval may lead to retention of unnecessary and possibly damaging information (such as personnel files containing irrelevant facts not related to an employee's performance).

Potential Management Problems

1. To remain competitive, employers may too readily exercise their prerogative to terminate their less desirable employees in a legal climate that has become more protective of employees.
2. Failure to abide by equal employment opportunity guidelines in the process of evaluating or laying off employees may lead to discrimination charges by employees in protected classes.
3. Unnecessary information in personnel files may harm an employer if it includes any notations that could be construed as having illegally discriminatory overtones.

Recommended Strategy

1. To retain the best-qualified personnel and preserve management's right to terminate unsatisfactory employees in a rapidly changing environment, the employment agreement should be in writing and clearly state that it is an employment at will contract. It is critical for an employer not only to state unequivocally that it is an employment at will situation, but also to ensure that handbooks, policy statements, and other communications to employees do not contain ambiguous statements that could be interpreted as implied promises. For example, listing behaviors that could lead to disciplinary actions and discharge could be interpreted to mean that discipline or discharge for any other reason violates the implied contract set out in a handbook.
2. To avoid wrongful discharge allegations, install a performance appraisal system that emphasizes accurate, objective evaluation of employees and that is demonstrably concerned with employee development and improvement. With a well-established and consistently applied performance appraisal system, accepted by and adhered to at all levels of the

organization, management will be in a better position to successfully defend against employee charges of unfair treatment.

3. Retain only job-related information in official personnel files. These files should be reviewed by several people and used for determination of an employee's future status, merit pay, transfer, or other employment decisions. Unrelated information (such as anecdotal information regarding an employee's behavior that is not job related) should be kept out of these files. Employers may face indefensible positions if evidence of discriminatory motives is presented in litigation or if it is unclear from the evidence whether an employee's dismissal or rejection was due to the job-related or the non–job-related factors. Under the 1991 Civil Rights Act, if the evidence in a case indicates that dismissal was the result of both discriminatory and nondiscriminatory reasons, the employer will be found in violation of the law, and the employer will be required to show that the nondiscriminatory reasons alone would have been sufficient to justify the firing decision. (See *Price Waterhouse v. Hopkins,* presented in Chapter 10, which was the decision that prompted Congress to enact this provision.)

C. *Assumptions*

An employee is hired as an administrative assistant. She performs well but occasionally becomes emotionally overwrought. She took 5 of her yearly allotment of 10 sick days in the first two months of her employment; these days were scattered throughout the two-month period.

Potential Management Problems

The employee's supervisor may note the excessive absenteeism and give the employee a warning of possible termination. If this is consistent with normal procedure or written policies, such action is usually defensible. If the supervisor ignores the absenteeism and makes no effort to inquire about possible problems, the company could face legal liability. If in fact the employee is suffering from a disability recognized by law, the employee may claim protection from discriminatory treatment or a failure on the part of the employer to accommodate the disability. The employee might argue that the company had reason to know about her health problems because of her frequent absences. Whether or not a court ultimately sides with the employer, it is wise to take such a matter seriously to prevent a lawsuit.

Recommended Strategy

Employers may not engage in medical testing before hiring, but they may insist on such testing after hiring as long as all employees are required to submit to such testing. If an employee's behavior indicates that there may be a medical problem—whether physical or mental—discreet inquiries may be made if the problem affects the performance of the employee. If it becomes apparent that the employee has a medical disability, discussions with the employee should be sought, and efforts to accommodate the disability should be made. Although it is clear that the courts will not require accommodation if an employer has no knowledge of a disability, employees have sued for accommodation based on factors that could have led an employer to know of the existence of such a disability. A case in point is *Miller v. National Casualty (1995)*[11], in which the employee presented a note from a nurse practitioner citing a diagnosis of "situational stress reaction" after an absence. During a subsequent absence, the employee's sister telephoned with the message, "She's falling apart. She's really lost it. We're trying to get her into a hospital." Although the court in this case held that these facts did not constitute sufficient information to tell the employer that the employee suffered from a manic depressive condition (thereby triggering the need to accommodate), another court might have reached a different result.

Global **Perspective**

Workplace Bullying—A Form of Harassment?

In the United States, if an employee is the subject of regular humiliation in front of colleagues, threats of dismissal, sarcasm, verbal abuse, intimidation, isolation, or similar types of targeted behavior, there could be a successful case against the employer based on sexual, racial, or other prohibited harassment. However, if the victim is not a member of a protected class, the case would probably be dismissed because there is no law prohibiting harassment per se. In other countries, such as New Zealand, Australia, and some European countries, such harassment itself is being discussed as the subject of express prohibition. Proponents of that view advocate that bullying should be included in legislation just like other forms of harassment.

N.Z. law already reflects a different perspective on the employment relationship than does U.S. law. Under the N.Z. Employment Relations Act of 2000, all workers can activate personal grievance charges for "being disadvantaged by some unjustifiable action by the employer." Even without legislation a judge could conclude that workplace bullying could be placed in the category of "disadvantage."

How much bullying goes on? In an article titled "Corrosive Leadership (Or Bullying by Another Name): A Corollary of the Corporatized Academy?"[12] academician Margaret Thornton writes, "A recent ACTU (Australian Council of Trade Unions) study found that the single most common source of workplace stress is bullying, and bossy and intimidating behavior from employers[13]. The ILO has found that complaints of bullying represent the fastest growing complaints of workers worldwide, with women especially at risk[14]. Bullying has been described as a 'new truth' about contemporary workplaces."[15]

Are many U.S. managers guilty of bullying? If so, unless done in connection with racial, sexual, or religious harassment, there is little likelihood of legal entanglement. However, a work environment that encourages or even permits such treatment contributes to lost productivity, poor morale, absenteeism, increased compensation claims, high staff turnover, and mistakes by workers who find it difficult to concentrate in such an environment.

Comparison of Protected Classes: United States and New Zealand	
New Zealand	**United States Federal Law**
Sex	Sex
Marital status	—
Religious belief	Religion
Ethical belief	—
Color	Color
Race	Race
Ethnic or national origin	National origin
Disability	Disability
Age	Age
Political opinion	—
Employment status	—
Family status	—
Sexual orientation	—

Note: There is lobbying in some U.S. states to pass a law that makes employment bullying illegal: "Legislation based on the model 'Healthy Workplace Act' has been proposed in approximately 12 states, including California, Connecticut, Hawaii, Kansas, Massachusetts, Missouri, Montana, New Jersey, New York, Oklahoma, Oregon, and Washington. Such a law would generally make abusive, bullying behavior tantamount to sexual harassment."[16]

Summary

Managers who perceive employment laws as a jungle of restraints that threaten the efficient operation of their business may inadvertently jeopardize their companies' success. But managers who understand the laws and their implications can design policies and programs that are fully effective as well as legally defensible, without regressing to needlessly bureaucratic and formalized systems.

Management personnel, educated in key aspects of the law, can share ideas and concerns more effectively with legal counsel and can incorporate legal perspectives into the company's strategic plan, ensuring a higher level of compliance with critical employment regulations.

Although managers need not be as well versed in legal detail as attorneys, any ambivalence or misunderstanding about the law and how it affects a business can lead to unnecessary dependence on legal counsel. Although employment laws are numerous and varied, they are a logical outgrowth of societal concerns with clearly stated purposes.

Because legal trends continue to favor greater protection for employees, employers should look closely at their human resource management systems, keeping in mind both the letter and the spirit of the laws regulating their organizations. Many firms are recognizing that good human resource strategy is valuable not only in preventing legal entanglements but also for an organization's long-term success. Furthermore, human resource management practices that respect the rights of workers are recommended not only because they are legally correct but also because they foster the loyalty and goodwill of employees—a major factor

23

in insulating organizations from costly litigation—and boost the standing of companies in social responsibility indexes.

The major points of this chapter are as follows:

1. Among the major sources of law that have an impact on human resource management in the United States are constitutional, statutory, and common law.

2. Constitutional law exists at both the federal and state levels. Government employees are protected by constitutional law, whereas private sector employees are minimally affected.

3. Statutory law at both the federal and state levels is codified law passed by legislative bodies, subject to executive veto power.

4. Definition of *employer* and *employee* in statutory laws is the most common way to determine whether a particular employer must comply with those laws.

5. Laws governing public sector workers differ from laws governing private sector workers. *Public sector* refers to government (civil service) employees. The public sector employee is protected primarily by civil service statutes, executive orders, and constitutional law. *Private sector* refers to employers with no ties to the government, and includes corporations, whether private or publicly traded.

6. Common law is judge-made law and is found only in court opinions. The most significant common law issues arising in employment cases involve exceptions to the employment at will doctrine.

7. The employment at will doctrine recognizes the right of employers to discharge an employee for any reason or no reason in the absence of an agreement to the contrary (such as that the employment is for a definite term). Likewise, this doctrine lets an employee end the employment relationship at any time and for any reason in the absence of a contrary agreement.

Questions

Note: For this chapter only, answers are provided for some of the questions because students have not yet been given sufficient information to fully address the issues raised.

1. In addition to the federal statutes prohibiting employment discrimination, state laws have similar prohibitions. Find out what some state laws are on employment discrimination in various states. Keywords with which to search include *civil rights, labor, industrial relations, employment, race discrimination, sex discrimination,* and so on.

   Find your own state's laws prohibiting employment discrimination by using traditional search engines such as Google and Yahoo! As a further exercise, try the following Web sites:

   a. Cornell Web site: http://www.law.cornell.edu/states (accessed February 17, 2008).

    b. Alabama law: How does Alabama deal with discrimination in employment? See http://www.wageproject.org/content/statelaw/al.php (accessed May 31, 2007).

    c. Florida law: How does Florida's antidiscrimination statute define *employer?* See http://www.FindLaw.com (accessed May 31, 2007). *Follow these instructions:* Go to the FindLaw Web site. Under "Research the Law," click on "Jurisdictions." Scroll down and click on "Florida." Scroll down and click on "Primary Materials—Cases, Codes, and Regulations." Click on "Florida Statutes." Scroll down and click on "Title XLIV." Under "Title XLIV," click on "Part 1." Click on "760.02."

2. David Ulrich (see the Management Perspective box) emphasizes the need to focus on employees. Does focusing on profit necessarily mean that employees or others must be shortchanged? Be prepared to discuss the implications of such a focus.

3. What are the effects of a policy that treats labor as a fixed cost rather than a vital resource?

4. The following scenarios and questions illustrate the fact that employment law varies from country to country. Here we compare U.S. laws with those of New Zealand. The first scenario reflects a U.S. case involving charges of sexual harassment, and the second involves a wrongful dismissal argument. Under U.S. law, the first is a statutory case and the second is a common law case.

Scenario One

Liz H. worked as a salesperson in a division of ABC Chemical. After 15 months she quit her job and subsequently filed suit claiming sexual harassment. Among other things, her boss, Andrew B., invited her to a hotel lounge on a business trip, at which time he made a comment about her breasts. When Liz gave him no encouragement, he said she should "loosen up" and warned, "You know, Liz, I could make your life very hard or very easy at ABC." Later, during an interview for promotion, Andrew expressed reservations because she was not "loose enough," after which he reached over and rubbed her knee. When Andrew called her to inform her she was promoted, he said to her, "You're gonna be out there with men who work in factories, and they certainly like women with pretty butts/legs." Although ABC had a policy prohibiting sexual harassment, Liz did not report these actions during her employment. This scenario is based on the *Burlington Industries v. Ellerth* Supreme Court decision presented in Chapter 10.

    a. If Liz brought a lawsuit based on these facts, what would be the legal basis (or cause of action) for Liz's complaint?

    Answer: Cause of action—sex discrimination under Title VII of the Civil Rights Act of 1964 (or a similar state law). This scenario is based on a U.S. Supreme Court decision. There are two types of sexual harassment: quid pro quo and hostile environment. *Quid pro quo* requires a finding that an employee was denied employment, a promotion, a raise, or the like because of his or her refusal to grant requested sexual favors. *Hostile environment* requires a finding that behavior of the harasser and/or the employer was pervasive or severe enough to interfere with the ability of the harassed person to perform his or her job functions.

b. What should the court decide?

Answer: The court should decide in Liz's favor. Although Liz was promoted and therefore was not clearly subjected to an adverse employment decision because she did not go along with her boss's desires, the behavior was found to be pervasive enough to cause her to quit—in other words, severe enough that a reasonable person in her situation would find it difficult to work.

Another issue that comes up in these cases and was put to rest by the Supreme Court was the fact that an employee who is subjected to sexual harassment need not prove psychological harm to succeed in this type of action.

c. List some practices, policies, and behaviors on the part of the company that could have prevented a lawsuit in this case.

Answer: (Many answers are possible. Here are some examples.) Be certain there is a reporting system that does not require complaints to be lodged with the immediate supervisor. Preferably there should be an objective third party with whom a person can register concerns of this type. Sexual harassment training should be implemented. Key personnel should be required to undergo such training.

Distinctions between N.Z. and U.S. Laws

N.Z. employment law would entertain a cause of action based on breach of contract or unjustifiable dismissal (constructive dismissal) for this type of case. There is no comparable statutory cause of action for sexual harassment. N.Z. law requires both parties to an employment contract to act in good faith.

Scenario Two

Gerard F. was employed for about six years as a technician for an oil company. At the time of hiring he was told that the employment would probably be available for approximately 20 years. The company gave Gerard a handbook that was revised from time to time during the years of Gerard's employment. The handbook described the company's progressive discipline system. Gerard had been summoned to a meeting once for reasons that were unclear, but they had to do with his "attitude." When a better position opened up and Gerard applied and was rejected, he was told that it was because of his obstinate and uncooperative behavior toward his supervisors and fellow employees. He was reassigned to a different position that required periodic meetings. When Gerard missed one of these meetings without notifying anyone, he was reprimanded and a letter was placed in his file. His explanation for missing the meeting was that he took medication for pain and passed out before the meeting. Others who had missed meetings had not received such reprimands. The company's handbook required a counseling session before a letter could be placed in an employee's file. Later Gerard was required to take instructions from a fellow technician (a lead technician on a project). He complained about this, and subsequently the company claimed that he failed to perform in accordance with the lead technician's instructions. Gerard denied any insubordination. After this event Gerard was fired. At the discharge session he was not given a written notice of termination as required by the supervisor's manual. Gerard requested a meeting with the next level of supervision to discuss matters. He was accompanied by his attorney. However, his attorney was not permitted to attend. Gerard filed suit charging wrongful termination and argued that the dismissal was in reality based on a personality conflict with his manager. This scenario is based on *ARCO v. Akers,* 753 P.2d 1150 (1988), a decision of the Alaska state courts.

a. What was the legal basis (or cause of action) for Gerard's complaint, and what type of law was involved?

Answer: The cause of action was wrongful discharge based on breach of contract and breach of the covenant of good faith and fair dealing. The type of law involved is common law, which is state law found only in state court precedent (past decisions) and not in statutory, constitutional, or administrative law.

b. What should the court decide?

Answer: The court must follow the precedent of the state (Alaska in the actual case on which this hypothetical situation is based) in common law. Alaska recognizes that a covenant of good faith and fair dealing exists in employment relationships where a contract controls. The fact that the position was expected to last for approximately 20 years and the fact that the employees were given handbooks governing the relationship were important criteria in finding for Gerard. The written progressive discipline procedures were not followed, and there was evidence that a jury could construe bad faith and unfairness on the part of the company managers.

c. In a case such as this, should the court award punitive damages?

Answer: In the actual case the trial court jury awarded punitive damages of $125,000 in addition to compensatory damages of $51,390. However, on appeal, the punitive damages were struck. The court held that this was a contract case, and as such punitive damages were inappropriate.

d. List some practices, policies, and behaviors on the part of the company that could have prevented a lawsuit in this case.

Answer: (Again, many answers are possible.) Employers can state unequivocally in writing that their handbook is not a contract that limits the discretion of management; that is, the company retains the right to discharge an employee for behavior that it deems disruptive, threatening, or the like. Also, when there is a clear set of progressive discipline procedures, these should be followed consistently.

Distinctions between N.Z. and U.S. Laws

U.S. law looks to the law of contract and the judicial exceptions to the employment at will doctrine; this is common law (not federal law) and lies within the jurisdiction of the state courts.

N.Z. law looks to its federal employment law, which requires good faith in all employment relationships. New Zealand focuses on the constructive dismissal aspect of a case under its employment law—whether there is a breach of implied duty of mutual trust and confidence and whether an employer treated an employee fairly.

References

1. R. L. Heilbroner, *The Worldly Philosophers,* 3rd ed. (New York: Simon & Schuster, 1967), p. 98.

2. P. J. Kitchen, "Managing Reputation on a Global Basis," *Competitiveness Forum* 1, no. 1 (2003), p. 573.

3. IRS Publication 15-A (1/2007 Employer's Supplemental Tax Guide). See http://www.irs.gov/publications/p15a/index.html (accessed July 8, 2007).

4. Civil Rights Act of 1964, 42 U.S.C. Subchapter 21, Sec. 2000e.

5. New Jersey Law against Discrimination, *N.J.S.A. Title 10:1–12.*

6. Fair Labor Standards Act of 1938 and National Labor Relations Act of 1935. See www.dol.gov/esa/whd/flsa and www.nlrb.gov/workplace_rights, (accessed July 8, 2007).

7. *Nu-Look Design Inc. v. Commissioner of Internal Revenue,* 543 U.S. 821, 125 S.Ct. 60 (2004).

8. R. F. Twomey, "Family and Parental Leave Statutes: A Status Report," *North East Journal of Legal Studies* 1, no. 1 (Spring 1993), pp. 80–102.

9. *Hennessey v. Coastal Eagle Point Oil Co,* 129 N.J. 81 (1992).

10. D. Ulrich, Speech at SHRM 2005 Conference. See www.citehr.com/what-is-next-for-hr-by-david-ulrich-phd-vt35732.html (accessed July 8, 2007).

11. *Miller v. National Casualty,* 61 F.3d 627 (1995), U.S. App. LEXIS 20190, at *629.

12. M. Thornton, "Corrosive Leadership (Or Bullying by Another Name): A Corollary of the Corporatized Academy?" *Australian Journal of Labour Law* 17 (August 2004), 2004 AJLL LEXIS 9.

13. ACTU, OHS Unit, "Stop Stress at Work (Draft for Discussion)," October 2000. See http://www.workstress.net/downloads/aussiestressguide.doc, (accessed July 8, 2007).

14. "When Working Becomes Hazardous," *World of Work: The Magazine of the ILO* 26 (1998). See also www.ilo.org/publicenglish/bureau/inf/magazine/26/violence.htm (accessed July 30, 2004).

15. C. Hatcher and P. McCarthy, "Workplace Bullying: In Pursuit of Truth in the Bully–Victim–Professional Practice Triangle," *Aust J Communication* 29 (2002), p. 45.

16. Taken from "What Employees Consider to Be Bullying Behavior May Surprise You," *Employment Law Today,* May 8, 2007. See http://www.ahipubs.com/newsletter/ht05.09.07.html (accessed June 1, 2007).

Bibliography

Portions of this chapter were printed first in *Business Forum:* Twomey, R. "Changing Environment Requires Strategic Human Resource Planning to Prevent Employee Lawsuits." *Business Forum* 22, no. 2 (Spring/Fall 1997).

Part Two

Basic Legal Concepts and Forums

2. Litigation
3. Alternative Dispute Resolution: Arbitration
4. Alternative Dispute Resolution: Mediation

Chapter **Two**

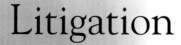

Litigation

Litigation: a machine which you go into as a pig and come out as a sausage.

From *The Devil's Dictionary,* Ambrose Bierce[1]

It is not illegality that fuels employee lawsuits, but rather employee anger arising from perceived unfair treatment. Placing a legal label, such as discrimination or retaliation, on the seeming unfairness occurs afterward.

Maxine Neuhauser[2]

INTRODUCTION

Legal disputes begin with complaints filed in courts of law by people who seek a redress of grievances, believing they have been harmed by another's violation of law. This method of dispute resolution is known as *litigation.* Litigation is also referred to as *adjudication* in a court of law or use of the *judicial process.* All other forms of dispute resolution are known collectively as methods of *alternative dispute resolution (ADR).*

Not every lawsuit filed results in a trial before a judge and jury. In fact, fewer than 2 percent of all cases filed in federal court end in trial. Many legal actions are settled before trial—many of these in an ADR forum such as arbitration or mediation, which can be quite successful[3].

This chapter describes the litigation process, particularly with regard to employment disputes.

LITIGATION OF EMPLOYMENT DISCRIMINATION CLAIMS

As just stated, the first step in a civil lawsuit is the filing of a complaint in the appropriate court. For most employment-related disputes, however, resort to the courts is somewhat indirect because the plaintiff–employee is required to file a charge with the Equal Employment Opportunity Commission (EEOC) before initiating a private lawsuit.

The EEOC is a federal administrative agency created by Congress to oversee and guide the enforcement of several federal statutes: Title VII of the Civil Rights Act (protection based on race, creed, color, national origin, and sex), the Americans with Disabilities Act (ADA), and the Age Discrimination in Employment Act (ADEA).

An employee with a cause of action arising under the Civil Rights Act, the ADA, or the ADEA must file his or her grievance with the EEOC within 180 days from the date of the violation. In legal terms, this period is known as the **statute of limitations.**

statute of limitations
Rule that specifies a maximum period for an aggrieved party to initiate a lawsuit. This time limit varies with the type of case presented; for example, the statute of limitations for filing a contract dispute in a court of law differs from an employment discrimination suit. In many jurisdictions the statute of limitations is six years for a contract action.

If a state has a law similar to the Civil Rights Act and has established an agency to enforce that law (referred to by the EEOC as a *fair employment practices agency* or FEPA), the employee can file with either that state agency or the EEOC. In cases filed with the EEOC, the EEOC will "dual file" with the corresponding state agency to avoid duplication of effort. The case will be handled by the agency with which the employee filed the charge.

When filing an employment discrimination claim, an employee must provide the following information[4]:

- The employee's name, address, and telephone number.
- The name, address, and telephone number of the respondent employer, employment agency, or union that is alleged to have discriminated, and the number of employees (or union members), if known.
- A short description of the alleged violation (the event that caused the complaining employee to believe that his or her rights were violated).
- The date(s) of the alleged violation(s).

The EEOC investigates the charges and determines whether there is reasonable cause to believe that discrimination has occurred. If it finds reasonable cause, it attempts to conciliate or mediate the dispute between the charging employee and the employer. If conciliation or mediation is not successful, the EEOC may litigate the suit in federal court. However, if the EEOC does not find reasonable cause, it issues a *notice of right to sue* to the employee. When a complainant receives such a notice, he or she can initiate a lawsuit in court.

CHARACTERISTICS OF LITIGATION

Adversarial Nature

Litigation is an adversarial process. Lawyers are taught that, under the attorneys' code of ethics, they must represent their clients "zealously." It is therefore not unusual for lawyers to encourage litigation over other methods of dispute resolution. The adversarial nature of lawsuits tends to drive parties further apart as they go deeper into the complexities and intricacies of the trial preparation phase and beyond. For this reason, if the parties desire to preserve the relationship, litigation is not the ideal path to follow.

Managers may or may not have a real choice of whether to settle a case rather than pursue it in court (litigation). The employee–plaintiff may insist on taking the matter to a jury and resist all attempts to settle. If the employer has taken all precautions to avoid a trial and has adequate documentation of facts to support its case against the employee, it may prevail at trial—but not without a loss of productive work time and possible reputation damage by the public exposure a trial can bring. Therefore, it is in the best interest of employers to operate their businesses in such a manner that employees will not be inclined to resort to lawsuits to resolve workplace disagreements with the company.

However, a compelling reason for employers to pursue a case through litigation, rather than settle the case, is to obtain a decision that will set precedent. For example, if a statute does not clearly say whether it pertains to certain situations, the company may want to try a case to get a definitive ruling on the matter. Likewise, if employees believe that bringing suit against their employer will result in a settlement award, regardless of whether or not they have good reason to sue, the employer may want to litigate to discourage such actions.

Formality

Litigation of a case in a trial court before a jury consists of numerous formal procedures, rules of evidence, and time-consuming efforts in retrieving records and supplying testimony of parties and witnesses, as well as stress for all parties involved. An appreciation of the nature of litigation and its process can help managers and key personnel prepare for trial when other alternatives are either undesirable or unavailable.

Litigation is governed by codified rules of procedure that apply at every stage of a lawsuit, from the initial filing of a complaint to the closing of a case by court decision or settlement by the parties. The primary purpose of these rules of procedure is to ensure fairness to all parties in the process.

Discovery

Unlike other methods of resolving legal disputes, litigation encourages and strongly supports a pretrial period in which the attorneys engage in a *discovery* process. The aim of discovery is to find out as much as possible about the facts of the case. The full power of the court can be brought to bear on parties who do not comply with requests for information during this process. In other words, the judge presiding over the case can issue orders to compel production of documents, order parties to cooperate in the discovery process, order parties to submit to medical examinations or to appear in court on a specific date, and so on. Failure to comply with a court order can lead to criminal sanctions for contempt of court, including jail terms. Additionally, a judge can simply decide a case against a party who fails to comply with court orders and can assess punitive damages for such behavior.

The more that is discovered about a case, the more likely the parties will settle before trial—an outcome that judges deem desirable. Through the process

deposition
Face-to-face session at which parties and witnesses are questioned by the attorneys in the presence of a court official who records the testimony so that it will be available for a trial.

of discovery, evidence is obtained and preserved for trial while it is fresh in witnesses' and parties' minds. Witnesses who might not be available for trial can answer questions in a formal **deposition,** which can be made available at trial in the absence of the witness. Depositions are also routinely taken from any party simply to preserve fresh evidence, obtain information relevant to a case, and have documented evidence of witnesses' and parties' statements that can be used to attack the credibility of those who give contradictory information when on the witness stand in trial.

When depositions are requested, the parties' attorneys will meet with the people who are to be deposed to prepare them for the session. It is critical that employees who will be witnesses for the employer understand the significance of the deposition and that they be adequately briefed before the date of the deposition. The deposition will be formally conducted, and the person being deposed will not have the luxury of asking for help from an attorney during the questioning.

Requests for information can take various forms. In addition to depositions, attorneys can request voluminous records from the opposing party by means of **interrogatories;** subpoenas of documents can be ordered; requests for mental and physical examinations can be made; and so on. Discovery sometimes provides an opportunity for more powerful parties to overwhelm opponents and wear them down to a point at which they will either give up or agree to a settlement. It is this abuse of discovery to which former California Attorney General EvelleYounger referred when she stated, "An incompetent attorney can delay a trial for months or years. A competent attorney can delay one even longer."[5]

interrogatories
Sets of written questions that are sent to the opposing party. The party must answer the questions and may obtain advice from counsel while doing so. Note that interrogatories are sent to the parties in the legal action, not to witnesses.

The formal rules of procedure during a trial require the services of an experienced, knowledgeable litigator—an attorney who is familiar with the facts of the case, the nature of the proceeding, the parties before the court, the judge, and the nuances of court strategies. There is no substitute for a competent, experienced litigator. Unless the employer and the HR manager trust and work well with their attorney, it may be advisable to seek a different legal representative.

With regard to document retrieval, in addition to the utility of adequate documentation to defend employers' decisions when they are challenged, the HR manager must be aware of the record-keeping requirements of several laws. (See Figure 2.1.) Also, the 2006 *EEOC v. Target Corp.* decision discussed in Case for Discussion 2-1 reveals new factors regarding the current state of the law on this issue.

The following advice regarding record keeping was presented by Elizabeth J. McNamee in an article titled "Avoiding Record Keeping Pitfalls."[6]

Litigation Rituals

- Ensure that requests for documents are specific and that there is appropriate follow-up (that the individual(s) assigned the task of locating the documents actually exhaust all avenues in their search for the documents).
- Distribute copies of document requests to all interested people. This action will limit the amount or level of miscommunication that may occur concerning requested documents.

FIGURE 2.1   **Federal Records Retention Chart**[7]

RECORDS TO BE RETAINED	PERIOD OF RETENTION
1. *Title VII, Civil Rights Act of 1964.*	
a. Application forms and records for hiring, promotion, demotion, transfer, layoff or termination, rates of pay or terms of compensation and selection for training, but not for temporary or seasonal work (29 CFR 1602.14).	a. Six months from date personnel action taken, whichever is later.
b. Records relevant to legal action by employee, e.g., test papers, application forms by all candidates for position.	b. Until final disposition of charge or action.
c. Apprenticeship programs: (1) Chronological list of names, addresses of applicants, dates, sex and minority group identification. (2) Any other record made solely for completing EEO-2 or similar reports (29 CFR 1602.20(b)).	c. (1) Two years from date application received, or period of successful applicant's apprenticeship, whichever is longer; (2) one year from date of report.
d. Employers with 100 or more employees: Copy of EEO-1, Employer Information Report (29 CFR 1602.7).	d. Most recent report to be kept at unit or division headquarters.
2. *Executive Order 11246.* Federal contractors, subcontractors: Affirmative action programs and supporting documents, including work force analysis and utilization evaluation; records and documents on nature and use of tests, validations of tests, and test results; records pertaining to construction industry EEO plans and requirements (41 CRF 60-1.7).	Not specified.
3. *Age Discrimination in Employment Act of 1967.*	
a. Payroll or records containing employee's name, address, date of birth, occupation, rate of pay and compensation per week.	a. Three years.
b. Records relating to (1) job applications, resumes or other replies to job ads, including for temp positions and records pertaining to failure or refusal to hire; (2) promotion, demotion, transfer, selection for training, layoff, recall or discharge; (3) job order to agencies or union; (4) aptitude or other employer-administered tests; (5) physical.	b. One year from date of personnel action to which record relates, except 90 days for application forms and other preemployment records of applicants for temporary jobs.
c. Examination results considered in connection with personnel actions; (6) job ads or notices to public or employees about openings, promotions, training programs, or opportunities for overtime work (29 CFR 1626.3).	
d. Benefit plans, written seniority or merit rating systems. Note: If not in writing, summary memorandum to be kept. (29 CFR 1627.3).	d. Full period that plan is in effect plus one year after termination.

FIGURE 2.1   Federal Records Retention Chart[7] (*Continued*)

e. Personnel records, including above, relevant to enforcement action brought against employer. Note: No particular form specified (29 CFR 1627.3).	e. Until final disposition of action.

4. Immigration Reform and Control Act of 1968.
INS Form I-9, Employment Eligibility Verification Form (8 USC 1324A(b)(3)). Note: INS Form I-9, signed by new-hire and employer, to be readily available upon request.

Three years after date of hire or one year after date of employee's termination, whichever is later.

5. Fair Labor Standards Act (and Equal Pay Act).
a. Basic records containing employee information, payrolls, individual contracts or collective bargaining agreements, applicable certificates and notices of Wage-Hour administrator, sales and purchase records (29 CFR 516, 29 CFR 1620.32).
b. Supplementary basic records, including basic employment and earnings records; wage rate tables; work time schedules; order, shipping and billing records; records of additions to or deductions from wages paid; and documentation regarding any wage differential to employees of opposite sex in same establishment (29 CFR 1620.32).
c. Certificates of age (29 CRF 516).
d. Written training agreements (29 CFR 516).

Note: No particular form specified (Microfilm permissible if employer is willing to provide adequate viewing facilities and make any extension, recomputation or transcript of film that may be requested. Punched tape is permissible if records can be readily converted to reviewable form).

6. Rehabilitation Act of 1973.
a. Federal contractors and subcontractors: For handicapped applicants and employees, complete and accurate employment records required. DOL suggests this may be met by notations on personnel forms of handicapped employees/applicants, including reasons for rejection that compare handicapped individual to qualifications of person selected, and accommodations considered (41 CFR 60-741.52).
b. Records of complaints and actions taken under Act (41 CFR 60-741.52).

a. and b. One year at minimum. Note: No particular form specified.

7. Vietnam-Era Veteran's Readjustment Act of 1974.
a. Contractors, sub-contractors with contracts of $10,000 or more: Copies of reports made to state employment services, e.g., number of Vietnam-era veterans hired during reporting period and related personnel records (38 USC 2012(d)).
b. Records of complaints and actions taken under Act (41 CFR 60-741.52).

a. Not specified. Note: No particular form specified. Must file annual report with EEOC. (Form VETS-100).

8. Americans with Disabilities Act of 1990.

Same as a. and b. for Title VII.

- Train and tutor management and supervisory-level employees concerning the importance of preserving documents and maintaining them in a uniform and easily accessible manner.
- Take steps to ensure that departments that experience high attrition rates are monitored concerning the preservation and destruction of documents.
- Exhaust all avenues when attempting to locate documents; even if you must advise the opposing side that the documents are lost or missing, continue to search for them—you might get lucky.
- Ensure that confidentiality policies exist that apply to all people handling the documents.

Public Nature

Litigation is a public process. When a case is filed at a courthouse, it can be broadcast to the world. The trial itself is a public stage on which dirty linen can be aired. For this reason, an employer might be tempted to settle a case rather than risk damage to its reputation.

Despite the public nature of litigation, there are ways for an employer to protect certain documents and information from public exposure. A competent attorney can at appropriate times assert privacy rights of employees, claim attorney–client privilege, or assert the "work product" defense (that is, that the information sought was secured by the efforts of the attorney in preparing the client's case.) It is also possible to request confidentiality agreements during discovery when agreeing to divulge sensitive information to opposing counsel.

Trial by Jury

summary jury trials
Abbreviated court sessions in which attorneys argue their cases before jurors who may be selected like a regular jury. By using such a forum, attorneys and parties become aware of the strengths and weaknesses of their cases.

With the exception of a few alternative dispute resolution forums, such as **summary jury trials,** only in litigation can a dispute be tried before a jury. Unless a case is one in which a jury would be sympathetic to the employer or one in which the law is clearly on its side, an employer risks losing a case in a trial by jury. Jurors are likely to be more sympathetic to an employee whom they perceive as having been given shoddy treatment by an employer than to a company that has exercised its rightful discretion even when the facts of the case favor the employer. Also significant is the fact that juries tend to give higher damage awards than would be granted by a judge sitting alone or an arbitrator.

Appellate Review

The rules of procedure also encompass the appellate process, by which parties can request review of a trial judge's actions and decisions. On appeal, the process of the trial court is examined to determine whether a trial judge committed errors of law or procedure. The trial court judge's decision can be reversed on appeal.

Review of a court decision differs significantly from review of decisions or agreements derived from other types of dispute resolution. For example, if parties submit their dispute to an arbitrator, the award of the arbitrator is binding, and the decision can be reversed only if there is evidence of corruption, conflict of interest, or other clearly prejudicial behavior on the part of the arbitrator. In contrast, during an appeal of a court decision, the appellate judges search for legal errors made by the trial court judge. Did the trial court judge err in understanding the law? Did the trial court fail to follow the principles of law in prior cases? These questions would not be asked of an arbitrator's decision.

Case for Discussion 2-1

The following 2006 federal appellate court case illustrates the role of the EEOC in resolving employment discrimination disputes. It also emphasizes the need for HR managers to keep adequate records and maintain such records for certain periods to comply with the law. The case involves various provisions of the Civil Rights Act of 1964.

This court opinion also demonstrates how cases are handled on appeal. For example, the trial court in *Target* granted what is known as **summary judgment** to Target on the issue of record retention (that is, the trial court decided that Target did not violate the law on this issue). At the appellate level, the reviewing judges looked at the evidence in the light most favorable to the losing party (in this case the EEOC and the plaintiff employees it was representing) to determine whether any genuine issue of material fact in dispute should have gone to a jury for resolution.

summary judgment
A decision made by a trial judge before trial. The judge says, in effect, that there is no genuine issue of material fact in dispute; therefore, all that is needed is to apply the law to the facts.

EEOC V. TARGET CORP., 460 F.3D 946 (2006)[8]

Facts

[A]t issue in this appeal is Target's practice of employment record retention. During the spring of 2001, Store Team Leader (STL) Walters estimated that he received 200 résumés for ETL positions and that STL Armiger reviewed 30 percent of them, or about 60 résumés. In the fall, slightly fewer résumés were submitted, and in other months, about 10 to 25 résumés were submitted each month. Armiger admitted to throwing out the résumés of applicants he deemed unqualified, including those of White, Edgeston, and Brown-Easley, rather than retaining them as required by law and by Target's document retention policy. Armiger claims he threw out the résumés to protect the applicants' privacy.

In an effort to comply with the EEOC's document retention requirement, Target currently uses Brass Ring, a nationwide employment recruitment Web site, to store applicant documents, including copies of applicants' résumés, applicants' PDI test results, and completed ELITE interview forms. . . . Target also has several policies to ensure that job applications and related documents are retained for the required time. Target uses its corporate intranet and e-mail messages to share its record retention policies with STLs. The human resource managers meet biannually to audit each Target store, to conduct training, and to remind employees of the record retention policy. The human resource managers instruct on-campus recruiters to retain all résumés, applications, and interview guides and notes, and to route the documents to the national head-quarters. Finally, the ETL for Team Relations is responsible for ensuring that the record-keeping policy is followed at each Target store.

The success of Target's record retention program through Brass Ring has been disputed. There is some indication that not all employees are following the program. As just discussed, STL Armiger threw out résumés that he should have retained. Additionally, Virginia Schomisch, the district team leader's administrative assistant, testified in June 2003 that she did not send applicant documents to Brass Ring, but instead she retained them herself for the required time. According to Target, the recruiters who send documents to Schomisch also send them to Brass Ring. Although Target's policy does not include a provision to ensure that relevant documents are retained from the time a discrimination charge is filed until that case is fully concluded, Target claims to address this requirement on a case-by-case basis, notifying employees to retain documents when a charge arises.

The EEOC's Investigation

On May 11, 2001, White and Edgeston filed EEOC discrimination charges against Target. White alleged that Target had discriminated against her and black applicants as a class by not considering them for ETL positions. Edgeston alleged that Target had discriminated against her because of her race.

The EEOC investigated the applicants' claims against Target. The EEOC issued a letter of determination for White and Edgeston's charges on September 13, 2001, finding reasonable cause to believe Target had discriminated against the applicants on the basis of their race. . . . The EEOC alleged that Target discriminated against the African-American applicants based on their race by refusing to hire them for ETL positions in District 110 since March 14, 2000. The EEOC also alleged that since at least March 14, 2000, Target had violated Title VII of the Civil Rights Act of 1964 by failing to make and preserve records relevant to the determination of whether Target engaged in unlawful employment practices.

The EEOC attempted to facilitate conciliation between Target and the applicants, but after four months of negotiations, they were unable to reach an agreement. The EEOC then filed its complaint in this lawsuit.

District Court's Action and Findings

A. *Record Retention*

The district court denied the EEOC's motion for summary judgment and granted Target's cross motion for summary judgment. . . . Summary judgment should be granted only if the record shows that there is no genuine issue of any material fact. When making such a determination a court must draw all reasonable inferences in favor of the nonmoving party.

1. Brass Ring

   Under Title VII, employers are required to "make and keep such records relevant to the determinations of whether unlawful employment practices have been or are being committed." The EEOC's record-keeping regulations require that employers retain applications and other documents related to hiring for one year. Additionally, if a charge of discrimination has been filed, an employer is required to retain all relevant personnel records until the final disposition of the charge.

   . . .

   While we agree that Target has put forth evidence that it has revised its record retention policies in an effort to comply with Title VII, we do not agree that such changes ensure "on [their] face" that Target will not commit further violations. . . . The reforms chosen do not address the particular problems that allowed violations to occur. Individual recruiters and administrative personnel destroyed records that were supposed to be retained because they did not know that they must retain them. In support of these allegations, the EEOC invoked the testimony of Virginia Schomisch, the person responsible for retaining employment documents for all of Target's District 110 applicants, who said that she did not know that she was required to retain an applicant's documents for more than one year if that applicant filed a charge with the EEOC. Additionally, Armiger failed to retain the records of the individual claimants in this suit and admitted that he destroyed records that should have been retained.

   Assuming that Armiger did not destroy employment documents in bad faith, his claim that he did not know he needed to retain these documents is problematic. . . . Because Target claims that its old policy could have allowed Armiger to recruit without knowing that he must retain recruitment documents, a reasonable fact finder could conclude that its new policy likewise will not prevent recruiters from being ill-informed. Although Target has assigned ETLs for team relations to ensure that each store is retaining documents (either onsite or with Brass Ring) in compliance with Target's record-keeping policy, a reasonable finder of fact might question whether this assignment will be sufficient if, for example, an STL (an ETL's superior) is assigned to help with recruiting in the same way that Armiger was assigned in early 2001. Thus, we find there is a genuine question of material fact as to whether Brass Ring has truly reformed Target's record retention policy in such a way as to ensure that violations will not continue.

2. Bad Faith

   Target argues that just because Armiger should have known better than to destroy résumés does not mean that he did know better; but this only underscores that this is a genuine issue of material fact to be resolved at trial. . . . The record evidence does not provide enough information for the question of bad faith to be resolved; but viewing all evidence in the light most favorable to the EEOC, there is certainly a genuine issue of material fact as to whether Armiger destroyed the résumés in bad faith.

If Target did not sufficiently prevent bad faith destruction of employment documents in the past, it should adopt some policy to prevent their destruction in the future. . . . Target has not claimed that it has adopted a system of penalties for failure to forward documents or in any other way provided new incentives to ensure compliance with the EEOC's record-keeping requirements.

Decision

Because these genuine issues of fact bear on whether Target's new record retention policy is sufficient to prevent future violations of federal law, Target's motion for summary judgment on this issue should not have been granted. Consequently, we reverse and remand for further proceedings.

Questions for Discussion

1. Note that the charging party in this litigation was the EEOC, not White and Edgeston, the aggrieved employees who filed claims with the EEOC. In this case the EEOC decided to take on the case. The trial court decided against the EEOC. Why did the appellate court reverse the trial court's decision?

2. The appellate court states there was not enough evidence to support a summary judgment in favor of Target. What evidence is available to an appellate court when a summary judgment has been granted by a trial court?

EEOC LITIGATION

The Equal Employment Opportunity Commission is an agency of the federal government with enforcement powers over several federal laws: the Civil Rights Act of 1964 (Title VII); the Americans with Disabilities Act of 1990; the Age Discrimination in Employment Act of 1967; the Equal Pay Act of 1963; and Sections 501 and 505 of the Rehabilitation Act of 1973, which prohibit discrimination against qualified individuals with disabilities who work in and for the federal government.

The EEOC is selective in determining which cases it will litigate. When it takes on certain cases, such as the *Target* case, the EEOC is the plaintiff (the one who initiates court action). There are several reasons the EEOC may opt not to take on a particular case; for example, with its limited resources, it tries to pursue issues that are significant and are of general concern for *all* employers. Figure 2.2[9] shows the number of cases litigated by the EEOC over a 10-year period ending in 2006 and the statutes involved.

FIGURE 2.2

The following table reflects EEOC enforcement suits filed and resolved in the federal district courts over 10 years. The table divides the suits by the various statutes enforced by the EEOC and provides aggregate data on monetary relief obtained. Note that many EEOC suits are brought on behalf of multiple aggrieved individuals. The lawsuits are filed under the various statutes enforced by the commission:

Title VII of the Civil Rights Act of 1964 (Title VII)

The Americans with Disabilities Act of 1990 (ADA)

The Age Discrimination in Employment Act of 1967 (ADEA)

The Equal Pay Act of 1963 (EPA)

Source: From www.eeoc.gov/stats/litigation.html (accessed March 2, 2008).

EEOC Litigation Statistics, Fiscal Year 1997 through Fiscal Year 2006

	FY 1997	FY 1998	FY 1999	FY 2000	FY 2001	FY 2002	FY 2003	FY 2004	FY 2005	FY 2006
Suits										
All suits filed	332	414	465	329	428	370	400	421	416	403
Merits suits	300	374	438	292	388	342	366	378	381	371
Suits with Title VII claims	182	254	341	236	289	268	298	297	295	294
Suits with ADA claims	83	87	55	29	66	44	49	46	49	42
Suits with ADEA claims	42	44	47	33	42	39	27	46	44	50
Suits with EPA claims	4	10	9	9	14	12	12	5	13	10
Suits filed under multiple statutes*	11	19	13	14	19	19	19	14	17	22
Subpoena and preliminary relief actions	32	40	27	37	40	28	34	43	35	32
All resolutions	243	331	350	440	362	381	381	380	378	418
Merits suits	214	295	320	407	321	351	351	346	338	383
Suits with Title VII claims	132	189	211	315	232	266	275	277	259	295
Suits with ADA claims	49	73	74	53	48	65	50	43	41	50
Suits with ADEA claims	38	38	51	41	39	26	35	34	45	50
Suits with EPA claims	7	4	7	6	15	9	13	9	12	8
Suits filed under multiple statutes	12	9	22	8	12	15	21	14	18	17
Subpoena and preliminary relief actions	29	36	30	33	41	30	30	34	40	35

FIGURE 2.2 (*Continued*)

	FY 1997	FY 1998	FY 1999	FY 2000	FY 2001	FY 2002	FY 2003	FY 2004	FY 2005	FY 2006
Monetary benefits ($ in millions)**	114.7	95.6	98.7	52.2	49.8	56.2	146.6	168.6	104.8	44.3
Title VII	95.0	62.0	49.2	35.0	33.6	29.2	85.1	158.5	98.0	34.3
ADA	1.1	2.8	2.9	2.9	2.3	15.1	2.3	2.5	3.4	2.8
ADEA	18.0	29.8	42.8	13.8	3.1	1.4	57.8	5.4	2.4	5.1
EPA	0.0	0.0	0.0	0.2	0.2	0.2	0.0	0.0	0.0	0.0
Suits filed under multiple statutes***	0.5	1.0	3.8	0.4	10.7	10.3	1.5	2.3	1.0	2.1

Note that to improve the clarity and completeness of the data on litigation activities, we have changed the format for presenting the count of cases filed and resolved by statute. Previously cases were included in a statute's count only if that statute was the only statute involved. Suits filed under multiple statutes were listed in a separate "concurrent" category. The new format includes suits under each statute alleged, resulting in some suits being counted in more than one statute. There is no longer a concurrent category.

In addition, recent data validation efforts have changed some of the counts and the annual amounts of monetary benefits.

Definitions:

Merits suits include direct suits and interventions alleging violations of the substantive provisions of the statutes enforced by the commission and suits to enforce administrative settlements.

Intervention occurs when the EEOC joins a lawsuit that has been filed by a private plaintiff.

Subpoena enforcement actions are filed during the investigation of a charge of discrimination where the respondent refuses to provide information relevant to the charge.

Suits to enforce administrative settlements involve a respondent's breach of an agreement with the EEOC to settle a charge during the administrative process.

This page was last modified on January 31, 2007.

*Suits filed under multiple statutes are also included in the tally of suits filed under the particular statutes.
**The sum of the statute benefits in some years will be less than the total benefits for those years due to rounding.
***Monetary benefits recovered in suits filed under multiple statutes are counted separately and are not included in the tally of suits filed under any particular statute.

HR managers should note that in many cases the EEOC will choose not to bring suit on behalf of an employee. In those cases the individual employee is issued a "right to sue" letter, enabling the employee to sue on her or his own behalf.

Note that employees can always bring suit on their own behalf when their claims are made under state laws prohibiting discrimination, rather than federal laws. State laws might allow greater damage awards—a matter of concern for employers.

EEOC Procedures for Initiating a Discrimination Case

All charges of employment discrimination brought under the provisions of federal laws enforced by the EEOC must be filed with the EEOC before an individual can file a private action.

How to File

An individual who believes that his or her employment rights have been violated under a federal law may file a charge of discrimination with the EEOC by doing the following:

- Filing a charge by mail or in person at an EEOC office.
- Providing the following information in writing:
  - The individual's name, address, and telephone number.
  - The name, address, and telephone number of the employer, employment agency, or union that is alleged to have discriminated, and the number of employees (or union members), if known.
  - A short description of the alleged violation (the event that caused the individual to believe that his or her rights were violated).
  - The date(s) of the alleged violation(s).

Time Period for Filing with the EEOC

A charge must be filed with the EEOC within 180 days from the date of the alleged violation. This 180-day filing deadline is extended to 300 days if the charge also is covered by a state or local antidiscrimination law.

Note: These time limits do not apply to claims under the Equal Pay Act because under that act people do not have to first file a charge with EEOC in order to have the right to go to court. However, because many EPA claims also raise Title VII sex discrimination issues, it is advisable for employees to file charges under both laws within the time limits indicated.

Time Period for Filing in a Court of Law

An individual may file a lawsuit within 90 days after receiving a "right to sue" letter from the EEOC. Under Title VII and the ADA, a charging party also can request a notice of "right to sue" from the EEOC 180 days after the charge was first filed with the commission, and may then bring suit within 90 days after receiving this notice.

Under the ADEA, a suit may be filed within 60 days after filing a charge with EEOC, but no later than 90 days after the EEOC gives notice that it has completed action on the charge.

Under the EPA, a lawsuit must be filed within two years (three years for willful violations) of the discriminatory act, which in most cases is payment of a discriminatory lower wage.

As previously indicated, litigation tends to present more problems than benefits for employers. Therefore, taking action to prevent lawsuits should be a high priority for employers. The potential damage to reputation, possible high damage awards by juries, and the productivity that is lost while preparing for a trial are all excellent reasons to do whatever is needed to prevent lawsuits being filed by employees. The following article lists some common managerial mistakes that lead to litigation[10]:

Oops, I Did It Again: The Ten Most Common Managerial Mistakes That Lead to Litigation

Employers that fail to adopt and follow basic good management practices will substantially increase their risk of litigation and liability.

It is not illegality that fuels employee lawsuits, but rather employee anger arising from perceived unfair treatment.

Placing a legal label, such as discrimination or retaliation, on the seeming unfairness occurs afterward.

Supervisors, managers, executives, and even human resources staff often engage in behaviors that, unwittingly, lead employees to feel misled, lied to, or otherwise unfairly treated. In doing so, they increase the likelihood of litigation. Ten common mistakes increase the likelihood of employee lawsuits and financial exposure.

1. **Forget about Training**

   Workplaces today are busier than ever. Devoting time to management training takes precious hours away from productive, money-making endeavors. A company, however, is its managers. What the managers say and do, the company says and does. Correct behavior prevents lawsuits. Missteps lead to liability. Managers who are not conversant in company policies, and who do not know the basics of setting goals and preparing performance appraisals and proper documentation, become the catalyst for lawsuits.

   Supervisors need training about how to handle difficult situations—what to say, whom to turn to for assistance, and what not to do. Failing to provide management training is shortsighted, and with the rise of potential individual liability, unfair to a company's supervisors.

2. **Disregard Company Policies**

   Policies establish a company's "rules for the road" for both employees and managers. They set company standards and inform employees of management's expectations. Well-drafted policies tied to an enterprise's business needs provide guidance to managers and employees. If followed, policies help ensure consistent treatment of employees.

   Disregarding policies heightens the potential for inconsistent treatment. It thus increases the risk that employees subjected to harsher action than their coworkers will interpret the discipline they received as unfair or discriminatory. Ignoring policies also sends the message that the employer believes they are unimportant, and gives license to employees to disregard them as well. An employer that fails to follow its policies not only loses the benefit of having them, but also sets itself up to be portrayed as mismanaged, uncaring, and willfully noncompliant with the law.

3. **Shoot from the Hip**

Firing without notice may occasionally be appropriate, but rarely. Acting without fair warning—or rashly or arbitrarily—invites resentment. Employees who feel ambushed may be led to seek their revenge through litigation.

Companies can reduce this risk by making employees aware of the probable consequences of misconduct through well-publicized and consistently enforced policies and progressive discipline. Before disciplining an employee, a company should be able to state

- The legitimate business reason for the action.
- Whether the action is consistent with other disciplinary actions the company has taken in similar situations, and if not, why not.

In addition, employers are usually well advised to give an employee the opportunity to give his or her side of the story before administering discipline. A meeting with the employee often provides a valuable safety valve for both employee and employer.

Often employees admit the misconduct (or some portion of it). Though unhappy with the discipline levied, employees often will be satisfied with the opportunity to have been heard. Managers need not agree with the employee, and should not argue or apologize. Meeting and listening alone can make employees feel that they have been treated fairly—because, in fact, they have been.

4. **Motivate Poor Performers with Raises and Bonuses**

The season for annual raises and bonuses brings with it the temptation to give underperforming employees some amount of increase or bonus. Withholding raises and bonuses is a tough decision. We all like to be liked. Withholding raises and bonuses seems contrary to a supervisor's goal of maintaining morale and staff loyalty.

Giving undeserved increases, however, does not spur poor performers to improve. Rather, it reinforces poor performance by telling employees that their performance merited an increase or bonus.

Terminating someone on the grounds of poor performance, after years of raises and bonuses (even small ones), creates concrete evidence of inconsistency between what the employer says now versus what it did then. It raises suspicion of ulterior motives for the adverse employment action and provides strong motivation for the employee to consult counsel.

5. **Criticize the Person**

Few jobs lend themselves to purely objective evaluation. Subjective criteria nearly always come into play. The challenge lies in relating performance criticism (and praise) to the job and not the person. Reviews that characterize the employee, rather than evaluating his or her performance, may become evidence of bias and discriminatory stereotyping.

Praise an employee for becoming the region's leading salesperson in just two months, but not for being "young and enthusiastic."

(Continued)

Similarly, criticize an employee for repeatedly failing to meet deadlines, not for being "lazy." Employees may need to "update their skill sets"; they do not, however, constitute "deadwood." To avoid such pitfalls, companies should encourage and assist managers in establishing measurable goals and creating business-related standards against which to evaluate employee performance.

6. Ignore Problems

Employers ask for trouble when they ignore problems and complaints. Failing to address performance issues has the practical effect of lowering performance standards. It leads employees to believe that they are performing at satisfactory levels because management has not told them otherwise.

Management may be dissatisfied with an employee's level of performance, and may truly believe that the employee ought to know he or she is missing the mark. Unless supervisors confront employees about performance deficiencies, however, and expressly state what employees need to do to meet expectations, change is unlikely. When after years of accepting poor performance a manager finally acts, perhaps by discharging the poor performer or perhaps by passing the employee over for promotion, the employee may react with surprise, hostility, and claims of discrimination.

7. Put Nothing in Writing

Without a written record documenting employee performance issues and management's response, employers increase the risks of "he said, she said" situations when taking adverse employment actions. Employees who have not been given (and required to sign) counseling memos or performance evaluations frequently claim that the counseling, the warning, or the evaluation was never received. Verbal warnings carry less weight than written warnings with employees, their lawyers, and juries.

Employees who have been repeatedly spoken to, but never written up, are likely to discount or even disregard the importance of the counseling. Employers who do not document employment issues leave themselves with little concrete evidence to prove a history of poor performance as the reason for discharge, instead of, for example, retaliation for taking medical leave.

8. Understand That Boys Will Be Boys

A hostile work environment, whether because of sexual harassment or harassment based on age, disability, or race, may arise from either severe or pervasive conduct. Jokes, e-mails, and passing comments when considered individually may be of little consequence. Accumulated and viewed as a whole, however, they can be used to show pervasive misbehavior that has converted a professional workplace into a frat house. That a harassing employee may not intend to harass his coworker does not constitute a defense; nor does it create a shield from being sued.

Employers who know of employee misconduct, such as use of the company's e-mail system to send sexually explicit jokes or photographs, and who fail to take action to stop the conduct, substantially increase their risk of litigation and liability for damages.

9. **Lie**

When management fails to tell the truth, employee disgruntlement inevitably follows, and with it a fast track to the courthouse—and potential liability.

Employers do not protect themselves by telling an older employee that he is being discharged because of job elimination when the true reason is poor performance. As soon as someone (younger) is hired to replace the discharged employee, the company's lie, even if intended to protect the employee from hurt feelings, will be seen as a pretext to hide discrimination.

10. **Cover Up**

Repeatedly, experience shows that a cover-up carries worse consequences than the initial misdeed. Shredding documents, deleting files, or throwing away drafts upon learning of an impending lawsuit can all add up to trouble. When confronted with a bad situation, it remains true that honesty is the best policy.

Information contained in this article is intended to provide useful information on the topic covered, but should not be construed as legal advice or a legal opinion. Also remember that state laws may differ from the federal law.

Source: M. Neuhauser, *Workforce Management* online (accessed March 2005).

Global **Perspective**

In December 2001 China revised its procedural law to make its rules uniform across all levels of its judiciary. The following excerpt compares the newly promulgated rules for the judicial system in China with U.S. federal rules. Note that "Fed. R. Evid" refers to U.S. federal rules of evidence, and "Article" refers to new Chinese rules of evidence.

A REVIEW OF CHINA'S NEW CIVIL EVIDENCE LAW[11]

***

E. *Witness Interrogation and Sequestration*

Article 58 and Fed. R. Evid. 614 both allow the court to interrogate witnesses. Article 58, in addition, provides for the automatic sequestration of

(Continued)

witnesses. In the United States, sequestration typically only occurs if a party requests it pursuant to Fed. R. Evid. 615.

Currently, U.S. courts are split on whether sequestration under Fed. R. Evid. 615 implicitly forbids witnesses from speaking to one another about their testimony outside of court. Some courts say such a prohibition is implied because the purpose of the rule is to prevent witness collusion, and, if witnesses could meet outside the courtroom to discuss their testimony, this purpose would be frustrated. Other courts say that the precise language of the rule only forbids witnesses from hearing the testimony of other witnesses, and to get involved in alleged out-of-court violations would lead to endless enforcement hearings. . . .

F. *Best Evidence*

China's best evidence rules are found in Articles 10, 20, 22, and 49; corresponding U.S. rules are found at Fed. R. Evid. 1001 through 1003. The Chinese rules require the production of the original document or thing as evidence. A duplicate may be allowed, but only if it is too difficult to present the original document or thing, or the original no longer exists but evidence shows that the duplicate is identical. In the United States, duplicates are allowed as evidence except when a genuine question is raised as to the authenticity of the original or, under the circumstances, it would be unfair to admit the duplicate in lieu of the original. . . .

G. *Hearsay*

Hearsay that would be inadmissible in U.S. courts is regularly allowed in Chinese courts. For instance, in China, written testimonial letters are routinely admitted as evidence. Even though it is understood that it is preferable to have the witness appear in court, this is not mandatory. . . .

***

V. *Evidence Production and the Exclusionary Sanction for Late Production*

The core of the new Chinese evidence law concerns a number of fundamental procedural rules, including, most importantly, provisions delineating mandatory evidence exchanges. . . . The equally critical process of examining and confronting an opponent's evidence, a process known as *zhizheng*, is also explored at length. . . .

The parties may agree on when the evidence will be exchanged, but if they cannot agree, then the court will set a deadline. . . . Most importantly, Article 34 mandates what is effectively an exclusionary sanction if evidence is not exchanged by the deadline. Evidence submitted by a party beyond the deadline will not be *zhizheng*-ed. Moreover, because evidence that is not *zhizheng*-ed cannot be considered by the court, the ultimate result is exclusion.

Source: P.J. Schmidt.

Summary

The use of the courts for resolving employment disputes is known as litigation. For several reasons, including cost, time, formality, liberal discovery, and clogged court dockets, there is a need to resolve disputes by alternative means.

Characteristics of litigation include the following:

- Litigation offers the option of jury trials.
- Litigation involves a formal process and formal rules set forth in legal statutes.
- Litigation involves liberal discovery that encourages and enables parties to seek information about the case. Parties can seek the help of the judge to order reluctant parties to comply with discovery requests.
- Litigation results in a decision that can be reviewed by an appellate court, which reviews the actions of the trial judge to determine whether any errors have been committed.
- Litigation can set precedent—that is, the case may lead to a legal determination that will be binding on future cases.
- Litigation is a public proceeding.
- Litigation is highly adversarial. It usually breaks whatever relationship existed before the lawsuit was initiated.

Questions

1. Go to www.eeoc.gov/abouteeo/overview_practices.html and answer the following questions:
   a. What discriminatory practices are prohibited by federal laws?
   b. Do federal laws prohibit discrimination based on sexual orientation, status as a parent, marital status, or political affiliation?
   c. Can employers reduce the wages of either sex to equalize pay between men and women?
2. If an employer wants to have an employee's supervisor sit in on the employee's deposition, is this permissible?
3. If an employee's attorney requests that the employer's vice president of human resources be deposed, can the VP send someone else in her place who she believes has better knowledge of the case? If the employee's attorney makes a convincing case to the judge that the VP's deposition is necessary, can the VP refuse to appear? What are the possible consequences of such a refusal?

References

1. A. Bierce, *The Devil's Dictionary,* 1911 (The Gutenberg Project).
2. M. Neuhauser, *Workforce Management Online,* March 2005, "Oops, I Did It Again: Ten Most Common Managerial Mistakes That Lead to Litigation." See www.workforce.com/archive/article/23/95/42.php (accessed July 3, 2008). Maxine Neuhauser is an attorney with Epstein Becker & Green in the labor and employ-

ment practice group. Prior to joining Epstein Becker & Green, Neuhauser was a deputy attorney general for the State of New Jersey, where she represented regulatory boards and agencies in both civil and administrative litigation.

3. Hobbs-Wright, Emily, Holland & Hart LLP, "Colorado Litigation: The Verdict Is In,"*Colorado Employment Law Letter,* January 2004 (M. Lee Smith Publishers & Printers, 2004).

4. See http://www.eeoc.gov/charge/overview_charge_filing.html (accessed March 2, 2008).

5. From *Michael Moncur's (Cynical) Quotations.* Search "Younger, Evelle J." at www.quotationspage.com (accessed March 2, 2008).

6. E. J. McNamee, "Avoiding Record Keeping Pitfalls." Published by the Colorado Bar Association, April 3, 2003 CLE Employment Issues in the Business World Program and previously posted on http://www.dgslaw.com/documents/articles/495305.PDF, (accessed July 17, 2007).

7. See http://www.da.ks.gov/ps/documents/aap/Federal%20EEO%20Record.pdf (accessed July 3, 2008).

8. *EEOC v. Target Corp.,* 460 F.3d 946 (2006).

9. See http://www.eeoc.gov/stats/litigation.html (accessed March 2, 2008).

10. M.Neuhauser, op. cit.

11. P. J. Schmidt, "A Review of China's New Civil Evidence Law," *Pacific Rim Law & Policy Journal,* March 2003, p. 12. See www.law.washington.edu/pacrim /abstract/12.2.htm (accessed June 12, 2007).

Alternative Dispute Resolution: Arbitration

If any suit or proceeding be brought in any of the courts of
the United States upon any issue referable to arbitration
under an agreement in writing for such arbitration, the court
in which such suit is pending, upon being satisfied that the
issue involved in such suit or proceeding is referable to
arbitration under such an agreement, shall on application of
one of the parties stay the trial of the action until such
arbitration has been had in accordance with the terms of the
agreement, providing the applicant for the stay is not in
default in proceeding with such arbitration.

The Federal Arbitration Act of 1925 [Title 9, U.S. Code, Sections 1–14]

INTRODUCTION

Congress, in enacting the Federal Arbitration Act in 1925, made an em-
phatic declaration that agreements to arbitrate disputes would be enforced
by the federal courts. Over the years, with few exceptions, U.S. courts have
followed the spirit of this law. Although early cases often involved unionized labor situations, today more and more contracts, including private employment contracts, contain arbitration clauses. Managers should know
what the arbitration process requires, how it compares with other methods
of dispute resolution, and whether arbitration is advisable when this choice
is available.

There are numerous alternatives to litigation, some of which offer the possibility of a win–win resolution and rely on agreement between the parties.
Others are simply advisory or investigative models. Some are formal, whereas
others are informal. Some are administered internally by a member of the

company; others rely on outside hires. Most, but not all, use neutral third parties. The best-known alternative dispute resolution (ADR) methods include negotiation, arbitration, mediation, med–arb (a combination of mediation and arbitration), minitrial, summary jury trial, (judicial) settlement conference, and peer review. ADR is so flexible that it can be designed to fit parties' particular needs. For example, mediation can be modified to include fact-finding. A more thorough analysis of mediation is given in Chapter 4.

This chapter will describe the process of arbitration—arguably the most common method of alternative dispute resolution, and one that has been utilized extensively in labor dispute resolutions for decades. Arbitration will be compared and contrasted to litigation.

Litigation and arbitration are the most well-known formal means of dispute resolution, and they have the most in common compared to other ADR methods. Briefly, litigation and arbitration both use the services of a neutral third party who, after hearing testimony and reviewing evidence given by the disputing parties in the case, renders a decision that is binding on the parties.

THE RISE OF ALTERNATIVES TO LITIGATION

As our population increases and our laws multiply, our courts have become overburdened with the volume of litigation. Alternative dispute resolution can take pressure off overloaded court dockets.

The courts are not the only beneficiaries of ADR, however. Traditional litigation is increasingly thought of as a lose–lose proposition. As Voltaire quipped, "I was never ruined but twice: Once when I lost a lawsuit, and once when I won one"[1]. That is still true at times today because litigation often involves high costs to both parties and significant amounts of time that could otherwise be devoted to productive work. Also, parties have so little control over litigation's outcome that everyone can be left disgruntled—even a person who receives a favorable verdict. With ADR parties generally save money and time. Also, greater control over the outcome translates into greater satisfaction for both parties. Some forms of ADR have the potential to improve or heal relationships. This is particularly important when the parties have an ongoing relationship, such as an employment situation in which, except for the dispute at hand, there is the potential of a mutually beneficial arrangement. The benefits the parties can expect from alternative forums depend, however, on which type of ADR is used and how it is implemented.

ARBITRATION

Arbitration has long been used in collective bargaining. Its use in private disputes has been a more recent and growing phenomenon. In the employment arena, more and more employers are including arbitration clauses in employment agreements. Employees who enter such an agreement forfeit their rights to sue these employers.

Whether or not an arbitration clause will be enforced is often one issue before a court. If an employee claims a violation of statutory law, an argument can be made that because the rights asserted by the employee are specifically granted by Congress, employees should not be barred from using the courts to enforce those rights. Courts are mixed in their treatment of this issue.

Characteristics of Arbitration

The Process

In appearance, arbitration generally looks like an informal, abbreviated court case. It is an adversarial proceeding where the parties often have counsel present their case, along with testimony of parties and witnesses, to a neutral person or panel of neutrals who then make a decision on the case. Arbitration is the alternative method that is most similar to traditional court-based litigation, but it has less formality.

The Agreement to Arbitrate

In general, parties come to arbitration in one of three ways: (1) by agreement at the time of the dispute (*voluntary arbitration*); (2) as a result of an arbitration clause in a contract (*mandatory contractual arbitration*); or (3) by order of a court (*mandatory arbitration*). The first two ways are considered private arbitration (parties enter arbitration independently of a court case). The third situation is sometimes referred to as *court-annexed arbitration* (during litigation, the court orders the parties to attempt resolution through arbitration).

Binding versus Nonbinding Arbitration

Binding arbitration refers to the traditional arbitration process in which an arbitrator renders a decision (known as an *award*) that is legally enforceable. The other type of arbitration is *nonbinding arbitration,* in which neither party is bound to accept and comply with the arbitrator's award. For example, when a judge, during litigation, orders parties to submit to arbitration, this is a nonbinding arbitration process.

The Question of Arbitrability

Whether a particular dispute should be resolved through arbitration or otherwise is one that has been addressed by the U.S. Supreme Court in several cases. The high court decided that the question of arbitrability is "an issue for judicial determination unless the parties clearly and unmistakably provide otherwise"[2]. In other words, if one party seeks to resolve a dispute in court and the other argues that the case must be arbitrated in accordance with an agreement to arbitrate, a court, not an arbitrator, must resolve that initial issue.

Selection of Arbitrator(s)

Generally, at the beginning of arbitration, the parties to a dispute obtain a list of potential arbitrators and negotiate the selection of the arbitrator or panel of arbitrators. In litigation, the parties have no control over which judge will hear the case. Nonetheless, some argue that the process of selecting an arbitrator gives frequent users of arbitration an unfair advantage. For example, most employees are not likely to repeatedly arbitrate with their employers and are unlikely to have any relationship with or knowledge of the arbitrators. On the other hand, an employer may arbitrate frequently, allowing the employer to build a relationship with certain arbitrators as well as have an idea of their viewpoints and biases.

Discovery of Evidence

Arbitrators often limit the amount of legal discovery. There is generally a brief period of fact-finding before an arbitration hearing begins. Because discovery is time-consuming and expensive, this is one way that arbitration has traditionally benefited both parties. However, two significant complaints are emerging regarding discovery in arbitration. The first is that without sufficient discovery, justice may not be served, and often the plaintiff—the less powerful party with less access to documentation—suffers as a result. The second complaint is that arbitrators are increasingly allowing more extensive discovery so that some arbitrations actually take longer than, and cost more than, traditional court resolution. A significant factor is that arbitrators, unlike judges, generally lack the authority to impose orders and sanctions if a party fails to cooperate in the discovery process.

Presentation of Case

During arbitration, the parties (or their representatives) present their cases to the arbitrator or panel. After both sides have presented their evidence, the arbitrator or panel renders a verdict or decision, known as an *award.*

Outcomes

As previously stated, an arbitrator's award can be binding or nonbinding depending, among other things, on the parties' agreement. If it is binding, the parties have no choice but to accept the award. If it is nonbinding arbitration, either party can ignore the ruling and proceed otherwise.

Appeals

The parties have the right to appeal the arbitrator's award in a court of law. However, as stated in Chapter 2, the right to appeal an arbitration award is more limited than the appeal of a court order. To succeed on an appeal of an arbitration award, one must generally show an abuse of process by the arbitrator, evidence of corruption or conflict of interest on the part of the arbitrator, or the failure of the arbitrator to act reasonably within the law. (See Case for Discussion 3-1.) In nonbinding arbitration, the parties can pursue the case anew in court or resolve the conflict in another manner.

Arbitration Clause

As already noted, in many areas it has become common practice to include arbitration clauses in contracts. Arbitration clauses usually require that any dispute arising from the contract or relationship between the parties be resolved through binding arbitration. Some critics have noted that when there is a standard arbitration clause, the parties may not be fully aware of how that clause affects their rights. Furthermore, although in theory contracts assume an "arms-length" relationship in which both parties have equal bargaining power, in reality this is not always the case—especially in employment contracts. Many statutory laws affect the employer–employee relationship, and critics claim that employees may not be aware of the effect of binding arbitration on their statutory rights, including the right to appeal and the ability to affect precedent.

Punitive Damages

When arbitration first became widely used in the employment setting (outside collective bargaining), arbitrators generally did not award punitive damages; indeed many believed they did not have that power. This is a vital issue for both parties. To the extent that it is known which arbitrators are prone to awarding punitive damages, this information will obviously influence the choice of arbitrator. To the extent that punitive damages awarded by arbitrators are upheld by the courts, the trend will either grow or diminish.

Case for Discussion 3-1

SCHOCH V. INFO USA, 341 F.3D 785 (2003)[3]

Facts

Schoch sold his business to InfoUSA for $20,000,000 in 1996 and entered a three-year employment agreement. InfoUSA also granted Schoch the option to purchase 360,000 shares of InfoUSA stock. The options could be exercised for up to three months after termination of the employment relationship. The employment agreement ended on September 9, 1999, and there was no renewal of the agreement. However, Schoch continued to do some work for InfoUSA through December 1999. During those last months Schoch attempted to have InfoUSA extend his agreement, but InfoUSA refused. On December 17 Schoch tried to exercise his options to purchase 360,000 shares. InfoUSA argued that his right to do so ended on December 9, and therefore he was not entitled to do so.

Schoch took the matter to arbitration pursuant to the arbitration clause in the contract. The arbitrator found in Schoch's favor, concluding that Schoch's continuation of work for InfoUSA through December in fact extended his employment period. The arbitrator awarded $1,632,000 to Schoch.

InfoUSA appealed the decision in the district court, arguing the following: (1) The arbitrator exceeded his contractual authority; and (2) the award was "completely irrational" and evidenced a "manifest disregard for the law."

The district court affirmed the arbitrator's award, and InfoUSA appealed.

Decision

The federal appellate court stated, in confirming the district court's decision, "Although an arbitrator has broad authority, the arbitrator is not wholly free from judicial review. An arbitrator's award can be vacated for the reasons provided in the Federal Arbitration Act (FAA). See 9 U.S.C. Sec. 10(a)." Those reasons include "corruption, fraud, undue means, evident partiality, misconduct, or **ultra vires** acts." The court further stated, ". . . our court has recognized two 'extremely narrow' judicially created standards for vacating an arbitration award. . . . First, an arbitrator's award can be vacated if it is 'completely irrational,' meaning 'it fails to draw its essence from the agreement.' . . . The second judicially created standard for vacating an arbitration award is when the award 'evidences a manifest disregard for the law.' . . . An arbitrator's award 'manifests disregard for the law' where the arbitrators clearly identify the applicable, governing law and then proceed to ignore it."

ultra vires

Ultra vires is Latin for "beyond powers." It refers to conduct by a person, organization, or corporation that exceeds the powers granted by law or by their own documents.

Questions for Discussion

1. What does the case tell you about the difference between an arbitrator's decision and a trial judge's decision?
2. What lessons can managers take from the *Schoch* case? Explain your answer.

THE FEDERAL ARBITRATION ACT[4]

In a number of cases decided by the U.S. Supreme Court involving interpretation of the Federal Arbitration Act of 1925, the purpose of the act was explained. Some of the Court's reasoning was as follows. The Arbitration Act of 1925, reversing centuries of judicial hostility to arbitration agreements, is designed to let parties avoid the costs and delays of litigation and to place arbitration agreements on the same footing as other contracts[5].

The Federal Arbitration Act confers a duty to enforce arbitration agreements. This duty is not diminished when a party bound by an agreement raises a claim founded on statutory rights; absent a well-founded claim that an arbitration agreement resulted from fraud or excessive economic power such as would provide grounds for revocation of any contract, the act provides no basis for disfavoring agreements to arbitrate statutory claims. The act's provisions may be overridden by Congress. The burden is on the party opposed to arbitration to show that Congress intended to preclude waiver of judicial remedies for statutory rights at issue [6].

Case for Discussion 3-2

The *Circuit City* case here is of great significance to human resource professionals. It essentially supports employers who include arbitration clauses in employment contracts. If a contract is clear regarding arbitration, the court will enforce it.

CIRCUIT CITY STORES V. SAINT CLAIR ADAMS, 532 U.S. 105, 121 S.CT. 1302 (2001)[7]

Facts

In this case the issue centered on the question of whether employment contracts were exempted from the provisions of the Federal Arbitration Act (FAA). The FAA basically requires that parties that have agreed to arbitrate disputes arising from contracts must therefore arbitrate disputes and cannot resort to the courts. Exempted from the FAA's provisions are "seamen" and "railroad employees" and "any other class of workers engaged in commerce." The meaning of the term "engaged in commerce" has, in other contexts, a broad application. In other statutory contexts the term "business engaged in commerce" has been held to mean a business whose activity "affects" commerce. In arguing that Circuit City employees do not come within the meaning of workers "engaged in commerce," Circuit City sought to force arbitration pursuant to the agreement to arbitrate.

Decision

The U.S. Supreme Court held in favor of Circuit City and wrote that the FAA exemption is confined to transportation workers. Had the Supreme Court applied the broader meaning of employers "engaged in commerce," employers would have been unable to rely on the provisions of the FAA to enforce arbitration clauses in employment contracts.

Questions for Discussion

1. The plaintiff, Adams, in looking at the language of the Federal Arbitration Act, gave the words "engaged in commerce" a broad meaning—a meaning that in other legislative contexts encompasses almost all business activity. In so doing, Adams argued that employees of Circuit City were exempt from the provisions of the FAA. How significant was this decision to American businesses?

2. What does the U.S. Supreme Court's decision tell you about how courts interpret statutory law?

RELATED ISSUES INVOLVING ARBITRATION

In sum, the courts favor arbitration when the parties have agreed to this form of dispute resolution. Three U.S. Supreme Court opinions have resolved other issues regarding arbitration of disputes. In *Green Tree Financial Corp. v. Bazzle,* 2003[8], the court held that a class action arbitration was permissible if the contract between the parties did not expressly forbid it. In that case the Court cited *Mitsubishi Motors v. Soler Chrysler,* 1985[9], stating, "any doubt about the scope of arbitrable issues should be resolved in favor of arbitration." In *Pacificare Health Systems v. Book,* 2003[10], the Court stated it would give the benefit of the doubt to the arbitrator in a case where the arbitrator's award was treble damages awarded under the federal Racketeer Influenced and Corrupt Organizations Act (RICO).

Case for Discussion 3-3

IN RE JOHNNY LUNA, RELATOR, 175 S.W.3D 315 (2004)[11]

Facts

Poly-America hired Luna on October 21, 1998, to work as an operator in Poly-America's plant in Mont Belvieu, Texas. When he was hired, Luna signed an arbitration agreement. Luna continued to work for Poly-America, and on July 18, 2002, Luna signed another document acknowledging that he had received the June 2002 employee handbook. The handbook contained another arbitration agreement with similar provisions. Luna was injured, and he filed a worker's compensation claim on December 7, 2002. On February 11, 2003, Poly-America terminated Luna's employment, and Luna subsequently sued Poly-America under the Texas Labor Code, alleging wrongful discharge and retaliation. The trial court granted Poly-America's motion to compel arbitration and to stay litigation on September 19, 2003.

***

Luna asserts that the arbitration agreement is unenforceable because several of its provisions are unconscionable.

***

A. *Costs of Arbitration*

Luna asserts that the arbitration agreement's cost-allocation provisions are unconscionable because they require him to pay more than a nominal fee for the arbitration. Specifically, the agreement in the employee handbook provides:

All fees charged . . . shall be divided equally between the Parties. All fees associated with the Arbitration (including, but not limited to, the Arbitrator's fee, court reporter fees, and fees to secure a place for the hearing, if any) shall be divided equally between the Parties. However, the total fees incurred by the Employee shall not exceed the gross compensation earned by the Employee in the Employee's highest earning month in the twelve months prior to the time the arbitrator issues his award.

***

Luna stated in his affidavit that two attorneys refused to take his case on a contingency basis due to the arbitration agreement, and he also stated that he would be unable to afford the arbitration fees. . . .

***

B. *Limitation of Remedies*

Luna asserts that the arbitration agreement's prohibition of punitive damages and reinstatement remedies is substantively unconscionable because those remedies are allowed under the Texas Labor Code.

***

Although preclusion of statutory remedies may not always weigh toward a finding that the provisions as a whole are substantively unconscionable, their preclusion does so with regard to the statutory remedies at issue in this case because Luna's claim is one brought for alleged retaliation for filing a worker's compensation claim as part of the overall Worker's Compensation Act. The Texas Supreme Court has held that the legislative policy behind the act dictates that its provisions be construed in favor of the injured worker. . . . Such a policy heightens the scrutiny that should be afforded to arbitration provisions that expressly limit statutory remedies afforded under the act. In particular, the act expressly confers upon a prevailing plaintiff a right to "reinstatement in the former position of employment," and the arbitration agreement at issue here expressly abrogates such a right.

***

Thus preclusion of the two substantive statutory remedies here tends to weigh toward a finding that the agreement's provisions as a whole are substantively unconscionable.

***

G. *Unconscionability of Agreement as a Whole*

Luna asserts that, even if none of the provisions in the agreement is unconscionable by itself, the agreement as a whole is so unfair as to be unconscionable.

***

It is not the number of provisions weighing toward an overall finding of substantive unconscionability that matters as much as the cumulative one-sidedness of the burden that those provisions place on a party.

***

Decision

Accordingly, we hold that the arbitration costs imposed on Luna, who provided evidence of the costs of arbitration and of his inability to pay, in addition to the limitations on Luna's opportunity to be reinstated and to recover punitive damages, render the arbitration agreement, when considered as a whole, so one-sided in Poly-America's favor and so oppressive to Luna as to be substantively unconscionable, given the strong legislative policy behind the Worker's Compensation Act.

Questions for Discussion

1. How important to the outcome of the case was the fact that Luna's grievance arose from a worker's compensation claim?
2. Explain the potential benefits that Luna would receive by having his grievance decided by a judge rather than an arbitrator. Be specific.
3. In some situations companies such as Poly-America impose one-sided agreements on employees—that is, clauses that favor the company over the employee. Evaluate the pros and cons of making one-sided agreements with employees. Consider Robert Bruce Shaw's advice in the "Management Perspective" box in this chapter.

THE AMERICAN ARBITRATION ASSOCIATION

The American Arbitration Association (AAA) has existed for many years and provides arbitration as well as other alternative dispute resolution services to individuals and organizations. The AAA also runs the International Center for Dispute Resolution for international dispute resolution. Its services include assisting in the appointment of mediators and arbitrators, setting up hearings, and providing information about dispute resolution options.

Additional AAA services include the design and development of alternative dispute resolution (ADR) systems for corporations, unions, government agencies, law firms, and the courts. The Association also provides elections services as well as education, training, and publications for those seeking a broader or deeper understanding of alternative dispute resolution.[12]

Plaintiff–employees who take their employers to court are motivated to do so for a variety of reasons. Certainly, if there has been a clear breach of a contract promise that is economically devastating to the employee and the employer is not willing to negotiate a resolution, litigation may be the most reasonable option.

On the other hand, some workers will take advantage of the legal system and sue their employers even in the absence of justification. In many situations, though, the fired employee or the candidate that is passed over for hire will not consider suing if he or she understands and appreciates the employer's position. The following excerpt from *Trust in the Balance* by Robert Bruce Shaw[13] offers advice on the necessity of building trust—a vital factor in the ongoing employee–employer relationship. Employees' trust will go a long way in preventing lawsuits and is therefore worthy of consideration.

Eliminating Trust-Eroding Practices

Moving beyond a culture of distrust requires diligence in changing old patterns of behavior. Many people in low-trust environments will continue to work in ways that fuel suspicion unless they are shown the need to behave differently. For example, a functional leader may refuse to collaborate with colleagues on key business initiatives, or a senior leader may refuse to push accountability into the organization (and instead keep it for himself or herself). The specifics will vary depending on a firm's culture. The response to those exhibiting "old behavior," however, should be consistent and, when needed, tough. A new way of operating cannot last if key individuals are allowed to function in ways that reinforce distrust and suspicion.

In addition, low-trust situations are often plagued by management systems that sustain distrust. These systems become lightning rods for suspicion. For example, some systems result in groups and individuals lowering their performance objectives in order to increase their likelihood of making their targets. If this is allowed, the organization ends up rewarding those who are less aggressive and, in some cases, less honest.

One of the most important policies to examine in relation to trust is the organization's reward system. The goal, in general, is to create reward systems that encourage individual achievement along with shared ownership for organizational performance. Systems must be crafted carefully to avoid simply creating new zero-sum situations (where individuals and groups believe they must outperform others in order to be successful). For example, many organizations have traditionally forced a bell-shaped distribution of performance ratings. This system ensures that superior performance across the board will not be rewarded (since some employees must fall on the lower end of the performance continuum). This forces employees to compete against

(Continued)

each other for recognition and rewards. To prevent this effect, the leadership needs to establish collective rewards that reinforce collaboration and identification with the entire firm. The nature of these reward systems will vary but typically will include profit sharing and group bonuses.

Motorola has taken a different tactic with its annual worldwide employee competition on quality and customer satisfaction. A set of well-known criteria (including involvement of all team members in the project) is used to evaluate the results of teams across the firm. The projects are screened, and at year-end, twelve finalists are recognized in a companywide event. Their accomplishments are publicized through employee newsletters that include photographs of the winners. The entire process, while resulting in a few winners, is designed to make all who enter feel like they have made a contribution and are making progress. [Footnote 4 in Shaw's book cites R. Pascale, *Managing on the Edge: How the Smartest Companies Use Conflict to Stay Ahead* (New York: Simon & Schuster, 1990), p. 244.]

The leadership task within low-trust organizations and teams is to scrap practices that provoke distrust and replace them, as necessary, with more collaborative processes. For example, some firms have systems that reward individuals for their suggestions. If not properly managed, a suggestion system can result in secrecy among employees. People keep their ideas to themselves in order to win financial awards, thus restricting the flow of information among individuals and groups. A restrictive suggestion system can be replaced with approaches that emphasize organizational learning and collective achievement of results.

Organizations can be well served by simply eliminating some systems and not putting others in their place. Consider, for example, one successful retailer's approach to an employee handbook. In most firms the handbook, containing all types of policies and restrictions, fills several large binders. At Nordstrom it is significantly smaller: half a page, to be exact. It reads,

Welcome to Nordstrom. We're glad to have you with our company. Our number one goal is to provide outstanding customer service. Set both your personal and professional goals high. We have great confidence in your ability to achieve them.

Nordstrom rules: Use your good judgment in all situations. Please feel free to ask your department manager, store manager, or division general manager any question at any time. [Footnote 5 in Shaw's book cites the GE Annual Report, 1991, p. 5.]

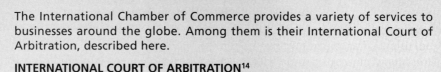

Global **Perspective**

The International Chamber of Commerce provides a variety of services to businesses around the globe. Among them is their International Court of Arbitration, described here.

INTERNATIONAL COURT OF ARBITRATION[14]

Arbitration Today

The ICC International Court of Arbitration is the world's leading institution for resolving international commercial and business disputes.

The total number of cases handled by the court since it was founded is more than 15,000. In 2006 alone, 593 cases were filed, involving 1,613 parties from 125 countries.

The proliferation of international commercial disputes, many of them involving several parties, is an inevitable by-product of the global economy. Today's business and operating conditions underscore arbitration's advantages over litigation, especially in cross-border disputes.

Often the parties are from markedly different national, cultural, and legal backgrounds.

They want to avoid litigation because they fear bias by national courts, are unfamiliar with national court procedures, and want to be spared damaging publicity. ICC arbitration is an attractive alternative because it is international and confidential. Usually it is less time-consuming and less expensive than litigation.

Summary

The use of the courts for resolving employment disputes is known as litigation. For several reasons, including cost, time, formality, liberal discovery, and clogged court dockets, there is a need to resolve disputes by alternative means. The most common alternative other than informal negotiation is arbitration. In both litigation and arbitration, a third party hears the evidence in a case and renders a decision.

Differences between litigation and arbitration include the following:

- Litigation offers the option of jury trials. Arbitration is heard by an arbitrator (or panel of arbitrators) without a jury.
- Litigation involves a formal process and formal rules set forth in legal codes. Arbitration is more informal.
- Litigation involves liberal discovery that encourages parties to seek information about the case. Arbitrators allow discovery but may curtail the process.
- Litigation results in a decision that can be reviewed by an appellate court, which reviews the actions of the trial judge to determine whether any errors have been committed. An arbitrator's award will stand unless there is evidence of corruption or abuse of the arbitrator's power.

- Litigation can set precedent—that is, the case's legal determination may be binding on future cases. Arbitration decisions do not establish precedent.
- Litigation is a public proceeding. Arbitration is private.

The Federal Arbitration Act of 1925 and cases that have interpreted that statute have strengthened the use of arbitration by requiring the enforcement of arbitration clauses in contracts, including employment contracts.

Questions

1. Access the American Arbitration Association's Web site: www.adr.org/arb_med. Select "Employment Rules." From the right column, select "Employment Arbitration Rules and Mediation Procedures." Answer the following questions:

   a. If you wanted to use the services of the American Arbitration Association, how would you initiate the process? See Item #4.

   b. How many arbitrators would hear the case? See Items #12 and #13.

   c. As a party in the dispute, can you call the arbitrator and discuss the facts of the case? See Item #17.

   d. How much does the AAA charge for its services? See Item #48(i) et seq.

2. Joannie C. had been employed as an accountant at Briscoll's Hardware Store for 20 years. Joannie's work had always been satisfactory, but she and Mr. Briscoll had their share of misunderstandings and disputes. At one time Briscoll actually took Joannie to court on a claim of harassing a customer and causing loss of business profits. Joannie won the suit. A formal employment agreement was drawn up when Andra was hired, and it contained an arbitration clause. In February 2000 Andrew B., a friend of Briscoll's, was brought in to supervise the staff, including Joannie. Andra and Andrew developed a romantic relationship, which later failed. Andrew and Briscoll subsequently harassed Joannie in numerous ways, such as doubling her workload and commenting on her incompetence. Joannie filed a charge with the state's civil service agency (similar to the EEOC) and was ultimately given a "right to sue" letter. Joannie then filed a complaint in the state court.

   What should the court decide?

3. Christopher D. signed an employment agreement that included an arbitration clause. When he was discharged, he believed the decision was motivated by age discrimination. He filed a charge with the EEOC. The EEOC investigated and sued the employer in district court for age discrimination. The employer argued that the case should be submitted to arbitration and was not properly before the court.

   What should the court decide?

4. Hannah L. was employed by Cone Mills and was a union member. Hannah complained to the union representative about sex discrimination at work. The union represented her through the collective bargaining agreement's four-step grievance process, after which a resolution was reached. Subsequently Hannah again complained about continuing sex discrimination activity and sought help from the union. She was advised to seek legal counsel. Eventually she instituted litigation by filing a charge with the EEOC. The company argued that the method of resolution was arbitration, not litigation. The terms of the agreement upon which the company based its case were as follows:

> Section XX of the CBA specifically stated that the company and the union "agree that they will not discriminate against any employee with regard to race, color, religion, age, sex, national origin, or disability. . . . The parties further agreed that they will abide by all the requirements of Title VII of the Civil Rights Act of 1964." Section XX further noted, "Unresolved grievances arising under this Section are the proper subjects for arbitration." Cone Mills urged the district court to dismiss the case, arguing that the CBA clearly and unmistakably permitted arbitration as the sole remedy for alleged violations of Title VII.

   a. Should Hannah be forced to submit her claim to arbitration? What factors are important to support your answer?

   b. In assessing whether to pursue this case in court, what advice would you give to the company? Why?

   c. If you knew that the company would lose the case at the appellate level (which would likely have entailed high litigation costs, attorney fees, lost work time for certain employees, possible loss of morale among some workers, and possible bad press for the company), would your advice be the same for Question 2? Explain.

5. In 1970 Jeevan F. began working as a longshoreman. He was a member of the AFL-CIO (union) local. Clause 15(B) of the CBA between the union and the local provides in part as follows: "Matters under dispute which cannot be promptly settled between the Local and an individual Employer shall, no later than 48 hours after such discussion, be referred in writing covering the entire grievance to a Port Grievance Committee. . . ." If the Port Grievance Committee, which is evenly divided between representatives of labor and management, cannot reach an agreement within five days of receiving the complaint, then the dispute must be referred to a District Grievance Committee, which is also evenly divided between the two sides. The CBA provides that a majority decision of the District Grievance Committee "shall be final and binding." If the District Grievance Committee cannot reach a majority decision within 72 hours after meeting, then the committee must employ a professional arbitrator.

Clause 15(F) of the CBA provides as follows:

The Union agrees that this Agreement is intended to cover all matters affecting wages, hours, and other terms and conditions of employment and that during the term of this Agreement the Employers will not be required to negotiate on any further matters affecting these or other subjects not specifically set forth in this Agreement. Anything not contained in this Agreement shall not be construed as being part of this Agreement. All past port practices being observed may be reduced to writing in each port.

Finally, Clause 17 of the CBA states, "It is the intention and purpose of all parties hereto that no provision or part of this Agreement shall be violative of any Federal or State Law."

Jeevan was also subject to the Longshore Seniority Plan, which contained its own grievance provision, reading as follows: "Any dispute concerning or arising out of the terms and/or conditions of this Agreement, or dispute involving the interpretation or application of this Agreement, or dispute arising out of any rule adopted for its implementation, shall be referred to the Seniority Board." The Seniority Board is equally divided between labor and management representatives. If the board reaches agreement by majority vote, then that determination is final and binding. If the board cannot resolve the dispute, then the Union and the Local each choose a person, and this "Committee of two" makes a final determination.

On February 18, 1992, Jeevan injured his right heel and his back at work. He sought compensation from the employer for permanent disability under the Longshore and Harbor Workers' Compensation Act and settled the claim for $250,000 and $10,000 in attorney's fees. He was also awarded Social Security disability benefits.

In January 1995 Jeevan returned to the union hiring hall and asked to be referred for work. (At some point he obtained a written note from his doctor approving such activity.) Between January 2 and January 11, he worked for four stevedoring companies, none of which complained about his performance. When, however, the stevedoring companies realized that he had previously settled a claim for permanent disability, they informed the union that they would not accept him for employment because a person certified as permanently disabled is not qualified to perform longshore work under the CBA. The union responded that the employers had misconstrued the CBA and suggested that the ADA entitled Jeevan to return to work if he could perform his duties.

When Jeevan found out that the stevedoring companies would no longer accept him for employment, he contacted the union to ask how he could get back to work. The union told him to obtain counsel and file a claim under the ADA. He hired an attorney and eventually filed charges of discrimination with the Equal Employment Opportunity Commission (EEOC) and the South Carolina State Human Affairs Commission, alleging that the stevedoring companies and the union local had violated the ADA by refusing him work. In October 1995 he received a right-to-sue letter from the EEOC.

In January 1996 Jeevan filed a complaint against the local and six individual stevedoring companies in the U.S. District Court. Among the defenses raised by the defendants was Jeevan's failure to exhaust his remedies under the CBA and the seniority plan.

The CBA and the seniority plan contain clauses that seem to indicate that Jeevan had agreed to arbitrate disputes that arose between himself, the union local, and the companies. Who has the better argument—Jeevan or the defendants? Why?

References

1. Quotation from *The 'Lectric Law Library Reference Room.* See www.lectlaw.com/ref.html, under "Litigation Issues—General" (accessed March 3, 2008).

2. *AT&T Technologies, Inc. v. Communications Workers,* 475 U.S. 643, 649 (1986).

3. *Schoch v InfoUSA,* 341 F.3d 785 (2003).

4. See 9 U.S.C.S. 1 et seq. Title 9, U.S. Code, Sections 1–14, was first enacted February 12, 1925 (43 Stat. 883), codified July 30, 1947 (61 Stat. 669), and amended September 3, 1954 (68 Stat. 1233). Chapter 2 was added July 31, 1970 (84 Stat. 692); two new sections were passed by the Congress in October 1988 and renumbered on December 1, 1990 (PLs 669 and 702); Chapter 3 was added on August 15, 1990 (PL 101-369); and Section 10 was amended on November 15.

5. Language taken from *Scherk v. Alberto-Culver Co.* (1974) 417 US 506, 41 L Ed 2d 270, 94 S Ct 2449, CCH Fed Secur L Rep P 94593, reh den (1974) 419 US 885, 42 L Ed 2d 129, 95 S Ct 157.

6. Language taken from *Shearson/American Express v. McMahon* (1987) 482 US 220, 96 L Ed 2d 185, 107 S Ct 2332, CCH Fed Secur L Rep P 93265, reh den (1987) 483 US 1056, 97 L Ed 2d 819, 108 S Ct 31.

7. *Circuit City Stores v. Saint Clair Adams,* 532 U.S. 105, 121 S.Ct. 1302 (2001).

8. *Green Tree Financial Corp. v. Bazzle,* 539 U.S. 444, 123 S.Ct. 2402 (2003).

9. *Mitsubishi Motors v. Soler Chrysler,* 473 U.S. 614, 626 (1985).

10. *Pacificare Health Systems v. Book,* 538 U.S. 401, 123 S.Ct. 1531 (2003).

11. *In re Johnny Luna, Relator,* 175 S.W.3d 315; 2004 Tex. App. LEXIS 8241; 21 I.E.R. Cas. (BNA) 1353.

12. Taken from the American Arbitration Association (AAA) Web site: www.adr.org (accessed July 17, 2007).

13. R. B. Shaw, *Trust in the Balance* (San Francisco: Jossey-Bass, 1997), pp. 191–192.

14. From the Web site of the International Chamber of Commerce: http://www.iccwbo.org/court/arbitration/id4584/index.html (accessed July 5, 2008).

Chapter **Four**

Alternative Dispute Resolution: Mediation

Mediation seems to have achieved the universal appeal of popcorn and it probably should have. Like popcorn, it's quick, it's cheap, it's homey, and, unlike popcorn, it tends not to raise your blood pressure.

Robert M. Smith[1]

INTRODUCTION

Mediation is the utilization of a third party to help disputants resolve a conflict. Beyond that simple definition, mediations can differ in several ways. For example, the third party can be an external neutral person or one who is employed in-house by a firm; the parties may voluntarily enter mediation or may be required to use a mediator (such as by court order or through contractual provisions—sometimes referred to as *mediated settlement conferences*); the mediator may or may not be trained in mediation; and the goals of the process can differ (for example, to help resolve conflict, to assess the parties' dispute, or simply to return the parties to a more satisfactory relationship). These are just some factors that distinguish one mediation type from another.

The differences between the various types of mediation are significant, and it is imperative that the parties understand and appreciate precisely the type of mediation in which they are engaged and what the process requires.

When mediation is mandatory, such as when a judge orders mediation, the mediator initially faces the problem of obtaining the trust of the parties. Without the establishment of trust, a mediator's effectiveness is seriously hampered, and the success of the process is jeopardized.

Although mediation is commonly thought of as one of several modes of alternative dispute resolution, it can be much more than that. For example, organizations might use in-house mediation as a readily accessible and effective risk management tool to address problems before they escalate into lawsuits. The timing of mediation is critical: The earlier the process is invoked, the greater the likelihood of its success. When disputes are not acknowledged or acted upon, parties take up positions. As they encounter protracted resistance, they tend to become entrenched in those positions and more antagonistic toward their adversaries. Parties then focus on winning and are less willing to seek a mutually satisfactory resolution.

MEDIATION VERSUS ARBITRATION

As stated in the previous chapter, the most common alternative to litigation is arbitration. Mediation is a close second. Unlike arbitration, ordinary mediation bears no resemblance to litigation but rather is a cooperative problem-solving method of dispute resolution that uses the skills of a neutral third party: the mediator.

In binding arbitration the arbitrator acts as a judge and makes a decision that is binding on the parties. In mediation a mediator facilitates a settlement between the parties that reflects a mutually satisfactory agreement fashioned by the parties themselves. In mediation, therefore, the parties have greater control over the outcome than in either litigation or arbitration.

TYPES OF MEDIATION

Ordinary Mediation

In addition to ordinary mediation, at least three other types of mediation exist. The goal of ordinary mediation is to facilitate a mutually acceptable resolution to a conflict. The goal of the process is what distinguishes the various types. The EEOC refers to ordinary mediation as *facilitative* mediation.

Transformative Mediation

Although the mediators' skills and the process itself help to improve or stabilize a relationship, this is not usually the stated goal. However, in *transformative mediation* the relationship is the primary issue, and settlement is reached as a natural by-product of the improved relationship. A description of transformative mediation, as compared to problem-solving mediation, is provided by Bush and Folger in *The Promise of Mediation*[2].

In particular, Bush and Folger contrast problem-solving mediation and transformative mediation. In the problem-solving type, the mediator focuses on what it would take to resolve the dispute. After assessing the facts gathered from the disputants, they more or less direct the parties toward a solution, often drawing up a settlement agreement for the parties and seeking their consent to that agreement. Areas of disagreement may be overlooked, and the settlement is achieved by concentrating on what appears to be the consensus of the parties.

On the other hand, the transformative approach to mediation looks beyond the problem at hand to explore the underlying relationship. The mediator seeks to enable the parties to view their dispute from differing perspectives, including the perspective of the opposing party. To the extent the disputants can see and understand the other's viewpoint, while not necessarily agreeing with it, they are in a better position to arrive at a mutually agreeable solution. In essence, the parties are empowered not only to solve the current issue, but also to preserve the relationship and work together more effectively in the future.

Evaluative Mediation

The general rule is that the mediator does not offer an opinion on the case or conflict. The exception to this rule is known as *evaluative mediation*. In this type of mediation, the role of the mediator is a limited one.

In evaluative mediation the mediator is selected, in part, for his or her knowledge of the subject matter. Thus the mediator can develop an informed opinion about the likely outcome or verdict in the case. The mediator may present his or her opinion in caucus or to the parties jointly. In essence, a mediator or a panel of mediators listens to both sides and prepares an evaluation of the case. The parties use this information to further negotiate settlement. The parties can either accept or reject the evaluation. If either party rejects the assessment of the mediator, the case can proceed to litigation or binding arbitration. Evaluative mediation bears some resemblance to nonbinding arbitration in as much as the parties can either accept or reject the decision maker's ruling.

Shadow Mediation

Shadow mediation refers to the simultaneous use of mediation and arbitration. It is a conscious utilization of both methods to encourage the settlement of a case at various times throughout the process. As the case unfolds, there is the possibility that the parties will resolve the issues themselves with the help of the mediator rather than relying on the binding decision of the arbitrator.

Unless otherwise noted, this chapter will focus on traditional or ordinary mediation.

BENEFITS OF MEDIATION

In management terminology, litigation and arbitration would be referred to as zero-sum games—situations in which the results are a winner and a loser. In contrast, mediation, a collaborative venture, would be referred to as a win–win situation. Whereas mediation can repair and improve relations, litigation can terminate and destroy them. Other benefits of mediation include the following:

1. *Mediation is a private process.* This is crucial for companies who might risk costly and sometimes irreparable reputation damage with public lawsuits and trials.

2. *Mediation provides confidentiality.* A confidentiality agreement can ensure that nothing stated in the process of mediation can be used in a court of law. It is a private matter. If the parties do not resolve their dispute in mediation and the case moves to trial, neither party can use the information revealed in the mediation process to their advantage in court. This is clearly beneficial if admissions are made in the mediation process. Furthermore, without the promise of confidentiality, parties would be reluctant to divulge information that the other party could use against them. This reticence to share information would undermine the mediation process.

   The requirement of confidentiality is also important in light of current heightened concerns about privacy. The HR manager is advised to be cognizant of any potential for legal entanglement regarding careless divulging of protected private information by any party involved in a dispute resolution process.

   Note: If internal mediators are used and information is divulged in mediation that creates an obligation on the part of the employer to take certain actions, the mediator should nevertheless take steps to protect the interests of the company (such as in the case of allegations of sexual harassment that had not been previously disclosed). Privacy interests of all parties concerned must be respected.

3. *Mediation focuses on mutuality of interests.* Because it is not an adversarial process, mediation can incorporate and integrate what is important to both parties. Litigation, on the other hand, is designed to be adversarial and tends to aggravate whatever poor relationship has arisen between the parties. Mediation is designed to achieve an amicable result that will be satisfactory to both parties. Only when both parties agree does the mediator draw up a contractual agreement that will bind the parties.

4. *Mediation is cost-effective.* Whether mediators are internally or externally obtained, the cost is likely to be a fraction of relevant litigation costs. The Equal Employment Opportunity Commission provides free mediation services in certain cases.

5. *Mediation results in an agreement that is enforceable in a court of law.* If a party does not live up to the agreement, action can be taken to force compliance.

6. *Parties maintain more control* over the outcome than is possible in either litigation or arbitration.

DRAWBACKS OF MEDIATION

When mediation is not successful, its breakdown can often be linked to a failure to utilize the process in a timely manner, failure to understand the need for effective and experienced mediators, and parties (or one party) who are unwilling to cooperate in the process—sometimes in the hope of a better outcome in court and often because the mediation process was thrust upon them rather than voluntarily embraced.

Other drawbacks include the following:

1. *No discovery process is available*. Parties must rely on each other's good faith to be forthcoming with information relevant to the situation.
2. *No court decision or arbitrator award results from mediation*. Thus there is no order or award that can be enforced by a court of law. The result of a successful mediation is an agreement. In the event the agreement is not honored, the other party would have to sue for enforcement.
3. *Mediation agreements have no precedent-making power*. These agreements are strictly private resolutions with no ability to influence similar disputes.

AN EXAMPLE OF A SUCCESSFUL MEDIATION PROGRAM

An excellent example of the successful use of mediation is a program instituted by the U.S. Postal Service known as the REDRESS program[3]. Employees can opt to use the program, which uses outside mediators who have been trained in the transformative mode of mediation. The mediation takes place during working hours, and the mediator is paid on a per-case basis. Statistics about the program were reported as follows:

> Postal Service statistics compiled through independently monitored exit surveys show a resolution rate that exceeds 70 percent, and of the 30 percent not resolved in mediation only 15 percent actually move on to further proceedings. This program also tracks more than a 98 percent satisfaction rate, by both management and line staff, with mediators and the mediation process. REDRESS's track record clearly shows a decrease in repeat filers.[4]

MEDIATION "SURPRISES"

An experienced mediator has shared some success stories that are presented here[5]. Because of the confidential nature of mediation, names have been changed and the contexts of the situations have been modified.

Sometimes in mediation the solution the parties reach surprises even the mediator. The following three true vignettes make this point:

1. Wesley T. occupied a room directly below Lola B.'s room and complained to her that he was experiencing physical and mental stress caused by the activities above him. After several complaints and requests to make changes that would alleviate his discomfort, Wesley filed a legal action alleging that Lola made no attempt to ameliorate the situation. The matter was referred to mediation. During the mediation, a frustrated Wesley asked Lola why she was not making any attempt to address the problem. Lola admitted that she simply was not aware of anything she could do within her restricted budget. The mediation resolved with Wesley proposing that

he assist Lola in locating secondhand materials (such as carpeting) and making changes to the room, even at a potential minimal cost to Wesley.

2. Maureen E. and Hannah L. were extremely hostile to each other. After reviewing the mediation ground rules and proceeding with the first phase of the process, the parties remained openly hostile. The mediator had to intervene several times to remind the parties to not interrupt each other. The mediator then instructed Maureen to repeat her story and instructed Hannah to listen to Maureen as if Maureen were Hannah's best friend. Hannah was instructed to respond only with advice that she would give a best friend and not with a rebuttal. Hannah was assured that after Maureen was finished, Hannah would have the same opportunity. Each party proceeded as instructed. By the time Maureen finished telling her story, the demeanor of each party had completely changed. When Hannah finished with her story, the parties proposed and agreed on a settlement agreeable to both and put it in writing in less than 10 minutes.

3. Tim W. (the plaintiff in an action) was, by choice, not represented by counsel. During mediation it became obvious to the mediator that the defendant's counsel was interpreting a relatively new law in a way that the mediator had reason to believe was incorrect. During a caucus with defense counsel the mediator shared her interpretation of the law and the basis for that interpretation. Under the mediator's interpretation, the law would favor the plaintiff. When the parties returned from caucus, it was agreed that the mediation would close and they would reconvene the following week. When the mediator called the defendant's lawyer to schedule the next session, she was told that there was no need. The attorney had researched the law and concluded that the mediator's interpretation of the law was correct. They offered a settlement to the plaintiff, which the plaintiff accepted.

Mediation also provides an opportunity to "enlarge the pie." The more information is divulged in the process, the more likely a settlement becomes. Even something as simple as an apology can make a difference. In one case the plaintiff was willing to walk away with less than a fifth of the damages he was seeking if the defendant offered an apology. The plaintiff's willingness to do so was not related to the relative merits of the case. It was a reflection of the real and common circumstance that the plaintiff and defendant had at one time been friends. Although there were valid legal issues on the table, the emotions of the parties were a major force behind the litigation.

MEDIATION AND THE NATIONAL LABOR RELATIONS BOARD (NLRB)

Mediation has had a long history in the area of labor–management relations. As early as 1947, when Congress passed the Labor–Management Relations Act, it also created the independent agency of the Federal Mediation and

Conciliation Service. This agency was set up to prevent or minimize the impact of labor–management disputes on interstate commerce through the use of mediation, conciliation, and voluntary arbitration.

MEDIATION AND THE EQUAL EMPLOYMENT OPPORTUNITY COMMISSION (EEOC)

The Equal Employment Opportunity Commission is the enforcement mechanism for several federal antidiscrimination statutes. Historically, if the EEOC determined, after investigation of a particular complaint, that an employer was in violation of those laws, it attempted to resolve the dispute by conciliation. Today the EEOC has turned to mediation as a major means of obtaining compliance. "Since April 1999, the agency has mediated 52,400 charges, about 69 percent of which were successfully resolved in an average of 85 days."[6]

More recently the EEOC has pushed the use of mediation by making available to employers a free videotape highlighting the benefits of mediation.

In a 1997 General Accounting Office Report on alternative dispute resolution, the EEOC's adoption of mediation and other methods of resolving employment disputes was discussed. Portions of that Report follow:[7]

> ...
> EEOC issued regulations in 1992 that encouraged the use of ADR in the federal discrimination complaint process. And in 1995, EEOC established a policy encouraging the use of ADR for dealing with discrimination complaints by private sector employees.
> ...
> Another factor in the widening adoption of ADR practices has been a recognition that traditional methods of dispute resolution do not always get at the real or underlying issues involved between disputants and that methods that focus on the disputants' interests may have advantages.
>
> Traditional methods of dispute resolution—lawsuits in the private sector— are predominately position-based. Simply stated, each disputant stakes out a position—such as a complaint of discrimination or a defense against a complaint—and hopes to win the case. But interest-based dispute resolution . . . focuses on determining the disputants' underlying interests and working to resolve their conflict at a more basic level, perhaps even bringing about a change in the work environment in which their conflicts developed.
>
> EEOC, among others, has noted the potential value of the interest-based approach to dispute resolution in reducing the number of formal discrimination complaints. Reflecting on the high number of discrimination complaints among federal employees, an EEOC study recently concluded that ". . . there may be a sizable number of disputes . . . which may not involve discrimination issues at all. They reflect, rather, basic communications problems in the workplace. Such issues may be brought into the EEO process as a result of a perception that there is no other forum available to air general workplace

concerns. There is little question that these types of issues would be especially conducive to resolution through an interest-based approach."

Statistics on EEOC Mediation

A 2000 study showed that 96 percent of employers who participated in EEOC mediation were willing to try it again[8]. Although this reflects a positive attitude toward the use of mediation, when the EEOC offered mediation as a means of resolving the disputes submitted to it in 2002, only 30.5 percent of employers accepted, compared to 83 percent of employees. Some employers view the EEOC as an institution skewed to benefit employees. Others think that mediation "places too much emphasis on making a payout to workers"[9]. Irene Hill, an attorney for the EEOC, explains that the EEOC uses "facilitative mediation, and under facilitative mediation the parties design their own settlement. . . . It's definitely not EEOC's intent that mediators pressure parties to settle cases for monetary benefits or for any other type of benefits"[10]. The commission is actively engaged in getting employers to sign "universal agreements to mediate" (UAM) all charges filed against them. An employee making a complaint need not agree to the mediation, however, and the employer retains the right to opt out of the agreement in any given case[11].

INTERNAL MEDIATION PROGRAMS

In addition to its use in resolving legal conflicts between employers and employees, mediation has been adopted by companies as an early intervention tool to deal with workplace conflicts before they develop into more serious situations affecting morale and productivity, or possibly even lawsuits. The following advice is given to employers who wish to set up an ongoing process for resolution of workplace problems.

Developing Internal Mediation Programs

Here is how employers can establish an effective internal mediation process[12]:

1. Determine the types of disputes that arise in the workplace, how often they crop up, how they are dealt with, and how costly they are.
2. Establish a process by which employees can request mediation, including forms to be used, rules to be followed, and a means of tracking the outcomes and the process for continuous improvement.
3. Get help from professional mediators in designing the program.
4. Set up a pool of mediators from which employees can choose, and specify the process used in selecting them.
5. Run a pilot project of the program.
6. Identify key internal people to act as liaisons with outside mediators.

EMPLOYER CONSIDERATIONS REGARDING MEDIATION

Whether to Mediate

There is rarely any reason to forgo mediation. Even when a case is taken to court solely to establish precedent, mediation can be useful to minimize costs by settling nonessential or peripheral issues. However, precedent is rarely the motive for litigation. Compared to most litigation, mediation can save time and money.

When to Mediate

Complaints are often more easily settled before litigation begins. Therefore, it may benefit an employer to hire a mediator whenever there is an issue that management has failed to resolve. However, mediation can be used at many different times and for many different reasons. It can begin as soon as a conflict or problem is discovered to avoid the onset of litigation. It can be used at the start of, or soon after, litigation is commenced, or during any part of litigation—even to reach a postverdict settlement to avoid an appeal. It is used primarily to reach a settlement, but it can also improve the relationship of the parties or assist the parties in reaching a "meeting of the minds" on various issues.

Agreement to Mediate and Selection of the Mediator

Parties may come to mediation through a mediation clause in a contract, through an in-house mediation program, through court referral, or by agreement at any time. One party may propose a mediator; the parties may negotiate the selection from a panel; or one may be provided, for example, through court-ordered mediation. Because the mediator does not render a verdict, decision, or opinion, the potential problem of bias that exists in arbitration is largely absent from mediation. However, if this is evaluative mediation in which the mediator renders an opinion, the problem of bias would still exist.

Role of the Mediator

Ideally the mediator is an individual who is skilled at facilitating communication and compromise while remaining neutral. The mediator helps the parties identify core issues and obstacles to settlement and actively engages with the parties to create possibilities for settlement. The mediator may meet with the parties separately to discuss the strengths and weaknesses of their cases and, if permitted, may communicate settlement proposals. The goal of mediation is to reach a settlement that is acceptable to both parties, although it has other uses as well.

Experienced mediators will give the parties written ground rules for the process they are about to undertake. See the sample ground rules in Figure 4.1.

Internal and External Mediators

A company may have an internal mediator or may rely on external mediators. An internal mediator may be an ombudsman, a manager, a corporate attorney, or someone hired specifically as an in-house mediator. A major benefit to

FIGURE 4.1[13]
Sample Ground Rules Agreement for Mediation

Competency

I certify that I am competent to engage in this mediation.

I certify that I am over 18 years of age, in sound mind and body, and that I wish to engage in mediation.

I do not have a psychological or emotional disability that could interfere with my ability to competently engage in this mediation.

Conflict of Interest

I certify that I have revealed to the mediator and to all parties any relationship I have that could be construed as leading to potential mediator bias.

Process

I understand that the purpose of this mediation is to identify and explore issues involved in the conflict that is the subject of the mediation and to move toward settlement of those issues.

I understand that this mediation is an alternative to litigation. I know that the mediator does not sit in the role of judge and will not impose any settlement or penalty. I understand that the role of the mediator is to facilitate the process of mediation. I realize that although the mediator may be a lawyer, neither I nor any other party present has a lawyer–client relationship with the mediator regarding the conflict at hand. I understand that although the mediator may have knowledge of the law, the mediator does not provide legal advice. I understand that any agreement reached is not imposed but is freely entered as an acceptable solution to the conflict. I understand that I am not required to enter any agreement that I do not find satisfactory.

I understand that the mediator may find it necessary to speak with each party privately (this is called a caucus). I understand the mediator may caucus more often with one party than with the other, as the mediator deems necessary. I understand that this may happen more than once and is a normal part of the mediation process.

I understand that any agreement reached during mediation will not be legally binding unless it is reduced to writing and signed by all parties. I understand that a signed agreement is binding and enforceable as a legal contract.

Conduct

I agree not to interrupt when others are speaking.

I agree to refrain from yelling, using profanity, issuing threats, or name calling.

I agree to act respectfully at all times.

Confidentiality

I agree to keep this mediation confidential. I understand that nothing said here will be used in court in the event that litigation follows. However, anything discovered or discoverable from what is said might be used in a court of law.

I certify that I have read and agree to all of the above, and any questions I may have had have been adequately answered by the mediator.

Signed: _____ Date: _____

Copyright © Teresa M. Twomey, Esq.

having an internal mediator is that the company is more likely to mediate conflicts early, which increases rates of settlement, improves satisfaction of the parties, helps retain valuable employees, and avoids the costs of litigation, as well as hidden costs such as replacing employees and maintaining worker morale. Unfortunately, many companies wait until a lawsuit is filed and in process before they seek to mediate. By that time the parties are more entrenched, and reaching an agreement is more difficult and may take more time.

An internal mediator may be seen as beholden to the company and may have a difficult time earning employees' trust. If a party feels the mediator is "on the other side," he or she is likely to resist the process. A skilled mediator may be able to overcome this attitude with trust-building techniques.

The danger of having an in-house mediator is that if she or he fails to earn the trust of the parties, the parties may develop a distrust of all mediation. This can deprive an employer of a valuable tool if litigation commences. The alternative is to hire an outside mediator—an independent contractor—who is mutually agreed on by the parties and who may have an easier time earning the parties' trust. Either way, a mediator must reveal any and all potential conflicts of interest to both parties.

Criteria for Selecting a Mediator

A mediator can be anyone. Although many mediators are lawyers, this is not a requirement. In the absence of a law requiring certain qualifications, any adult can take on this role. Therefore, a mediator can be an external person hired by the disputants directly, an external individual hired by an employer to mediate disputes, or an internal mediator whose function is to help resolve workplace disputes.

There is a split of opinion regarding whether it is necessary for a mediator to have expertise or experience in the subject matter of a dispute. Some feel that such a mediator can talk more knowledgeably with the parties and help them gauge where they really stand in the case. Others feel that the process and desires of the parties are most important, and therefore expertise as a mediator, not expertise in a subject area, is most important.

Mediators who are also lawyers will have expertise that may benefit the parties. Their knowledge of the relevant law can help parties understand and appreciate their potential of succeeding in a case if it goes to trial.

Discovery of Evidence

Because the focus of mediation is on helping parties come to a mutually acceptable solution, there is generally little need for discovery. At times one party may refer to evidence that the other party has not "discovered"—information that was not previously revealed. When that happens, the ground rules of mediation generally state that evidence divulged during mediation cannot be referred to in a court of law unless that evidence was obtained otherwise. This insistence on confidentiality is crucial to the success of mediation. Without it, parties will be reluctant to reveal sensitive information.

Presentation of the Case

During mediation each party presents his or her side of the story. (Although attorneys may be present at mediation, their function is generally limited to advising the client.) Because this is a cooperative process, it is not necessary to present evidence and legal arguments. Nor does mediation follow the same formal processes as litigation and arbitration. In mediation the mediator may use many different skills and methods to help the parties reach an agreement.

caucus
In mediation a caucus is a private, closed meeting restricted to specific individuals who are pledged to confidentiality with regard to the information divulged at the meeting.

The Caucus

The most common tool that is used by mediators to improve chances of reaching a mutually satisfactory resolution is a *caucus*. During a caucus the mediator will meet with one side to discuss the conflict. Everything discussed in caucus remains private unless the party gives the mediator permission to reveal it to the other party. After caucus, the parties return to the table. When mediators learn privately from the parties what their concerns, fears, and objectives are, they are better able to help the parties fashion a win–win solution to the dispute.

MEDIATION OUTCOMES AND APPEALS

When a settlement is reached, the mediator records the terms of the settlement, which, upon the final agreement of the parties, becomes a binding contract. If no settlement is reached, nothing binds the parties. The courts generally afford mediation the same privacy rights as other settlement conferences. As previously indicated, any offer of settlement, discussion, or presentation of evidence is confidential and is not admissible in court. Furthermore, courts generally would not require or permit a mediator to testify in court regarding the substance of the mediation.

To reiterate, once the parties have reached an agreement through the services of a mediator or have accepted the evaluation submitted to the parties following mediation, the mediation resolution becomes binding. There is no right to revisit the issues in court. Case for Discussion 4-1 illustrates this point.

Case for Discussion 4-1

REDDAM V. CONSUMER MORTGAGE CORPORATION, 182 MICH. APP. 754 (1990)[14]

The trial court entered judgment in favor of the plaintiff in the amount of $35,000 pursuant to an accepted mediation evaluation, and the plaintiff appealed.

Facts

Plaintiff was employed by defendant under a written contract that included a provision for bonuses and also provided for a cap on bonuses of $50,000 per year. According to plaintiff, he was orally told not to worry about the cap and that he would be paid whatever bonus he had earned. During the second fiscal year of plaintiff's employment, his bonus was calculated to be $307,050. However, defendant's board of directors determined that it would not pay any bonus above the $50,000 provided for in the agreement. Around the same time, defendant's board of directors became aware of problems allegedly caused by plaintiff's selling bad mortgages to various mortgage purchasers, most prominently Fannie Mae (Federal National Mortgage Association). In fact, on January 26, 1986, Fannie Mae informed defendant that it was being terminated as an eligible lender to sell mortgages to Fannie Mae. Shortly thereafter, plaintiff was suspended pending an investigation and was subsequently terminated for cause pursuant to the contract.

Plaintiff thereafter filed suit, alleging various counts against defendant. The trial court dismissed all counts except the claims based on written contract and granted plaintiff leave to amend the complaint to allege entitlement to bonuses even if terminated for cause. However, the trial court thereafter also dismissed claims in the amended complaint based on the oral modification or supplement to the written contract. . . .

Plaintiff filed an application for leave to appeal in this Court seeking review of the dismissed claims. Two weeks after filing the application, the trial court submitted the matter to mediation, which resulted in the plaintiff's claim being evaluated at $35,000, and all parties accepted the evaluation. This Court thereafter dismissed plaintiff's application for leave to appeal as being moot in light of the accepted mediation evaluation. . . .

The entry of a judgment pursuant to the acceptance of a mediation evaluation is, in essence, a consent judgment. One may not appeal from a consent judgment, order, or decree. Finally, we agree with defendant that the mediation rule envisions the submission of an entire civil action to mediation where monetary damages are involved and that the mediators shall evaluate the total valuation of the case. That is, absent a showing that less than all issues were submitted to mediation, a mediation award covers the entire matter, and acceptance of that mediation award settles the entire matter. Accordingly, plaintiff's acceptance of the mediation award settled all claims, including those that had been dismissed by partial summary disposition.

Decision

Simply put, this Court has jurisdiction only over appeals filed by an "aggrieved party." Having accepted a mediation award, plaintiff is not an aggrieved party. Accordingly, this Court is without authority to entertain plaintiff's appeal. That is, absent particular facts justifying a contrary conclusion, which are not present in this case, the general rule to be applied is that there is no appeal from a judgment entered upon the acceptance of a mediation evaluation. Appeal is dismissed.

Questions for Discussion

1. Assume that the plaintiff had reason to believe that his discharge was groundless. Is it fair that the plaintiff was barred from defending his position regarding whether the employer had reasonable grounds to discharge him?

2. What would the plaintiff have had to do to preserve his right to appeal on the issue raised in Question 1?

3. What does this case tell you about the use of, and preparation for, mediation?

HOW MEDIATION FITS IN THE LEGAL FRAMEWORK

National Conference of Commissioners on Uniform State laws (NCCUSL)
An organization that provides model laws to the states from time to time in areas of concern to society; it is then up to each state to decide whether to adopt the legislation.

Current federal and state laws do not regulate mediation. The primary exception occurs when laws regulate who may serve as a mediator. For example, state-certified mediators are usually required in custody cases because these agreements must comply with child custody and support guidelines. However, in other situations mediation is treated as informally as negotiation, with the exception of statutes addressing the need for confidentiality in the mediation process. No state has as yet passed a law to regulate mediation in any other aspect. However, a model mediation statute has been drawn up by the **National Conference of Commissioners on Uniform State Laws (NCCUSL)**, excerpts of which are given here. This model statute provides guidance to anyone interested in using this form of dispute resolution. If a state adopts this law, employers in that state must be aware of its provisions.

Excerpts from the Model Uniform Mediation Act (1999)[15]

SECTION 1. DEFINITIONS. In this Act:

(a) "Mediation" means a process in which disputants negotiate a dispute with the assistance of a mediator toward a resolution that is to be the disputants' decision.

(b) "Mediator" means an impartial person or persons appointed by a court or government entity, or engaged by disputants through an agreement evidenced by a record.

(c) "Disputant" means a person who attends a mediation and:
   (1) has an interest in the outcome of the dispute or whose agreement is necessary to resolve the dispute, and
   (2) was asked by a court, governmental entity, or mediator to appear for mediation, or entered an agreement to mediate and that agreement was evidenced by a record.

(d) "Mediation communication" means a statement made as part of a mediation unless the disputant would not be reasonable in expecting that the mediation is confidential. It may also encompass a communication for purposes of considering, initiating, continuing, or reconvening a mediation or retaining the mediator.

SECTION 2. CONFIDENTIALITY: PROTECTION AGAINST COMPELLED DISCLOSURE; WAIVER.

(a) A disputant may refuse to disclose, and prevent any other persons from disclosing, mediation communications in a civil, juvenile, criminal misdemeanor, arbitration, or administrative proceeding. These protections may be waived, but only if waived by all disputants explicitly or through conduct inconsistent with the continued recognition of the protection.

. . .

SECTION 4. QUALITY OF MEDIATION.

(a) A mediator shall disclose information related to his or her qualifications or possible conflicts of interest if requested by a mediation disputant or representative of a disputant.

(b) If immunity from liability is not extended to mediators by common law judicial immunity doctrine, rules of court, or other law of this state, any contractual provision purporting to disclaim the mediator's liability shall be void as a matter of public policy.

(c) A disputant has the right to be represented at any mediation session. A predispute waiver of representation prior to mediation is ineffective.

Management **Perspective**

The role of a human resource manager is, to a great extent, to do what is needed to provide competent and appropriate employees to perform work that is needed to accomplish a company's objectives. The more the employees' goals are aligned with the goals of the employer, the more likely the success of the enterprise. A skilled manager will be cognizant of the degree to which this alignment exists and will know how to achieve the needed mutuality of purpose. One method available to managers is that proposed by Bill Torbert in his book *Action Inquiry*. A manager's use of this manner of communication could fend off disputes that might lead to litigation. Note how use of action inquiry communications could be especially beneficial to a mediator. The following are excerpts from Torbert's book:[16]

> In relationships . . . the value-explicit aim of action inquiry is to generate a critical and constructive *mutuality*. Power differences and the unilateral use of power by either party reduce the likelihood of trust and honest communication. Mutuality is generated through two dynamics. The first dynamic is an increasingly open inquiry into the play of power between parties, with mutuality as a goal. . . . The second dynamic that generates

mutuality . . . is more and more creative actions to develop shared visions and strategies, increasingly collaborative ways of conversing, and jointly determined ways of learning the worth of what is created together[17].

Speaking is the primary and most influential medium of action in the human universe. . . . Our claim is that the four parts of speech—framing, advocating, illustrating, and inquiring—represent the very atoms of human action. If we can cultivate a silent, listening, triple-loop awareness to our own actions and to a team's current dynamics . . ., we can arrange and rearrange the interweaving of these atoms as we speak, peacefully harnessing the human equivalent of technological, unilateral nuclear power.

* **

Here are the definitions and examples of the four parts of speech:

1. *Framing* refers to explicitly stating what the purpose is for the present occasion, what the dilemma is that everyone is at the meeting to resolve, what assumptions you think are shared or not shared (but need to be tested out loud to be sure). . . .
2. *Advocating* refers to explicitly asserting an option, perception, feeling, or strategy for action in relatively abstract terms. . . .
3. *Illustrating* involves telling a bit of a concrete story that puts meat on the bones of the advocacy and thereby orients and motivates others more clearly.
4. *Inquiring* obviously involves questioning others in order to learn something from them. In principle, the simplest thing in the world; in practice, one of the most difficult things in the world to do effectively. Why? One reason is that we often inquire rhetorically, as we just did. We don't give the other the opportunity to respond; or we suggest by our tone that we don't really want a *true* answer.[18]

A manager orients new employees to the workplace, describing their roles in the organization, and subsequently keeping them informed about what they must know to perform their duties in the workplace. This interface is crucial to maintaining a productive workplace. Torbert provides guidance on communication strategies that can strengthen a manager's effectiveness.

As cases are presented throughout this book, ask whether an "action inquiry" approach to the problems that led to the legal actions presented might have been instrumental in averting the lawsuits. How were communications conducted in the organization? To what extent was the supervisor's (or other party's) way of being a contributing factor to the plaintiff–employee's complaint? Successful, effective mediators will make inquiries and create an environment in which the parties will listen to each other so that each party will feel that he or she has been heard.

TIPS FOR MEDIATORS INVOLVED IN DISPUTES TRANSCENDING NATIONAL BORDERS

When human resource management functions can transcend geographic borders, a look at international mediation is warranted. In a recent publication, successful international mediators listed tips for those engaged in international mediation. Excerpts from that article are given here[19]:

International disputes are often complicated by long distances, cultural misunderstanding, political intervention, and shifting commercial agendas . . .

Premediation—Selling the Benefits of Mediation

Mediation might be treated by inexperienced advisers and managers as a last resort, so the first task of the advocate is to sell the process to in-house colleagues. Try presenting the following benefits to support the argument for international mediation:

Preservation of business relationships.

Business reputation and face-saving, confidentiality, and avoiding loss of face (a key goal in some cultures).

Savings on transaction costs: The direct and indirect costs of litigation and arbitration are multiplied by a factor of at least 1.5 in international cases. . . .

A fresh mind/objectivity: Mediation offers the best feature of litigation/arbitration—a third-party neutral—but does so within a framework of greater flexibility for the neutral and greater safety and control for the parties. The normal sensitivities of the parties in negotiation may be multiplied at an international level by an additional level of cross-cultural suspicions or misunderstandings. Mediator neutrality is therefore an even more valuable commodity, although may also be more difficult to achieve in international cases.

Holistic approach: Effective mediation requires giving attention to all of the dimensions of a dispute (legal, technical, commercial, etc.)—conducting a "dispute diagnosis." Particularly important in complex international disputes. . . .

A complementary tool: Mediation can be woven into other dispute resolution approaches, or be used as a parallel process alongside existing arbitration or litigation proceedings. . . .

Confidentiality

. . . Parties should consider whether they want to opt for a mediation agreement governed by the law of a jurisdiction that protects confidentiality. If so, they should ensure that the mediation takes place in that favorable jurisdiction.

Select a mediator whose training and professional code of ethics supports adherence to mediation confidentiality.

Documents: Distinguish between those documents created specifically for the mediation (protected from later disclosure in legal proceedings) and those contemporaneous to the dispute that evidence factual and technical issues (not protected). If in doubt, use the protection of mediation confidentiality to disclose a document to the mediator only.

Law of the Mediation Agreement

. . . A mediation agreement should normally provide that any settlement will not be legally binding unless it is reduced to writing and signed.

E. Carroll and K. Mackie, "Tips for Lawyers Working in International Mediation," *CEDR*, May 2005. This article is abstracted from E. Carroll and K. Mackie, "International Mediation—The Art of Business Diplomacy" (Kluwer, 1999). See also http://www.cedr.com/about_us/library/ (accessed March 3, 2008).

Summary

Mediation is a useful tool for managers, whether dealing with employees who have begun legal action against an employer or simply as a means of attempting to resolve a workplace disruption that threatens to develop into such a lawsuit. Effective intervention at a critical time can prevent legal entanglements.

The major benefits of mediation include the following: (1) The process is private, and statements made during the process are confidential; (2) the mediation process promotes mutual interests and concerns and is not adversarial; (3) it is a cost-effective means of resolving disputes; and (4) it can result in an agreement that is enforceable in court.

The Equal Employment Opportunity Commission has stepped up its use of mediation in resolving many disputes that are submitted to it. The EEOC is in the process of getting employers to sign "universal agreements to mediate" all charges filed against them. It is up to the employee, however, to agree or disagree with the use of mediation, and the employer retains the right to opt out of mediation for any given case.

There are three major types of mediation: (1) ordinary mediation (also known as traditional or facilitative mediation), in which the mediator strives to bring about a mutually acceptable resolution of a dispute between the parties; (2) evaluative mediation, in which one or more mediators hears the stories of the parties, assesses the case, and presents an evaluation of the case to the parties; and (3) transformative mediation, in which the primary goal is the healing and improvement of a relationship, and the secondary goal is resolution of a conflict.

Mediation can occur at any point in a relationship. Employers can use a mediation process to deal with routine problems that arise in the workplace. This may be an effective way of reducing exposure to unnecessary legal actions. Often, after legal action has been taken, a court may order the parties to mediation before a trial is held. If mediation fails to result in a satisfactory agreement, the case will proceed as if no mediation had taken place. Mediation can also be used during a trial or even after a trial court has issued a decision.

Once a matter has been resolved by mediation in a litigated case, there is no right to appeal unless the parties made it clear that the mediation was entered to resolve only certain issues. In such a case the parties can preserve their right to continue to litigate and/or appeal other issues in the case.

In the event of a breach of the confidentiality agreement involved in mediation, the breaching party may lose the right to litigate the case. The court can dismiss the case against the breaching party. Also, the confidentiality clause ensures that, in the event of a failed mediation, statements made in the process cannot be used in court.

Class Exercise: Mediation Role Play

The instructor will prepare students to engage in a mediation process.

Questions

1. Dorothy W. alleged that she deposited $200,000 in Citizens Bank and opened two certificates of deposit, each for $100,000. Several months later Dorothy sued the bank because she discovered that her statements showed only one CD for $100,000, and the bank denied that it ever received the additional $100,000. The court ordered mediation, and the parties signed a mediation agreement with a confidentiality clause. During mediation Dorothy was offered $25,000 to settle the case. Dorothy refused the offer and called the local newspaper, which ran an article about the matter. The bank then requested a dismissal of the case in its favor based on the breach of the confidentiality agreement.
   a. Should the court grant the bank's request?
   b. What are the benefits of confidentiality in mediation?

2. Andra V. filed a claim against her local telephone company based on Title VII and state law discrimination allegations as well as retaliation grounds that occurred while she was an employee. The court ordered that the matter be sent to mediation. In the meantime Andra filed for bankruptcy. After the mediation Andra argued that the mediator pressured her to accept a $50,000 settlement because her case against the telephone company was not listed in her bankruptcy petition, and if she took the case to trial any damages she recovered would go directly to creditors. This statement was made in front of Andra's attorney. Shortly thereafter she learned from her bankruptcy attorney that her Title VII claim was in fact insulated from the creditors of her bankruptcy estate. Andra sought to avoid enforcement of the mediated settlement agreement.
   a. Will Andra succeed?
   b. What issues are raised in this case?

3. Andrew B., an African-American employee of ABC Gas, instituted action against the company alleging various forms of racial discrimination in

violation of federal and state laws. He claimed that he was denied training and promotion opportunities afforded to employees who were not African-American, and he also alleged that he was subjected to racially offensive remarks for which the supervisors failed to take corrective action. The court ordered mediation. Several matters were negotiated between the parties, and finally a written agreement was drawn up. Andrew refused to sign, stating, among other things, that there was no clause assuring him that he would no longer be subjected to racial discrimination—an assurance that he was led to believe would be in the agreement. When ABC took the matter to court to enforce the agreement, the court ruled in ABC's favor. The attorneys, the mediator, and ABC all testified that the agreement contained all the terms to which there had been verbal consent by the parties. Andrew appealed the decision.

a. What are the issues?

b. Is Andrew likely to succeed?

c. How would a case such as this be decided?

4. Weiwei Y. sued her employer on the basis of race and national origin discrimination, a violation of New Jersey statutory law. She also sued for retaliation. After a failed evaluative mediation attempt, the matter went to trial on the issue of the employer's failure to promote the plaintiff to a managerial position. After a week-long trial, before the trial court made its decision, the parties were asked to submit proposed findings of fact to clarify for the judge the factual matters that were in dispute. In her proposal, Weiwei revealed the mediation evaluation amount and that she had accepted the evaluation and the employer had rejected it. The employer requested a dismissal of the lawsuit based on the fact that making such a revelation was prejudicial and a violation of New Jersey law.

a. How would you evaluate this case?

b. What decision is the court likely to make, and why?

References

1. Robert M. Smith is a full-time commercial mediator and arbitrator in San Francisco. He is the author of *Alternative Dispute Resolution for Financial Institutions,* 2nd ed. (West Group, 1998). He was senior litigation counsel for Bank of America and special assistant to the U.S. Attorney General.

2. R. A. Baruch Bush, and J. P. Folger, *The Promise of Mediation* (San Francisco: Jossey-Bass, 2005). From an online summary by Heidi Burgess at www.colorado.edu/conflict/transform/tmall.htm (accessed July 17, 2007).

3. A. Begler, "How Mediation Can Resolve Workplace Disputes—The Benefits of Mediation, How to Start a Program, Pick a Mediator, and More," March 28, 2001. See also www.workforce.com/archive/feature/22/28/28/index.php (accessed March 3, 2008).

4. Begler, ibid.

5. As relayed to the author by Teresa M. Twomey, Esq., attorney/mediator.

6. A. Brynelson, *Employment Roundup* (M. Lee Smith Publishers LLC, 2004).

7. GAO Report to the Chairman, Subcommittee on Civil Service, Committee on Government Reform and Oversight, House of Representatives, August 1997. http://www.gao.gov/cgi-bin/getrpt?GGD-97-157 (accessed August 27, 2008).

8. M. Barrier, "The Mediation Disconnect: If the EEOC's Program Is Working so Well, Why Aren't More Employers Willing to Try It?" *HR MAGAZINE,* May 2003, p. 1.

9. Ibid. at p. 2.

10. Ibid. at p. 3.

11. Ibid. at p. 4.

12. Begler, op cit.

13. Copyright © Teresa M.Twomey, Esq.

14. *Reddam v. Consumer Mortgage Corporation,* 182 Mich. App. 754 (1990).

15. *National Conference of Commissioners on Uniform State Laws,* April 1999. Copyright National Conference of Commissioners on Uniform State Laws.

16. B. Torbert, and Associates, *Action Inquiry: The Secret of Timely and Transforming Leadership* (San Francisco: Berrett-Koehler, 2004).

17. Ibid. at p. 7.

18. Ibid. at pp. 27–30.

19. E. Carroll and K. Mackie, "Tips for Lawyers Working in International Mediation," *CEDR,* May 2005. This article is abstracted from E. Carroll and K. Mackie, "International Mediation—The Art of Business Diplomacy" (Kluwer, 1999). See also www.cedr.co.uk/index.php? location+library/articles/tips_lawyers_intmed.htm (accessed March 3, 2008).

Bibliography

Portions of this chapter were printed first in *Competition Forum.* R. Twomey, "Mediation and Its Merits as an Alternative Method of Employer-Employee Dispute Resolution," *Competition Forum,* Vol. 4, No. 2, 2006.

Employment Law and the Common Law

5. Employment at Will

6. Privacy Rights, Restrictive Covenants, and Intellectual Property

Employment at Will

Over the past century, the United States has moved from a society, which had primarily adopted Adam Smith's laissez faire view of employment, into a society that regulates, often quite extensively, the employment relationship. . . . The current century brought, again in a somewhat tumultuous fashion, the Fair Labor Standards Act, labor laws, civil rights laws, a vast collection of employee protection statutes, as well as the erosion of the employment at will doctrine.[1]

INTRODUCTION

In the United States, contrary to the employment laws of many other countries, employers and employees can, with impunity, terminate an employment relationship at any time, whether for good cause, bad cause, or no cause at all, unless they have agreed otherwise, as in a contract for a definite time[2]. This doctrine, referred to as *employment at will,* is part of each state's common law.

Employers clearly have the right to reprimand or discharge an employee for misconduct, insubordination, incompetence, failure to follow company policies and rules, excessive absences, and many other justifiable causes. Hence a manager can fire an employee for violating the company's dress code or for poor employee evaluations. The employment at will principle, which originated in court opinions, adds to that right the power to dismiss an employee for whatever reason the employer wishes, including no reason at all. Therefore, in an at-will situation an employee can be dismissed if the manager perceives that the employee does not fit in well or because she wants to hire a replacement with a livelier personality. To be sure, in many situations that right is limited, as will be discussed later in this chapter and the following chapters.

The common law principle of employment at will has been challenged in the courts of all the states, and the result is a patchwork of state laws that vary from strong adherence to many exceptions. When the doctrine is upheld, employees claiming wrongful discharge must resort to basic contract principles or statutory laws prohibiting discharge for discriminatory or other clearly articulated reasons. In short, the United States has no recognized general rule that an employer must show good cause for dismissing an employee.

Two states have passed legislation regarding wrongful dismissal; one has embraced the employment at will concept and the other has rejected it. Arizona has codified the employment at will doctrine[3]; in that state an employee must prove a violation of statutory law to win a wrongful discharge action. This effectively vitiates many arguments made by employees that their employers' conduct violates established public policy (but not necessarily a specific law). In Arizona employees would also fight an uphill battle in claiming breach of an implied covenant of good faith and fair dealing, which is essentially a breach of contract claim that has been made successfully in many states even in the absence of an otherwise clear employment contract.

Whereas Arizona has codified the employment at will principle, Montana has legislatively abrogated it. Montana legislators rejected this doctrine by passing the Wrongful Discharge from Employment Act of 1987, which prohibits discharge of employees without good cause. Specifically barred is firing in retaliation for an employee's refusal to violate public policy or for reporting such a violation, and terminating an employee in direct violation of the provisions of an employer's written personnel policy.[4]

In the state of Arkansas efforts are being made to pass a law that would abolish the employment at will doctrine and replace it with an employee-favorable wrongful employment termination act. The anticipated text of that bill is as follows[5]:

SECTION 1.

(a) This act shall be known and may be cited as The Arkansas Wrongful Employment Termination Act. The common law doctrine of employment at will no longer applies to any employment contract, arrangement, agreement, or circumstance, within the State of Arkansas nor to any situation wherein the law of Arkansas applies, unless that employment contract, arrangement, agreement, or circumstance has been expressly exempted or excepted by act of the Arkansas State Legislature.

(b) Within any and all situations of employment, which are not specifically exempted nor excepted by express legislative enactment of the Arkansas General Assembly, any discharge from employment of an employee by that employee's employer, must meet, comport and comply with fundamental notions and standards of fairness, justice, reason, rationale, justification, even-handedness, nondiscrimination, and nondisparate treatment.

(c) The breach of this act shall ipso facto give rise to causes of action in law, equity, declaratory proceedings, and court directives, including restraining orders and injunctive relief. A cause may be brought by any aggrieved and non-exempt employee, the authorized agent or representative of such employee, or by an employer on behalf of a recalcitrant or reluctant employee. Where the ends of substantial justice require, a cause of action hereunder may be brought by a municipality, by the State of Arkansas, or a department or agency thereof, by an agency or a department of the United States, or by the United States.

(d) Punitive damages shall be awardable within appropriate cases wherein the conduct of the employer has been egregious. By "egregious" is meant that the employer acted with malice, or with wantonness, or with reckless disregard of the rights of the employee. The punitive damages, if appropriate to the case, shall be in addition to the just and reasonable recompense to the aggrieved and injured employee.

(e) Within its sound judicial discretion, a court of competent jurisdiction may award a just and reasonable attorney's fee to an aggrieved employee who prevails in a cause of action brought under this act.

(f) Any claimed, purported, attempted, or alleged waiver of the terms or of the application of this act, whether written, expressed, or implied, shall not be afforded either force nor effect by a court of competent jurisdiction.

Global **Perspective**

The unemployment rate in France has been quite high for several years; and in response to a government remedy targeting the high rate of unemployment for youths, there was major rioting in the streets. Some argue that this high rate of unemployment is linked to French law that makes it extremely difficult for employers to fire workers.

The following excerpt from an article published in January 2006 gives a sense of the French situation[6]:

Dominique de Villepin, France's prime minister, wants to loosen job protection rights for young workers. A recent *Financial Times* article (de Villepin labor reforms) highlights de Villepin's labor proposal. Existing French labor laws make it difficult and expensive for French firms to fire workers. The laws intend to prevent companies from dismissing employees on a whim. But job protection rights have some unintended consequences as well.

To analyze the effects of the laws, imagine yourself as a French business owner. Suppose a young, inexperienced worker applies for a position with your firm. There's a 50 percent chance she will work hard and a 50 percent chance she will slack off. You might be less willing to take a chance on this inexperienced worker if you face high dismissal costs in the event that she's a slacker. In short, French laws designed to protect workers actually create a disincentive for businesses to hire young, inexperienced workers in the first place. Some argue that this accounts for the sky-high youth unemployment rate in

France, which currently stands at 23 percent—and even higher among immigrant populations.

De Villepin's reform would allow companies to hire workers aged 26 and under on a two-year trial basis. If a young worker excels during the two-year trial, she gets a full-time contract and all of the job protection rights that come with it. But if she doesn't, the employer could let her go at no cost. De Villepin argues that these looser firing restrictions would encourage firms to hire more young workers, driving down the youth unemployment rate.

Source: From Aplia Econ Blog (www.Aplia.com). Reprinted by permission from Aplia Learning.

WHEN DOES THE EMPLOYMENT AT WILL DOCTRINE COME INTO PLAY?

Some circumstances the employment at will doctrine does not apply. When the employer and employee have agreed to a specified period of employment or to the performance of a specified project, neither party has the right to terminate the relationship arbitrarily during the term of the agreement. Union workers are protected from unjust dismissal by a collective bargaining agreement containing a provision requiring just cause for termination. Government employees have the added protection of the constitutional guarantees of due process and therefore are not employees at will. Figure 5.1 graphically describes the applicability of the employment at will doctrine.

FIGURE 5.1
Applicability of the Employment at Will Doctrine

Type of Employment Agreement	Public Sector	Private Sector	Union	Nonunion
Written contract for a *definite* term of employment.	O	O	O	O
Written contract for an *indefinite* term of employment.	X*	X	O**	X
No written contract; agreement is *indefinite* as to term of employment.	X*	X	O***	X
No written contract; agreement is *definite* as to term of employment.	O	O	O	O

Key: X = Doctrine is applicable. Management can fire employee without cause, unless otherwise agreed.
     O = Doctrine is not applicable. Management must abide by agreement for definite term.
*Even if the doctrine applies, public employees might be protected by a constitutional right of due process before termination.
**With rare exception, union employees are covered by comprehensive collective bargaining agreements that protect them from discharge without cause.
***With rare exceptions, the collective bargaining agreement will be a written document.

EROSION OF THE EMPLOYMENT AT WILL DOCTRINE

The employment at will doctrine, a function of common law, was adopted by state judges in cases that pitted employers' termination decisions against employees 'rights to continued employment. The judges determined in case after case that both the employer and the employee could end the employment relationship at any time unless they had agreed otherwise. Over time, however, this principle has been eroded by numerous statutory protections for employees in protected classes, such as people with disabilities and those in specified minority groups. In addition to the protected classes, the unionized labor force and civil servants enjoy protection from wrongful dismissal. Unions' collective bargaining agreements (contracts between labor and management) contain clauses that require good cause for discharge. Civil servants benefit from statutory protection provided to government workers, such as the Civil Service Reform Act as well as the federal and state constitutions.

The various statutes, both federal and state, that prohibit discrimination on the basis of sex, creed, national origin, race, color, disability, pregnancy, and other categories are the subject of later chapters in this book. This chapter explores the growing number of other legal exceptions to the employment at will doctrine. Employment at will cases are a type of wrongful discharge case. They involve factual situations and arguments that range from claims that an employer violated an implied contract to claims that an employer violated established notions of public policy.

EXCEPTIONS TO THE EMPLOYMENT AT WILL DOCTRINE

As we just noted, the common law principle that employers can legally dismiss employees for any reason unless otherwise agreed is not as straightforward as it once was. Here are situations in which the employment at will principle will not protect an employer against a wrongful dismissal challenge:

1. *The public policy exception:* The employer's action is contrary to established public policy, which could be grounded in common law, statutory law, or constitutional law.
2. *Breach of implied contract:* The employer's action is a breach of an implied contract between the employer and the employee, such as might be evidenced in a company handbook.
3. *The implied covenant of good faith and fair dealing:* In commercial dealings there is an implied contract obligation that parties will observe standards of good faith and fair dealing. In employment situations there is no such implied obligation. However, in some states this requirement is being imposed on employment relationships, either by judges in case decisions or by legislators enacting statutory laws to that effect.

4. *Violation of statutory law:* The employer's action violates a statutory law, such as those prohibiting workplace discrimination. Other examples include these:

   - The employer's action violates a whistleblower protection law.
   - The employer's action violates statutory law that prohibits retaliation against an employee who utilizes the benefits of a particular law.
   - The employer's action violates the Civil Service Reform Act regulating the employment relationship between the government and its workers.
   - The employer's action violates labor laws.

5. *Tort allegations:* The employer's action gives rise to a tort allegation. Although the probable success of any such allegation may be small, employers must nonetheless exercise caution to avoid the disruption and cost of defending themselves. Examples of possible allegations include these:

   - The employer defamed the employee, such as by unfairly accusing the employee of sexual harassment of a fellow worker and then firing him.
   - The employer's manner of dismissing the employee amounts to intentional infliction of emotional distress, such as first demoting an employee, humiliating her several times in front of colleagues, or requiring her to do demeaning work before dismissal.
   - The employer impermissibly invaded the employee's privacy, such as in a suspicion of theft circumstance or an unnecessarily invasive drug test.
   - The employer acted with malice or bad faith in discharging the employee, constituting the tort of abusive or wrongful discharge.
   - The employer's action amounted to fraud.
   - The employer's action constitutes an intentional interference with contractual relations.

These items are neither exhaustive nor mutually exclusive; the facts of a case may give rise to more than one of these arguments. For example, if an employee is terminated in retaliation for refusing to give false facts in a sexual harassment investigation, it could be classified as a public policy case, a common law tort case, a violation of statutory law protecting whistleblowers, and so on. There can be, and often is, overlap among the various exceptions to employment at will.

The Public Policy Exception

The public policy exception to the at-will principle recognizes that an employee occasionally gets into an ethical or legal dilemma because of an employer's request. For example, a nurse might be ordered by a doctor to falsify or alter a diagnosis or a prescription dosage that has been made in error to the detriment of a patient. If her refusal to do so results in dismissal, she could sue for wrongful termination. Her legal argument would be that the act of firing her under such circumstances violates established public policy.

In a public policy case of wrongful dismissal, courts generally analyze state law to determine whether there was indeed an established public policy recognized in that state that would support the employee's case. In the previous example, an employee could rely on the common law tort of fraud or on a specific statutory law regarding a patient's right to know. In the absence of such laws, a public policy argument may fail even if the employee's action was clearly prompted by ethical considerations.

A 1992 California Supreme Court case recognized the public policy exception to employment at will relationships, and made this comment:

> For at root, the public policy exception rests on the recognition that in a civilized society the rights of each person are necessarily limited by the rights of others and of the public at large; this is the delicate balance which holds such societies together. Accordingly, while an at-will employee may be terminated for no reason, or for an arbitrary or irrational reason, there can be no right to terminate for an unlawful reason or a purpose that contravenes fundamental public policy. Any other conclusion would sanction lawlessness, which courts by their very nature are bound to oppose.[7]

Public policy violations generally fall into one of four categories. An employee could argue that termination was caused by his (1) refusing to violate a statute, such as refusing to participate in a price-fixing scheme; (2) performing a statutory obligation, such as serving on jury duty or telling the truth under oath; (3) exercising a statutory right or privilege, such as engaging in union activities; or (4) reporting an alleged violation of a statute of public importance, such as reporting illegal activity of the employer[8].

These listed exceptions to the employment at will doctrine are not all-inclusive, and whether any of the circumstances that give rise to a wrongful dismissal case will result in a successful outcome for an aggrieved employee ultimately depends on the common law of the state that has jurisdiction over the case.

In an early case, *Tameny v. Atlantic Richfield Co.* (1980), 27 C3d 167, employee Tameny, who had worked for Arco for 15 years with a satisfactory record and a promotion, was fired for refusing to carry out illegal activity on the defendant's behalf and direction. Arco was setting prices in violation of antitrust laws, and Tameny, a sales representative, refused to pressure service stations to reduce prices in conjunction with the price-setting scheme. The plaintiff sought recovery from Arco on a number of theories, asserting, among other things, that Arco's conduct in discharging him for refusing to commit a criminal act was a tort violation and subjected the employer to liability for compensatory and punitive damages under normal tort principles. Arco contended, however, that the employee's remedy was restricted to a contract claim and not tort. The trial court accepted Arco's argument. On appeal, the court wrote, ". . . [T]he relevant authorities both in California and throughout the country establish that when an employer's discharge of an employee violates fundamental principles of public policy, the discharged employee may maintain a tort action and recover damages traditionally available in such actions."

Case for Discussion 5-1

GANTT V. SENTRY INSURANCE, 824 P.2D 680, 686-87 (CAL. 1992)[9]

Facts

This case involved a sales manager, Gantt, hired to develop the Sacramento sales force for this insurance company. Joyce Bruno, the liaison between trade associations and two of Sentry's offices, reported to both Gantt and Desser. Bruno complained to Gantt of sexual harassment by Desser. Gantt promptly reported the matter to appropriate people in the company, but the harassment continued. After Gantt spoke up a second time on the matter, Desser was demoted and Bruno was transferred to a sales representative position. A month later she was fired.

Bruno filed a complaint with California's Department of Fair Employment and Housing (DFEH). Sentry's house counsel investigated the charges. It gradually became apparent to Gantt that his support of Bruno was not appreciated by some of Sentry's executives. Less than three months after the DFEH official interviews, Gantt attended an awards ceremony to accept a life insurance sales award on behalf of his office. The next morning he was demoted to sales representative. His new supervisor warned him that he would be fired if he attempted to undermine his authority, and that he would not be given a "book" of existing accounts to start his new job. According to Gantt, such a book was necessary to survive.

Gantt experienced illnesses the following month and missed days at work. He took a position a couple of months later with another company and shortly thereafter filed suit alleging that "as a result of the pressure applied by the defendants . . . he was forced to resign."

The jury returned a verdict in favor of Gantt. Among other things, they believed he was *constructively discharged.* Furthermore, the jury concluded that Sentry acted in retaliation for Gantt's refusal to testify untruthfully or to withhold testimony, and that Sentry therefore acted with malice, oppression, or fraud.

constructive discharge
An employee leaves a position because a situation at work has made it difficult if not impossible to perform his or her work effectively.

Decision

The Supreme Court of California found in favor of Gantt and stated the following: "The instant case fits squarely with the rubric of Petermann and Tameny. The FEHA specifically enjoins any obstruction of a DFEH investigation. Government Code section 12975 provides: 'Any person who shall willfully resist, prevent, impede or interfere with any member of the department or the commission or any of its agents or employees in the performance of duties pursuant to the provisions of this part relating to employment discrimination, . . . is guilty of a misdemeanor' punishable by fine or imprisonment. Nowhere in our society is the need greater than in protecting well motivated employees who come forward to testify truthfully in an administrative investigation of charges of discrimination based on sexual harassment. It is self-evident that few employees would cooperate with such investigations if the price were retaliatory discharge from employment."

Question for Discussion

Assume that Bruno and Gantt were marginal employees whose personalities were a source of annoyance to other employees. What policies and practices might have prevented this legal action?

Breach of Implied Contract

consideration
The bargained-for element that motivates parties to enter a contract. It involves an exchange of legal benefits or legal detriments. For example, Susan agrees to pay Paul $100 in exchange for his old computer. The consideration is Susan's promise to part with $100 (money she is otherwise legally entitled to keep) and Paul's promise to give up his legal right to keep his old computer.

capacity
The recognition that a contracting party has no legal limitations on the right to enter a binding contract. For example, a person for whom a court has appointed a legal guardian to manage money and property has no capacity to contract.

The employment relationship can be a formal one evidenced by a written document signed by employer and employee, stating the terms and conditions of employment. Or it can be quite informal, created by the spoken words and actions of the parties.

When there is a breach of a clear provision in a contract, the nonbreaching party can initiate action against the other to enforce the terms of the agreement. The court will seek evidence that the parties agreed to those terms, that the parties exchanged *consideration* for their mutual promises, that there was *capacity* on the part of both parties to enter the contractual relationship, and that the contract was for a legal purpose and did not otherwise violate any laws. If the legally required components of a valid contract exist, and the evidence proves there was a breach, the courts will provide a remedy for the nonbreaching party. Courts generally seek to put the nonbreaching party into the economic position she or he would have been in if the other had not breached the contract.

In many employment situations there is no formal written contract setting forth the terms and conditions of employment. One provision that might not be spelled out is the time period for which the employee will be retained. In such a situation, with no period specified, unless the understanding is that the position will end at the completion of a specific project or undertaking, or unless the agreement requires good cause for dismissal, it is an employment at will relationship.

A finding that an implied contract is an exception to employment at will often involves company manuals or handbooks that were created by the employer but not considered by the employer as a contract. Employers did not treat the provisions of the handbook as contract obligations, but rather intended them to be guides for supervisors and employees. Employers are often surprised when judges side with employees who point out that the employers did not follow the provisions in their handbooks and that they were therefore in breach of an implied contract obligation. For example, employers may not believe that by listing specific reasons for dismissal, they could lose a wrongful dismissal action because the reason given for a dismissal was not listed there. Likewise, they may not believe that by describing a progressive disciplinary policy, they could lose a case for firing an employee without following the designated procedures. Employees have used these arguments successfully in cases across the country, claiming that employer actions have violated an implied contractual agreement. To protect their right to fire at will, astute employers are now careful to state clearly in manuals and handbooks that they offer at-will employment.

One issue that arises in cases of this nature is whether the element of consideration is present when a company unilaterally changes the employment relationship after an employee has been hired. For example, Ann had been an administrative assistant for ABC Company for several years before ABC drew up a new handbook. Ann subsequently accrued more absences than the new handbook allowed and was terminated. Ann argued that the new handbook provisions did not constitute a contract because there was no consideration to support such a finding (she was promised no more in exchange for accepting the terms of the new handbook, and ABC offered no more to her). Courts do not agree about whether the act of continuing to work for ABC and ABC's continuing to pay Ann represent the requisite consideration for finding a valid implied contract.

Case for Discussion 5-2 is an example of the implied contract exception to employment at will, and it shows the importance of a clear disclaimer in a company manual.

Case for Discussion 5-2

NICOSIA V. WAKEFERN FOOD CORPORATION, 136 N.J. 401, 643 A.2D 554 (1994)[10]

The issue in this New Jersey Supreme Court case was whether the employer's "Human Resources Policies and Procedures Manual" constituted an enforceable implied contract that changed what would otherwise be an employment at will relationship to one in which the employer was limited in its ability to discharge the employee.

Facts

In this case a low-level supervisor was fired for mishandling merchandise. He filed a wrongful discharge action against his employer. . . . [T]he employee denies that his employer had any grounds to terminate him and claims that his discharge was wrongful because the employment manual distributed by the employer constitutes an implied contract that bars termination without cause under *Woolley v. Hoffmann-La Roche,* 99 N.J. 284, 491 A.2d 1257, modified, 101 N.J. 10 (1985). The employer contends that the employee is "at will" and therefore can be fired without cause and, further, that its employment manual does not constitute an implied employment contract, particularly in light of its disclaimer. . . . Following a jury trial, the trial court entered judgment in favor of the employee. On appeal, the Appellate Division upheld the judgment entered on the jury's verdict. . . .

Plaintiff, Anthony Nicosia ("Nicosia"), was hired by defendant, Wakefern Food Corporation ("Wakefern"), in 1971. Nicosia was promoted several times during his eighteen-and-one-half years of employment. When Nicosia was terminated, he held the position of warehouse shift supervisor. The termination was carried out without resorting to the disciplinary procedures set forth in the employer's manual. Wakefern countered that the infraction was listed as one that permitted summary dismissal, i.e., theft of company property.

The manual's disclaimer that Wakefern relied on to support the position that Nicosia was an at-will employee stated the following: "This manual contains statements of Wakefern Food Corp. and its subsidiaries' Human Resource policies and procedures. (Hereafter referred to as "the Company"). The terms and procedures contained therein are not contractual and are subject to change and interpretation at the sole discretion of the Company, and without prior notice or consideration to any employee."

Decision

The Supreme Court of New Jersey, in upholding the judgment of the trial court, stated, "Wakefern's disclaimer language fails to constitute an 'appropriate statement' under *Woolley* because it does not use 'straightforward terms.' . . . Instead, it contains 'confusing legalese,' such as the terms 'not contractual,' 'subject to . . . interpretation,' and 'consideration.' . . . As the trial court noted, Wakefern uses 'language that a lawyer would understand, but that an employee would not equate with the objectives of . . . *Woolley*.' Nicosia should not be expected to understand that Wakefern's characterization of its manual as 'not contractual' or 'subject to change and interpretation at the sole discretion of the Company' meant that the employer, despite the discipline and termination provisions of its manual, reserved the 'absolute power to fire anyone with or without cause' without actually changing those provisions. . . . *Woolley* also held that the disclaimer must be in a 'a very prominent position.' . . . Disclaimers in employee manuals fail for lack of prominence when the text is not set off in such a way as to bring the disclaimer to the attention of the reader." . . . We concur in the finding of the Appellate Division that Wakefern had failed to meet the prominence test in part because its 'statement is not highlighted, underscored, capitalized, or presented in any other way to make it likely that it would come to the attention of an employee reviewing it.'

Questions for Discussion

1. Analyze this case under the laws of Montana and Arizona. Would the outcome have been different? Why or why not?
2. When an employee is suspected of embezzlement, what steps should management take?

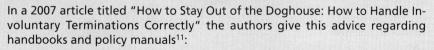

In a 2007 article titled "How to Stay Out of the Doghouse: How to Handle Involuntary Terminations Correctly" the authors give this advice regarding handbooks and policy manuals[11]:

1. Have a prominent statement (in larger letters, underscored, highlighted, in all caps, or in a different color or font) declaring that the handbook is not to be construed as a contract and that the employer and employee have an *employment at will* relationship.

2. State clearly the policies, practices, and rules that are to be followed by employees, supervisors, and other relevant people in the workplace.

3. List the violations that are subject to progressive discipline and state clearly the specific discipline related to each infraction, and what the ramifications for each additional infraction will be.

4. List separately the violations that are excluded from the progressive discipline list that will result in immediate dismissal.

5. Include a provision that allows the employer to immediately dismiss an employee for behaviors not specifically included in the immediate dismissal list, such as violating a state or federal law while on the job.

6. Enforce the provisions of the handbook or manual in a nondiscriminatory manner, making certain that it is consistently implemented. Haphazard utilization of the provisions can easily lead to the loss of a lawsuit.

7. Train supervisors in the use and implementation of the handbook or manual, stressing the importance of consistency in application.

The Implied Covenant of Good Faith and Fair Dealing

In both common law and statutory law governing contracts for the sale of goods, there is a requirement that parties deal with one another fairly and in good faith. This requirement, however, did not carry over to employment contracts. Only in recent years have certain state courts carved out an exception to employment at will in circumstances where a judge believes that a discharge violates notions of good faith and fair dealing on the part of the employer. Eleven states now recognize this exception. (See Figure 5.2.)

Examples of cases involving a violation of the implied covenant of good faith and fair dealing include (1) the firing of an airline employee who had worked satisfactorily for 18 years for American Airlines and who was given no reason for his dismissal [*Lawrence M. Cleary v. American Airlines, Inc.,* 111 Cal.App.3d 443 (1980), a California decision]; and (2) a tenured Kmart employee, terminated before retirement, who the court believed was discharged to avoid paying him retirement benefits [*Kmart Corporation v. Ponsock*, 103 Nev. 39, 732 P.2d 1364 (1987), a Nevada decision].

Recognizing an implied obligation to exercise good faith in dealing with employees opens the door to many dismissal situations that a court might find impermissible. Although this obviously might place a burden on employers, the wise company and manager will have clear rules and practices in place

101

FIGURE 5.2
Recognition of Employment at Will Exceptions, by State as of October 1, 2000[12]

Source: D.J. Walsh and J.L. Schwarz, "State Common Law Wrongful Discharge Doctrines: Update, Refinement, and Rationales," *Am. Bus. L.J.* 33 (Summer 1996), p. 645. Case law was shepardized (verified) to update the recognition of exceptions through October 1, 2000.

	Public Policy	Implied Contract	Covenant of Good Faith and Fair Dealing
	43	38	11
Alabama	No	Yes	Yes
Alaska	Yes	Yes	Yes
Arizona	Yes	Yes	Yes
Arkansas	Yes	Yes	No
California	Yes	Yes	Yes
Colorado	Yes	Yes	No
Connecticut	Yes	Yes	No
Delaware	Yes	No	Yes
District of Columbia	Yes	Yes	No
Florida	No	No	No
Georgia	No	No	No
Hawaii	Yes	Yes	No
Idaho	Yes	Yes	Yes
Illinois	Yes	Yes	No
Indiana	Yes	No	No
Iowa	Yes	Yes	No
Kansas	Yes	Yes[1]	No
Kentucky	Yes	Yes	No
Louisiana	No	No	No
Maine	No	Yes	No
Maryland	Yes	Yes	No
Massachusetts	Yes	No	Yes
Michigan	Yes	Yes	No
Minnesota	Yes	Yes	No
Mississippi	Yes[1]	Yes	No
Missouri	Yes	No[1]	No
Montana	Yes	No	Yes
Nebraska	No	Yes	No
Nevada	Yes	Yes	Yes
New Hampshire	Yes	Yes	No
New Jersey	Yes	Yes	No
New Mexico	Yes	Yes	No
New York	No	Yes	No
North Carolina	Yes	No	No
North Dakota	Yes	Yes	No

FIGURE 5.2
(Continued)

	Public Policy	Implied Contract	Covenant of Good Faith and Fair Dealing
Ohio	Yes*	Yes	No
Oklahoma	Yes	Yes	No
Oregon	Yes	Yes	No
Pennsylvania	Yes	No	No
Rhode Island	No	No	No
South Carolina	Yes	Yes	No
South Dakota	Yes	Yes	No
Tennessee	Yes	Yes	No
Texas	Yes	No	No
Utah	Yes	Yes	Yes
Vermont	Yes	Yes	No
Virginia	Yes	No	No
Washington	Yes	Yes	No
West Virginia	Yes	Yes	No
Wisconsin	Yes	Yes	No
Wyoming	Yes	Yes	Yes

*Overturned previous decision that was contrary to current doctrine.

regarding expectations, rewards, and punishments, as well as an effective communication system to ensure basic understandings between the employee and the employer. Moreover, the rules must be followed consistently, and documentation of appropriate information must be carefully kept. In other words, establish a system that ensures the bare minimums of good faith and fair dealing.

Contract versus Tort: Variation in State Laws

The exceptions to the employment at will principle involve both contract issues and tort issues. For example, an exception involving a handbook provision and its treatment by courts as constituting an implied contract provision is an interpretation of contract law. Exceptions involving defamation, fraud, and others are clearly applications of tort law. An exception that applies the covenant of good faith and fair dealing does not fall neatly under either contract or tort law but has aspects of both.

The implications of falling within contract or tort law can be significant for the parties involved; for example, courts will not award punitive damages for breach of contract. The evidence needed for a successful contract action differs from the evidence needed for a tort case. In a contract case, the court analyzes the evidence to determine whether the elements of contract are present. (For example, was there evidence of an agreement? Was there consideration? Was the agreement for a legal purpose? Did the parties have capacity to contract?) In a tort case, the court analyzes the evidence to determine whether the wrongdoer had a duty to not harm the injured party under the circumstances, whether that duty was breached, and whether the breach of duty was the proximate cause of the injury.

Contract damages are more limited than tort damages. In a contract action, the objective is to put the nonbreaching party in as good a position as he or she would have enjoyed had the other not breached the contract. In a tort action, the goal is to compensate the victim for the harm done. Historically tort cases have led to some very high awards, including compensation not only for the actual expenses incurred by the injured person, but also for mental and physical pain and suffering, loss of the ability to earn an annual income multiplied by the number of years the party is expected to live, and many other types of relief, such as "loss of consortium," which can be requested by the spouse of the injured party, and of course punitive damages designed to punish the wrongdoer when the action was intentional, malicious, or otherwise reprehensible. In comparison, a successful litigant in a contract case can recover only the "loss of the bargain" and cannot seek damages that are speculative—such as lost profits that cannot be readily documented.

Both contract and tort are variations of common law, and common law is a function of state law; therefore, it varies from state to state. Some situations give rise to actions that can be argued as either contract or tort cases and can be brought in more than one state. In such cases the court must address initial issues such as whether the case will be treated as a tort or contract case, and which state's common law is to be applied to the facts. The Case for Discussion 5-3 illustrates this type of lawsuit.

Case for Discussion 5-3

CATON D/B/A CATON SALES COMPANY V. LEACH CORPORATION, 896 F.2D 939 (1990)[13]

Ralph Caton sued Leach Corporation, which had terminated him after 22 years as an employee and a sales representative, to recover damages for breach of contract and implied contract, wrongful discharge, and amounts allegedly owed as restitution. . . .

Facts

Leach Corporation ("Leach") manufactures electronic and mechanical products for use in the aerospace industry. Leach marketed and sold its products for many years throughout the country through local sales representatives such as Ralph Caton ("Caton").

From 1963 until June 15, 1985, Caton worked for Leach in several capacities. . . . Caton eventually became Leach's exclusive representative to solicit relay switch sales in Texas.

In July 1983 Leach and Caton executed a sales representative agreement that defined the parties' relationship through provisions that addressed Caton's responsibilities, sales territory, and compensation structure. The 1983 agreement recognized that Caton was to be compensated for his services on a commission basis . . .

. . . During 1984, Caton notified Leach that General Dynamics expected a large government order of F-16 aircraft ("Multi-Year Buy"), for which General Dynamics would need relay switches. Fulfilling his sales representative responsibilities, Caton maintained and solidified Leach's position as a General Dynamics supplier.

By letter dated May 14, 1985, however, Leach notified Caton that the sales representative agreement would be terminated 30 days later. . . .

By a remarkable coincidence, the termination occurred after Leach had received quotation requests from General Dynamics regarding relay switches for the Multi-Year Buy and after Caton prophesied the success of Leach's efforts on this contract. A table submitted in evidence indicates that Leach had bid to supply over $12,000,000 of relay equipment by June 15, 1985. Caton contends that Leach was awarded $4.9 million in relay orders by September 6, 1985, and eventually received $8.6 million of relay business.

Although the reasons for Caton's termination are, naturally, disputed, Caton has directed us to evidence suggesting that he contributed significantly to obtaining the General Dynamics contract. . . . In a letter dated March 6, 1985, Whitcomb . . . commended Caton for developing the "obvious rapport and good relations with G.D. [General Dynamics], T.I. and Electro Space." A later Whitcomb memo discussing possible changes in sales personnel acknowledged that Caton could potentially cost Leach $300,000 in commissions during fiscal year 1986 . . .

Choice of Law

Either the law of California or Texas applies to Caton's various claims. . . .

The parties' choice of law clause provides that "[this] Agreement shall be construed under the laws of the State of California." Texas choice of law principles give effect to choice of law clauses if the law chosen by the parties has a reasonable relationship with the parties and the chosen state, and the law of the chosen state is not contrary to a fundamental policy of the state. . . .

We will give effect to the parties' determination that their agreement be construed under California law. Likewise, Caton's claim for relief under the implied contractual covenant of good faith depends on the construction of the contract under California law, and California law will govern this claim.

The parties' narrow choice of law clause does not address the entirety of the parties' relationship, however, and hence does not end our inquiry. Caton's other claims for relief involve the tort duty of good faith and fair dealing and a claim for restitution . . ., and, as such, do not arise out of the contract. Because the choice of law clause does not address the general rights and liabilities of the parties, we must return to Texas choice of law rules to determine which law applies. [*Footnote:* In contrast to broad clauses, which choose a particular state's law to "govern, construe and enforce all of the rights and duties of the parties arising from or relating in any way to the subject matter of this contract," the instant clause denotes only that California law will be applied to "construe" the contract.]

In Texas, where the parties have not agreed to the application of law to a particular issue, "the law of the state with the most significant relationship to the particular substantive issue will be applied to resolve that issue.". . .

Caton resides in Texas, served Leach in Texas by soliciting sales from companies in Texas, and was terminated by Leach in Texas. Leach is a Delaware corporation, which has its principal place of business in California. Caton and Leach agree that Texas law should be applied to Caton's claims that arise independently from the sales representative agreement. Finally, Texas has a significant interest in remedying civil injury to Texas citizens through tort liability and also in defining the outer limits of tort liability. Therefore, Caton's wrongful discharge claim based on breach of the alleged tort duty of good faith should be governed by Texas law.

***

The Contract

The trial court held succinctly that because the sales representative agreement allowed for Caton's termination at will, on 30 days' notice, Caton had no claim for commissions. We view the matter as more complex, based on a careful review of the contract. As was just stated, we shall construe the sales agreement according to California law.

The relevant portions of the sales agreement are these:

> 8C. *Payment of Commissions:*
> No commission shall be earned until shipment is made. Commissions shall be payable within twenty (20) days after the close of the Company's monthly accounting period on all shipments made during the prior monthly accounting period. Payment of commissions due shall be subject to the following deductions, if applicable:. . . .

> 17. *Termination:*
> This Agreement may be terminated by either party, without cause, upon thirty (30) days' prior written notice to the other party.

> . . . . . .

> Upon any termination Representative shall be entitled to all or the allocable portion of commission on any orders for shipment to his Territory accepted by the Company prior to the date of termination, payable when the Company receives payment from its customers.

The termination provision creates an at-will arrangement that either party may end upon 30 days' notice, without cause. The termination provision entitles the representative "upon any termination" to all or the allocable portion of certain commissions. Leach contends that this provision defines Caton's commission rights at termination and limits commissions to orders accepted by the Company prior to the date of termination. The construction urged by Leach would cut off Caton's right to commissions on orders that Caton may have procured or provided engineering services for but that were not accepted by the company before his termination.

Significantly, however, Caton's right to receive all or an allocable portion of the applicable commission also appears in an earlier part of the agreement.

***

We find these provisions ambiguous and not dispositive of the question of Caton's right to at least an allocable portion of the commissions from the General Dynamics Multi-Year Buy after his termination.

***

The California Supreme Court has articulated several rules of construction relevant to this dispute. In *Universal Sales Corp. v. California Press Mfg. Co.*, 20 Cal. 2d 751, 128 P.2d 665, 671 (Cal. 1942), as in this case, separate contractual provisions applied together created an ambiguity on the face of the contract. The court stated that "The whole of a contract is to be taken together, so as to give effect to every part, if reasonably practicable, each clause helping to interpret the other." Furthermore, the interpretation of specific terms in a particular case "is controlled by the context of the writing, and the whole instrument must be examined." . . .

***

Consistent with these rules, the district court should admit evidence of the parties' intent as to the ambiguous provisions. This may be derived from evidence of negotiations, "the circumstances surrounding the contract's execution" and "the parties' conduct subsequent to contract formation." . . . The court should determine whether the parties intended for Caton to acquire rights or benefits upon the performance of engineering or procurement services and whether the parties intended for such rights, if any, to be eliminated if orders, although expected to be received, were not accepted by Leach until after the representative's termination. . . .

. . .

Breach of Implied Covenant of Good Faith

The next issue is whether the district court erred in granting summary judgment against Caton's claim that Leach violated an implied covenant of good faith in his sales representative agreement. The district court determined that because the agreement was terminable on 30 days' notice, Caton could not recover on this claim. Perceiving at least part of Caton's argument to reach the question of his right to receive compensation for work he performed toward the Multi-Year Buy, which was denied only because he was fired shortly before Leach accepted orders for those sales, we disagree.

The California courts recognize that "[every] contract imposes upon each party a duty of good faith and fair dealing in its performance and its enforcement." . . . This good faith obligation applies to effectuate the promises, terms, and purposes of the parties' agreement. . . . We agree with the district court that the implied good faith covenant may not obliterate rights, such as at-will termination, expressly embodied in a written contract. "Because the implied covenant protects only the parties' right to receive the benefit of their agreement, and, in an at-will relationship there is no agreement to terminate only for good cause, the implied covenant standing alone cannot be read to impose such a duty."

. . .

Nevertheless, where obligations are imposed and rights are created by a contract, the implied covenant of good faith protects the parties' expectations to receive the contractual benefits. . . . Caton contends that Leach acted in bad faith in denying him benefits, *i.e.* an allocable share of commissions, to which he was entitled under the agreement.

If the entitlement language in paragraph 8D created rights or benefits for a sales representative upon the performance of specified services, then Caton may be able to recover damages for breach of California's implied covenant. In other words, even if the parties clearly intended for post-termination acceptance of orders to eliminate a right to commissions, fact questions remain whether Leach breached the implied covenant of good faith and fair dealing by accepting Caton's engineering and procurement services on the Multi-Year Buy while maneuvering to terminate Caton and cut off his right to receive an allocated commission for his work. The breach of the covenant would be limited to Leach's actions in accepting services without ever intending to compensate Caton, rather than for his termination. Caton's recovery for a breach of the implied covenant of good faith would be restricted to a contract measure. . . . In this case, contract damages would be based on an allocation of commissions under paragraph 8D. This theory of liability would not restrict the parties' contractual right to at-will termination of the agreement, but would nevertheless "protect the express covenants or promises of the contract." . . .

Tort of Wrongful Discharge

The district court held that the tort of wrongful discharge does not provide a viable theory of relief in the context of the at-will contractual relationship and granted summary judgment against Caton's tort claim. We agree.

The Texas courts have refrained from imposing a contractual covenant of good faith and fair dealing in every contract. . . .

The Texas courts have injected the tort duty of good faith in discrete, special relationships, earmarked by specific characteristics including long-standing relations, an imbalance of bargaining power, and significant trust and confidence shared by the parties. *Aranda,* . . . (compensation carrier occupies position of control over dependent employee, who places trust in carrier); *Arnold,* . . . (special relationship between insurer and insured is based on unequal bargaining power and insurer's position of control); *see also Lovell v. Western Nat'l Life Ins. Co.,* . . . (Tex.App.—Amarillo 1988, writ denied) . . . The Texas appellate courts, as yet, have not found the employment relationship to present an adequate basis upon which to impose the duty of good faith.

***

Decision

We have held that after the introduction of extrinsic evidence, Caton may be able to recover an allocable portion of commissions under the express contract with Leach. He may alternatively be able to sustain a claim based upon breach of California's implied contractual covenant of good faith, if it is found that Leach understood its obligation to compensate Caton for services under paragraph 8D and followed a course of conduct designed to avoid that compensation. The equitable theory of quantum meruit is not available to Caton, nor does Texas recognize a tort duty of good faith that would give him succor in these circumstances.

Questions for Discussion

1. Did the appellate court consider the covenant of good faith and fair dealing to be a contract issue or a tort issue? Explain your answer.
2. In what significant ways did Texas and California law differ with regard to employment at will exceptions?
3. The appellate court applied both California law and Texas law to the case. Explain why this was done.

Violation of Statutory Law

Many statutes, both federal and state, impact an employer's personnel decisions. The more prominent of these laws include (1) antidiscrimination laws, (2) whistleblower protection laws, and (3) prohibitions on retaliatory behavior.

Antidiscrimination Statutes

In later chapters of this textbook several federal statutes prohibiting discrimination against employees and prospective employees will be described. Those statutes specify certain classes of people who are protected from illegal discrimination: people of a particular race, creed, color, sex, and so on. At-will employers must be careful in dealing negatively with such employees and must be well prepared to defend their decisions. If there is any evidence of illegal discriminatory motives, employers will be found in violation of the law.

Whistleblower Protection Statutes

In the wake of corporate scandals, such as arose in the Enron and Tyco cases involving executive wrongdoings, Congress passed the Sarbanes–Oxley Act. Included in the act's provisions is language that encourages employees to report illegal activities in the workplace to designated officials in the Occupational Safety and Health Administration (OSHA). Such whistleblowers are protected from retaliation. This is an example of several statutory laws that protect whistleblowers. In one of the earliest cases to test the effectiveness of Sarbanes–Oxley's whistleblower provisions, the Department of Labor entered a ruling against CheckFree Corp. of Norcross, Georgia, in October 2004[14]. CheckFree's product marketing director, Larry Hogan, complained to superiors and others that the company was engaging in deceptive marketing, overstating income, and defrauding both customers and investors. As a result of his complaints, CheckFree fired him. The agency ordered the company to compensate Hogan for back pay, interest, counseling and job search expenses, and loss of professional reputation as well as mental pain and suffering. The amount of the award was over $103,000.

There are also numerous state statutes protecting whistleblowers. The NJ Conscientious Employee Protection Act [N.J.S.A. 34:19-1, et seq] is an example. An employee who successfully argues that an employer's action against her or him was the result of actions protected under CEPA can recover compensatory and punitive damages, job reinstatement, attorney's fees, and injunctive relief (an order of the court enjoining the employer from taking certain actions). Among other things, under CEPA an employee has a protected right to disclose to a supervisor or to a public body a practice of the employer that the employee reasonably believes violates a law, rule, or regulation. CEPA also protects an employee from retaliation if she or he provides information or testifies before a public body conducting an investigation of the employer's business.

Prohibitions on Retaliatory Actions

In addition to the whistleblower statutes, several federal and state statutes have provisions that give to employees who avail themselves of this legal protection an added means of recourse if the employer subsequently takes negative actions against that employee. For example, if an employee complains of sexual harassment by a supervisor and the company, instead of addressing the problem, fires or demotes the victim, she or he has at least two legal violations to charge against the employer—the harassment and the retaliation, each with its own unique remedy, including the possibility of punitive damages.

These statutory laws illustrate only some of the restrictions placed on employers, whether or not the employment relationship is at will.

COMMON LAW TORT VIOLATIONS

Tort claims are predicated on the notion that harm has been done to someone, whether intentionally or negligently, and that the law will compel the tortfeasor to compensate the victim for that harm. A concern for employers is that when an employee succeeds in a tort action, punitive damages can be assessed against the employer. Punitive damages will result if the conduct is held to be malicious, willful, intentional, reckless, or the like.

Whether an act amounts to a tort depends on the judges and juries that decide these cases. As stated earlier, tort law is part of common law—the law that is found in court decisions. Common law is a function of state law, not federal law; therefore, tort cases follow different paths from one state to another. The precedent provided by past cases emanates from the highest courts of each state and is binding only within that state. As a result, employers operating in more than one state face great variation when it comes to tort exceptions to employment at will.

The tort principles discussed here represent the majority of tort cases brought in wrongful discharge cases, but our discussion is not all-inclusive. Other tort claims can be argued.

Abusive (Wrongful) Discharge

This tort is based on conduct of an employer that is harmful to the employee and is done with malice or bad faith. In the absence of malice or bad faith the termination of an at-will employee, even if for no good reason, would not constitute abusive discharge.

The tort of wrongful discharge was raised in *Staggie v. Idaho Falls,* an Idaho case decided in 1986 and presented in Case for Discussion 5-4.

Case for Discussion 5-4

STAGGIE V. IDAHO FALLS CONSOL. HOSP., INC., 110 IDAHO 349, 715 P.2D 1019 (CT. APP. 1986)[15]

Facts

The plaintiff argued that his firing was in bad faith. His firing occurred after he engaged in unauthorized time-swapping with another employee. His request for review of the decision through a grievance procedure was not acknowledged or granted.

Decision

The court said that the plaintiff had failed to produce any evidence that the employer had acted in bad faith or that the discharge was based on an improper motive. No handbook or manual was put in evidence by the plaintiff to support his claims. Therefore, the court held in favor of the employer, finding that there was no wrongful discharge.

Intentional Infliction of Emotional Distress

To succeed in this tort claim, also referred to as the tort of outrage, the plaintiff must produce evidence that the employer's actions were beyond malice, willfulness, intent, reckless disregard for the employee's health or safety, or the like. Courts look for behavior that shocks the conscience, is outrageous, or goes beyond the bounds of decency. See Case for Discussion 5-5.

Case for Discussion 5-5

WAL-MART STORES, INC. V. LUIS A. CANCHOLA, 64 S.W.3D 524 (TEX. APP. 2002)[16]

Facts

Canchola was a deli manager at a Wal-Mart store in Texas. According to his supervisors, Canchola was an excellent employee . . . In July 1993 Canchola experienced chest pains and underwent bypass surgery on six arteries. Following surgery, Canchola missed work for 13 weeks, then was allowed to return to work for four hours daily with restrictions that he forgo heavy lifting and handle only paperwork. . . . In April 1994 Canchola again suffered chest pains . . . Following treatment, Canchola remained at home for a month, then returned to work, again at a reduced schedule. According to Canchola, Wal-Mart's management was very supportive during the period of time while Jessie Frias was store director.

However, in July 1994 David Drastrata replaced Frias as store director of the Mission Wal-Mart. Canchola testified that Drastrata's attitude toward him was hostile.

***

Carmen Gonzalez, a part-time worker in the deli department under Canchola's supervision, initiated the complaint against Canchola. . . . Gonzalez testified that Canchola's sexual harassment of her began before she started working at Wal-Mart. Gonzalez nevertheless approached Canchola for his assistance in procuring a job with Wal-Mart, and Canchola helped her obtain a position in Wal-Mart's deli department. . . .

Irene Flores, a support manager in the clothing department, witnessed Canchola approach Gonzalez, stand close to her, and appear to be whispering in her ear. Flores reprimanded Gonzalez for her "unprofessional" and "unladylike" behavior. In response, Gonzalez told Flores that Canchola had been making advances toward her. Flores took Gonzalez to report her allegations to Drastrata.

***

[D]uring the month before Gonzalez's accusation against Canchola, Light had offered Gonzalez full-time work in the men's department, but Gonzalez declined the position on grounds she did not want to leave the deli. According to Light, a full-time position in his department offered more benefits than a similar job in the deli department.

***

Drastrata obtained written statements from Carmen Gonzalez, Irene Flores, Graciela and Katherine Solis, and Antonia "Toni" Cobios, a female subordinate of Canchola's who worked in the deli department. These statements were the key to Wal-Mart's claim that it terminated Canchola for nondiscriminatory reasons. At trial, however, Cobios testified that Drastrata pressured her to provide a written statement. According to Cobios, Drastrata instructed her to include specific factual allegations against Canchola in her statement despite her protestation that she knew nothing about the matters he wanted her to include. Cobios subsequently wrote a letter to the president of Wal-Mart explaining that she was pressured into providing a statement including false claims against Canchola. A copy of her letter, introduced at trial, states that Canchola was a "very respectable" supervisor who gave his subordinates "space and respect."

***

Intentional Infliction of Emotional Distress

. . . Wal-Mart contends that the evidence was legally or factually insufficient to support the jury's finding that it intentionally inflicted emotional distress on Canchola. To recover damages for intentional infliction of emotional distress, a plaintiff must establish that (1) the defendant acted intentionally or recklessly; (2) the defendant's conduct was extreme and outrageous; (3) the defendant's actions caused the plaintiff emotional distress; and (4) the emotional distress suffered by the plaintiff was severe. . . .

Wal-Mart first argues that its conduct was not extreme and outrageous. Extreme and outrageous conduct is conduct "so outrageous in character, and so extreme in degree, as to go beyond all possible bounds of decency, and to be regarded as atrocious, and utterly intolerable in a civilized community." . . . Generally, insensitive or even rude behavior does not constitute extreme and outrageous conduct. . . . Similarly, mere insults, indignities, threats, annoyances, petty oppressions, or other trivialities do not rise to the level of extreme and outrageous conduct.

A claim for intentional infliction of emotional distress does not lie for ordinary employment disputes. . . . When reasonable minds may differ, it is for the jury, subject to the court's control, to determine whether, in the particular case, the conduct has been sufficiently extreme and outrageous to result in liability.

Wal-Mart contends that the evidence establishes nothing more than an ordinary employment dispute. However, the jury heard evidence suggesting that Wal-Mart's investigation of the charges against Canchola was incomplete and biased. The jury also heard conflicting evidence about Wal-Mart's policy on harassment, and heard that Wal-Mart failed to uniformly implement its policy regarding sexual harassment by demoting one individual accused of harassment, yet terminating Canchola. Most significantly, the jury had before it evidence that Drastrata instructed a witness to falsify her statement implicating Canchola. Under these circumstances, we conclude that the evidence before the jury was legally and factually sufficient to support the jury's finding of extreme and outrageous conduct on the part of Wal-Mart.

Next, Wal-Mart argues that any distress Canchola may have suffered was not severe. Emotional distress includes all highly unpleasant mental reactions such as embarrassment, fright, horror, grief, shame, humiliation, and worry. Severe emotional distress is distress that is so severe that no reasonable person could be expected to endure it. In considering Canchola's emotional distress, we consider evidence of his distress in the days and months following the accident, as well as evidence concerning Canchola's emotional state during the harassment investigation.

Canchola was hospitalized due to stress at least twice following his termination. Canchola testified that his termination was "really, really devastating." He talked to his wife about it and prayed about it. He sought guidance from his minister and a friend.

[A]ppellee's wife of 29 years testified that the termination caused her husband, and in fact, her whole family, problems. According to Mrs. Canchola, the termination took Canchola's respect away. Canchola was "totally shocked" by the accusation, and testified that he was not given an opportunity to defend himself.

Decision

This evidence is legally and factually sufficient to support the jury's finding that Canchola suffered from severe emotional distress.

We overrule Wal-Mart's third issue.

Negligent Infliction of Emotional Distress

Some states have recognized a less egregious offense of inflicting emotional distress. To be successful in this tort claim, the usual requirements of negligent tort must be proven: that the defendant owed a duty to the plaintiff; the defendant breached that duty; injury resulted; and injury was more or less directly caused by the defendant's breach of duty. Cases for Discussion 5-6 and 5-7 are illustrations of this tort; one is a 2001 Washington State case and the other a 2005 Connecticut case. States differ in their analyses of tort cases.

Case for Discussion 5-6

SNYDER V. MEDICAL SERVICE CORPORATION OF E. WASH., 35 P.3D 1158 (2001)[17]

Facts

Plaintiff Snyder began working as a case manager in 1996. A few months later Celestine Hall was hired as her supervisor. Shortly thereafter several people resigned from the employer (MSC) citing Ms. Hall as the reason for their departure. Employees describe Hall as an "authoritarian," "belligerent," and "harassing-type supervisor" who routinely embarrassed her subordinates in front of their peers.

As Ms. Snyder took on more and more workplace responsibility she frequently discussed with Ms. Hall the possibility of having her salary increased. In May 1996 Ms. Snyder was given a raise but was told by Hall that if she sought a further increase in salary she would be disciplined. Nevertheless when Snyder filled out her supervisor evaluation form in July 1996, she described Ms. Hall as wonderful, understanding, and not "out of line."

In February of the following year Ms. Hall told Ms. Snyder she would receive another raise, but said she would literally hunt Ms. Snyder down and "kill her" if she told anyone at MSC about that raise.

The events that form the basis of this litigation occurred on February 13, 1997. On that day Ms. Hall convened a staff meeting at which she proposed a "push-day" where all employees would come in and work on a Saturday without extra compensation. Ms. Snyder objected, stating she was expecting to spend the weekend with her children. Ms. Hall mocked her in front of the group, and Ms. Snyder left the meeting.

After the meeting Ms. Hall confronted Ms. Snyder. She poked Ms. Snyder in the chest and accused her of being insubordinate. That afternoon Ms. Snyder went to see her therapist and did not return to the office. Her doctor advised her to take two weeks off work. On February 26, 1997, MSC was advised Ms. Snyder would be out of the office for an additional two weeks.

During the second week in March Ms. Snyder met with Dr. Norman Charney, Ms. Hall's supervisor. She indicated she could no longer work under Ms. Hall and asked if she could either report directly to him or be transferred to another department. Dr. Charney stated he would like to have Ms. Snyder back in the office but that she would have to report to Ms. Hall as Hall was still the manager of Snyder's department, and he said he had not yet determined whether disciplinary action should be taken against Hall.

On April 10, 1997, Ms. Snyder took a full-time position with another company. She did not return to MSC claiming she could not, and her physician would not allow her to, work under Ms. Hall's supervision.

Snyder filed suit against MSC alleging handicap discrimination, constructive discharge, outrage, and negligent infliction of emotional distress. MSC then moved for summary judgment of dismissal.

Decision

While the court acknowledged that Washington does recognize the tort of negligent infliction of emotional distress, it emphasized that employers are under no obligation to remove stress from the workplace. The court stated that because the utility and risk of harm of an action must be weighed, actions taken as a result of disciplinary decisions or in response to workplace personality disputes cannot support a cause of action for negligent infliction of emotional distress.

Case for Discussion 5-7

DAVIS V. MANCHESTER HEALTH CTR., INC., 88 CONN. APP. 60, 867 A.2D 876 (2005)[18]

Facts

The plaintiff, a certified nursing assistant, had informed her employer that she was pregnant. One night when she reported for work, she was assigned to work on the wing of the nursing home that involved the most physically demanding work. Because she had experienced cramping during her shift the day before, the plaintiff requested to be reassigned to another wing. An employee who overheard the exchange offered to trade stations with the plaintiff, but the supervisor refused, telling the plaintiff that she could either work in the assigned wing and " 'deal with it' or leave and never come back."

Decision

The employer's order that the plaintiff choose between losing her job or performing work that she reasonably believed would endanger her pregnancy was "patently unreasonable," and the jury's verdict for the plaintiff on her claim for negligent infliction of emotional distress was upheld.

Fraud

Fraud is a difficult tort to prove. An employer commits fraud when it knowingly makes a false representation of a material nature with the intent to deceive the employee and the employee justifiably relies on the representation to his or her detriment. All the elements of fraud must be in evidence to have a successful claim. The equitable contract theory of promissory estoppel often accompanies fraud claims in wrongful discharge cases. A typical case involves an employee who takes a position based on statements made by the employer that subsequently prove to be false. For example, an employer told an employee that he would have the job for life as long as his work was satisfactory and that he could expect to be promoted within a year. In fact, the employee was terminated for no just cause after six months. These facts could give rise to an action for fraud and/or promissory estoppel. Cases for Discussion 5-8 and 5-9 illustrate this type of tort.

Case for Discussion 5-8

OSBORN V. UNIVERSITY MED. ASSOCS. OF MED. UNIV. OF S.C., 278 F. SUPP. 2D 720 (D.S.C. 2003)[19]

Facts

In 1997 defendant had conducted a financial evaluation and decided to pursue the goal of attaining a profitable commercial status. With this goal in mind, they recruited Osborn, and Osborn accepted the position. They entered into an employment agreement that stated, among other things, that Osborn would have the responsibility of moving the PDC "up to the next business level," and more specifically, it charged him with the duty to "grow the revenues and develop sufficient professional staff to profitably expand the enterprise into a 'for profit' operation." However, they failed to reach profitability after two years under Osborn's direction. Osborn was terminated in 2001. No explanation for termination was given, but the implication was that removal was not for cause.

Osborn filed suit against defendants alleging a total of six causes of action: (1) fraud in the inducement; (2) negligent misrepresentation; (3) breach of contract accompanied by a fraudulent act; (4) breach of contract; (5) breach of implied covenant of good faith and fair dealing; and (6) a violation of the South Carolina Payment of Wages Act.

At the trial level the court held against Osborn on summary judgment—that is, without a trial.

First among Osborn's claims on appeal is the allegation that "Defendants committed fraud in the inducement by misrepresenting critical facts about the organization at the time he was hired." A party asserting a claim for fraud in the inducement to enter into a contract must establish (1) a representation; (2) its falsity; (3) its materiality; (4) either knowledge of its falsity or a reckless disregard of its truth or falsity; (5) intent that the representation be acted upon; (6) the hearer's ignorance of its falsity; (7) the hearer's reliance on its truth; (8) the hearer's right to rely thereon; and (9) the hearer's consequent and proximate injury. A failure to prove any of these elements is fatal to recovery. Additionally, "fraud cannot be presumed; it must be proved by clear, cogent, and convincing evidence."

Specifically, Osborn argues that during his recruitment he was told that the PDC was financially stable, possessed a state-of-the-art facility very near completion and ready for validation, and that he would receive an equity interest in the enterprise that would provide him with a "significant accumulation" of wealth. According to Osborn, however, when he began running the PDC he quickly discovered that none of these things were true. In fact, Osborn contends that upon his hire, the facility was "utterly useless," the financial condition of the PDC was "utterly abysmal" and, moreover, although defendants had promised him an "equity, or an ownership position . . . in the PDC[,]" they "had no intention of providing him with such an interest." In short, Osborn claims that he "stepped into a nightmare."

The defendant asserts that any representations made to Osborn constituted mere expressions of intention or statements concerning the future, neither of which are actionable as fraud. For instance, they argue that "these alleged 'representations' fall well short of what is required by South Carolina law to make them actionable, but rather they amount only to an expression of intention. . . . [and] Osborn has presented no evidence to support the contention that the defendants knowingly or recklessly made a false representation at the time they hired [him]."

Decision

After reviewing the factual record in the light most favorable to Osborn, the court agreed with defendant employer and held against Osborn.

Case for Discussion 5-9

HORD V. ERIM, 228 MICH. APP. 638, 579 N.W.2D 133 (1998)[20]

Facts

Plaintiff interviewed for a job with defendant in 1992. At that interview, he was given a copy of defendant's operating summary for the fiscal year ending September 30, 1991. According to the plaintiff, defendant's financial position had weakened significantly between the time of the 1991 operating summary and the time he was hired. He argued that he would not have accepted the job if he had known defendant's actual financial status. The case was submitted to the jury on theories of fraudulent misrepresentation, among others. The jury awarded plaintiff $175,000 in damages.

On appeal defendant repeatedly argued that the 1991 operating summary was clearly labeled "For the Fiscal Year Ending September 30, 1991," and, therefore, that it could not have constituted a misrepresentation regarding defendant's financial position in 1992, and that plaintiff could not have been misled by it. The flaw in this argument is exposed by simply asking, Why did defendant give plaintiff a copy of its 1991 operating summary? Clearly the act of giving plaintiff the operating summary constituted an endorsement of its contents and a representation that the summary was somehow a reflection of defendant's current financial strength. This was obviously a material representation, and the act of giving the operating summary to plaintiff during a job interview allowed the jury to infer that defendant intended that plaintiff act on it. In addition, there was evidence that, at the time defendant gave plaintiff the 1991 operating summary, it had more current financial information suggesting that it was in a much weaker financial position than it was in September 1991. From this evidence, the jury could have concluded that the representation regarding defendant's financial strength was false and that defendant knew that it was false when made. Finally, plaintiff testified that he relied on this representation in making his decision to accept defendant's offer of employment, and there was evidence that plaintiff suffered injury.

Decision

The appellate court found no error in the trial court's decision, and held in favor of the plaintiff.

Defamation

Defamation occurs when an employer makes statements about an employee that injure his or her character, reputation, ability to obtain employment, or the like. It consists of two basic types: slander and libel. *Slander* refers to written statements and *libel* to oral statements. To be actionable, the statements must be false and must be "published" to third parties. Truth is a defense to the tort of defamation.

Many statements about employees are "privileged"; that is, even if they are false, they do not amount to defamation if they are made in good faith and without malice. Communications between and among persons within a firm or department that are connected with the operation of the company and made for business purposes come within the privilege defense. Likewise, statements made in conjunction with judicial or quasi-judicial proceedings are also privileged. Case for Discussion 5-10 illustrates this type of tort.

Case for Discussion 5-10

MINO V. CLIO SCHOOL DISTRICT, 255 MICH. APP. 60, 661 N.W.2D 586 (2003)[21]

Facts

Dr. Mino began his employment as superintendent of the Clio School District in June 1997. In September 1997 problems developed in Dr. Mino's performance as superintendent. Superintendent secretary Diane Schaupp felt that Dr. Mino did not take charge of the position because he did not attempt to meet with staff and did not attend organizational meetings. She also testified that Dr. Mino received excessive telephone calls from his former place of employment. In addition, Schaupp observed Dr. Mino speaking loudly and angrily with public relations director Wanda Emmerling regarding a district publication and heard Dr. Mino say he could fire her despite the fact that her husband was a school board member. Among other things, there were also difficulties between Dr. Mino and assistant superintendent Fay Latture. According to Schaupp, Latture had to assume extra duties that Dr. Mino was supposed to perform.

In January 1998 Dr. Mino decided to look for work outside the school district. In April 1999 Dr. Mino and the district entered into a "letter of understanding" establishing a severance agreement. It stated, in part, "Unless *required by law* to do so, the Clio Area Schools will not disseminate negative information about Dr. Mino to any person or organization inside or outside of the Clio Area Schools." (Emphasis in original.) The severance agreement also included a release of claims against both parties and effected a "buyout" of Dr. Mino's three-year contract.

In May 1999 Dr. Mino went to Pocatello, Idaho, to interview for a superintendent position. The Pocatello Board of Education appointed four people to a search committee to go to Michigan in order to investigate Dr. Mino. One committee member testified that board members at Dr. Mino's former place of employment said that they would not hire Dr. Mino again. Many of the committee members testified that, at first, Clio employees did not say anything negative about Dr. Mino. However, committee member Gwendalyn C. Lloyd testified that Jolene Peacock eventually told her that they might hear rumors and that there was an agreement not to provide any negative information about Dr. Mino. Peacock also informed some of the committee members that there were community concerns about Dr. Mino's leadership style, his management of the budget, and other unsubstantiated rumors.

Because Dr. Mino is a public figure, he "must prove by clear and convincing evidence that the publication was a defamatory falsehood and that it was made with actual malice through knowledge of its falsity or through reckless disregard for the truth." "Actual malice is defined as knowledge that the published statement was false or as reckless disregard as to whether the statement was false . . . Ill will, spite, or even hatred, standing alone, do not amount to actual malice." Whether actual malice exists is a question of law that must be determined by clear and convincing evidence.

Decision

On this claim, the circuit court determined that it was impossible to conclude from the record that anyone made alleged defamatory statements, and that there was no evidence of actual malice. In addition to citing the release of claims provision, the circuit court further found that there was a qualified privilege to speak in meetings. Regarding the statements made to the Pocatello search committee after the severance agreement was signed, the circuit court determined that they were insubstantial. Therefore, on the allegation of defamation, Dr. Mino lost his case.

Self-Compelled Defamation

In some jurisdictions employees have advanced the theory of "self-compelled defamation," in which a former employee felt the necessity of divulging to prospective employers the negative reasons for leaving their former job. One example is illustrated in Case for Discussion 5-11.

Case for Discussion 5-11

CWEKLINSKY V. MOBIL CHEM. CO., 267 CONN. 210, 837 A.2D 759, 766-67, 20 IER 1281, 1285 (2004)[22]

Facts

Cweklinsky, who had worked for the defendant for 25 years, was given approximately six weeks of paid medical leave in November of 1998 to undergo carpal tunnel syndrome surgery on his wrist. In December plaintiff's treating physician gave him a return-to-work letter that cleared him to return to full-time work on December 11. On December 11, however, he requested that the doctor's office manager, Giacondino, extend his return-to-work date from December 11 to December 14. The change was made to accommodate him. Significantly, Giacondino did not amend the office copy of Dr. Cambria's December 8 letter, nor indicate the change in the plaintiff's file.

When plaintiff reported to work on December 14, he gave his amended copy of Dr. Cambria's December 8 return-to-work letter to his supervisor. The discrepancy between documents came to light and the matter was investigated. After checking with several people, including staff in the doctor's office, it was concluded that the plaintiff himself must have altered Dr. Cambria's December 8 letter, and the defendant decided to fire the plaintiff.

The plaintiff denied altering Dr. Cambria's letter, but did not state that it was actually Giacondino who had changed the note at the plaintiff's request. After further investigation, defendant concluded that although the plaintiff had not falsified his return-to-work letter, his employment should nonetheless be terminated because he had taken paid medical leave without a medical basis.

Cweklinsky stated that he had had to repeat these facts over and over in his quest for a new job, and that this amounted to self-compelled defamation.

A defamatory statement is defined as a communication that tends to "harm the reputation of another as to lower him in the estimation of the community or to deter third persons from associating or dealing with him. . . ." To establish a case of defamation, the plaintiff must demonstrate that (1) the defendant published a defamatory statement; (2) the defamatory statement identified the plaintiff to a third person; (3) the defamatory statement was published to a third person; and (4) the plaintiff's reputation suffered injury as a result of the statement. As a general rule, however, no action for defamation exists if the defendant publishes the defamatory statements to only the plaintiff, and the plaintiff subsequently disseminates the statements to a third person.

Several courts in other states, however, have carved out an exception to that rule in the context of employment. These courts have concluded that publication to the third party by the defamed former employee, or "self-publication," may satisfy the publication requirement because the person effectively is "compelled" to publish the defamatory statement to prospective employers when the person is asked why he or she left his or her former employment. These courts reason that it is fair to hold an employer liable for compelled self-publication because it is reasonably foreseeable that the employee, in seeking new employment, will inevitably be asked why he or she left his or her former employment.

The most compelling public policy consideration against recognition of the doctrine is that acceptance of the doctrine would have a chilling effect on communication in the workplace, thereby contradicting society's fundamental interest in encouraging the free flow of information. Open and honest communication in the workplace is a laudable public policy, in that "an employer who communicates specific feedback, gives reasons for actions, and communicates those reasons to other employees will [foster] a happier . . . and [more] efficient [working environment]." [R. Prentice and B. Winslett, "Employee References: Will a 'No Comment' Policy Protect Employers against Liability for Defamation?" *Am. Bus. L.J.* 25 (1987), pp. 207, 234.] Recognition of compelled self-publication defamation, however, would encourage employers to curtail communications with employees, and the employees' prospective employers, for fear of liability.

Decision

We are persuaded that undermining open and honest communication in the workplace, to the detriment of both employers and employees, is a substantial public policy reason that weighs heavily against recognizing a cause of action for compelled self-publication defamation. The court held in favor of the employer.

Intentional Interference with Contractual Relations

A claim of intentional interference with contractual relations can be raised by an employee against his or her supervisor or other person who intentionally causes a breach between that employee and the employer. Case for Discussion 5-12 is an example.

Case for Discussion 5-12

ZIMMERMAN V. DIRECT FEDERAL CREDIT UNION AND BRESLIN, 121 F. SUPP. 2D 133 (2000)[23]

Facts

In *Zimmerman,* a case filed in the U.S. District Court of Massachusetts, Celia Zimmerman worked for Direct Federal Credit Union. In 1997 she filed a discrimination claim with the Massachusetts agency (MCAD) that handles such cases. She claimed that her supervisor Breslin engaged in retaliatory behavior between the time of her filing the action to the year 2000. She filed this action against Breslin and Direct on grounds of retaliation and violation of the Family and Medical Leave Act, and against Breslin alone, on grounds of intentional interference of an advantageous relationship between Direct and herself. The evidence on which the jury based its verdict included the following:

- After having received the MCAD complaint, Zimmerman observed Breslin "storming toward the front lobby very angry" and later saw him calling people into the board room. . . . Zimmerman discovered that, alone among her colleagues, her early departures and late arrivals at work were being tracked. . . . [H]er attempts to participate in meetings were brushed aside and Breslin essentially ignored her. After a few months, Breslin stopped including Zimmerman at the meetings.

- Whereas in 1996 Zimmerman had been the planner, manager, and facilitator of an off-site strategic planning meeting, in 1997 she was not included at all.

- A company meeting attended by all employees was held at some point shortly after Zimmerman gave notice of her intent to pursue her discrimination charge in court. Zimmerman was humiliated at that meeting by Breslin's comments about integrity and . . . about people that he would have expected would have already left the employ of the credit union. According to her testimony, she felt as though "a spotlight was shining on" her "and that the comments were directed specifically at" her. Other employees similarly thought that Breslin's comments were specifically directed at Zimmerman. For instance, Karen Clougher expressed her belief that Breslin's remarks were aimed at Zimmerman and she, Clougher, considered the meeting to have been a public humiliation for the plaintiff.

- Zimmerman had begun keeping a journal in early December 1996, when she returned to work after her leave. She learned in 1997 that she would have to produce that diary to Breslin and Direct during the discovery phase of this litigation. The journal "contained records of events and conversations and employees that had been very supportive of [Zimmerman] whom she identified in there."

- After the diary had been produced, Zimmerman observed senior managers and other people mentioned in the journal frequently entering Breslin's office and exiting "visibly shaken." Zimmerman began being treated "like [she] had the plague."

- Zimmerman's testimony is buttressed by that of Hagerstrom. Hagerstrom described Zimmerman as being "stressed and upset," actually breaking down several times at work. According to Hagerstrom, Breslin and Capalbo treated Zimmerman "like the enemy" after she filed her charge of discrimination.

- Hagerstrom confirmed that Breslin assigned Zimmerman the task of underwriting the 100 percent home equity loans. It was estimated that it would take an inexperienced person approximately 40 minutes to write a home equity loan, and that Zimmerman was being faced with 20 to 30 such loans daily.

- Another Direct employee, Cotter, was quoted in the diary as saying that "the reason [Zimmerman] was being treated the way she was by Mr. Breslin was the fact that she was a woman, a woman, and a woman, three times straight."

***

Jury Verdict

joint and several liability
Joint and several liability is used in civil cases where two or more people are found liable for damages. The winning plaintiff in such a case may collect the entire judgment from any one of the parties, or from any and all of the parties in various amounts until the judgment is paid in full.

On claims submitted to the jury Zimmerman was awarded $200,000 in compensatory damages on her claim of retaliation under state law against both defendants, $400,000 in punitive damages jointly and severally against both defendants, and $130,000 in damages on her claim for intentional interference with advantageous relations against Breslin. Direct and Breslin successfully defended against claims of gender/pregnancy discrimination and violation of the Family Medical Leave Act.

The defendants now move for judgment as a matter of law with respect to the tortious interference claim and the award of punitive damages contending that no adequate evidentiary basis existed to support those aspects of the jury verdict.

. . . [A]lthough the court should review the record as a whole, it must disregard all evidence favorable to the moving party that the jury is not required to believe. That is, the court should give credence to the evidence favoring the nonmovant as well as that "evidence supporting the moving party that is uncontradicted and unimpeached, at least to the extent that that evidence comes from disinterested witnesses."

***

Ms. Zimmerman's last claim is against only David Breslin. She claims that she had an employment relationship with Direct which was advantageous to her and that Mr. Breslin intentionally interfered with that relationship. In order to prove that claim, Ms. Zimmerman must prove by a preponderance of the evidence that, one, she had an advantageous employment relationship with Direct; two, Mr. Breslin knew about the relationship; three, Mr. Breslin knowingly interfered with the relationship; four, the interference was improper in motive or means; and five, that Mr. Breslin's interference was the cause of an injury or damage to her.

. . . Under Massachusetts law, "in the employment and discharge context, the law of this jurisdiction seeks to protect a corporate official's freedom of action by requiring proof that the official acted with actual malice." Painting the picture a bit more completely: to make out the tort of intentional interference with a contractual relationship, a plaintiff must present evidence of "actual malice" or a "spiteful, malignant purpose, unrelated to the legitimate corporate interest." . . . In addition, "when an employer or supervisor is acting within the scope of his employment responsibilities, the hiring and firing decisions are privileged unless he acted with malevolence."

As earlier noted, the defendants are not challenging the jury verdict on the retaliation claim in their post-trial motion. In finding that Zimmerman had proven her claim of retaliation under Massachusetts laws, the jury must have concluded that Zimmerman suffered adverse employment actions as a result of having filed an MCAD claim, that the lawful, nondiscriminatory reasons articulated by the defendants for having taken those actions were false, and that an objective, determinative reason that the adverse employment actions were taken was retaliation. In this case, the same adverse employment actions that the jury found constituted retaliation supply the "improper motive or means" in the intentional interference claim.

***

[U]nder Massachusetts law, it is unlawful for any employer to discriminate against any person because she has filed a complaint in any proceeding alleging unlawful employment discrimination, including discrimination based on sex or pregnancy.

***

Instructions to the jury on punitive damages: Punitive damages are damages awarded for the purpose of condemning a defendant's unlawful conduct and deterring such conduct in the future. However, punitive damages are not available unless a further burden of proof is met. Ms. Zimmerman may receive an award of punitive damages if, and only if, you find that she has proven by a preponderance of the evidence that the defendant's conduct was outrageous because of its evil motive and/or because it exhibited a reckless disregard for the rights of others.

Decision

The Court upheld the jury's verdicts against Direct regarding retaliation, and against Breslin for intentional interference with an advantageous relationship. The punitive damage awards were also affirmed.

THE MODEL EMPLOYMENT TERMINATION ACT

Because the employment at will concept is a function of state common law, companies need to comply with a complex variety of employment at will exceptions that exist in different states. The rationale for the Model Employment Termination Act is to come up with a law that would ease the burden for enterprises that span several states. It is important to note that this Model Employment Termination Act is merely a proposed law. It is up to each state's legislative body to review it and consider whether to make it part of the state's statutory law. Arguments against passage have been advanced by advocates for both employees and employers. Neither side finds its provisions completely acceptable. Under the act employers cannot terminate employees at will. However, in the event of an unfair dismissal, the act provides that the dispute will be submitted to arbitration and that the damages will be capped.

In their summary of the Model Employment Termination Act (META), the National Conference of Commissioners on Uniform State Laws wrote the following[24]:

> In 1991 it is not possible to return to the original common law rule. The common law development of the last two decades indicates neither the desirability nor the possibility of that option. At the same time, a reasonable, uniform solution that fairly balances the equities of both employers and employees seems essential to eliminate the social and economic costs inherent in the current confused situation. The Uniform Law Commissioners propose to remedy these defects in the growing law of employment termination, beginning in 1991, with the Model Employment Termination Act (META). It offers the states, for the first time, a fair solution to the problems inherent in the recent common law revolution of employment law.
>
> Any qualified employee under META may not have his or her employment terminated without "good cause." An employee is anyone who works for hire. But not all employees are covered by META. An employer that employs fewer than five employees is not subject to META, for example. Each state is left to decide whether to apply META to employees of local government, and should make the determination based upon existing law protecting municipal employees. In addition, an employee must serve an employer for a significant enough time to be qualified for "good cause" termination. An employee must be employed by the firing employer for one year or longer. Moreover, the employee has to have worked for the employer at least 520 hours during the 26 weeks

preceding the termination. An employee, so qualified, is entitled to protection under META.

The good cause standard can be waived or modified, also, in specific agreement. However, a complete waiver is obtainable only if the employer agrees to severance pay upon dismissal equal in amount to one month's pay for each full year of employment—up to a maximum amount of 30 months' pay. If there is a contract of employment for specific duration related to the completion of a specified task, project, undertaking, or assignment, the termination of employment based upon the running of that contract, also, is not subject to the good faith standard.

Also, nothing in META displaces rights and claims arising under collective bargaining agreements. But at the same time, employees under collective bargaining agreements are not deprived of their rights under META. State and federal government employees are treated the same way as employees subject to collective bargaining agreements. They are deprived of nothing in the law and regulations pertaining to their employment. They have their rights under META.

"Good cause" is carefully defined in META. Basically, it can be one of two things. The employee's own inadequate or improper conduct in the performance of the job is one kind of "good cause." The second involves the economic or institutional goals of the employer. If these goals require reorganizations, discontinuing functions, and changing the size and character of its workforce, employees discharged as a result are discharged with "good cause." Of course, such determinations must be in "good faith," which means that they must be honestly made. Thus an employer, who must in good faith curtail operations because of lost markets or any downturn in business, can discharge employees to survive these adverse business conditions.

If a qualified employee is terminated without "good cause," META provides a remedy for that discharge. The remedies that may be sought under META are reinstatement, back pay, lost benefits, or, in the alternative, a lump sum severance payment. META excludes recovery for pain and suffering, emotional distress, defamation, fraud, punitive damages, compensatory damages, or any other monetary award. Attorney's fees are recoverable, so that employees with modest incomes have an opportunity to obtain legal assistance in bringing legitimate claims.

Perhaps the most significant aspect of the provisions is the reliance upon arbitration for determination of any award under META. Enforcement in META is entirely by arbitration. Judicial review of arbitration awards is permitted only for various abuses of the discretion or office of the arbitrators. Review is not in any sense "de novo."

META also protects employees who participate in termination proceedings. No employer can retaliate against an employee for filing a complaint, giving testimony, or otherwise lawfully participating in proceedings under META. Any retaliation can make the employer subject to damages, including punitive damages.

Neither employees nor employers appear to embrace the Model Act. Proponents hold that META would provide fairer and more efficient adjudication of employment termination cases in any adopting jurisdiction. Employee–opponents object to the limitation of remedies and the mandated arbitration, precluding the opportunity for an employee's "day in court."

As noted earlier, the laws of many other countries do not permit employers to terminate employees without good reason or without a prescribed notification and/or grievance procedure. One example is Norway, a European country that has not yet joined the European Union. In a 2006 publication, questions were posed to attorneys knowledgeable about Norway's employment law. Here are some questions and responses related to Norway's employment at will status:

Is there employment at will, or some other rule, in your jurisdiction? What are the exceptions?

Regarding the hiring process, an employer's freedom to choose which person to employ is only limited by the statutory discrimination regulations. As for termination of employment, there is no "at will" termination in Norway; termination initiated by the employer requires "good" or "valid" cause.

What are the legal obligations upon terminating an employee in your jurisdiction?

According to the WPA, employees may not be dismissed without notice unless this is objectively justified on the basis of circumstances relating to the undertaking, the employer, or the employee. As a minimum procedure, all terminations must be preceded by an individual discussion meeting with the employee. Furthermore, the notice must satisfy certain formal requirements in order to be valid. The employee is entitled to stay in his/her position, perform his/her duties, and receive salary during the notice period.

Are there any family and/or medical leave laws in your jurisdiction, and if so, what do they require?

According to the Norwegian National Insurance Act, an employee who has been employed for at least 2 weeks and has a certain minimum yearly salary is entitled to sick pay. The employer is obliged to pay sick pay for the first 16 days, whereafter the National Insurance takes over. The sick pay equals the employee's salary, up to a defined maximum (approximately NOK 420,000). An employee is also entitled to different types of leaves (with or without pay), such as maternity/paternity leave and parental leave, leave of absence in case of caring for close relatives in the terminal stage, or in case of child's or child minder's sickness.

Please list any miscellaneous, interesting, or oddball laws in your jurisdiction, and state under what circumstances they pertain.

There are no single oddball laws in Norway. However, according to the WPA, an employee who challenges the validity of a dismissal has, unless the court decides otherwise, a right under the WPA to remain in his/her job and perform the normal tasks and receive salary during the entire hearing of the legal dispute. With an appellate hearing, that may easily take up to 1–2 years. Such an extensive right for the employee is, as far as we know, quite unique.

Disclaimer: The descriptions set forth in this survey are intended only as a general overview of the law. The information presented in this survey is not intended to constitute legal advice as to any specific case or factual circumstance. Readers requiring legal advice on any of the specific case or circumstance should consult with counsel admitted in the relevant jurisdiction.

In many wrongful discharge cases, the needs, concerns, or potential of the aggrieved employee are not given sufficient attention by the employer. This is especially true in those instances in which the employee was, in fact, a highly desirable and productive person. Putting "people first" and appreciating the unique value of human capital in the enterprise is the focus of work by Jeffrey Pfeffer[26]. He advocates the establishment of three guiding principles for management: building trust, encouraging change, and measuring what matters.

Building trust: This means, among other things, sharing information with everyone, treating people with respect and dignity, and taking the organization's values seriously. Pfeffer cites companies that abide by these principles. For example, Whole Foods Market prominently presents the results of its employee satisfaction survey. Other examples include honest discussion in an annual report of how well an organization is doing in living up to its core values of fun, fairness, integrity, and social responsibility.

Encouraging change: Organizations can encourage change by putting people in new roles in a different organizational structure—"doing things that break old ways of organizing." The example given is that of the *New Zealand Post,* which required employees to do things differently and not be limited by old habits and assumptions. Among other things, the *Post* physically reconfigured the workplace, changing the dress code so that ties were no longer worn, moving the equipment, and rearranging the production process. Pfeffer notes that new initiatives are often greeted with skepticism, but when demonstrable change is applied to the workplace, it can result in new ways of thinking and acting.

Measuring what matters: Not only does Pfeffer believe that serious attention should be given to measuring employee activity; he also advocates that what should be measured is not only what the current information system happens to routinely track, but such things as how subordinates evaluate managers' behavior and adherence to company values, what training is provided to employees, how effective it is and how it is tracked, how well the managers track employee turnover, and even the number of job applicants the company handles. In other words, measure the components of the firm's people management practices.

Discussion Questions Apply the Pfeffer principles to the defendant companies in the cases described in this chapter. For example, is there evidence that those principles were part of management's strategy? How might the principles have been manifested in practice? Be specific. How realistic is Pfeffer in advocating that firms trust their employees?

WHAT ABOUT BULLYING?

In the United States it may seem to some that bullying by a supervisor or even a coworker is illegal and can be the subject of a lawsuit against an employer who allows it to go on unimpeded. That is not the case. If the person or people who are being "bullied" are members of one of the statutorily protected classes, however, a claim can be made that the bullying violates a statutory prohibition. For example, the Civil Rights Act of 1964 prohibits discrimination against people based on race, creed, color, sex, religion, and national origin; other laws prohibit discrimination against people based on age or disability; and so on. Therefore, bullying by a manager that is aimed solely at females or black employees is actionable, but bullying aimed indiscriminately at all workers is not.

There is a movement, however, that seeks to make bullying illegal, regardless of who is being bullied. Several countries already have laws that are interpreted to prohibit bullying, and several states in the United States are considering such bills. As of October 2007, 13 U.S. states have proposed legislation[27]:

- New Jersey (2007)
- Washington (2007, 2005)
- New York (2006)
- Vermont (2007)
- Oregon (2007, 2005)
- Montana (2007)
- Connecticut (2007)
- Hawaii (2007, 2006, 2005, 2004)
- Oklahoma (2007, 2004)
- Kansas (2006)
- Missouri (2006)
- Massachusetts (2005)
- California (2003)

Summary

Employment at will is a common law principle that essentially allows employers to fire employees even when there is no good cause to support such a move. Also, employees have the right to quit when they wish without owing anything to the employer.

Because this doctrine arises in common law, it is state law and is created and modified by judges in individual cases. Each state fashions its own judge-made common law and sets its own precedents in cases that come before the states' courts. Therefore, the exceptions to employment at will differ from one state to another.

This principle has been eroded in the past few decades in all the states, and employers must be aware of the differing degrees by which the employment at will doctrine has changed in each of the states in which they operate their businesses.

The employment at will principle applies only to employment relationships in which there is no contract to the contrary. Two examples in which such contracts exist are (1) in a union setting where there is a collective bargaining agreement protecting employees from discharge without just cause; and (2) when there is a contract for a definite period.

Exceptions to the employment at will principle include the following:

- When dismissal is contrary to public policy.
- When dismissal violates an implied contract.
- When dismissal violates an implied covenant of good faith and fair dealing.
- When dismissal violates statutory law.
- When dismissal gives rise to a tort claim.

Tort claims include, but are not limited to, the following:

- Intentional infliction of emotional distress, also known as the tort of outrage.
- Defamation.
- Invasion of privacy.
- Fraud.
- Interference with a contractual relationship.

To address the dilemma facing employers because the unfair dismissal rules involving employment at will differ from state to state, the National Conference of Commissioners for Uniform State Laws has put together the Model Employment Termination Act. Its basic provisions are that a dismissal can be made only when there is good cause; when such a case arises, it will be submitted to arbitration; and there are limitations to the awards that a plaintiff can recover. Among other things, the META excludes recovery for pain and suffering, emotional distress, defamation, fraud, punitive damages, compensatory damages, or the like. Instead the successful plaintiff may be awarded reinstatement, back pay, lost benefits, or, in the alternative, a lump sum severance payment.

Questions

1. Ambler M. was a union employee who was told upon hire that as long as her work was satisfactory she would be retained. Ambler's work had been rated as "highly satisfactory" just one day before she was subpoenaed to testify before the Assembly Interim Committee on Governmental Efficiency and Economy of the California Legislature. Ambler alleged that she was instructed by Kevin S., the secretary–treasurer of the union and the person who did hiring and firing, to make certain false statements in the testimony. She refused to do so and answered truthfully all questions asked of her. The next day she was discharged by Kevin S. The defendant argued that it had the right to terminate the employment under the principle of employment at will.

   a. What facts would Ambler have to present to the court to successfully challenge her dismissal?

   b. What should the court decide? Support your answer.

2. Paul M. was employed by Hershey Chocolate–Memphis as an at-will employee. He had been an employee for more than 16 years and had a good work record. As part of mandatory company policy, he consented to and took a urinalysis drug test. The results were inconclusive, and he was asked to submit to an additional test. He had never tested positive for drugs in previous years of employment with Hershey, and he was not in a "safety-sensitive" position. After Paul declined to submit to the additional test, he was fired by Hershey. He had never been informed that failure to agree to a drug test could result in termination. Paul sued for wrongful discharge.

   a. What legal argument would Paul use to win his case?

   b. What are his chances of success? Explain your answer.

3. Katherine H. worked for Durand as a quality inspector for over four years. Her supervisor admitted that she was a dependable and conscientious employee and acknowledged telling the plaintiff on several occasions that her job was secure. It was also stated, however, that she was antagonistic, argumentative, and disruptive. One week before Katherine was fired, her entire crew was experiencing problems with Amy B., another supervisor, and Amy told the department head that she "wanted Katherine off my shift." Katherine asked why she was being fired. "I've done nothing wrong. I've never been warned. I've never been written up." The unwritten policy at the workplace was that employees would be told "[t]his is your first warning, this is your second warning" and so on. Also, Katherine's supervisor told her that the only cause for "immediate discharge" was insubordination. The written "Rules of Conduct" for Durand did not include a warning procedure. Katherine did not have a formal contract of employment with Durand. Katherine sued Durand for wrongful discharge.

   a. What are Katherine's chances of success?

   b. What exception to employment at will should Katherine argue here? Explain your answer.

   c. What management practices could have prevented this litigation?

4. Laurie E., Linda H., and Jill F. worked for ABC Company under a supervisor named F. Falmouth. The supervisor began regularly using the harshest vulgarity shortly after his arrival at the facility where Laurie, Linda, and Jill worked. In response, they informed him that they were uncomfortable with obscene jokes, vulgar cursing, and sexual innuendo in the office. Despite these objections, he continued to use exceedingly vulgar language on a daily basis. Several witnesses testified that he used the word "f---" as part of his normal pattern of conversation, and that he regularly heaped abusive profanity on the employees. Linda testified that Falmouth used this language to get a reaction. Another ABC employee testified that he used the words "f---" and "motherf---er" frequently when speaking with employees. On one occasion when a female employee asked him to curb his language because it was offensive, he positioned himself in front of her face and screamed, "I will do and say any damn thing I want. And I don't

give a s--- who likes it." Another typical example occurred when a male worker asked Falmouth to stop his yelling and vulgarity because it upset the female employees, and Falmouth replied, "I'm tired of walking on f---ing eggshells, trying to make people happy around here." There was further evidence that Falmouth's harsh and vulgar language was not merely accidental but seemed intended to abuse the employees.

The plaintiffs complained to ABC and ABC investigated these complaints, after which ABC issued Falmouth a "letter of reprimand." After the reprimand, he discontinued some of his egregious conduct but did not end it completely. Eventually the plaintiffs sought medical treatment for emotional distress caused by Falmouth's conduct. Subsequently the employees filed suit, alleging that ABC intentionally inflicted emotional distress on them through Falmouth. The jury awarded $100,000.00 plus interest to Linda, $100,000.00 plus interest to Laurie, and $75,000.00 plus interest to Jill. ABC appealed.

a. What would Laurie, Linda, and Jill have to prove to be successful in their claim of intentional infliction of emotional distress?

b. What is the likelihood of their success?

c. What could ABC have done to avoid this lawsuit?

d. Would ABC be liable if it had a sexual harassment policy?

e. Is it necessary for the behavior of the supervisor to have a detrimental effect on the plaintiffs for them to succeed in their legal action?

f. Would workers' compensation benefits be allocated to the employees under these circumstances?

5. On April 3, 1996, Sal S., the plaintiff in this case, was engaged in a conversation with Tom T., a supervisor at LMN. In this conversation, plaintiff was acting defensively in response to Tom's earlier suggestion in a meeting that she needed to handle more claims. Tom suggested that the two continue the conversation outside, where plaintiff continued to act defensively. At this point Tom stated that she should relax and that she was not being investigated. He then added that "if we caught you in bed with a dead man or a live woman, then we might have to investigate you." Plaintiff reported this comment to Patrick S., a coworker who had been plaintiff's former direct supervisor. Patrick subsequently notified Sarper T., Tom's supervisor.

Sal took a leave of absence for three months and within two weeks of her return received a verbal reprimand for improperly using her e-mail to spread rumors. Defendant also reprimanded plaintiff for improperly contacting a supervisor in the New York office even though she was expressly given permission to do so.

Subsequently, several events occurred that plaintiff alleged were in retaliation for her reporting Tom's comment in April:

LMN threatened to place Sal on a work program; LMN did not assign plaintiff a sufficient number of cases with which to achieve her critical success goals; an in-house attorney, during an interview with Tom, asked whether Tom and plaintiff were having an affair; LMN issued two verbal reprimands that had no basis in fact; her supervisor issued an inaccurate performance evaluation; Patrick promised plaintiff he would be there when she returned to work from her leave of absence, but was absent upon her return. Two months after returning from her leave of absence, plaintiff resigned and brought legal action against LMN.

a. What legal arguments would Sal make against LMN to support a wrongful discharge action?

b. What are her chances of success?

6. Laura T. was employed at Manor House, a nursing home. At some point Laura became aware that Elaine Z., the executive director of Manor House, had been engaging in various illegal and improper practices. Specifically Laura claims to have learned that Elaine misappropriated the property of deceased residents, stole funds from the home's petty cash drawer, charged personal long distance telephone calls to the employer, and used other employer resources, including an automobile and food service, for personal benefit.

Subsequently the vice president of human resources encouraged Laura to explain to him what she knew about the improper conduct. He also requested that she provide him with the names of any other employees who might have information regarding Elaine's conduct. After seeking and obtaining assurances that if she disclosed this information she would be protected from any reprisals, Laura disclosed the information she had learned, as well as the names of coworkers who were also aware of the alleged misconduct.

In response to Laura's information, the CEO personally interviewed the other employees named by Laura. The nursing home eventually determined that Elaine had in fact engaged in improper conduct. As a result, she was reprimanded and directed to cease such practices.

Elaine soon learned, or began to suspect, that Laura had provided the information regarding improper practices to upper management. Laura contends that the employer was reckless in not keeping the matter confidential, and Elaine became very critical of Laura's work. Soon thereafter, Laura's employment was terminated at the behest of Elaine.

Laura was told that she was being discharged because her position was being eliminated. Laura, however, contends that she was discharged for providing information regarding Elaine's misconduct despite assurances that there would be no reprisals.

a. State the legal arguments that Laura might make to support a lawsuit against the nursing home.

b. What would she have to prove?

c. How likely is her success?

d. If you were asked to advise the HR department, what changes would you recommend?

7. On March 19, 2002, Ted F. was called to a meeting with Pete C., Yellow Cross's director of human resources, and the vice president of innovation, quality, and cost. Pete informed Ted that a complaint had been received from Williamstown Hospital to the effect that Ted, while in the presence of representatives from the other hospitals, had divulged the details of a confidential financial settlement between Yellow Cross and Williamstown Hospital. Pete told Ted he would be discharged immediately because of this conduct. Ted denied the accusation and claims he did not even know about any settlement between Yellow Cross and Williamstown Hospital, let alone divulge its details to anyone. Despite Ted's request that Yellow Cross investigate the matter further, Pete did not do so, allegedly acting on the advice of a lawyer.

When Ted sought employment elsewhere, he felt obliged to describe the circumstances of his termination and consequently was unable to obtain employment in his chosen field.

Does Ted have a good legal argument to bring against Yellow Cross? Explain.

References

1. J. E. Macdonald and C. L. Beck-Dudley, "A Natural Law Defense to the Employment Law Question: A Response to Richard Epstein," *Am. Bus. L. J.* 38 (Winter 2001), p. 364.
2. *Adair v. U.S.*, 208 U.S. 161 (1908). See also *Payne v. Western Atlantic RR,* 81 Tenn. 507 (1884).
3. 1996 Employment Protection Act, Ariz. Rev. Stat. § 23-1501 (3)(b)(i) (Supp. 1998). For discussion of this law, see *Cronin v. Arizona*, No. CV-98-0495-5A and No. CV-98-0580-5A, 1999 Ariz. LEXIS 125 (Dec. 17, 1999).
4. Mont. Code Ann. 39-2-901-914.
5. State of Arkansas, 83rd General Assembly, Regular Session, 2001, HR 1053, by Representative Thomas.
6. B. Fuller, "Youth Unemployment in France," *Aplia Econ Blog News for Econ Students* (January 27, 2006). See also www.econblog.aplia.com/2006/01/youth-unemployment-in-france.html (accessed July 10, 2007).
7. *Gantt v. Sentry Insurance,* 824 P.2d 680, 686-87 (Cal. 1992).
8. For (1) see *Tameny v. Atlantic Richfield Co.* (1980) 27 Cal.3d 167 and *Petermann v. International Brotherhood of Teamsters* (1959), 174 Cal.App.2d; for (2) see *Nees v. Hocks* (1975), 272 Ore. 210; for (3) see *Wetherton v. Growers Farm Labor Assn.* (1969), 275 Cal.App.2d 168; and for (4) see *Hentzel v. Singer Co.* (1982), 138 Cal. App.3d 290. See also *Gantt v. Sentry Insurance,* id.
9. *Gantt v. Sentry Insurance,* id.
10. *Nicosia v. Wakefern Food Corporation,* 136 N.J. 401, 643 A.2d 554 (1994).
11. L. L. Sullivan, A. F. Sullivan, Boyar & Miller [s3], and C.R.B. Stowe, "How to Stay Out of the Doghouse: How to Handle Involuntary Terminations Correctly," *Journal of Business and Public Affairs* 1, no. 1 (2007).

12. C. J. Muhl, "The Employment-at-Will Doctrine: Three Major Exceptions," *Monthly Labor Review,* January 2001, p. 3. See also www.bls.gov/opub/mlr/2001/01/art1full.pdf (accessed March 4, 2008).

13. *Caton d/b/a Caton Sales Company v. Leach Corporation,* 896 F.2d 939; 1990 U.S. App. LEXIS 3980; 115 Lab. Cas. (CCH) P56, 263.

14. *Lawrence Hogan v. CheckFree Corporation,* D.O.L. case, October 7, 2004, taken from National Whistleblower Center press release. See www.whistleblowers.org/html/past_press_releases.htm (accessed July 10, 2007).

15. *Staggie v. Idaho Falls Consol. Hosp., Inc.,* 110 Idaho 349, 715 P.2d 1019 (Ct. App. 1986).

16. *Wal-Mart Stores, Inc. v. Luis A. Canchola,* 64 S.W.3d 524 (Tex. App. 2002).

17. *Snyder v. Medical Serv. Corp. of E. Wash.,* 35 P.3d 1158 (2001).

18. *Davis v. Manchester Health Ctr., Inc.,* 88 Conn. App. 60, 867 A.2d 876 (2005).

19. *Osborn v. University Med. Assocs. of Med. Univ. of S.C.,* 278 F. Supp. 2d 720 (D.S.C. 2003).

20. *Hord v. ERIM,* 228 Mich. App. 638, 579 N.W.2d 133 (1998).

21. *Mino v. Clio School District,* 255 Mich. App. 60, 661 N.W.2d 586 (2003).

22. *Cweklinsky v. Mobil Chem. Co.,* 267 Conn. 210, 837 A.2d 759, 766-67, 20 IER 1281, 1285 (2004).

23. *Zimmerman v. Direct Federal Credit Union and Breslin,* 121 F. Supp. 2d 133 (2000).

24. *National Conference of Commissioners for Uniform State Laws,* Summary of the Model Employment Termination Act, from www.nccusl.org/Update/uniformact_summaries/uniformacts-s-meta.asp (accessed July 18, 2007). See also the Model Employment Termination Act (1991), reprinted in 9A Individual Employment Rts. Manual (BNA) 540:21-540:46 (Aug. 8, 1991); and D.A. Ballam, "Employment-at-Will: The Impending Death of a Doctrine," *American Business Law Journal* 37 (Summer 2000), p. 653.

25. Lex Mundi Labor and Employment Desk Book Prepared by the Lex Mundi Labor and Employment Law Group Norway Chapter prepared by Lex Mundi member firm Thommessen Krefting Greve Lund AS (www.thommessen.no) Authors: Kristine Schei, Partner, and Håvard Sandnes, Senior Associate *Lex Mundi Labor and Employment Desk Book* (Lex Mundi Ltd., 2006). See also lexmundi.com/images/lexmundi/PDF/LaborEmployment/Labor_Employment_DeskBook/LaborEmployment_Norway.pdf, (accessed February 17, 2008).

26. J. Pfeffer, "The Real Keys to High Performance," *Leader to Leader* 8 (Spring 1998).

27. *Workplace Bullying Institute* (HarperCollins, 2006). See http://en.wikipedia.org/wiki/Workplace_bullying#United_States (accessed February 14, 2008).

Privacy Rights, Restrictive Covenants, and Intellectual Property

> . . . [A]s we enjoy great advantages from the inventions of others, we should be glad of an opportunity to serve others by any invention of ours; and this we should do freely and generously.
>
> Benjamin Franklin[1]

INTRODUCTION

Benjamin Franklin, in making the statement that opens this chapter, reflected an attitude that is almost nonexistent in today's competitive business world. Fortunes are made and lost today based on a patent, copyright, or other form of intellectual property, and those property rights are adamantly protected from infringement by competitors or even potential competitors.

With all their benefits to industry and to individuals in their personal and professional lives, rapidly changing technologies give rise to numerous legal issues. In the relationship between employers and employees, these issues include, but are not limited to, employee privacy rights, the right to capitalize on personal knowledge by having an unfettered right to work for competitors or compete with a former employer, and ownership rights to intellectual property. In each of these areas, the challenge for the employer is to keep up with changing law as the courts seek to address technological progress and all its ramifications.

This chapter explores each of these three areas—employee privacy, noncompete agreements, and intellectual property—in an attempt to assess the status of the law and how companies are handling these issues. We will also refer to the issues as they appear in situations outside the United States.

EMPLOYEE PRIVACY RIGHTS

Employee privacy rights are not a new phenomenon; but the form in which those rights might be violated has changed. Access to the Internet, use of e-mail messages, new surveillance technology, and other available methods of potential intrusion into employees' personal lives can all lead to claims of invasion of privacy.

Public Sector versus Private Sector

Privacy rights of civil servants (employees of the government—the *public sector*) differ from those of employees in the private sector. (*Note: Private sector* here refers to enterprises not operated by the government. Do not confuse the public sector with publicly traded corporations, which are listed on stock exchanges. Such publicly traded companies are referred to in this chapter as private employers operating in the private sector.)

The major difference between employees in the public and private sectors is the impact of the Constitution. The constitutionally guaranteed rights enjoyed by U.S. citizens include the government's guarantee that it will not deprive citizens of life, liberty, and property without due process (Fifth Amendment); that the government will refrain from unreasonable search and seizure of its citizens (Fourth Amendment); and that citizens have the right to speak freely and exercise their right to religious freedom without government interference (First Amendment). Drug testing of government employees is considered a form of search and seizure and therefore can violate an employee's constitutional rights if the government does not follow due process in its drug testing methods. Similarly, if the government does not have justifiable reason to engage in such testing, it could be considered a constitutional violation. The U.S. Supreme Court has held that random drug testing for employees in safety-sensitive positions is not a constitutional violation. Although private employers can enforce dress codes and speech codes with impunity as long as they do not have an adverse impact on a protected class, the government must be circumspect about imposing such rules on its workers unless there is a job-related or other justifiable reason for such a rule. Reasons for restricting the guaranteed rights of citizens can include national security, safety of self and others, and so on.

In the private sector employers need not concern themselves with constitutional rights because those rights are guarantees made by the government, not by private enterprises. However, there *is* a right to privacy in tort law, and that *is* a concern for private employers.

Essentially the tort of invasion of privacy occurs in one of several ways. Most states' courts find invasion of privacy in the following circumstances: intrusion on the seclusion of another, appropriation of another's name or likeness without consent, unreasonable publicity about another's private life, or unreasonably and publicly placing another in a false light. What the law recognizes as unreasonable may differ from state to state because tort is common law. For example, in many states a plaintiff must meet the following requirements to show invasion of privacy involving unreasonable publicity of private life: (1) the facts disclosed must be private; (2) the disclosure must be made to the public; (3) the disclosure must be one that would be highly offensive to a reasonable person; (4) the facts disclosed cannot be of legitimate concern to the public; and (5) the defendant acted with reckless disregard of the private nature of the facts disclosed.

The potential for violation of privacy rights in the workplace is complicated by new and changing technologies such as e-mail communications, Internet use, camera phones, and more sophisticated means of surveillance.

E-Mail

There are at least two potential pitfalls regarding e-mail use in the workplace. First, legal liability on the part of the company may arise from information that is exchanged through company-provided e-mail. Messages might contain defaming or harassing statements made by or about employees, competitors, or others. For those reasons and others, such as monitoring communications between customers and the employees, employer access to e-mail is warranted. The second problem is related to the first. If a company limits its e-mail system to business use and monitors that use, a violation of privacy may result when the employer unreasonably taps into personal exchanges. Telephone use by employees for personal reasons has been held to be permissible up to a point; and if an employer taps into personal calls, courts have held that listening beyond what is necessary to ascertain the personal nature of a call is considered invasion of privacy. A similar analysis is likely to prevail regarding e-mail use.

Suggestions for E-Mail Monitoring Policy

There are a number of concerns to be addressed when establishing a monitoring policy covering the use of technology in the workplace. Major concerns of the employer should be the focus of such policies. The employer might consider the following rules, or variations of these rules, when writing up an e-mail monitoring policy. Similar rules can be written to address use of camera phones, instant messaging, or other devices on company premises or during working hours.

- E-mail usage is subject to monitoring.
- When sending e-mails or instant messages (if permitted by the employer) for any purpose, employees are prohibited from making disparaging comments about the company and its products and/or services.
- When sending e-mails or instant messages (if permitted by the employer) for any purpose, employees are prohibited from making defamatory or harassing statements about anyone, including, but not limited to, other employees, suppliers, visitors, or the organizations they represent.
- Monitoring of e-mail usage will be limited to [insert number] session(s) per day/month. [Specify the duration, and whether it will be random.]
- Instant Messaging software is [or is not] permitted to be downloaded to company computers.
- Internet use for personal matters is limited to [insert number] minutes per day/month.

- Violation of the E-mail/Internet policy can result in disciplinary action, possibly resulting in discharge, if it involves jeopardizing company interests. This includes, but is not limited to, harassment, defamation, divulging of trademark or other intellectual property infringement.

Internet

Employers have a legitimate expectation that employees will be engaged in company-related activity while at work. The Internet contains tools and information that employees can and do access for work purposes, but it also provides a wide array of distracting sites that can quickly usurp employees' time. Should employers restrict personal use of the Internet? If so, how will this be done? Just as monitoring of e-mail runs the risk of privacy invasion, so too does monitoring of Internet use.

Internet use outside the workplace also raises legal issues for an employer. Employee use of company electronics, whether in or out of the office, can expose an employer to viruses, theft, electronic eavesdropping, and other threats. Bloggers (employees or others) can share information with people worldwide and in some cases have been problematic. "Numerous bloggers who maintain blogs outside the workplace have been fired for publicly posting sensitive information or defaming their employers on the Internet, or just for posting inappropriate content with an actual or implied connection to their employer"[2]. It is recommended that employers include blogging and chat room use in their Internet use policies.

Monitoring e-mail and Internet use could easily make available to the employer information that is legally protected, such as medical records. Furthermore, although it is clearly a right of employers to regulate workplace procedures, including phone calls, computer use, and work schedules in general, the law recognizes certain rights to privacy even within the physical premises of the employer. There are no laws in the United States prohibiting employers from accessing or reading employees' e-mail, but caution must be observed to avoid unlawful intrusions on privacy that could be the subject of state common law violations. Other countries view this matter more stringently. For example, Australia is considering passage of a bill that would make it a criminal offense for employers to read employee e-mail[3].

Camera Phones

Employee use of camera phones in the workplace can obviously threaten security regarding trade secrets, client lists, product formulas, marketing strategies, and the like. In addition, inappropriate use of cameras at work can lead to charges of harassment, invasion of privacy, or similar claims by affected employees.

Privacy issues can also be the subject of complaints involving disability discrimination laws. Genetic screening technology makes possible an entirely different manner of weeding out employees who might be costly to an employer. Under the Americans with Disabilities Act and the Rehabilitation Act of 1973, employer use of such tools would likely run afoul of the law. The position of the EEOC regarding genetic testing in employment situations was made clear in a mediated resolution of a case brought by the EEOC against Burlington Northern and

Santa Fe Railway Company (BNSF) in 2002. The EEOC alleged that BNSF violated the Americans with Disabilities Act of 1990 (ADA) by genetically testing or seeking to test 36 of its employees without their knowledge or consent. The testing was part of a medical examination that was required of employees who filed claims or reported work-related carpal tunnel syndrome injuries. Some of the employees claimed that they faced disciplinary measures for refusing to submit to the examination. BNSF settled for the sum of $2.2 million[4].

In response to such concerns, new company privacy policies have proliferated across the country. Hewlett-Packard, for example, has created a privacy office to enforce a global master privacy policy that establishes privacy and data protection principles for its worldwide operations. "The policy applies to the collection, storage, transportation, and use of personal information obtained from customers, prospects, business partners, employees, job applicants, and retirees. All HP employees and contracted parties working on behalf of HP must comply with these policies, even if local law is less restrictive"[5].

Government employers walk a tightrope between the privacy rights of their employees and the public's right to know. A recent relevant case is *Teamsters Local 856 et al. v. Priceless, LLC et al.* (2003)[6]. Priceless, a publisher, sought to publicize the names and compensation figures of municipal employees from several cities. As a result of union objections, the employers obtained an injunction against the publisher. On appeal, the issue centered on the right of the public to have this information and the privacy rights of the employees. The state court, relying in part on judicial interpretations of the Freedom of Information Act and the U.S. Supreme Court's 1989 decision in the *Reporters Committee* case[7], held that to compel disclosure of individual public employees' information, it must pertain to the government's performance of its duties, and that when the name of an individual reveals nothing about the public employer, private data should not be made public[8]. If the information Priceless sought to publish included names of individuals with corresponding information, it must argue that naming individuals is integral to its discussion of the government activity. In the absence of such evidence, disclosure of names is prohibited.

The American Civil Liberties Union, concerned about employee privacy, has created the Model Electronic Privacy Act, which consists of guidelines that employers can use to conduct electronic monitoring of their workers. The model act covers the nature of the information that is to be collected, the requirements for notice to employees about such monitoring, the disclosure of information collected, and more. Employers can also find valuable sample policies online[9].

DILEMMA FOR MANAGERS

Insufficient safeguards on the flow of information through e-mail, the Internet, camera phones, and the like can lead to privacy violations concerning medical records or unique information regarding personal identity, such as

Social Security numbers. Because of increasing identity theft, employers need to protect their employees' personal data by instituting security measures that were unnecessary in the past. Conversely, employers find themselves caught between the assertion of privacy rights by employees and the government's demand for employee data relating to national security. The Patriot Act passed by Congress in 2001 created an overarching Homeland Security agency with authority to collect personal information about employees in an effort to uncover terrorist activity. For example, financial institutions must report "suspicious" activity, and more stringent record keeping about foreign national employees is required[10].

Case for Discussion 6-1

The *Chimarev* case here shows how the state of New York handles privacy issues in the workplace. Students should note the references in the first few paragraphs to the Title VII claim that the plaintiff raised and why it was dismissed.

CHIMAREV V. TD WATERHOUSE INVESTOR SERVICES, INC., 280 F. SUPP.2D 208 (2003)[11]

Facts

Chimarev was terminated for disciplinary reasons after an investigation concerning inappropriate use of computer servers and records. He filed suit, alleging, among other things, discrimination based on his nationality and invasion of privacy. Chimarev's supervisor had met with him to discuss several work-related concerns, such as problems with coworkers, insubordination, failure to complete projects, and other disciplinary issues. The employer decided to investigate some of these concerns and went into his computer and e-mail records to see whether, among other things, he had abused computer and e-mail privileges. Chimarev was ultimately dismissed when his performance and behavior did not improve.

Decision

Because New York's limited right of privacy does not prohibit an employer from accessing employee e-mail and other documents produced on the company's system, Chimarev has no invasion of privacy claim to adjudicate.

Questions for Discussion

1. What is the significance of the fact that there is a limited common law of privacy in New York State?
2. How might the case be decided if New York followed a more liberal common law of privacy?
3. Why was the Title VII claim dismissed?

HIPAA: FEDERAL LEGISLATION ON PRIVACY RIGHTS

The Health Insurance Portability and Accountability Act of 1996 (HIPAA)[12] sets forth privacy rules regarding matters of health. The "covered entities" under HIPAA (those that must comply with its provisions) include health care providers, health care clearinghouses, and health plans (including self-funded and insured group health plans of public and private employers). Employers must determine whether they meet the law's definition of "covered entities" to determine whether HIPAA applies to them. However, even companies that are not technically covered entities are nonetheless responsible for the manner in which they use "protected health information" (PHI) of their employees. This arises, in particular, with worker's compensation matters or employees seeking leave for disability or other reasons under federal or state family leave laws. In these cases an employer must receive written authorization from the affected employee before obtaining health information from health care providers. Only the minimum necessary information can be disclosed. Furthermore, employee health information must be kept separate from the employee's regular personnel file. HIPAA provides that some employers must use firewalls around protected health information. However, if a self-insured group health plan has fewer than 50 participants, it is exempt from HIPAA requirements.

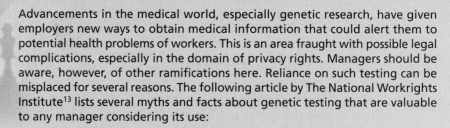

Management **Perspective**

Genetic Testing in the Workplace

Advancements in the medical world, especially genetic research, have given employers new ways to obtain medical information that could alert them to potential health problems of workers. This is an area fraught with possible legal complications, especially in the domain of privacy rights. Managers should be aware, however, of other ramifications here. Reliance on such testing can be misplaced for several reasons. The following article by The National Workrights Institute[13] lists several myths and facts about genetic testing that are valuable to any manager considering its use:

Myth: Genetic testing is an accurate way to predict disease.
Fact: Although some genetic tests can accurately predict that an individual will develop a certain disease or condition (for example, Huntington's disease or sickle cell anemia), even those tests often do not indicate when the individual will develop symptoms or how severe the symptoms will be.

Many genetic tests now commercially available, including tests for such complex conditions as breast cancer, cannot predict whether a person will actually develop the disease, but only if they have a genetic predisposition and a greater likelihood of developing cancer. Many people who test positive for genetic mutations associated with certain conditions will never develop those conditions. Moreover, while individuals with genetic mutations associated with certain diseases like cancer may be at higher risk, many factors determine whether someone will actually develop the disease. For example, most women who develop breast cancer (85–90 percent) do not have an inherited genetic susceptibility to the disease.

Most health care providers do not have training in genetics, and many who order genetic tests may not know how to interpret the results. There is no requirement for genetic counseling in commercial or many clinical settings, so individuals and their doctors often do not understand what the results of a genetic test really mean for the individual or family members.

Myth: Genetic tests are reliable and safe.

Fact: Currently the U.S. Food and Drug Administration (FDA) has declined to regulate genetic tests, despite the fact that many are commercially available and aggressively marketed by biotech firms. The absence of regulation means that there is no government oversight or quality control, and the accuracy and reliability of the tests are unproven.

While taking blood or tissue samples for genetic testing may cause minimal risk of physical harm, the results of genetic tests often create enormous psychological problems for individuals tested and their families. Information gathered from genetic tests is not just about individuals—it has implications for all of the individual's blood relatives as well. Sometimes genetic tests have implications for whole communities because some genetic conditions are associated (sometimes inappropriately) with certain racial or ethnic groups. For example, sickle cell anemia is associated with African-Americans, and predisposition for breast cancer has been associated by some with Ashkenazi Jews, even though it is not clear that they as a group are at greater risk.

Myth: Genetic testing is not really a serious workplace issue.

Fact: Genetic testing in the workplace is on the rise. In 1982 a federal government survey found that 1.6 percent of companies who responded were using genetic testing for employment purposes.[a] In a similar survey conducted by the American Management Association in 1997, 6–10 percent of employers were found to be conducting genetic testing.[b]

Moreover, there have been many documented cases of genetic discrimination.[c] In a survey of nearly 1,000 individuals who were at risk for genetic conditions, over 22 percent reported that they had experienced some form of discrimination based on their risk status.[d] The U.S.

[a] "The Role of Genetic Testing in the Prevention of Occupational Disease," Office of Technology Assessment, April 1983.

[b] American Management Association.

[c] P. Billings et al., "Discrimination as a Consequence of Genetic Testing," *American Journal of Human Genetics* 50 (1992), pp. 476–82.

[d] L. N. Geller et al., "Individual, Family, and Social Dimensions of Genetic Discrimination: A Case Study Analysis," *Science and Engineering Ethics* 2, no. 1 (1996).

(*Continued*)

Department of Labor has found genetic information to be a very serious workplace issue.[e]

Myth: Certain work environments may hasten the onset of genetically based diseases, and genetic testing can protect employees who are at risk. *Fact:* Currently no one knows whether some work environments hasten the onset of genetic disease. According to the American Medical Association, "there is insufficient evidence to justify the use of any existing test for genetic susceptibility as a basis for employment decisions."[f] There are no empirical data showing that "the genetic abnormality results in an unusually elevated susceptibility to occupational injury."[g]

Myth: Federal laws like the Americans with Disabilities Act (ADA) protect employees from genetic discrimination in the workplace. *Fact:* The extent of federal protection against genetic discrimination is unclear, and limited at best.[h] The federal appeals courts are divided on the scope of protection of the ADA, particularly for employees who have not yet manifested symptoms of illness.[i] In any event, the ADA addresses workplace discrimination but not privacy. There is currently no federal law prohibiting an employer from requesting genetic information or testing employees, and no law protecting the privacy of genetic information.[j]

Myth: State employment discrimination laws protect workers against genetic discrimination. *Fact:* Currently only 12 states have enacted laws that protect employees from genetic discrimination in the workplace (including California, Connecticut, Illinois, Iowa, New Hampshire, New Jersey, New York, North Carolina, Oregon, Rhode Island, Texas, and Wisconsin); a handful of other states have legislation pending.

[e] "Genetic Information and the Workplace," U.S. Department of Labor Report, January 20, 1997.

[f] Council on Ethical and Judicial Affairs, "Use of Genetic Testing by Employers," *Journal of the American Medical Association* 266, no. 13 (October 2, 1991).

[g] Id.

[h] 42 U.S.C.A. Sec. 12111 et seq.

[i] There is a case, *Bragdon v. Abbot,* pending in the U.S. Supreme Court that raises the issue of whether the ADA covers such conditions as asymptomatic HIV infection; the Court's decision in that case may have broader implications regarding the applicability of the ADA to asymptomatic genetic conditions.

[j] Recently the Ninth Circuit Court ruled that Lawrence Berkeley Laboratory may have violated its employees' constitution right to privacy by subjecting workers to genetic testing without their knowledge or consent, and remanded the case to the trial court. See *Norman-Bloodsaw et al. v. Lawrence Berkeley Laboratory et al.,* No. 96-16526, 9th Cir., Feb 3, 1998. This is the first U.S. appeals court decision on genetic privacy in the workplace.

Note: As of April 30, 2007, the U.S. House of Representatives voted favorably (420 to 3) on a bill, the Genetic Information Nondiscrimination Act of 2007, to prohibit discrimination in employment based on genetic testing. However, until the Senate votes favorably on it and the president approves it, this is not U.S. law.[14]

Global **Perspective**

Concerns about personal information passing from company to company, and from country to country, have been the subject of guidelines drawn up by the U.S. Department of Commerce. In an attempt to resolve discrepancies between European Union standards of privacy and those of the United States, the "Safe Harbor" principles were drawn up.[15] In October 1998 the European Union passed the Data Protection Directive prohibiting transfers of personal data to countries without "adequate" data protection. U.S. privacy laws did not adequately meet the EU's criteria. As a result of negotiations between the EU Commission and the U.S. Department of Commerce, the Safe Harbor program was created. Companies that agree to the Safe Harbor principles can freely transfer personal information, including employee information, to the United States from any of the EU nations.

The U.S. Department of Commerce provides on its Web site the following questions and answers to aid human resource managers who are interested in the Safe Harbor program:

Q and A for Human Resources on "Safe Harbor Principles"

1. *Q:* Is the transfer from the EU to the United States of personal information collected in the context of the employment relationship covered by the safe harbor?
1. *A:* Yes; where a company in the EU transfers personal information about its employees (past or present), collected in the context of the employment relationship, to a parent, affiliate, or unaffiliated service provider in the United States participating in the safe harbor, the transfer enjoys the benefits of the safe harbor. In such cases, the collection of the information and its processing prior to transfer will have been subject to the national laws of the EU country where it was collected, and any conditions for or restrictions on its transfer according to those laws will have to be respected.

    The Safe Harbor Principles are relevant only when individually identified records are transferred or accessed. Statistical reporting relying on aggregate employment data and/or the use of anonymized or pseudonymized data does not raise privacy concerns.

2. *Q:* How do the notice and choice principles apply to such information?
2. *A:* A U.S. organization that has received employee information from the EU under the safe harbor may disclose it to third parties and/or use it for different purposes only in accordance with the notice and choice principles. For example, where an organization intends to use personal information collected through the employment relationship for non–employment-related purposes, such as marketing communications, the U.S. organization must provide the affected individuals with choice before doing so, unless they have already authorized the use of the information for such purposes. Moreover, such choices must not be used to restrict employment opportunities or take any punitive action against such employees.

(Continued)

It should be noted that certain generally applicable conditions for transfer from some member states may preclude other uses of such information even after transfer outside the EU, and such conditions will have to be respected.

In addition, employers should make reasonable efforts to accommodate employee privacy preferences. This could include, for example, restricting access to the data, anonymizing certain data, or assigning codes or pseudonyms when the actual names are not required for the management purpose at hand.

To the extent and for the period necessary to avoid prejudicing the legitimate interests of the organization in making promotions, appointments, or other similar employment decisions, an organization does not need to offer notice and choice.

3. *Q:* How does the access principle apply?

3. *A:* The FAQs on access provide guidance on reasons that may justify denying or limiting access on request in the human resources context. Of course, employers in the European Union must comply with local regulations and ensure that European Union employees have access to such information as is required by law in their home countries, regardless of the location of data processing and storage. The safe harbor requires that an organization processing such data in the United States will cooperate in providing such access either directly or through the EU employer.

4. *Q:* How will enforcement be handled for employee data under the safe harbor principles?

4. *A:* Insofar as information is used only in the context of the employment relationship, primary responsibility for the data vis-à-vis the employee remains with the company in the EU. It follows that, where European employees make complaints about violations of their data protection rights and are not satisfied with the results of internal review, complaint, and appeal procedures (or any applicable grievance procedures under a contract with a trade union), they should be directed to the state or national data protection or labor authority in the jurisdiction where the employee works. This also includes cases where the alleged mishandling of their personal information has taken place in the United States and is the responsibility of the U.S. organization that has received the information from the employer and not of the employer and thus involves an alleged breach of the safe harbor principles, rather than of national laws implementing the directive. This will be the most efficient way to address the often overlapping rights and obligations imposed by local labor law and labor agreements as well as data protection law.

A U.S. organization participating in the safe harbor that uses EU human resources data transferred from the European Union in the context of the employment relationship and that wishes such transfers to be covered by the safe harbor must therefore commit to cooperation in investigations by and to comply with the advice of competent EU authorities in such cases. The DPAs that have agreed to cooperate in this way will notify the European Commission and the Department of Commerce. If a U.S. organization participating in the safe harbor wishes to transfer human resources data from a member state where the DPA has not so agreed, the provisions of FAQ 5 will apply.

RESTRICTIVE COVENANTS

restrictive covenants
Contractual provisions that limit a person's right to compete with another. They include promises to refrain from setting up a competing company within a certain period or a certain geographical area. They also include promises by exiting employees not to use trade secrets or other intellectual property in their next employment.

In today's high-tech and highly competitive environment, employers are turning to **restrictive covenants** more than ever before. For many years employers have required employees to sign *noncompete agreements* and *confidentiality agreements,* which are forms of restrictive covenants. An employee may have to sign an agreement that, as an ex-employee, she or he will not set up shop or work for a competing firm within a prescribed period or within a designated geographic area. This is an example of a noncompete clause or agreement.

U.S. Policy against Restraint of Trade

Although it is well understood in the United States that competition is favored and that practices inhibiting competition and limiting an individual's opportunities are regarded with suspicion, the law is also interested in reasonable protection of a company's proprietary interests. If a barber's assistant quits his job, it would be reasonable to restrain him from setting up a competing shop within the same town for a year. However, in today's highly competitive high-tech world, valuable knowledge regarding software, trade secrets, client lists, and the like is jealously guarded. Allowing employees to rotate among competing companies could wreak havoc on the competitiveness of the firms in that industry. Under some circumstances, banning employees from working with competitors within a city for a year would not sufficiently protect the former employer.

Restrictive covenants can be broad or narrow in scope. They may consist of a broad ban on a particular individual's ability to work in an industry (a covenant not to compete) or may limit an employee's use of or disclosure of a trade secret, client list, or other form of intellectual property. This is an example of a confidentiality clause or agreement. One thing is clear: What a court considers reasonable will be determined case by case. The limitations should be no more restrictive than necessary and reasonable to protect the legitimate concerns of the employer. Each case sheds some light on this issue, and wise managers will keep abreast of how such issues are dealt with in their particular industry in the states in which they operate.

Cases that involve breach of restrictive covenants are state law claims and are usually resolved in state courts. For example, Case for Discussion 6-2 was brought to a New Jersey court and concerns an employer's argument that two former employees launched a corporation in direct competition with it and took client information in violation of a confidentiality and noncompete agreement.

Case for Discussion 6-2

LAMORTE BURNS & CO., INC. V. WALTERS ET AL., 167 N.J. 285, 770 A.2D 1158 (2001)[16]

Facts

Lamorte provided services as a claims adjuster and investigator for marine and nonmarine liability insurers and others. Walters and Nixon were employed by Lamorte. Shortly after hire, the employees signed an employment agreement containing, among other things, the following provisions:

- You agree to devote your full time and best efforts to the performance of your duties for the Company and not to engage in any other business activities without the prior written consent of the Company.

- You agree to maintain in confidence all proprietary data and other confidential information (whether concerning the Company, or any of its affiliated companies, or any of their respective clients or cases being handled for clients) obtained or developed by you in the course of your employment with the Company. Such information and data shall include, but not be limited to, all information covering clients and cases being handled for clients. All such information and data are and shall remain the exclusive property of the Company and/or affiliated companies. In addition you assign to the Company all right, title, and interest in and to any and all ideas, inventions, discoveries, trademarks, trade names, copyrights, patents, and all other information and data of any kind developed by you during the entire period of your employment with the Company and related to the work performed by you for the Company.

  You covenant and agree that upon termination of this Agreement for whatever reason, you will immediately return to the Company any and all files, documents, records, books, agreements, or other written material belonging to or relating to the Company or its affiliated companies and any of their respective clients, together with all copies thereof in your possession or control. . . .

  Your obligation under this paragraph shall survive any termination of your employment.

- Employee agrees that so long as you are an employee of the Company, and for a period of twelve (12) months after your termination, whether voluntary or involuntary, you will not solicit or accept any claim, case, or dispute that is being handled or directed by the Company or any of its affiliated companies during the term of your employment with the Company. You agree that you will not solicit or accept any such claim, case, or dispute directly in your individual capacity, nor indirectly as a partner of a partnership, and as an employee of any other entity, nor as an officer,

> director, or stockholder of a corporation, a joint venturer, a principal, or
> in any other capacity.
>
> You further agree not to solicit or induce any employee of the Company
> or any of its affiliated companies to leave its employ, nor to hire or attempt
> to hire any such employee. . . .

Walters never believed the contract was enforceable against him because he was an at-will employee, and Lamorte did not sign it. An attorney corroborated his view, and Walters never expressed his beliefs to anyone at Lamorte out of fear that he would be fired.

After Walters left the company and set up a competing firm, Lamorte brought a legal action against him on several grounds: breach of contract, breach of the employee's duty of loyalty, tortious interference with an economic advantage, misappropriated confidential and proprietary information, and unfair competition.

One of the arguments Walters raised was that customer lists of service businesses did not rise to the level of a trade secret.

Decision

restatements
Authoritative, but not official, treatises of common law. There are restatements for each of the various types of common law—tort, contract, agency, and so on. Litigators refer to a restatement as a means of persuading a judge to change the common law of the state to reflect a section in the restatement that has been adopted by other states.

The N.J. Supreme Court noted that information need not rise to the level of a trade secret to be protected, and, in fact, prior cases had recognized that the names and addresses of customers are not public knowledge and are the private property of a service company.

Lamorte was also successful in the claim of breach of the duty of loyalty. N.J. courts follow the provision in the **Restatement** (Second) on Agency, which states that an agent must not take "unfair advantage of his position in the use of information or things acquired by him because of his position as agent or because of the opportunities which his position affords"[17].

Questions for Discussion

1. What management practice or policy could Lamorte have utilized to prevent the actions taken by Walters?

2. In addition to the signed contract, what more could Lamorte have done to eliminate the need to sue Walters?

3. Articulate more fully Walters' argument that because this was an employment at will situation, the contract was unenforceable. Is it a persuasive argument? Why or why not?

OWNERSHIP OF INTELLECTUAL PROPERTY

Copyright, patent, trademark, and service mark protection is a vital concern for all firms of any size, especially those in high-tech industries.

In the employment context, a number of cases have been litigated over the question of whether an individual or his or her employer owns intellectual property created while the individual works for that employer. The concept of *work for hire* arose to deal with this issue. The U.S. Supreme Court fleshed out the meaning of the work for hire principle in *Community for Creative Nonviolence v. Reid (1989)*[18]. In this case (see Case for Discussion 6-3) the CCNV had a sculpture created by Reid in accordance with CCNV's ideas. A dispute of ownership developed. The law the court was interpreting is the Copyright Act, which is federal statutory law. Note the distinctions the court makes between employees and independent contractors in applying the Copyright Act to the facts of this case.

Work for Hire: Independent Contractor

Advice for employers of independent contractors hired to create certain works includes, at a minimum, the following:

1. Draw up a written agreement before any work begins.
2. State in the agreement that the creator of the work shall grant all rights, title, and interest in and to the work to the company.
3. State that the work is to be made exclusively for the company.
4. State that in the event the provisions of copyright law do not recognize the work as having been done in a work-for-hire arrangement, the creator agrees to do whatever is necessary to assign the intellectual property to the company and transfer exclusive title in the work to the company.

Work for Hire: Employee

When an employee creates intellectual property in her or his normal work for a company, there is no need to draw up an agreement. There is a presumption that such efforts are the equivalent of a work-for-hire arrangement. Nevertheless, to eliminate any ambiguities, an agreement can be drawn up as a precaution.

Case for Discussion 6-3

COMMUNITY FOR CREATIVE NONVIOLENCE V. REID, 490 U.S. 730 (1989)[19]

In this case an artist, Reid, was hired by the Community for Creative Nonviolence (CCNV), a nonprofit organization, to create a sculpture for them. There was no written contract to reflect their agreement. Reid created the sculpture, but later a dispute arose over its ownership. Subsequently a member of the CCNV filed for a copyright, as did Reid. Eventually the association filed an action in the U.S. District Court for the District of Columbia against the sculptor and sought a return of the sculpture and a determination of copyright ownership. The court reviewed the language of the federal Copyright Act and principles of common law to make its decision.

Facts

Snyder and fellow CCNV members conceived the idea for the nature of a display: a sculpture of a modern nativity scene in which, in lieu of the traditional holy family, the two adult figures and the infant would appear as contemporary homeless people huddled on a streetside steam grate. The family was to be black (most homeless people in Washington are black); the figures were to be life-sized; and the steam grate would be positioned atop a platform pedestal, within which special-effects equipment would be enclosed to emit simulated steam through the grid to swirl about the figures. They also settled on a title for the work—*Third World America*—and a legend for the pedestal: "and still there is no room at the inn."

***

We . . . conclude that the language and structure of §101 of the [Copyright] Act do not support either the right to control the product or the actual control approaches. The structure of §101 indicates that a work for hire can arise through one of two mutually exclusive means, one for employees and one for independent contractors, and ordinary canons of statutory interpretation indicate that the classification of a particular hired party should be made with reference to agency law.

***

We turn, finally, to an application of §101 to Reid's production of *Third World America*. In determining whether a hired party is an employee under the general common law of agency, we consider the hiring party's right to control the manner and means by which the product is accomplished. Among the other factors relevant to this inquiry are the skill required; the source of the instrumentalities and tools; the location of the work; the duration of the relationship between the parties; whether the hiring party has the right to assign additional projects to the hired party; the extent of the hired party's discretion over when and how long to work; the method of payment; the hired party's role in hiring and paying assistants; whether the work is part of the regular business of the hiring party; whether the hiring party is in business; the provision of employee benefits; and the tax treatment of the hired party. See Restatement § 220(2) (setting forth a nonexhaustive list of factors relevant to determining whether a hired party is an employee). No one of these factors, standing alone, is determinative.

Decision

Reid was not an employee, and this was not a work for hire.

Note: The above factors came to be known as the "Reid test"—the work for hire criteria by which courts assess whether a hired person who creates intellectual property is an employee or an independent contractor, and, consequently, whether the creator or the employer owns the work.

Questions for Discussion

1. How relevant is it, in a case like this, that the parties had no written agreement stating the terms of the employment arrangement?
2. What role can HR managers play in situations like this to prevent or discourage legal disputes?

In a later case, *Simon v. Marvel Characters* (see Case for Discussion 6-4), a federal appellate court in 2002 dealt with the work for hire issue in a case that hinged on the interpretation of the Copyright Act of 1976. The act gives authors the inalienable right to terminate a grant of copyright 56 years after the original grant, notwithstanding any agreement to the contrary[20]. This right to terminate does not apply in a work for hire situation.

In light of the cases that have interpreted and applied the work for hire issue, employers who hire people to create intellectual property (writing software, inventing products, patenting processes, and so on) should be prepared to compose agreements that will adequately protect the employers' investments.

Case for Discussion 6-4

SIMON V. MARVEL CHARACTERS, 310 F.3D 280 (2D CIRC. 2002)[21]

Facts

Simon created Captain America in 1943. He filed actions in state and federal court at that time concerning the renewal term of his work with the Marvel Characters book company. The actions were resolved by a settlement agreement in which he conceded that he created the character in a work-for-hire situation. In 1999, pursuant to provisions of the 1976 Copyright Act, Simon filed a termination notice to Marvel claiming that he was "neither an employee for hire nor a creator of a work for hire." Marvel sued, alleging that the termination notice was invalid because of the agreement.

Application of Section 304(c) of the 1976 Act

Having concluded that Simon is not precluded from asserting that he is the author of the works for purposes of exercising his statutory termination right, we turn, at length, to the issue of first impression presented by this case: whether an agreement made subsequent to a work's creation that declares that it is a work created for hire constitutes an "agreement to the contrary" under § 304(c)(5) of the 1976 act. The district court never addressed this question. Instead, it simply assumed that because Simon had conceded in the unambiguous settlement agreement that the works were created for hire, he could not now assert that he was the works' author for purposes of exercising the termination right in this action. While the district court was undoubtedly correct that the settlement agreement is not ambiguous, this is not the relevant analysis of this issue. Instead, we must analyze the legislative intent and purpose of § 304(c) of the 1976 act to determine its application to this case.

Simon contends that the district court's failure to give effect to § 304(c)'s mandate that authors can terminate copyright grants "notwithstanding any agreement to the contrary" contravenes the legislative intent and purpose of § 304(c). Further, because Simon has submitted testimony that he was not in fact an employee for hire when he created the Captain Marvel character, he maintains that a genuine issue of material fact exists regarding Marvel's claims that the termination notices are invalid and it is the sole owner of the copyright in the works. . . .

The Supreme Court has elucidated the intent and purpose behind the termination provision of the 1976 act:

> The principal purpose of the amendments in § 304 was to provide added benefits to authors. The . . . concept of a termination right itself was obviously intended to make the rewards for the creativity of authors more substantial. More particularly, the termination right was expressly intended to relieve authors of the consequences of ill-advised and unremunerative grants that had been made before the author had a fair opportunity to appreciate the true value of his work product. . . .

Decision

In sum, we hold that an agreement made subsequent to a work's creation that retroactively deems it a "work for hire" constitutes an "agreement to the contrary" under . . . 304(c)(5) of the 1976 act. Therefore, Simon is not bound by the statement in the settlement agreement that he created the works as an employee for hire. Because Simon has proffered admissible evidence that he did not create the works as an employee for hire, the district court's grant of summary judgment to Marvel was erroneous. It will be up to a jury to determine whether Simon was the author of the works and, therefore, whether he can exercise § 304(c)'s termination right.

Questions for Discussion

1. What might the companies in *Reid* and *Simon* have done differently?
2. What policies or procedures could have been in place to prevent these issues from going to litigation?

In Mexico, in 1997, a new copyright law, the FCRL[22], went into effect strengthening authors' rights. The changes were necessitated by the requirements of NAFTA. Mexico's new copyright law has provisions for a work for hire rule that states the circumstances under which an employee/creator cedes intellectual property rights to an employer. Among other things, if the work results from a written, individual employment contract, the rewards are divided equally between employer and employee unless their contract provides differently. The employer may disclose the work without employee authorization. The employee has no corresponding right. If there is no written employment contract between the employee/creator and the employer, all rewards belong to the employee.

With regard to transfers of rights, the Mexican law provides that the creator must be given either a proportional share in the profits emanating from the work or a fixed amount of compensation. The copyright holder cannot waive this requirement. Moreover, the law places time limits on all transfers. Unless agreed otherwise, all transfers will last for 5 years. A transfer that, by agreement, will exist for more than 15 years will not be upheld except in limited circumstances depending on the nature of the work or other justification[23].

Summary

Rapidly changing technology has had a significant impact on employer–employee relations—in particular on privacy rights, restrictive covenants, and ownership of intellectual property.

Invasion of privacy claims can arise when information about someone's personal life is unreasonably publicized without her or his consent and without justified reasons. Use of computers, whether at work or offsite, allows employees to send and receive e-mail, engage in blogging and chat rooms, browse the Internet, and essentially be in touch with the world. Employers have the capacity to obtain personal information about employees through those computers. How that information is accessed and utilized can be grounds for an invasion of privacy claim. Monitoring the use of company computers is advisable, but policies must be carefully drawn up.

Restrictive covenants have always been viewed unfavorably by U.S. courts because there is a bias toward free competition. Any attempt to restrict competition is suspect. Nonetheless, courts recognize the legitimate concerns of employers in protecting their intellectual property, customer lists, reputations, and other rights that might be threatened by a former employee working nearby or for direct competitors. In a high-tech marketplace restrictive covenants are more extensively used, and their enforcement is handled case by case to determine whether their provisions are reasonable.

There has also been a sea of change in the realm of intellectual property law in the employment relationship. The Copyright Act has been amended, and the common law concept of work for hire has been reviewed and reinterpreted to reflect changes in industry and the workplace. The work for hire principle asserts that under specified circumstances a work created by an employee belongs to the employer.

Questions	1. Explore the meaning of patents, trademarks, service marks, and copyrights by viewing the U.S. Patent Office Web site: http://www.uspto.gov/web/offices/pac/doc/general/whatis.htm.

1. Explore the meaning of patents, trademarks, service marks, and copyrights by viewing the U.S. Patent Office Web site: http://www.uspto.gov/web/offices/pac/doc/general/whatis.htm.

   a. What rights does a registered patent holder have?

   b. How long does a patent holder retain those rights?

   c. What is the difference between a trademark and a service mark?

   d. Distinguish between a copyright and a patent.

2. On July 1, 1994, Dr. Jay More began to work as a neurosurgeon at JFK Institute following his residency at Mt. Sinai Hospital in New York City. Thereafter Dr. More entered three separate employment agreements with the institute, the most recent one being a five-year agreement effective July 1, 1999. Under the terms of the 1999 agreement, either party could terminate the agreement upon 365 days' written notice to the other party. Critical to this appeal, each of the three employment agreements contained postemployment restrictive covenants that prohibited Dr. More from engaging in certain medical practices within a 30-mile radius of JFK for two years. The agreement provided that in the event of a breach, JFK would suffer irreparable harm and damage and would be entitled to injunctive relief to enforce the postemployment restraints. Dr. More ceased working at JFK on July 17, 2002. He had received offers to join other practices that were located beyond the 30-mile restrictive area, but he declined each one. Between the date of his notice of resignation and his separation date, Dr. More removed documents from the institute identifying patients' names and addresses, as well as the identity and location of the institute's referral sources.

   On July 22, 2002, Dr. More affiliated with another neurosurgeon, James M. Chimenti, M.D., as an employee of Neurosurgical Associates at Park Avenues, P.A. (NAPA), located in Plainfield, New Jersey. In addition, Dr. More received medical staff privileges at Somerset Medical Center (Somerset), which is located approximately 13½ miles from JFK. When Dr. More joined NAPA, Dr. Chimenti was the only neurosurgeon taking emergency room calls at Somerset. With the addition of Dr. More,

Somerset was able to provide complete neurological coverage through the two neurosurgeons.

Believing that Dr. More was in violation of the 1999 agreement, on September 6, 2002, JFK filed a complaint against him, seeking among other things a preliminary injunction prohibiting him from the practice of neurosurgery with NAPA or Somerset. On November 21, 2002, the trial court denied JFK's request for a preliminary injunction.

    a. Was the trial court wrong in denying JFK's preliminary injunction?

    b. On what basis would an appellate court reverse the decision? Be explicit in your answer.

3. Plaintiff Comprehensive Psychology Systems, P.C., a corporation that provides professional neuropsychological service to individuals under the trade name LifeSpan, appeals from an order of the Chancery Division that denied its application to enforce a restrictive covenant limiting the ability of a former employee, defendant Brett Prince, PhD, from practicing his profession within 10 miles of plaintiff's facility and from soliciting any of plaintiff's patients.

The relevant provisions of the restrictive covenant were as follows:

> (a) *Restrictions:* During the term of and for two years following the termination of this agreement, Dr. Prince shall not solicit any patient of LifeSpan nor solicit referrals from any referral source of LifeSpan, nor without approval remove any property including patient charts from the offices of LifeSpan, nor employ any employee of LifeSpan who has been employed by LifeSpan during the term of this agreement.
>
> (b) During the term of this agreement, in the event of termination, then for a period of 2 years from date of termination, Dr. Prince shall not practice within a 10-mile radius of any facility or office location of LifeSpan existing at the time of termination and at any hospital utilized by LifeSpan. The parties acknowledge that this geographic area constitutes the geographical area in which LifeSpan's patients and sources of referral reside or maintain their offices.

    a. Are the provisions of the restrictive covenant reasonable?

    b. Would a court enforce them?

    c. Why or why not?

4. Barry P., a driver for ABC Trucking and a member of the International Brotherhood of Teamsters, instituted legal action against the company for invasion of privacy. ABC had installed video cameras and audio listening devices behind two-way mirrors in the restrooms at the terminal in an effort to detect and deter the use of drugs by its drivers. A provision in the collective bargaining agreement stated, "The employer may not use video cameras to discipline or discharge an employee for reasons other than theft of property or dishonesty," and stipulated a procedure to be followed if video tapes were used to support discipline or discharge. Other provisions acknowledged concern about substance abuse, prescribed drug

testing procedures, and established a grievance process for disputes arising under the agreement.

a. Is legal action the proper manner in which to resolve this dispute? Why or why not?

b. Decide the case and give reasoning to support your answer.

5. An employer faxed to its 16 terminal managers a list of the names and Social Security numbers of 204 employees. The employees' union decried the dissemination, and the defendant ordered the recipients to destroy or return the lists. The plaintiffs filed an invasion of privacy/publication of private facts class action suit, and the defendant countered by arguing that the plaintiffs failed to establish the "publicity" element of their cause of action.

Decide the case ands support your answer.

6. Roy A. worked for 12 years as a senior executive for ABC Insurance Services Corporation. In his employment he used two computers owned by ABC—one at the office, the other at his residence. Roy signed ABC's "electronic and telephone equipment policy statement" in which he agreed, among other things, that he would use the computers "for business purposes only and not for personal benefit or noncompany purposes, unless such use [was] expressly approved. Under no circumstances [could the] equipment or systems be used for improper, derogatory, defamatory, obscene, or other inappropriate purposes." Roy consented to have his computer "use monitored by authorized company personnel" on an "as needed" basis, and agreed that communications transmitted by computer were not private. He acknowledged his understanding that his improper use of the computers could result in disciplinary action, including discharge.

Roy and ABC entered a "shareholder buy–sell agreement," pursuant to which ABC sold 4,000 shares of its stock to Roy at $.01 per share; one-third of the stock was to vest on December 1, 1999, one-third on December 1, 2000, and one-third on December 1, 2001, each vesting contingent upon Roy's continued employment; if Roy's employment terminated before all the shares had vested, ABC had the right to repurchase the nonvested shares at $ .01 per share. As part of the buy–sell transaction, Roy signed a confidentiality agreement and gave ABC a two-year covenant not to compete. One-third of Roy's shares vested on December 1, 1999. In March 2000 ABC's shareholders (including Roy) sold a portion of their shares to Nationwide Insurance Companies; more specifically, Roy sold 1,230 of his 1,333 vested shares to Nationwide for a cash price of $1,278,247.

On November 28, 2000, three days before another 1,333 shares were to vest, Roy's employment was terminated. According to ABC, Roy "had violated ABC's electronic policies by repeatedly accessing pornographic sites on the Internet while he was at work." According to Roy, the pornographic

Web sites were not accessed intentionally but simply "popped up" on his computer. Roy sued ABC, alleging that his employment had been wrongfully terminated "as a pretext to prevent his substantial stock holdings in ABC from fully vesting and to allow ABC to repurchase [his] nonvested stock" at $ .01 per share.

ABC asked Roy to return the home computer and cautioned him not to delete any information stored on the computer's hard drive. Roy said he would either return it or purchase it, but said it would be necessary "to delete, alter, and flush or destroy some of the information on the computer's hard drive, since it contains personal information which is subject to a right of privacy." ABC refused to sell the computer to Roy and demanded its return without any deletions or alterations.

Does the company have the right to demand the return of the computer without deletions or alterations to the information on the hard drive? Explain your answer.

7. In June 1990 Borquez began working as an associate attorney for Ozer & Mullen, P.C. He received three merit raises, the last of which was awarded 11 days prior to his termination.

On February 19, 1992, Borquez, who is homosexual, learned that his partner was diagnosed with AIDS. Borquez's physician advised him that he should be tested for HIV immediately. Borquez was anxious about his health and attempted to arrange for a colleague to fill in for him at a deposition and hearing. Borquez disclosed his situation to Ozer, the president, and asked him to keep it confidential, but Ozer made no reply. Ozer stated that he would handle the deposition and arbitration hearing and that Borquez should "do what [he needed] to do."

After speaking with Borquez, Ozer telephoned his wife, Renee Ozer, and told her about Borquez's disclosure. Additionally, Ozer informed the law firm's office manager and discussed it with two of the law firm's secretaries. On February 21, 1992, Borquez returned to the office and became upset when he learned that everyone in the law firm knew about his situation. Later that afternoon, Ozer met with Borquez and told him that Ozer had not agreed to keep Borquez's disclosure confidential. One week after Borquez made his disclosure to Ozer, Borquez was fired.

The law firm asserted that Borquez was terminated due to the law firm's poor financial circumstances. Borquez filed suit against the Ozer law firm and against Ozer as an individual, claiming wrongful discharge and invasion of privacy. Among other things, Borquez asserted that Ozer violated his right to privacy by disseminating private facts that Borquez had revealed and requested remain confidential.

Did Ozer violate Borquez's right to privacy? Explain your reasoning.

8. Andrew W. used his work computer to share pictures over the Internet of his 10-year-old stepdaughter in nude and seminude positions. He also downloaded other images of child pornography onto his work computer.

On several occasions the company's management received complaints that this employee had viewed pornographic Web sites. After inspection of the computer confirmed that Andrew had visited such pornography sites, the company reprimanded the employee for having done so. The employee's wife filed a negligence lawsuit against the employer on behalf of the child–victim, based on the employer's failure to investigate and report to authorities that its employee was downloading and distributing child pornography on his work computer. According to the lawsuit, had the employee been reported to authorities, the daughter would not have been victimized.

What will the court decide? State your reasons.

References

1. *The Private Life of the Late Benjamin Franklin, LL.D* (known as *The Autobiography of Benjamin Franklin*), Chapter X (London: J. Parsons, 1793). (This was his reply when refusing to patent his invention of a new stove.)

2. V. Alfieri and G. Lemley, "What Employers Should Know about Blogs," *Workforce Management Online,* March 2005, at www.workforce.com. by V. Alfieri and G. Lemley are partners in the labor and employment practice at Bryan Cave LLP.

3. "New Australian Law to Ban E-Mail Monitoring." See http:www.itworld.com/Man/2690/050504emailprivacy/ (accessed July 18, 2007).

4. *Equal Employment Opportunity Commission vs. The Burlington Northern and Santa Fe Railway Company,* Civil Action File No. 02-C-0456. See also http://www.bnsf.com.

5. *HP Global Master Privacy Policy.* See www.bsr.org/CSRResources/IssueBriefDetail.cfm?DocumentID=50970 (accessed July 18, 2007).

6. *Teamsters Local 856 et al. v. Priceless, LLC et al.,* 1112 Cal.App.4th 1500, 5 Cal. Rptr. 3d 847 (2003).

7. *U.S. Dept. of Justice v. Reporters Committee,* 489 U.S. 749, 103 L.E.2d 774, 109 S. Ct. 1468 (1989).

8. Ibid. 489 U.S. at p. 766, fn. 18.

9. *ACLU,* "Legislative Briefing Kit on Electronic Monitoring" (3/11/2002). See www.aclu.org/privacy/gen/14798res20020311.html (accessed March 4, 2008).

10. See "Patriot Act—Section by Section Analysis" at www.senate.gov/~leahy/press/200110/102401a.html (accessed July 18, 2007).

11. *Chimarev v. TD Waterhouse Investor Services, Inc.,* 280 F.Supp.2d 208 (2003).

12. Public Law 104-191, 104th Congress. See also "Employer's Guide to HIPAA" at www.smc.org/Pdfs/Discounts/HIPAA1.pdf (accessed July 18, 2007).

13. See www.workrights.org/issue_genetic/gd_fact_sheet.html (accessed July 18, 2007).

14. See www.genome.gov/10002328 (accessed July 13, 2007).

15. Export Portal, U.S. Department of Commerce, Safe Harbor Documents, #9 Human Resources. See www.export.gov/safeharbor/sh_overview.html (accessed July 18, 2007).

16. *Lamorte Burns & Co., Inc. v. Walters et al.,* 167 N.J. 285, 770 A.2d 1158 (2001).

17. Restatement (Second) of Agency Sec. 387 comment b (1958).

18. *Community for Creative Nonviolence v. Reid,* 490 U.S. 730 (1989).

19. *Community for Creative Nonviolence v. Reid,* ibid.

20. 17 U.S.C.S. Sec.304 (c).

21. *Simon v. Marvel Characters,* 310 F.3d 280 (2d Circ. 2002).

22. Article 84 of the FCRL. See M. Michaus, "Mexico Strengthens Copyright Protections," *IP Worldwide* (The New York Law Publishing Company, August 1997). See also http://www.lexis.com/research/retrieve?_m=e67ecd89c0f1127760d6205eea 201d69&docnu.

23. Ibid.

Bibliography

Portions of this chapter were first printed in *Competition Forum.* R. Twomey, "Privacy, Restrictive Covenants, and Intellectual Property: Technology and Its Impact on the Employment Relationship," *Competition Forum,* Vol. 3, No. 1, 2005.

Reaching for Equal Opportunity Based on Sex and Race

7. Civil Rights Act of 1964 (Title VII)

8. Race and Color Discrimination

9. The Civil Rights Act of 1991, the Glass Ceiling Act, and the Pregnancy Discrimination Act

10. Sex Discrimination, the Equal Pay Act, and the Civil Rights Act

Civil Rights Act of 1964 (Title VII)

> The purpose of the law is simple. Those who are equal
> before God shall now also be equal in the polling booths,
> in the classrooms, in the factories, and in hotels, restaurants,
> movie theaters, and other places that provide service to
> the public.
>
> President Lyndon B. Johnson, July 2, 1964[1]

INTRODUCTION

President Lyndon B. Johnson made the remarks that open this chapter in a speech to the American people about the bill he was about to sign into law—the Civil Rights Act of 1964. The Civil Rights Act is a comprehensive federal statute aimed at reducing discrimination in public accommodations and employment situations. The portion of the act that covers employment is Title VII. Employers of 15 or more people must comply with its provisions. Title VII also applies to state and local governments, employment agencies, and labor organizations, as well as to the federal government.

The initial focus of the bills that led to the passage of this groundbreaking federal law was the prejudicial treatment of people based on stereotypes of race and color. Other prohibited classifications of discrimination under this law are national origin, religion, and sex.

The Civil Rights Act of 1964 has been amended several times, most notably by the Pregnancy Discrimination Act of 1978 and the Civil Rights Act of 1991, which are the subjects of later chapters. In January 2008 a proposal was made to amend it once again with several sweeping changes, among them the elimination of the damage caps created in the 1991 amendment. It remains to be seen whether this law will be approved by Congress, and if so to what extent.

LEGISLATIVE HISTORY AND THE ROLE OF THE COURTS

When legislators pass a law (statute), they try to be clear about its purposes and specific about its provisions. To the extent that the law contains ambiguities or is otherwise unclear, judges and lawyers rely on *legislative history,* which consists of the recorded comments made by legislators and others in committee or in other venues as they deliberated on the content and language of the proposed legislation. This history helps shed light on what the lawmakers meant. If the matter remains unclear, the second means of interpreting a statute is to consider the overall objectives of the act and make a decision accordingly. The interpretation that best carries out that intention would likely be the one adopted by a court.

As can be seen in the cases that have been tried under the Civil Right Act of 1964, the courts have used what Congress has written to develop a number of principles and concepts in their analyses of these cases. Examples include the notions of disparate treatment and disparate impact, shifting burdens, the need for a plaintiff to establish a pretext to prove intentional discrimination in a disparate treatment case, and the criteria needed to establish a prima facie case of discrimination. In other words, the statute says nothing specific about these matters. Rather, the courts review the facts of each case to fashion a cohesive and consistent framework in which to apply the law in a way that best carries out congressional intentions.

DISPARATE TREATMENT AND DISPARATE IMPACT CASES

The cases of discrimination argued in the courts that were based on violations of the Civil Rights Act eventually led the courts to distinguish between two basic types of illegal discrimination: those that can be argued under a disparate treatment analysis and those that can be argued under a disparate impact analysis. In a *disparate treatment* case the plaintiff–employee must prove that the employer's negative action was motivated by illegal discriminatory intent. For example, if an employee believes that her boss fired her on the basis of her race, she must produce evidence that the firing was based on illegal discrimination. If she can prove, for example, that there were supervisory comments such as "you people have no sense" (in a context clearly referring to people of color) or something equally racially derogatory, her claim of discriminatory motive would be supported, and a judge or jury could therefore believe that the termination was prompted by illegal discrimination. Words that company personnel use can come back to haunt them as potent evidence of discriminatory intent.

On the other hand, if a black male has been overlooked for promotion in favor of a white male, and there is no concrete evidence of discriminatory motive, but he can prove statistically that black males in that company have little chance of success, his case might better be argued under a disparate impact analysis. In a *disparate impact* case the focus would be on the policies and practices of the company that led to an adverse impact on a statutorily protected class (such as race, national origin, or sex). The plaintiff's statistics must show the percentage of employees in the protected class (for example, African-Americans) working for the company as compared to the percentage of qualified African-Americans in the **relevant labor market.** If the employee can link a policy or practice of the employer with statistics that show the workforce is disproportionately constituted, there is a presumption that the company is illegally (even if unintentionally) limiting the opportunities for members of that protected class. The employee would likely win the lawsuit, and the company would be required to compensate for the wrong, either monetarily or otherwise. It is likely that the company would also be required to take affirmative measures to remedy the disparities. Note that it is unnecessary to prove discriminatory intent in a disparate impact case.

relevant labor market
The population of the geographic area from which employees are (or ought to be) recruited.

Defenses for Disparate Treatment Cases

When a plaintiff–employee successfully proves a disparate treatment case, an employer has one defense: The employer must show that it had a legitimate and nondiscriminatory reason for its decision, or it must credibly show that a **bona fide occupational qualification (BFOQ)** warrants the discriminatory treatment. If the issue is sex discrimination, the employer must have a genuine (bona fide) rationale for favoring a male over a female or vice versa. For example, to be a candidate for a female modeling job, the person must be a woman—that is a BFOQ for the position.

bona fide occupational qualification (BFOQ)
A defense that permits discrimination when it is reasonably necessary to the normal operation of that particular business.

Note: The BFOQ defense is not available when the discrimination at issue is based on race.

Defenses for Disparate Impact Cases

An employer faced with a disparate impact case can defend itself by producing evidence that the practices and policies that have an adverse impact on a protected class are necessary to the business and are job-related.

The Prima Facie Case and Shifting Burdens

The U.S. Supreme Court, in *McDonnell Douglas Corp. v. Green,* 411 U.S. 792 (1973), fashioned the **prima facie case** for cases alleging discrimination, whether it be under the Civil Rights Act, the Age Discrimination in Employment Act, or another such law. In a case alleging failure to hire based on discrimination, these facts must be in evidence to establish a presumption of discrimination[2]:

prima facie case
When certain facts have been alleged by a plaintiff, there is a presumption that illegal discrimination has taken place. This is known as establishing the *prima facie case.* The burden of proof then passes to the defendant to rebut this presumption.

- The plaintiff is in a protected class (for example, a particular racial or national origin classification).
- The plaintiff applied and was qualified for the position.
- The plaintiff was not hired.
- The position remained open, and the employer continued to seek applicants.

Once the plaintiff has established a prima facie case, the burden of proof shifts to the defendant, who must give evidence of a legitimate, nondiscriminatory reason for its decision not to hire (or to terminate, or other negative decision). If such evidence is provided, and a jury is not convinced of its veracity, the plaintiff will probably win. For example, if the plaintiff counters with evidence that the defendant's reasons are merely a pretext for discrimination and that the decision was actually motivated by illegal discrimination, the jury is likely to decide for the plaintiff. Basically the plaintiff has the ultimate burden of proving disparate treatment (intentional) discrimination.

The prima facie case differs for a disparate impact case. In a disparate impact case, the plaintiff must prove the following:

- There is a statistical imbalance of members of a particular protected class in the workplace when the percentage of that class in the workplace is compared with the percentage of qualified class members in the relevant labor market.
- One or more practices or policies of the employer are causing the imbalance.

Once the plaintiff has established this presumption of illegal discrimination, the defendant must prove a business necessity for the suspect practice or policy. Failure to convince the fact finder of such business necessity can lead to a decision for the plaintiff on the grounds that the reason given was a pretext for actual discrimination.

Case for Discussion 7-1

Disparate Treatment

ASH ET AL. V. TYSON FOODS, INC., 546 U.S. 454 (2006)[3]

Facts

Two African-American employees brought a claim of disparate treatment against Tyson Foods arguing that they were passed over for promotion in favor of less qualified white employees. Although a prima facie case was established, there were conflicting opinions about whether each of the plaintiffs had proven actual discrimination. In other words, had they been successful in establishing that the defendant's reasons for not promoting them were, in reality, pretexts for intentional discrimination, they would have won their case.

The trial court (U.S. District Court), after finding in favor of both plaintiffs and awarding compensatory and punitive damages, ultimately granted a new trial. The appellate court held in favor of Tyson, deeming the trial evidence insufficient to show pretext (and thus insufficient to show unlaw-ful discrimination). As for Hithon, the appellate court found there was enough evidence to go to the jury. The appellate court, however, affirmed the district court's alternative remedy of a new trial, holding that the evidence supported neither the decision to grant punitive damages nor the amount of the compensatory award, and thus that the district court did not abuse its discretion in ordering a new trial.

[T]here was evidence that Tyson's plant manager, who made the disputed hiring decisions, had referred on some occasions to each of the petitioners as "boy." Petitioners argued this was evidence of discriminatory animus. The court of appeals disagreed, holding that "[w]hile the use of 'boy' when modified by a racial classification like 'black' or 'white' is evidence of discriminatory intent, the use of 'boy' alone is not evidence of discrimination." Although it is true the disputed word will not always be evidence of racial animus, it does not follow that the term, standing alone, is always benign. The speaker's meaning may depend on various factors including context, inflection, tone of voice, local custom, and historical usage. Insofar as the court of appeals held that modifiers or qualifications are necessary in all instances to render the disputed term probative of bias, the court's decision is erroneous.

Second, the court of appeals erred in articulating the standard for determining whether the asserted nondiscriminatory reasons for Tyson's hiring decisions were pretextual. Petitioners had introduced evidence that their qualifications were superior to those of the two successful applicants. (Part of the employer's defense was that the plant with the openings had performance problems and petitioners already worked there in a supervisory capacity.) The court of appeals, in finding petitioners' evidence insufficient, cited one of its earlier precedents and stated, "Pretext can be established through comparing qualifications only when 'the disparity in qualifications is so apparent as virtually to jump off the page and slap you in the face.'"

Under this court's decisions, qualifications evidence may suffice, at least in some circumstances, to show pretext. See *Patterson v. McLean Credit Union,* 491 U. S. 164, 187–188 (1989) (indicating a plaintiff "might seek to demonstrate that respondent's claim to have promoted a better qualified applicant was pretextual by showing that she was in fact better qualified than the person chosen for the position. . . .") The visual image of words jumping off the page to slap you (presumably a court) in the face is unhelpful and imprecise as an elaboration of the standard for inferring pretext from superior qualifications. Federal courts, including the Court of Appeals for the Eleventh Circuit in a decision it cited here, have articulated various other standards, see, e.g., *Cooper, supra,* at 732 (noting that "disparities in qualifications must be of such weight and significance that no reasonable person, in the exercise of impartial judgment, could have chosen the candidate selected over the plaintiff for the job in question." . . . This is not the occasion to define more precisely what standard should govern pretext claims based on superior qualifications. Today's decision, furthermore, should not be read to hold that petitioners' evidence necessarily showed pretext. The district court concluded otherwise. It suffices to say here that some formulation other than the test the court of appeals articulated in this case would better ensure that trial courts reach consistent results.

Decision

The court of appeals should determine in the first instance whether the two aspects of its decision here determined to have been mistaken were essential to its holding. On these premises, the judgment of the court of appeals is vacated, and the case is remanded for further proceedings consistent with this opinion.

Questions for Discussion

1. Did the U.S. Supreme Court decide that use of the term "boy" is evidence of a discriminatory motive? Explain your answer.
2. Did the U.S. Supreme Court decide that evidence of disparities in qualifications between plaintiffs and the people who were given positions or promotions instead of them will always be sufficient to show that the employers' proffered reasons for failure to hire or promote are pretexts for actual discrimination? Support your answer.
3. Does the *Ash* case provide valuable lessons for HR managers? If so, what are they?

Case for Discussion 7-2

Disparate Impact

The following case concerns discrimination based on race. It was the first U.S. Supreme Court case to recognize the theory of disparate impact.

Note that after a statute has been passed by Congress, it is open to interpretation by the courts. There was nothing in the express language of the Civil Rights Act regarding disparate treatment and disparate impact. These terms were created by the courts in analyzing cases.

GRIGGS V. DUKE POWER 401 U.S. 424 (1971)[4]

The Civil Rights Act provides the following:

> Sec. 703. (a) It shall be an unlawful employment practice for an employer—
>
> . . . (2) to limit, segregate, or classify his employees in any way which would deprive or tend to deprive any individual of employment opportunities or otherwise adversely affect his status as an employee, because of such individual's race, color, religion, sex, or national origin.

... (h) Notwithstanding any other provision of this title, it shall not be an unlawful employment practice for an employer ... to give and to act upon the results of any professionally developed ability test provided that such test, its administration, or action upon the results is not designed, intended, or used to discriminate because of race, color, religion, sex, or national origin. . . ."

***

Facts

The District Court found that prior to July 2, 1965, the effective date of the Civil Rights Act of 1964, the company openly discriminated on the basis of race in hiring and assigning employees at its Dan River plant. The plant was organized into five operating departments: (1) Labor, (2) Coal Handling, (3) Operations, (4) Maintenance, and (5) Laboratory and Test. Negroes were employed only in the Labor Department, where the highest-paying jobs paid less than the lowest-paying jobs in the other four "operating" departments, in which only whites were employed. . . .

In 1955 the company instituted a policy of requiring a high school education for initial assignment to any department except Labor, and for transfer from the Coal Handling to any "inside" department (Operations, Maintenance, or Laboratory). When the company abandoned its policy of restricting Negroes to the Labor Department in 1965, completion of high school also was made a prerequisite to transfer from Labor to any other department. . . .

The company added a further requirement for new employees on July 2, 1965, the date on which Title VII became effective. To qualify for placement in any but the Labor Department it became necessary to register satisfactory scores on two professionally prepared aptitude tests, as well as to have a high school education.

***

The court of appeals . . . concluded . . . that in this case there was no showing of a discriminatory purpose in the adoption of the diploma and test requirements. On this basis, the court of appeals concluded there was no violation of the act.

It held that, in the absence of a discriminatory purpose, use of such requirements was permitted by the act. In so doing, the court of appeals rejected the claim that because these two requirements operated to render ineligible a markedly disproportionate number of Negroes, they were unlawful under Title VII unless shown to be job-related.

***

The objective of Congress in the enactment of Title VII is plain from the language of the statute. It was to achieve equality of employment opportunities and remove barriers that have operated in the past to favor an identifiable group of white employees over other employees. Under the act, practices, procedures, or tests neutral on their face, and even neutral in terms of intent, cannot be maintained if they operate to "freeze" the status quo of prior discriminatory employment practices.

***

Decision

On the record before us, neither the high school completion requirement nor the general intelligence test is shown to bear a demonstrable relationship to successful performance of the jobs for which it was used. Both were adopted, as the court of appeals noted, without meaningful study of their relationship to job performance ability. Rather, a vice president of the company testified, the requirements were instituted on the company's judgment that they generally would improve the overall quality of the workforce.

. . . We do not suggest that either the district court or the court of appeals erred in examining the employer's intent; but good intent or absence of discriminatory intent does not redeem employment procedures or testing mechanisms that operate as "built-in headwinds" for minority groups and are unrelated to measuring job capability.

. . . The Equal Employment Opportunity Commission, having enforcement responsibility, has issued guidelines interpreting § 703 (h) to permit only the use of job-related tests. The administrative interpretation of the act by the enforcing agency is entitled to great deference. . . . The commission accordingly interprets "professionally developed ability test" to mean a test that fairly measures the knowledge or skills required by the particular job or class of jobs the applicant seeks, or that fairly affords the employer a chance to measure the applicant's ability to perform a particular job or class of jobs. The fact that a test was prepared by an individual or organization claiming expertise in test preparation does not, without more, justify its use within the meaning of Title VII.

. . . These guidelines demand that employers using tests have available "data demonstrating that the test is predictive of or significantly correlated with important elements of work behavior that comprise or are relevant to the job or jobs for which candidates are being evaluated."

***

Nothing in the act precludes the use of testing or measuring procedures; obviously they are useful. What Congress has forbidden is giving these devices and mechanisms controlling force unless they are demonstrably a reasonable measure of job performance. Congress has not commanded that the less qualified be preferred over the better qualified simply because of minority origins. Far from disparaging job qualifications as such, Congress has made such qualifications the controlling factor, so that race, religion, nationality, and sex become irrelevant. What Congress has commanded is that any tests used must measure the person for the job and not the person in the abstract.

The judgment of the court of appeals is, as to that portion of the judgment appealed from, reversed.

Questions for Discussion

1. The Supreme Court justices are basically stating that a company can violate the Civil Rights Act even though it is clear that its practices were created without any discriminatory intent. Do you believe this is fair? Discuss.
2. Based on the decision in *Griggs,* write and discuss a list of recommendations for HR managers and recruiters.

AFFIRMATIVE ACTION

The concept of *affirmative action* arose from the recognition that there was a historical pattern of discrimination against people belonging to certain groups—in particular racial minorities and women. In the public sector (government as the employer), pressure was applied to institute programs to overcome the effects of past discrimination. In the private sector, employers also felt a need to establish programs that would result in hiring more members of the protected classes. These programs are collectively referred to as *affirmative action programs or plans.*

The government, as an employer, must abide by the Constitutional provision of equal protection. That means it must not make laws (or decisions) that have a disproportionate negative effect on any class of people without a legitimate (or sometimes a "compelling") reason. Thanks to the Civil Rights Act of 1964, private employers are also prohibited from discriminating against statutorily designated protected classes.

Reverse Discrimination

The major problem with affirmative action programs is this: If they are not designed appropriately, they may contradict the constitutional (for government employers) or statutory prohibitions against discrimination. Assume that ABC Corporation decides to give hiring preferences to black women. A qualified white male who applies for a job at ABC and loses out to a black woman similarly qualified, but with less experience, might raise the charge of reverse discrimination. To address this conundrum, the U.S. Supreme Court has spelled out the criteria for what it deems to be a valid affirmative action program for both the public and private sectors in the *Wygant* and *U.S. Steelworkers* cases, discussed later in this chapter.

Public Sector: Constitution and Executive Order 11246

Constitutional law requires the government to treat citizens equally (see the Fourteenth Amendment, which declares that the government shall not deny to citizens equal protection of the law). Therefore, attempts by public sector (government) employers to manipulate the hiring and promotion of employees by granting priorities to individuals based on their race, sex, or other protected characteristics run the risk of violating the Constitution.

Executive Order 11246

In 1965 President Johnson issued Executive Order 11246, requiring federal agencies and all federal contractors to prohibit discrimination based on race, color, religion, sex, or national origin and to take "affirmative action" to accomplish these objectives. The Office of Federal Contracts Compliance Programs (OFCCP) was thus established in the U.S. Department of Labor. Federal contractors were required to develop written affirmative action plans in cases where minorities and women were underutilized. It was up to the courts to determine the limits, if any, that could be placed on affirmative action programs in order to reconcile constitutional restrictions and the requirements of Executive Order 11246.

Originally Executive Order 11246 required government contractors and subcontractors to take affirmative action favoring minorities. In 1967 this language was amended to include affirmative action for women. Contractors must make good-faith efforts to expand employment opportunities for women as well as minorities.

The U.S. Supreme Court in 1986 ruled in *Wygant v. Jackson Board of Education,* 476 U.S. 267 (1986), that the public school system violated the Constitution when it instituted a layoff plan. This plan was the result of a collective bargaining agreement, and its goal was to increase the employment of minority personnel in light of past societal discrimination. The Court held that the public school district must provide a compelling state interest to justify the action it took. In other words, in a constitutional case such as this the school's action is subject to "strict scrutiny" by the courts. To show a compelling state interest in this case, evidence of actual racial discrimination by the school district would have to be presented in order to initiate a valid affirmative action plan. Furthermore, under a strict scrutiny analysis, the action of the government (the public school district in this case) in establishing an affirmative action plan must accomplish its intentions in a manner that is "least restrictive." The school district would have to consider the effect of the plan on nonminority employees. Here the plan resulted in layoffs of white employees with more seniority.

According to the U.S. Supreme Court decision in *Wygant,* affirmative action programs (AAPs) instituted by the government or by federal contractors must meet the following criteria:

- The AAP must be created for the purpose of remedying actual discrimination by the employer.
- The AAP must foster a compelling state interest.
- The AAP must be "narrowly tailored to accomplish its goals in the 'least restrictive'" manner.
- The AAP must not unnecessarily trammel the interests of nonminorities.

Cases for Discussion 7-3

Michigan's Affirmative Action Cases (2003)

GRUTTER V. BOLLINGER, 539 U.S. 306 (2003)[5]

GRATZ V. BOLLINGER, 539 U.S. 244 (2003)[6]

Facts

The University of Michigan was challenged in two separate cases on the grounds that its admission procedures were impermissible affirmative action programs that violated the Civil Rights Act of 1964. The two cases were heard in tandem in what are sometimes referred to as *companion cases.*

One case focused on the law school admissions criteria (*Grutter v. Bollinger*) and the other on the undergraduate admissions criteria (*Gratz v. Bollinger*). It was the aim of the University of Michigan to effect greater diversity in its student body.

Of particular concern was the fact that the university's undergraduate admissions process automatically distributed 20 points, or one-fifth of the points needed to guarantee admission, to every single "underrepresented minority" applicant solely because of race.

The long-standing precedent set in *Regents of the University of California v. Bakke,* 438 U.S. 265 (1978), held that race can be a factor in an admissions process, but it cannot be a "deciding factor."

The admissions process for the University of Michigan Law School, in its attempt to diversify the student body, utilized a different method than the university's undergraduate college. The words of the Supreme Court's opinion describe the law school's methods:

Excerpts from *Grutter*

The law school ranks among the nation's top law schools. It receives more than 3,500 applications each year for a class of around 350 students. Seeking to "admit a group of students who individually and collectively are among the most capable," the law school looks for individuals with "substantial promise for success in law school" and "a strong likelihood of succeeding in the practice of law and contributing in diverse ways to the well-being of others." More broadly, the law school seeks "a mix of students with varying backgrounds and experiences who will respect and learn from each other." In 1992, the dean of the law school charged a faculty committee with crafting a written admissions policy to imple-ment these goals. In particular, the law school sought to ensure that its efforts to achieve student body diversity complied with this Court's most recent ruling on the use of race in university admissions. Upon the unanimous adoption of the committee's report by the law school faculty, it became the law school's official admissions policy.

The hallmark of that policy is its focus on academic ability coupled with a flexible assessment of applicants' talents, experiences, and potential "to contribute to the learning of those around them." The policy requires admissions officials to evaluate each applicant based on all the information available in the file, including a personal statement, letters of recommendation, and an essay describing the ways in which the applicant will contribute to the life and diversity of the law school. In reviewing an applicant's file, admissions officials must consider the applicant's undergraduate grade point average (GPA) and Law School Admissions Test (LSAT) score because they are important (if imperfect) predictors of academic success in law school. The policy stresses that "no applicant should be admitted unless we expect that applicant to do well enough to graduate with no serious academic problems."

The policy makes clear, however, that even the highest possible score does not guarantee admission to the law school. Nor does a low score automatically disqualify an applicant. Rather, the policy requires admissions officials to look beyond grades and test scores to other criteria that are important to the law school's educational objectives. So-called soft variables such as "the enthusiasm of recommenders, the quality of the undergraduate institution, the quality of the applicant's essay, and the areas and difficulty of undergraduate course selection" are all brought to bear in assessing an "applicant's likely contributions to the intellectual and social life of the institution." The policy aspires to "achieve that diversity which has the potential to enrich everyone's education and thus make a law school class stronger than the sum of its parts." The policy does not restrict the types of diversity contributions eligible for "substantial weight" in the admissions process, but instead recognizes "many possible bases for diversity admissions." The policy does, however, reaffirm the law school's longstanding commitment to "one particular type of diversity"—that is, "racial and ethnic diversity with special reference to the inclusion of students from groups which have been historically discriminated against, like African-Americans, Hispanics, and Native Americans, who without this commitment might not be represented in our student body in meaningful numbers." By enrolling a "'critical mass' of [underrepresented] minority students," the law school seeks to "ensure their ability to make unique contributions to the character of the law school."

The policy does not define diversity "solely in terms of racial and ethnic status." Nor is the policy "insensitive to the competition among all students for admission to the law school." Rather, the policy seeks to guide admissions officers in "producing classes both diverse and academically outstanding, classes made up of students who promise to continue the tradition of outstanding contribution by Michigan graduates to the legal profession."

Decision in *Grutter*

The law school admissions process is not a violation of Title VII.

Decision in *Gratz*

The undergraduate admissions process is a violation of Title VII.

Significance of the Michigan Cases

In both cases the U.S. Supreme Court reiterated the *Bakke* precedent, holding that race can be a factor in admissions decisions. In addition, the Court held that student body diversity is a legitimate goal in initiating an affirmative action plan. The problem with the undergraduate process was that it was not sufficiently "narrowly tailored" to meet the requirements set out in previous public sector affirmative action cases.

Public Sector Update on Affirmative Action

In 2000 the U.S. Department of Labor created regulations to promote equal pay by requiring federal contractors to report hiring, termination, promotion, and compensation data by minority status and gender.

Private Sector: Affirmative Action and the Civil Rights Act

Because it is in the nature of an affirmative action plan to take race, color, religion, sex, or national origin into consideration in hiring, promotion, termination, or other decisions regarding employee status, such programs, to a certain extent, contradict prohibitions against discrimination. For that reason, employers are cautioned that to have a valid and enforceable affirmative action plan, they should remember the following criteria, emanating from the U.S. Supreme Court decision *United Steel Workers of America v. Weber*, 443 U.S. 193 (1979):

- The AAP should be designed to remedy an imbalance in the company workforce.
- The AAP should not contain rigid and inflexible goals or quotas.
- The AAP should be temporary, not indefinite, and should contain reasonable targets that can be attained with good-faith efforts.
- The AAP should not unnecessarily or unreasonably discriminate against an employee or applicant because of race, color, religion, sex, or national origin.

Retaliation for Exercising Rights under the Civil Rights Act

The Civil Rights Act of 1964 contains provisions that prohibit employers from retaliating against employees who exercise their rights under antidiscrimination laws. Just what constitutes retaliation was the subject of the 2006 U.S. Supreme Court decision *White vs. Burlington Northern and Santa Fe Railway*. In that case the plaintiff was the only woman on the defendant's maintenance crew in Memphis, Tennessee. She complained of sexual harassment by her supervisor, including a statement that a woman did not belong there. Although the supervisor was suspended for 10 days, the plaintiff was reassigned to a less desirable position (at the same rate of pay). She notified the EEOC, claiming the reassignment amounted to illegal retaliation. After a dispute with another supervisor, she was suspended without pay for 37 days. She filed a second claim with the EEOC. Eventually a jury awarded the plaintiff compensatory damages of $43,500 for retaliatory action on the part of Burlington Northern. The U.S. Supreme Court affirmed. Justice Breyer wrote, in part, "Common sense suggests that one good way to discourage an employee such as White from bringing discrimination charges would be to insist that she spend more time performing the more arduous duties." Future retaliation cases will be decided case by case, and employers are on notice that retaliation claims will be dealt with seriously by the courts.

The Civil Rights Act of 1866: Retaliation

In 1866 (long before the Civil Rights Act of 1964) Congress enacted the first Civil Rights Act, which essentially extended equal protection to all people regardless of race with respect to the making and enforcing of contracts. Workers who suffer from discrimination in employment situations because of their race or ethnic origin can file a claim under this statute. As noted earlier, a claim of discrimination under Title VII of the Civil Rights Act of 1964 requires the aggrieved employee to file a claim with the EEOC and to abide by specific statutory timelines in doing so. However, filing a claim under Section 1981 of the 1866 statute does not have the same restrictions. In addition, there are limits on damages that can be awarded under the 1964 law, but no such limits exist under the 1866 law.

In recent years cases have been brought under the 1866 statute containing retaliatory discrimination charges. Although most federal appellate courts agree that this statute can be interpreted to protect workers from retaliation for exercising their rights under the law, some courts take a contrary position, arguing that nothing in the statute speaks to such protection. Furthermore, they argue, because the Civil Rights Act of 1964 specifically includes this protection in its language, the fact that it is omitted in the earlier law is evidence of congressional intent to exclude it. In February 2008 this issue was the subject of oral argument in the U.S. Supreme Court in the case of *CBOCS West, Inc. vs. Humphries* (see Case for Discussion 7-4).

Case for Discussion 7-4

Section 1981 of the Civil Rights Act of 1866

CBOCS WEST, INC. V. HUMPHRIES, 474 F.3D 387 (2007)[7]

Facts

The plaintiff in the CBOCS case, Hedrick G. Humphries, is a black man who was employed at a Cracker Barrel restaurant. He claims that he was fired for complaining about the firing of a black food server and for speaking out about other remarks of a supervisor that he regarded as racially discriminatory. The district court held in favor of Cracker Barrel, stating that Section

1981 of the Civil Rights Act of 1866 does not cover retaliation claims. Humphries initially made his claims under both Title VII of the Civil Rights Act of 1964 and Section 1981. Because the district court dismissed the Title VII claims for procedural violations, he proceeded with only the 1981 claim.

Decision

The Court of Appeals for the Seventh Circuit disagreed with the district court's decision and held in favor of Humphries. Cracker Barrel then appealed to the U.S. Supreme Court.

Note: The U.S. Supreme Court granted certiorari and ruled in favor of the plaintiff in May of 2008, agreeing with the appellate court that a retaliation claim is covered by the 1866 Act.

Questions for Discussion

1. Discuss the ramifications of this case for HR managers. What impact will the decision have on the employment relationship?
2. The 1866 act essentially stated that citizens of the United States were "of every race and color" and "without regard to any previous condition of slavery or involuntary servitude." As citizens they could make and enforce contracts; sue and be sued; give evidence in court; and inherit, purchase, lease, sell, hold, and convey real estate and personal property. For what reasons should HR managers be concerned about this very old statute?

Management **Perspective**

THE U.S. EQUAL EMPLOYMENT OPPORTUNITY COMMISSION: EEOC PARTNERS WITH BUSINESS TO BUILD BEST PRACTICES FOR INCREASING DIVERSITY. [8]

WASHINGTON—In its continuing efforts to boost equal opportunity and corporate diversity through stronger partnerships with businesses, the U.S. Equal Employment Opportunity Commission (EEOC), Diversity Best Practices (DBP) and the Business Women's Network (BWN) hosted a landmark symposium Tuesday at the EEOC's downtown headquarters. More than 80 corporate officers and other executives from such companies as Lockheed Martin Corp., Coca-Cola and Eastman Kodak Co. were on hand to share their unique perspectives. . . .

The symposium participants resolved to:

- Build executive support, beginning with chief executive officers, for developing and advancing best practices. "For us, diversity is a business imperative," said Marillyn A. Hewson, President of Kelly Aviation Center, of Lockheed Martin Corp.

- Encourage companies and associations to apply for the EEOC's annual Freedom to Compete Award, which was designed to showcase, recognize and reward specific practices and concrete activities that produce results and reflect an abiding commitment to access and inclusion in the workplace. . . .

Edie Fraser, DBP president, founder and chief executive, welcomed Tuesday's participants. "Diversity Best Practices is proud of this historic collaboration with the EEOC as the agency strives to build unique and lasting partnerships with America's corporations to enhance equal opportunity and diversity in the workplace through identifying and implementing best practices," she said. . . .

"Just as diversity boosts companies' bottom lines, we have found that proactive prevention is money well spent for the agency," she said. "By devoting resources to stopping discrimination before it occurs, we gain by freeing up staff time and money to concentrate on the serious discrimination that still affects too many of our nation's workers."

Former EEOC Chairman Gilbert F. "Gil" Casellas, . . . added: "I am so pleased to participate in a program that reaffirms the EEOC's overarching mission of fostering equal opportunity in the workplace and celebrates those employers whose diversity practices are models for unleashing the enormous talent of our richly diverse population."

. . . Commissioner Griffin praised the program and expressed hope that all future diversity efforts will include people with disabilities.

Global **Perspective**

It is interesting to consider and compare the evolution of antidiscrimination laws in various countries. Whereas in America the initial focus of civil rights laws and the objective of equal opportunity for all citizens was centered on racial biases that took root in the existence of slavery, other countries encounter lingering biases against certain groups based more on ethnic, religious, or national identity possibly rooted in past wars that broke up and redrew geographical and political boundaries.

The European community has imposed guidelines for member nations regarding elimination of discrimination based on a variety of factors and covering many spheres of activity. The following excerpt is from an article that

(Continued)

describes the 2001 passage of new antidiscrimination laws in France.[9] Note the change in the burden of proof that the French law establishes for the employee–plaintiff and the employer–defendant.

Grounds for Discrimination and Discriminatory Practices

The list of prohibited grounds for discrimination previously provided for—including origin, sex, family situation, and membership of an ethnic group, nation, or race—is now expanded to include physical appearance (height, weight, attractiveness, etc.), surname, sexual orientation, and age. Martine Aubry (the Minister for Employment and Solidarity until 17 October 2000) stated that "all victims of discrimination, women, people with disabilities, foreigners and immigrants, gay men and lesbians" must be given the message "that our Republic is there to ensure that their rights are respected." She labeled all forms of discrimination "unacceptable violence."

The introduction of the principle of no discrimination based on age aims to bring French law into line with EU Council Directive 2000/78/EC of 27 November 2000, establishing a general framework for equal treatment in employment and occupation (EU0102295F). However, the criteria for applying this principle are detailed in order to avoid a challenge being mounted to employment policies targeted on certain age groups.

The relevant section of the Labor Code now reads, "No person can be eliminated from a recruitment process (. . .) due to their age, sex, lifestyle, sexual orientation, family situation, nonmembership, whether genuine or assumed, of an ethnic group, nation or race, political beliefs, trade union activities, religious beliefs, physical appearance, surname, state of health, or disability." Moreover, the definition of discriminatory practices provided by Article L. 122-45 of the Labor Code has been broadened to cover an employee's entire career. From now on, the ban on discrimination extends throughout a person's working life, covering recruitment; access to a placement or in-company training program; pay; training; redeployment within a company; posting; qualifications; job classification; promotion; transfer from one workplace to another; and renewal of contract.

A key point of the new law deals with the amendment of the provisions on the burden of proof in discrimination cases. The burden of proof has been amended so that if a legal case is brought, it is no longer only the employee's responsibility. Hitherto it had been the responsibility of the employee to prove that he or she had been the victim of discrimination, hence the very low number of successful convictions. The burden of proof will now fall equally upon the employer.

Summary

Title VII of the Civil Rights Act of 1964 prohibits discrimination in employment on the basis of race, color, religion, national origin, and sex. There have been several amendments to the Civil Rights Act, in particular the Pregnancy Discrimination Act of 1978 and the Civil Rights Act of 1991.

The statute has been interpreted to include two basic types of discrimination: disparate treatment and disparate impact. Disparate treatment cases usually involve an individual who claims that he or she has been the victim of discrimination at work. To be successful, the plaintiff–employee must prove that the discrimination was intentional. Disparate impact cases usually involve more than one person, and the claim is that the employer uses practices that have a disparate adverse impact on one or more protected classes. To be successful, the plaintiffs–employees must prove that such a practice exists and that statistical evidence proves the practice has a significant adverse impact on the protected group. It is not necessary to prove intentional discrimination. Therefore, even if the employer can argue successfully that the practice is a neutral one that was established with no discriminatory motive, the employer can still be held liable for illegal discrimination under the Civil Rights Act.

When a plaintiff alleges sufficient facts to establish a presumption that a law has been violated, the courts refer to this as establishing a prima facie case. After a prima facie case is established, the defendant must rebut the allegations to avoid liability. Facts needed to establish a prima facie case for discrimination were set out by the U.S. Supreme Court in the *McDonnell Douglas v. Green* case in 1973. For a prima facie case on disparate treatment, the plaintiff must allege

- That he or she is a member of a protected class.
- That he or she applied for and was qualified for a position.
- That he or she was not hired (or promoted or the like).
- That the position remained open, and the employer continued to seek applicants.

For a prima facie case on disparate impact, the plaintiffs must allege

- That practices of the employer create an adverse impact on a protected group.
- That statistical evidence shows that the adverse impact is caused by these practices.

Affirmative action programs have been instituted by both government (public sector) and private employers to address historical employment discrimination. Affirmative action programs that are not properly designed can generate actions alleging reverse discrimination.

The U.S. Supreme Court has set forth criteria for valid affirmative action programs for both the public and private sectors. In the public sector, the case of *Wygant* requires the following for valid affirmative action programs:

- The AAP must exist for the purpose of remedying actual discrimination by the employer.
- The AAP must foster a compelling state interest.
- The AAP must be "narrowly tailored to accomplish its goals in the 'least restrictive' manner."
- The AAP must not unnecessarily trammel the interests of nonminorities.

For the private sector, the case of *U.S. Steelworkers* requires the following for valid affirmative action programs:

- The AAP should be designed to remedy an imbalance in the workforce of the company.
- The AAP should not contain rigid and inflexible goals or quotas.
- The AAP should be temporary, not indefinite, and should contain reasonable targets that can be attained with good-faith efforts.
- The AAP should not unnecessarily or unreasonably discriminate against an employee or applicant because of race, color, religion, sex, or national origin.

Questions

1. Dana P. was employed by RST Lumber Co. for several years as the only female manager out of a total of eight in the company. When she became manager her salary was equal to that of other managers. However, by the time of her retirement, her salary was $600 less per month than any of the male managers. She had been paid less than the male managers for a few years before she retired. After retirement Dana brought a suit under Title VII for pay discrimination based on sex. RST claims that pay was based on merit raises, and there was no illegal discrimination. A jury decided in favor of Dana, and the case went to appeal.

   Are there any good legal arguments that RST can raise in its defense? Be prepared to discuss your answer.

2. Austin B. worked for FGH Computer Components. FGH, in an effort to create a culture of inclusiveness, encouraged the formation of "affinity groups," which would receive recognition by the company and would be permitted to use company facilities for various group activities. Accordingly, several groups were formed, including People with Disabilities, African Ancestry Network, GM Plus for gays and lesbians, and the Hispanic Initiative Team. Austin asked to begin a Christian Employee Network group, and FGH denied his request. The company relied on the guidelines that had been set up for these affinity groups, which precluded recognition of

affinity groups based on any religious position, including agnosticism, atheism, and secular humanism.

Austin filed a claim against FGH alleging religious discrimination under Title VII of the Civil Rights Act of 1964.

What facts would the two parties present in their arguments? Which party is likely to prevail? Support your decision.

3. John M. lost his position at the University of Delta and brought suit under Title VII of the Civil Rights Act of 1964 on the grounds that his firing was based on gender discrimination. He believed that his complaints about Tracy S., the chief information and planning officer, were the basis of a retaliatory discrimination decision to eliminate his position. Tracy S., he alleged, was given her position only because she was having an affair with a university administrator.

Discuss the merits of John's case. Is it likely that he will prevail? Why or why not?

4. Heather L. brought suit against West Co. on the basis of sexual harassment. After she alerted the company about the unwelcome physical conduct of a coworker, the company reprimanded the alleged harasser and moved him to another shift. Subsequently the harassment ceased. Heather, believing that the company's response was not adequate, filed an action.

Does Heather have adequate grounds to successfully hold West Co. liable for damages in this case? Why or why not?

References

1. President Lyndon B. Johnson, in a broadcast from the East Room at the White House on July 2, 1964. See www.lbjlib.utexas.edu/johnson/archives.hom/speeches.hom/640702.asp (accessed February 26, 2008).

2. As established in *McDonnell Douglas Corp. v. Green,* 411 U.S. 792, at 802 (1973).

3. *Ash et al. v. Tyson Foods, Inc.,* 546 U.S. 454 (2006).

4. *Griggs v. Duke Power,* 401 U.S. 424 (1971).

5. *Grutter v. Bollinger,* 539 U.S. 306 (2003).

6. *Gratz v. Bollinger,* 539 U.S. 244 (2003).

7. *CBOCS West, Inc. v. Humphries,* 474 F.3d 387 (2007).

8. The U.S. Equal Employment Opportunity Commission. "EEOC Partners with Business to Build Best Practices for Increasing Diversity." See http://www.eeoc.gov/press/3-8-06.html (accessed July 29, 2008).

9. Copyright European Foundation for the Improvement of Living and Working Conditions, 2008, Wyattville Road, Loughlinstown, Dublin 18, Ireland. First published in 'New antidiscrimination law adopted', in EIROnline at www.eurofound.europa.eu/eiro/2001/12/feature/fr0112152f.htm.

Chapter **Eight**

Race and Color Discrimination

Every year my parents would write away for the *Ebony Travel Guide,* published by *Ebony* magazine. During segregation *Ebony* would publish an annual guide for blacks' use when traveling across the country. The guide told you where you could eat, where you could stay, where you could purchase gas, what cities you should not stop in, what cities or sections of cities were hospitable to blacks, and other relevant information. Thus, as you were moving across the country, you would know what to do and what not to do.[1]

INTRODUCTION

As discussed in the previous chapter, the Civil Rights Act of 1964 and its amendments prohibit discrimination based on several categories, including discrimination motivated by race. In this chapter race discrimination is our focus.

The EEOC reported that complaints alleging discrimination based on race and sex accounted for most EEOC action in 2004—about the same percentages as in 2003. Race was cited in 27,696 cases (34.9 percent of the total) and sex was cited in 24,249 cases (30.5 percent of the total)[2]. These statistics underscore the importance of addressing practices and policies that may directly or indirectly affect people who are racially different from the dominant pool of employees in any given organization.

Statistics

In fiscal year (FY) 2006 the EEOC received 27,238 charges of race discrimination. The EEOC resolved 25,992 race charges in FY 2006 and

FIGURE 8.1   Race-Based Charges in Fiscal Year 1997 through Fiscal Year 2006

	FY 1997	FY 1998	FY 1999	FY 2000	FY 2001	FY 2002	FY 2003	FY 2004	FY 2005	FY 2006
Receipts	29,199	28,820	28,819	28,945	28,912	29,910	28,526	27,696	26,740	27,238
Resolutions	36,419	35,716	35,094	33,188	32,077	33,199	30,702	29,631	27,411	25,992
Resolutions by Type										
Settlements	1,206	1,460	2,138	2,802	2,549	3,059	2,890	2,927	2,801	3,039
	3.3%	4.1%	6.1%	8.4%	7.9%	9.2%	9.4%	9.9%	10.2%	11.7%
Withdrawals with Benefits	912	823	1,036	1,150	1,203	1,200	1,125	1,088	1,167	1,177
	2.5%	2.3%	3.0%	3.5%	3.8%	3.6%	3.7%	3.7%	4.3%	4.5%
Administrative Closures	8,395	7,871	7,213	5,727	5,626	5,043	4,759	4,261	3,674	3,436
	23.1%	22.0%	20.6%	17.3%	17.5%	15.2%	15.5%	14.4%	13.4%	13.2%
No Reasonable Cause	24,988	24,515	23,148	21,319	20,302	21,853	20,506	20,166	18,608	17,324
	68.6%	68.6%	66.0%	64.2%	63.3%	65.8%	66.8%	68.1%	67.9%	66.7%
Reasonable Cause	918	1,047	1,559	2,190	2,397	2,044	1,422	1,189	1,161	1,016
	2.5%	2.9%	4.4%	6.6%	7.5%	6.2%	4.6%	4.0%	4.2%	3.9%
Successful Conciliations	248	287	382	529	691	580	392	330	377	292
	0.7%	0.8%	1.1%	1.6%	2.2%	1.7%	1.3%	1.1%	1.4%	1.1%
Unsuccessful Conciliations	670	760	1,177	1,661	1,706	1,464	1,030	859	784	724
	1.8%	2.1%	3.4%	5.0%	5.3%	4.4%	3.4%	2.9%	2.9%	2.8%
Merit Resolutions	3,036	3,330	4,733	6,142	6,149	6,303	5,437	5,204	5,129	5,232
	8.3%	9.3%	13.5%	18.5%	19.2%	19.0%	17.7%	17.6%	18.7%	20.1%
Monetary Benefits (Millions)*	$41.8	$32.2	$53.2	$61.7	$86.5	$81.1	$69.6	$61.1	$76.5	$61.4

*Does not include monetary benefits obtained through litigation.

This chart represents the total number of charge receipts filed and resolved under Title VII alleging race-based discrimination. The data are compiled by the Office of Research, Information, and Planning from the EEOC's national database.

The EEOC total workload includes charges carried over from previous fiscal years, new charge receipts, and charges transferred to the EEOC from Fair Employment Practice Agencies (FEPAs). Resolution of charges each year may therefore exceed receipts for that year because the workload being resolved is drawn from a combination of pending cases, new receipts, and FEPA transfer charges. The total of individual percentages may not always sum to 100 percent due to rounding.

This page was last modified on January 31, 2007.

recovered $61.4 million in monetary benefits for charging parties and other aggrieved individuals (not including monetary benefits obtained through litigation). Figure 8.1 shows a breakdown of the charges received between 1997 and 2006.

In January 2008 the EEOC won the largest settlement to date for an individual claim of race discrimination when Lockheed Martin agreed to pay

$2.5 billion to Charles Daniels, an African-American[3]. Daniels was the only black electrician at his Florida job and alleged that he was repeatedly called the "N-word" and was subjected to racial taunts by both coworkers and supervisors. When the removal of the Confederate flag was in the news, some of his coworkers made derogatory statements about blacks, such as "We should do to blacks what Hitler did to the Jews." When he complained about the harassment, the situation became worse for him, including death threats. Under the settlement, Lockheed Martin also agreed to terminate the harassers and make significant policy changes to address future discrimination.

Lockheed Martin's position was summed up as follows: "The conduct in question involved a small number of first-line employees in a small, single operating unit of the company. When management became aware of the allegations, it conducted investigations and took the appropriate remedial actions based on the facts presented at that time. At no time was the operating unit aware of or did it ignore any unlawful conduct. All individuals involved in this matter have either left the company or are being terminated. Additionally, as a result of this settlement, we've barred the individuals allegedly involved in this matter from future work with the company."

Having harassment policies in place and posters clearly setting out the rights of workers, as well as doing what the law requires, will not insulate employers from charges of discrimination. Smart companies will be alert to the potentially damaging effects of the behavioral and cultural dynamics of their workforces, and they will actively establish a climate of respect at all levels.

DEFINING RACE AND COLOR

Race and color discrimination are two classifications designated in Title VII of the Civil Rights Act of 1964. Although the original focus of the terms *race* and *color* was on African-Americans, these classifications have been extended to include people of any race or color who are discriminated against in a workplace on the basis of those characteristics. For example, a Caucasian male might successfully claim discrimination based on race or color if he has been the victim of discrimination in a corporation that is composed of all Japanese executives and employees operating on American soil.

The Meaning of Race

What is it that brings an individual within the classification of race? Designations such as Caucasian, white, black, African, Asian, Oriental, Slavic, European, and others are terms that have been used to denote race, but such terms are not altogether clear. The EEOC uses the following categories for race and color discrimination[4].

Race Discrimination

Racial discrimination is present when people are treated differently than others who are similarly situated because they are members of a specific race. It can occur when individuals are treated differently because of unalterable characteristics, such as physical features, indigenous to their race. The courts have also found that racial discrimination in employment can occur when employees are treated differently than other employees similarly situated because of their interracial dating or marriages, racially oriented expression of attitudes and beliefs, or membership in racially oriented groups.

The courts have been careful to state that minority races are not the sole victims of discrimination. Whites, if treated differently than others who are similarly situated, have also been found to have been discriminated against.

The Equal Employment Opportunity Commission (EEOC) defines these racial categories:

- American Indian or Alaskan Native: A person having origins in any of the original peoples of North America.
- Asian or Pacific Islander: A person having origins in any of the original peoples of the Far East, Southeast Asia, the Indian subcontinent, or the Pacific islands. This area includes China, India, Japan, Korea, the Philippine Islands, and Samoa.
- -Black, not of Hispanic origin: A person having origins in any of the original peoples of Africa.
- -Hispanic: A person having origins in any of the original peoples of Mexico, Puerto Rico, Cuba, Central or South America, or other Spanish cultures regardless of race.
- -White, not of Hispanic origin: A person having origins in any of the original peoples of Europe, North Africa, or the Middle East.

Color Discrimination

Color discrimination occurs when individuals are treated differently than others who are similarly situated because of the color of their skin. This is a separately identifiable type of discrimination that can occur in conjunction with race discrimination. Color discrimination can also occur in the absence of race discrimination when members of the same race are treated differently because of their skin color. In *Felix v. Manquez,* 24EPD 279 (D.C.D.C. 1980), the court held that color discrimination is actionable under Title VII. The court stated that because of the mixture of races and ancestral origins in Puerto Rico, where the defendant employee was located, color was the most practical claim to present.

The Race Relations Act of 1976 makes it unlawful to discriminate against a person, directly or indirectly, in employment. Direct discrimination consists of treating a person, on racial grounds, less favorably than others are or would be treated in the same or similar circumstances. Segregating a person from others on racial grounds constitutes less favorable treatment.

Note: Racial grounds are the grounds of race, color, nationality—including citizenship—or ethnic or national origins, and groups defined by reference to these grounds are referred to as *racial groups*[5].

EEOC FACTS ABOUT RACE AND COLOR DISCRIMINATION

The provisions of the Civil Rights Act of 1964 pertaining to race-related discrimination were summed up by the U.S. Equal Employment Opportunity Commission in "Facts about Race/Color Discrimination" as follows[6]:

> It is unlawful to discriminate against any employee or applicant for employment because of his/her race or color in regard to hiring, termination, promotion, compensation, job training, or any other term, condition, or privilege of employment. Title VII also prohibits employment decisions based on stereotypes and assumptions about abilities, traits, or the performance of individuals of certain racial groups. . . . Equal employment opportunity cannot be denied because of marriage to or association with an individual of a different race; membership in or association with ethnic based organizations or groups; or attendance or participation in schools or places of worship generally associated with certain minority groups.

Race-Related Characteristics and Conditions

Discrimination on the basis of a characteristic associated with race, such as skin color, hair texture, or certain facial features, violates Title VII even though not all members of the race may share the same characteristic.

Title VII also prohibits discrimination on the basis of a condition that predominantly affects one race unless the practice is job related and consistent with business necessity. For example, because sickle cell anemia occurs predominantly in African-Americans, a policy excluding individuals with sickle cell anemia must be job related and consistent with business necessity. Similarly, a no-beard employment policy may discriminate against African-American men who have a predisposition to pseudofolliculitis barbae (severe shaving bumps) unless the policy is job related and necessary for business.

Language or behavior that clearly denotes animus or bias against people of a particular race (or color) constitutes the proverbial smoking gun that can connect a negative employment decision to illegal race discrimination. Most employers today realize the need to educate their workers in order to prevent liability based on such language or behavior.

Certain words are clearly viewed as discriminatory, but employers must also guard against less obvious words or behaviors to ensure compliance—for example, words that implicitly reveal bias. For example, one federal appellate court in Pennsylvania ruled that allegations by plaintiffs that they were referred to as "another one," "that one in there," "one of them," and "all of you," when spoken within a particular context, could raise disputed factual issues of substance and, therefore, the plaintiffs' case should not be dismissed without a trial. The court stated, "A reasonable jury could find that statements like the ones allegedly made in this case send a clear message and carry the distinct tone of racial motivations and implications. They could be seen as conveying the message that members of a particular race are disfavored and that members of that race are, therefore, not full and equal members of the workplace"[7].

Case for Discussion 8-1

The case here illustrates the fact that the plaintiff–employee bears the ultimate burden of proving intentional discrimination in a disparate treatment case.

ST. MARY'S HONOR CENTER ET AL. V. MELVIN HICKS, 509 U.S. 502 (1993)[8]

Facts

Petitioner St. Mary's Honor Center (St. Mary's) is a halfway house operated by the Missouri Department of Corrections and Human Resources (MDCHR). Respondent Melvin Hicks, a black man, was hired as a correctional officer at St. Mary's in August 1978 and was promoted to shift commander, one of six supervisory positions, in February 1980.

In 1983 . . . John Powell became the new chief of custody (respondent's immediate supervisor) and petitioner Steve Long the new superintendent. Prior to these personnel changes respondent had enjoyed a satisfactory employment record, but soon thereafter became the subject of repeated, and increasingly severe, disciplinary actions. He was suspended for five days for violations of institutional rules by his subordinates on March 3, 1984. He received a letter of reprimand for alleged failure to conduct an adequate investigation of a brawl between inmates that occurred during his shift on March 21. He was later demoted from shift commander to correctional officer for his failure to ensure that his subordinates entered their use of a St. Mary's vehicle into the official logbook on March 19, 1984. Finally, on June 7, 1984, he was discharged for threatening Powell during an exchange of heated words on April 19.

Respondent brought this suit . . . alleging that St. Mary's violated Title VII of the Civil Rights Act of 1964. . . . [T]he district court found for St. Mary's. The United States Court of Appeals for the Eighth Circuit reversed and remanded . . . and we granted certiorari.

We granted certiorari to determine whether, in a suit against an employer alleging intentional racial discrimination, . . .the trier of fact's rejection of the employer's asserted reasons for its actions mandates a finding for the plaintiff.

. . . Petitioners do not challenge the district court's finding that respondent satisfied the minimal requirements of such a prima facie case by proving (1) that he is black, (2) that he was qualified for the position of shift commander, (3) that he was demoted from that position and ultimately discharged, and (4) that the position remained open and was ultimately filled by a white man.

***

Under the *McDonnell Douglas* scheme, "establishment of the prima facie case in effect creates a presumption that the employer unlawfully discriminated against the employee." . . . Thus, the *McDonnell Douglas* presumption places upon the defendant the burden of producing an explanation to rebut the prima facie case—i.e., the burden of "producing evidence" that the adverse employment actions were taken "for a legitimate, nondiscriminatory reason." "The defendant must clearly set forth, through the introduction of admissible evidence," reasons for its actions which, *if believed by the trier of fact,* would support a finding that unlawful discrimination was not the cause of the employment action. It is important to note, however, that although the *McDonnell Douglas* presumption shifts the burden of *production* to the defendant, "the ultimate burden of persuading the trier of fact that the defendant intentionally discriminated against the plaintiff remains at all times with the plaintiff."

***

The district court, acting as trier of fact in this bench trial, found that the reasons petitioners gave were not the real reasons for respondent's demotion and discharge. It found that respondent was the only supervisor disciplined for violations committed by his subordinates; that similar and even more serious violations committed by respondent's coworkers were either disregarded or treated more leniently; and that Powell manufactured the final verbal confrontation in order to provoke respondent into threatening him. It nonetheless held that respondent had failed to carry his ultimate burden of proving that *his race* was the determining factor in petitioners' decision first to demote and then to dismiss him. In short, the district court concluded that "although [respondent] has proven the existence of a crusade to terminate him, he has not proven that the crusade was racially rather than personally motivated."

Footnote 2 in opinion: Various considerations led it to this conclusion, including the fact that two blacks sat on the disciplinary review board that recommended disciplining respondent, that respondent's black subordinates who actually committed the violations were not disciplined, and that "the number of black employees at St. Mary's remained constant."

The court of appeals set this determination aside on the ground that "once [respondent] proved all of [petitioners'] proffered reasons for the adverse employment actions to be pretextual, [respondent] was entitled to judgment as a matter of law." The court of appeals reasoned, "Because all of defendants' proffered reasons were discredited, defendants were in a position of having offered no legitimate reason for their actions. In other words, defendants were in no better position than if they had remained silent, offering no rebuttal to an established inference that they had unlawfully discriminated against plaintiff on the basis of his race."

***

But the court of appeals' holding that rejection of the defendant's proffered reasons *compels* judgment for the plaintiff disregards the fundamental principle of Rule 301 that a presumption does not shift the burden of proof, and ignores our repeated admonition that the Title VII plaintiff at all times bears the "ultimate burden of persuasion."

***

Decision

[In essence, the U.S. Supreme Court underscored the principle that the plaintiff in a discrimination case retains the burden of proving intentional discrimination for a disparate treatment claim. Once the prima facie case is made, the defendant–employer has the opportunity to show that the real reason for the action taken against the employee was not discriminatory. If a jury does not find the employer's reason to be credible, that does not mean an automatic victory for the plaintiff–employee. The jury can still find that the plaintiff has not satisfied his burden of proving intentional discrimination.]

Dissent

JUSTICE SOUTER, joined by JUSTICE WHITE, JUSTICE BLACKMUN, and JUSTICE STEVENS

At the outset, under the *McDonnell Douglas* framework, a plaintiff alleging disparate treatment in the workplace in violation of Title VII must provide the basis for an inference of discrimination. In this case, as all agree, Melvin Hicks met this initial burden by proving by a preponderance of the evidence that he was black and therefore a member of a protected class; he was qualified to be a shift commander; he was demoted and then terminated; and his position remained available and was later filled by a qualified applicant. . . . Hicks thus proved what we have called a "prima facie case" of discrimination, and it is important to note that in this context a prima facie case is indeed a proven case. . . . Given our assumption that "people do not act in a totally arbitrary manner, without any underlying reasons, especially in a business setting," we have explained that a prima facie case implies discrimination "because we presume [the employer's] acts, if otherwise unexplained, are more likely than not based on the consideration of impermissible factors."

Questions for Discussion

1. Are you more persuaded by the majority ruling or the dissent? Why?
2. Although St. Mary's won the case, the cost of taking a case all the way to the U.S. Supreme Court is substantial—not only in terms of money expended but also in terms of lost productivity, decline in worker morale, the emotional toll on all involved, and other related costs. What might the administrators of St. Mary's Honor Center had done differently to prevent this lawsuit?

Management **Perspective**

In an article in *The Wall Street Journal,* reporter Carol Hymowitz[9] wrote in 2005 about the wisdom of seeking diversity in a firm. The rationale for this initiative has little to do with legal requirements or affirmative action and more to do with the value to the profitability of the company:

> As companies do more and more business around the world, diversity isn't simply a matter of doing what is fair or good public relations. It's a business imperative.
>
> If companies are going to sell products and services globally, they will need a rich mix of employees with varied perspectives and experiences. They will need top executives who understand different countries and cultures. They will need executives around the world who intuitively understand the markets they are trying to penetrate.
>
> A wide swath of corporations, however, don't yet realize that. That fact is evident in the numbers, which show that management ranks and boardrooms remain almost exclusively white-male enclaves. African-Americans made up 13.8 percent of the U.S. workforce in 2003 but just 6.5 percent of managers, while Hispanics were 11.1 percent of the workforce and 5 percent of managers. Whites, by contrast, made up 69.9 percent of the workforce but 84.5 percent of managers—and dominate even more among top managers. Just 7.9 percent of top earners at *Fortune* 500 companies are women.
>
> Something dramatically different, however, is happening at a select group of corporations with the broadest global reach. Top executives at these companies know they need a workforce that reflects the changing

demographics of their customers. Rather than try to hire a certain number of African-Americans or Hispanics and then encourage these groups to blend together and conceal their differences, they're trying to tap into the differences to capture new business and increase the bottom line.

***

That is what PepsiCo Inc. is trying to do. The beverage and snack food giant has made big strides from a decade or two ago, when it had a reputation as a mostly white male fraternity. At the end of 2004, people of color held 17 percent of management jobs at midlevel and above, up from 11 percent in 2000, and women held 29 percent of those management jobs, up from 24 percent in 2000.

. . . PepsiCo estimates that in 2004 about one percentage point of the company's 8 percent revenue growth came from new products inspired by diversity efforts. Among these: guacamole-flavored Doritos chips and Gatorade Xtreme, aimed at Hispanics; Mountain Dew Code Red, which appeals to African-Americans; and a newly launched wasabi-flavored snack aimed at Asians.

Leading this initiative is chief executive Steve Reinemund, whose belief that diversity promotes innovation and better decision making is evident in his senior team. His president and number 2 executive is Indra Nooyi, who grew up in India and wears saris to work.

Starting this year, each member of PepsiCo's executive committee is required to sponsor a different employee affinity group. . . .

The goal is an inclusive culture where employees feel free to express their views, even if those are sometimes negative or involve confronting top executives. . . .

An employee affinity group generally consists of people of a particular race, gender, ethnic minority or sexual orientation, or people with a disability—with the idea that they share certain perspectives and needs within a company that can be best addressed through group discussion. Companies benefit from diversity, Mr. Reinemund believes, only if people of diverse races, ethnic backgrounds, gender or sexual orientation aren't required to act or think the same.

Disparate Treatment and Harassment in a Race Discrimination Case

There are several types of cases involving race discrimination under Title VII of the Civil Rights Act: disparate treatment, disparate impact, harassment (quid pro quo or hostile environment), and affirmative action cases. In Case for Discussion 8-2 one question is whether the plaintiff established a prima facie case of disparate treatment based on race. The case also addresses the elements required to succeed in a racial harassment charge involving hostile environment. Finally, the case involves a claim of retaliation and a discussion of what is needed for a successful retaliation claim under Title VII.

Case for Discussion 8-2

KEVIN A. MOORE V. UNITED PARCEL SERVICE, INC., 150 FED.APPX. 315 (2005)[10]

Facts

Moore joined UPS as a part-time worker in April 2000. He was a member of the Local 767 union, and the terms of his employment were governed under a collective bargaining agreement between UPS and the union. Under the agreement, employees may be discharged for absenteeism after they have been given one initial written warning. Also under the agreement, at the employer's discretion, employees may be issued more than one written warning to correct performance or attendance problems.

Moore started his employment at UPS as a preloader but began training as a driver in April 2001. Due to repeated performance failures, as well as an accident, however, Moore was disqualified from driving on May 12, 2001. In addition to his poor performance as a driver, Moore was absent or tardy more than 80 times during his last 10 months of employment. Moore received his first warning letter for poor attendance after failing to report to work on May 29, 2001.

On June 1, 2001, Moore filed a grievance contesting his disqualification as a driver. As a result of the grievance, a settlement was reached between the union and UPS in which UPS agreed to give Moore another opportunity at a driver position when an opening became available. On July 11, 2001, after being late or absent four times in the previous two weeks, UPS issued Moore a second warning letter for poor attendance. . . . Between July 25, 2001 and August 31, 2001, Moore was late or absent eight more times. On September 7, 2001, UPS issued Moore an intent to terminate notification. In response, on September 12, 2001, Moore filed a grievance challenging the second warning letter, the intent to suspend notification, and the intent to terminate notification. Following a hearing between the union and UPS on September 26, 2001, Moore agreed to withdraw his grievance and serve a suspension for his attendance infractions. In exchange, UPS withdrew its intent to terminate.

Just two days later, on September 28, 2001, Moore once again reported late to work. In response, UPS issued Moore another intent to terminate notification. On October 10, 2001, Moore reported late to work once again. On October 19, 2001, UPS notified Moore that his employment was being terminated for poor attendance. In response to the notification, Moore instead decided to sign a separation notice, which voluntarily terminated his employment.

***

A. *Disparate Treatment.*

. . . Moore argues that he provided direct evidence of discriminatory remarks made by his immediate supervisors as required under Title VII.

***

To establish a prima facie case of race discrimination in an employment termination case, Moore must prove that he "(1) is a member of a protected class; (2) was qualified for his position; (3) was subject to an adverse employment action; and (4) was replaced by someone outside the protected class, or, in the case of disparate treatment, show that others similarly situated were treated more favorably."

***

In an effort to satisfy the fourth element of the test, Moore argues that two white employees were not disciplined for poor attendance. The documents Moore provided to the district court, . . . were not authenticated or identified as UPS business records . . . and were not accompanied by any explanatory information to aid the court in understanding the statistical information contained in the documents.

***

B. *Hostile Work Environment*

Moore argues that he established the elements of a prima facie case for a racially hostile work environment under Title VII. To establish a prima facie case, Moore must prove that (1) he belongs to a protected group; (2) he was subjected to unwelcome harassment; (3) the harassment complained of was based on race; (4) the harassment complained of affected a term, condition, or privilege of employment; (5) the employer knew or should have known of the harassment in question and failed to take prompt remedial action.

***

Moore argues that several supervisors made a few racial comments that created a hostile environment. Moore, however, admitted that he never complained to UPS's human resource department or another supervisor about the comments. Moore failed to provide evidence to establish that the few isolated comments were so severe or pervasive that they affected a term, condition, or privilege of employment, or unreasonably interfered with his work performance. Moore also argued that the discipline he received for being tardy or absent was further evidence of a hostile work environment. As noted earlier, however, Moore failed to establish that the discipline was racially motivated. Consequently, Moore failed to provide evidence sufficient to create a material issue that his workplace was an abusive or hostile working environment.

C. *Retaliation*

Moore finally contends that he established the elements of a prima facie case of retaliation. This claim requires proof that (1) he engaged in a protected activity, (2) he experienced an adverse employment action following the activity, and (3) there was a causal link between the protected activity and the adverse employment action. Under Title VII, an employee has engaged in protected activity if he has "opposed any practice made an unlawful employment practice by this subchapter," or "made a charge, testified, assisted, or participated in any manner in an investigation, proceeding, or hearing under this subchapter."

Decision

Moore argues that he was retaliated against for filing a grievance on June 1, 2001, for his disqualification as a driver. Moore, however, was not engaged in a protected activity, as his grievance did not oppose or protest racial discrimination or any other unlawful employment practice under Title VII. . . . Therefore, the district court correctly granted summary judgment to UPS on Moore's retaliation claim.

Questions for Discussion

1. Did Moore testify in court to support the evidence that he claimed against UPS? Explain your answer.
2. Evaluate the fairness of the decisions of the trial and appellate courts.
3. What management practices and policies were modeled by UPS in this case? Evaluate those practices and policies.

DISPARATE IMPACT AND RACE DISCRIMINATION

The cases of *Hicks v. St. Mary's Honor Center* and *Moore v. UPS* involved disparate treatment claims. In a *disparate treatment* case the plaintiff argues that he or she was the specific target of intentional discrimination. In such cases the plaintiff must prove the element of intent, either directly or by inference. In a *disparate impact* case the plaintiff claims that people within his or her protected class have been precluded from particular jobs, or otherwise suffered as a class, from advantages that other employees enjoy in the organization. The plaintiff(s) need not prove intent in a disparate impact case. It is sufficient to show by statistical evidence that the practices of the employer have the effect of disproportionately and adversely affecting members of that class. The U.S. Supreme Court recognized the disparate impact form of discrimination in the landmark case of *Griggs v. Duke Power Co.,* 1971[11]. The Court stated, "The objective of Congress in the enactment of Title VII is plain from the language of the statute. It was to achieve equality of employment opportunities and remove barriers that have operated in the past to favor an identifiable group of white employees over other employees. Under the act, practices, procedures, or tests neutral on their face, and even neutral in terms of intent, cannot be maintained if they operate to 'freeze' the status quo of prior discriminatory employment practices."[12]

Case for Discussion 8-3

U.S. Supreme Court on Disparate Impact

WATSON V. FORT WORTH BANK & TRUST, 487 U.S. 977 (1988)[13]

Facts

Petitioner Clara Watson, who is black, was hired by respondent Fort Worth Bank and Trust (the Bank) as a proof operator in August 1973. In January 1976 Watson was promoted to a position as teller in the Bank's drive-in facility. In February 1980 she sought to become supervisor of the tellers in the main lobby; a white male, however, was selected for this job. Watson then sought a position as supervisor of the drive-in bank, but this position was given to a white female. In February 1981, after Watson had served for about a year as a commercial teller in the Bank's main lobby, and informally as assistant to the supervisor of tellers, the man holding that position was promoted. Watson applied for the vacancy, but the white female who was the supervisor of the drive-in bank was selected instead. Watson then applied for the vacancy created at the drive-in; a white male was selected for that job. The Bank, which has about 80 employees, had not developed precise and formal criteria for evaluating candidates for the positions for which Watson unsuccessfully applied. It relied instead on the subjective judgment of supervisors who were acquainted with the candidates and with the nature of the jobs to be filled. All the supervisors involved in denying Watson the four promotions at issue were white.

Watson filed a discrimination charge with the Equal Employment Opportunity Commission (EEOC). After exhausting her administrative remedies, she filed this lawsuit.

Trial and Appellate Court Decisions

The district court . . . concluded, on the evidence presented at trial, that Watson had established a prima facie case of employment discrimination, but that the Bank had met its rebuttal burden by presenting legitimate and nondiscriminatory reasons for each of the challenged promotion decisions. [T]he action was dismissed.

***

Watson argued that the district court had erred in failing to apply "disparate impact" analysis to her claims of discrimination in promotion. Relying on precedent, the majority held that "a Title VII challenge to an allegedly discretionary promotion system is properly analyzed under the disparate treatment model rather than the disparate impact model."

***

In *Griggs v. Duke Power Co.*, 401 U.S. 424 (1971), this Court held that a plaintiff need not necessarily prove intentional discrimination in order to establish that an employer has violated [the Civil Rights Act]. In certain cases, facially neutral employment practices that have significant adverse effects on protected *groups* have been held to violate the Act without proof that the employer adopted those practices with a discriminatory intent. . . . The evidence in these "disparate impact" cases usually focuses on statistical disparities, rather than specific incidents, and on competing explanations for those disparities.

***

Petitioner contends that subjective selection methods are at least as likely to have discriminatory effects as are the kind of objective tests at issue in *Griggs* and our other disparate impact cases. Furthermore, she argues, if disparate impact analysis is confined to objective tests, employers will be able to substitute subjective criteria having substantially identical effects, and *Griggs* will become a dead letter.

***

. . . If an employer's undisciplined system of subjective decision making has precisely the same effects as a system pervaded by impermissible intentional discrimination, it is difficult to see why Title VII's proscription against discriminatory actions should not apply. In both circumstances, the employer's practices may be said to "adversely affect [an individual's] status as an employee, because of such individual's race, color, religion, sex, or national origin.". . . . We conclude, accordingly, that subjective or discretionary employment practices may be analyzed under the disparate impact approach in appropriate cases.

***

. . . [W]e note that the plaintiff's burden in establishing a prima facie case goes beyond the need to show that there are statistical disparities in the employer's workforce. The plaintiff must begin by identifying the specific employment practice that is challenged. Although this has been relatively easy to do in challenges to standardized tests, it may sometimes be more difficult when subjective selection criteria are at issue.

   Once the employment practice at issue has been identified, causation must be proved; that is, the plaintiff must offer statistical evidence of a kind and degree sufficient to show that the practice in question has caused the exclusion of applicants for jobs or promotions because of their membership in a protected group. Our formulations, which have never been framed in terms of any rigid mathematical formula, have consistently stressed that statistical disparities must be sufficiently substantial that they raise such an inference of causation.

***

A second constraint on the application of disparate impact theory lies in the nature of the "business necessity" or "job relatedness" defense. Although we have said that an employer has "the burden of showing that any given requirement must have a manifest relationship to the employment in question," . . . such a formulation should not be interpreted as implying that the ultimate burden of proof can be shifted to the defendant. On the contrary, the ultimate burden of proving that discrimination against a protected group has been caused by a specific employment practice remains with the plaintiff at all times. Thus, when a plaintiff has made out a prima facie case of disparate impact, and when the defendant has met its burden of producing evidence that its employment practices are based on legitimate business reasons, the plaintiff must "show that other tests or selection devices, without a similarly undesirable racial effect, would also serve the employer's legitimate interest in efficient and trustworthy workmanship." Factors such as the cost or other burdens of proposed alternative selection devices are relevant in determining whether they would be equally as effective as the challenged practice in serving the employer's legitimate business goals. The same factors would also be relevant in determining whether the challenged practice has operated as the functional equivalent of a pretext for discriminatory treatment. . . .

***

Decision

The judgment of the court of appeals is vacated, and the case is remanded for further proceedings consistent with this opinion.

Questions for Discussion

1. In light of the *Watson* decision, what practices should managers establish to prevent liability based on a disparate impact theory of race discrimination?
2. If we assume that Watson established a sound disparate impact case, how can Ft. Worth Bank establish a successful rebuttal? What arguments can be made to satisfy a court (under the *Watson* framework of the U.S. Supreme Court) that it has justification for its subjective methods? (Students are not restricted to the facts presented in this case but are encouraged to consider other possible facts.)

AFFIRMATIVE ACTION: RACE DISCRIMINATION

As noted in the previous chapter, affirmative action is an issue that arises under both the Constitution and Title VII of the Civil Rights Act. Hence legal issues can arise for programs set up to encourage employment opportunities for women or for other protected classes. Many affirmative action cases involve AAPs to advance opportunities for racial minorities.

The Federal Sector

The *Adarand* case, decided by the U.S. Supreme Court in 1995[14], involves reverse discrimination resulting from an affirmative action plan designed by the government to expand employment opportunities for minority workers. In *Adarand* the Court held that federal affirmative action programs using racial and ethnic criteria for decision making are subject to strict judicial scrutiny. Under strict scrutiny, such programs must serve a compelling governmental interest and must be narrowly tailored to serve that interest. *Adarand* extended to the federal sector the reasoning of the Supreme Court's decision in *City of Richmond v. J.A. Croson Co.* (1989)[15]. The *City of Richmond* case held for the first time that race-based affirmative action by state and local government is subject to strict scrutiny.

Management **Perspective**

The EEOC Works to "E-RACE" Discrimination[16]

The EEOC has adopted the Eradicating Racism and Colorism from Employment (E-RACE) initiative.

The Equal Employment Opportunity Commission has championed equal opportunity in employment since its inception, shortly after the signing of Title VII of the Civil Rights Act of 1964. Although the Commission has been successful in its enforcement efforts, race and color discrimination continues to exist in the workplace. In an effort to identify and implement new strategies that will strengthen its enforcement of Title VII and advance the statutory right to a workplace free of race and color discrimination, EEOC is instituting the E-RACE Initiative.

E-RACE Objectives

The E-RACE Initiative is designed to improve EEOC's efforts to ensure workplaces are free of race and color discrimination. Specifically, the EEOC will identify issues, criteria and barriers that contribute to race and color discrimination, explore strategies to improve the administrative processing and the litigation of race and color discrimination claims, and enhance public awareness of race and color discrimination in employment. As a framework for implementing the E-RACE Initiative, EEOC has developed a set of detailed E-RACE goals and objectives to be achieved within a 5-year timeframe from FY 2008 to FY 2013.

Additionally, the Commission will combine the objectives of E-RACE with existing EEOC initiatives. For example, the Commission will integrate the goals of the Systemic Initiative by addressing race and color issues with class and systemic implications. It will incorporate the principles of the Youth@Work Initiative by combating disparate treatment of youth based on race and color. And, the Commission will complement the outreach and enforcement efforts of the LEAD Initiative by challenging exclusionary employment policies that adversely impact people of color who also have disabilities (in both the private and public sectors).

Finally, the Commission will strengthen partnerships with employee advocates and state and local human rights commissions and increase its outreach to human resource professionals and employer groups to address race and color discrimination in the workplace.

Summary

Race and color discrimination are prohibited by Title VII of the Civil Rights Act of 1964. According to the EEOC, race discrimination includes treating people differently because of

- Their membership within a specific race.
- Unalterable characteristics such as physical features indigenous to a particular race.
- A relationship with members of a particular race as through dating or marriage.
- Membership in a racially oriented group.
- Racially oriented expressions of attitudes and beliefs.

The EEOC defines racial categories as

- American Indian or Alaskan Native.
- Asian or Pacific Islander.
- Black, not of Hispanic origin.
- Hispanic.
- White, not of Hispanic origin.

According to the EEOC, color discrimination includes treating people differently because of the color of their skin.

Title VII prohibits discrimination based on stereotypes and assumptions about abilities, traits, or performance of individuals of certain racial groups.

Discrimination on the basis of immutable characteristics associated with race, such as skin color, hair texture, or certain facial features, violates Title VII even though not all members of a race share such characteristics.

Title VII prohibits discrimination on the basis of a condition that predominantly affects one race unless the practice is job related and consistent with business necessity.

The U.S. Supreme Court in the *Watson* case decided that an employee can use a disparate impact analysis if an employment practice creates a subjective adverse impact. Prior to *Watson,* disparate impact cases involved objective criteria (such as the high school diploma requirement in *Griggs*).

Promoting and seeking diversity in the workplace has been recognized by some scholars, practitioners, and companies as necessary not only for compliance but also for bottom-line success. For example, top executives are becoming aware of the competitive edge gained by having a workforce that reflects the changing demographics of customers.

Questions	1. Marjorie H., a black woman, began working at Game Stop in August 1999 as a clerk in the Return-to-Vendor (RTV) department. She received a pay raise one year later. In January 2001 Game Stop promoted Marjorie to the position of RTV lead, a promotion that brought with it a raise. In August 2002 Marjorie received yet another pay raise. At various points she requested training on the WMS computer system; she received only limited training. In November 2002 Stephanie McKee, a white woman employed in the RTV department, was promoted to co-lead.

On November 11, 2002, Marjorie took a leave of absence to care for her injured son. When Marjorie returned to work on December 9, 2002, she heard rumors that she was no longer a lead, but no official action had been taken. Game Stop managers presented Marjorie with a letter indicating their intention to eliminate one of the two lead positions. However, Game Stop managers eventually met and determined that the lead elimination plan would not be implemented and that Marjorie could remain a lead in the RTV department.

On January 8, 2003, Lori Wolf, now manager of the RTV department, met with Marjorie and Stephanie to inform the two that the position of lead in the RTV department would be eliminated due to internal restructuring. Game Stop reduced the salaries of both women. The position of lead remained eliminated until mid-2004, when Sharrel, a black woman, was hired to be the lead.

In April 2003 Marjorie injured her foot. She took leave again and exhausted her FMLA-protected leave. On June 18, 2003, Game Stop terminated Marjorie for missing work beyond the legal leave limit.

Marjorie H. sued Game Stop, alleging race discrimination under Title VII of the Civil Rights Act of 1964. The district court granted Game Stop's motion for summary judgment, and Marjorie appealed.

a. Could Marjorie establish a prima facie case of race discrimination? Explain fully.

b. Analyze management's behavior and tactics. Sometimes a new employee performs well but over time becomes lackluster in performance. Management has the opportunity to hire someone who promises to be an excellent replacement. What are management's options, especially if the replacement is white and the lackluster performer is black?

2. Joe L., an African-American male, began working for ABC Sugar Co. (ASC) as a janitor in 1982. He was promoted to shift foreman and then, in 1987, to warehouse manager. Joe was responsible for overseeing all warehouse operations during his shift, including shipping, receiving and storing sugar, and maintaining accurate inventory counts. His immediate supervisor at ASC was Hugh Mendenhall, who became director of operations in September 1987. In fact, it was Mendenhall who recommended Joe's promotion to warehouse manager.

In May 1989, when ABC Sugar Co. was experiencing significant losses of sugar from its inventory, Mendenhall issued a memo to all employees announcing that ASC would begin random searches of employees and their possessions. Twice Joe L. was accused of stealing sugar, and each time his property was subjected to a search by company officials. Once Mendenhall searched his garage; another ASC manager later searched Joe's truck for stolen sugar and called Joe a "black thief." In neither search was anything found. Joe reported this second incident to his superior, but no disciplinary action was taken. He then filed a complaint with both the EEOC and the state's Civil Rights Commission on January 14, 1993, alleging race-based disparate treatment. On March 8, 1993, Mendenhall sent Joe a letter of apology for any offense caused by the company's investigations of the thefts. On April 30, 1993, Joe filed another complaint, alleging retaliation when a white management trainee was given overtime work and he was not.

In mid-June of 1994 Mendenhall sent a memo asking the operations managers to list their five main performance goals. The list was to be used for evaluation purposes at the next performance reviews of the managers. However, Joe believed he was being singled out to do this listing. Mendenhall reported that Joe came to his office and became very loud and angry. Joe stated that although he was angry at first, he did not raise his voice during this conversation. Mendenhall assured Joe that all operations managers were required to provide a list of goals and asked Joe to "tone it down." However, Joe did not believe that everyone was being required to list goals. He told Mendenhall that it was not a fair request, but that he would comply. According to Mendenhall, Joe stated that he could do or say whatever he wanted as long as he did not use vile language or threaten Mendenhall, and that he had a right to consult with someone before responding to Mendenhall's directive. Joe denied making such a statement. Nevertheless, he admits that he did tell Mendenhall that he would consult with someone before complying with the memo; he explained in his deposition that he meant he needed someone to explain what he was supposed to do or not to do. Joe stated that he did make the "goals" list he had been asked to make. He also testified that he did not recall any mention made, during this meeting with Mendenhall, of his race, the EEOC charges he had filed, or a lawsuit.

On June 27, 1994, the EEOC issued a right to sue letter. Joe then filed a timely complaint in the district court.

On September 16 there was another altercation. Mendenhall gave Joe a written warning stating that any future incidents of insolent or disrespectful behavior would not be tolerated and would result in disciplinary action, including possible termination. Joe responded with a memorandum, dated September 23, 1994, to Mendenhall concerning his conduct.

On the afternoon of September 23, 1994, Yonover (another company officer) met with Joe and Mendenhall in his office. Yonover stated in his affidavit that he intended to reprimand Joe for his insubordinate conduct on September 16 and to warn him that ABC Sugars would not tolerate insubordination. Yonover explained to Joe that ASC depends on its employees to follow their supervisors' orders and that an employee's refusal to perform a job can hinder operations. Yonover asked Joe what he would do if a warehouse employee refused his request to load a truck until he talked to a lawyer; Yonover claimed that Joe answered argumentatively and loudly that the employee should question his orders if asked to do something that was unsafe. Yonover then explained that Mendenhall had simply asked Joe to respond to a routine memo. At that point Joe became louder, according to Yonover, and stated that Mendenhall had no judgment and that he would not do anything that Mendenhall asked him to do without first "checking it out." In his affidavit, Yonover described what next transpired: "I then attempted to speak, but Joe interrupted me. Joe once again raised his right to seek outside consultation before doing anything. I told Joe that it was my turn to speak and that he could speak when I was finished. Joe answered by stating that he could talk when he wanted and that he was going to talk at that time." Yonover then told Joe that he was not going to engage in a shouting match. Because of Joe's grossly insubordinate conduct during the meeting, Yonover terminated Joe on September 23, 1994 in a letter, stating, "As a result of a very unpleasant meeting with you today your employment with ABC Sugar has been terminated immediately."

In his deposition, Joe explained his claim that he was retaliated against for filing a lawsuit:

> A. Well, I had been there 13 years, and that 13 years should have counted for something. I had never been disciplined one time in 13 years. I did what I was asked and sometimes above and beyond the call of duty. I helped everyone I could.
>
> And as you compare my work record to [coworker] Mr. Moreland, Mr. Moreland can go around and call people niggers and coons and all this and never be written up or disciplined, but as soon as ABC Sugar receives a lawsuit document from me I'm terminated two days after.
>
> Q. Other than what you've mentioned, do you have any other facts to support your claim that you were retaliated against for filing a lawsuit?
>
> A. No, ma'am.

a. Has Joe established a prima facie case of race discrimination against ABC Sugars? Be explicit in your answers.

b. Will the court rule in favor of Joe or ABC on the claim of race discrimination? Explain your answer.

c. Will the court rule in favor of Joe or ABC on the claim of retaliation?

d. How would you describe the management behavior of Yonover? Of Mendenhall? Would you advise different behavior? Why or why not?

3. George L., an African-American, worked in the department of corrections for the city of New York. After several years of commendable service and attempts at promotion, he filed suit against the city on the basis of national origin. Among his allegations was a claim that employees who were members of an Irish society were given priority treatment and promotions, while he was passed over.

a. Do you believe George has established a prima facie case? Is this race discrimination or national origin discrimination?

b. Does it matter whether George alleged race, color, or national origin in his complaint?

4. Thirty-two African-American employees of Apollo Pigment Co. complained of a series of racially motivated incidents in the workplace. They filed an action with the EEOC; and in January 2000 the EEOC sued Apollo under Title VII of the Civil Rights Act of 1964 on grounds of racial harassment after the failure of attempts to reach a voluntary prelitigation settlement with the employer. The case alleged several harassing activities, including racist graffiti, display of hangman's nooses, and racial epithets at the employer's facility.

a. What will the court decide?

b. What posture should the employer take at this point in the case?

c. What would constitute a satisfactory outcome for the plaintiffs?

5. Oscar A., a black male, filed a claim of hostile work environment based on race. Over the entire course of his employment with Amtrak he argued that a number of unrelated incidents occurred that could be characterized as racially motivated slurs, negative comments, and other means of putdowns directed at him. After the latest of these incidents, he filed his claim. He alleged that all of the racially motivated behaviors constituted the existence of a racially hostile environment in violation of Title VII. Only the last incident was within the statutory time limit imposed for claims of this type.

a. If you assume that the latest incident by itself is insufficient to rise to the level of a Title VII violation, but some of the past incidents, taken together with the last, could rise to such a level, should Oscar prevail in his suit?

b. If the court dismisses the case for failure to file on time, what message does this send to employers?

6. Keith D. started a new job as a server at an Applebee's restaurant in Atlanta. Less than a month later a new manager arrived. After fewer than 90 days of Keith's employment there, the new manager fired him. According to a lawsuit filed by Keith against the restaurant chain, he was a victim of discrimination. Keith is a dark-skinned African-American, and the

restaurant manager is a light-skinned African-American. When Keith complained about his treatment to the chain's corporate headquarters in Overland Park, Kansas, he was fired, according to the U.S. Equal Employment Opportunity Commission.

In light of the fact that the manager and the aggrieved employee are both black, does Keith have a viable case against Applebee's under Title VII of the Civil Rights Act of 1964?

References

1. P. D. McClain, Preface of *Legacies of the 1964 Civil Rights Act,* ed. B Grofman (University Press of Virginia, 2000).

2. D. Superville, "EEOC Collects Record $420M for Workers." See the Equal Employment Opportunity Commission Web site at http://www.eeoc.gov (accessed February 14, 2005).

3. L. Chiem, "Lockheed Martin Settles Hawaii Race Discrimination Suit for $2.5 Million," *Pacific Business News* (Honolulu), January 2, 2008.

4. See www.fmc.gov/bureaus/equal_employment_opportunity/basisfordiscrimination. asp.

5. See www.cre.gov.uk/gdpract/employ_cop.html.

6. U.S. Equal Employment Opportunity Commission, "Facts about Race/Color Discrimination."

7. *Aman v. Cort Furniture Rental Corp.,* 85 F.3d 1074 (3d Cir. 1996). See also B. Ingersoll, "'Code Words' May Support a Finding of Discrimination, Decides Third Circuit," *Pennsylvania Employment Law Letter* 6, no. 2 (August 1996).

8. *St. Mary's Honor Center et al. v. Melvin Hicks,* 509 U.S. 502; 113 S. Ct. 2742; 125 L. Ed. 2d 407 (1993).

9. C. Hymowitz, "The New Diversity." *The Wall Street Journal,* November 14, 2005, p. R1.

10. *Kevin A. Moore v. United Parcel Service, Inc.,* 150 Fed.Appx. 315 (2005), No. 04-11403, U.S. Court of Appeals for the Fifth Circuit, U.S. App. LEXIS 21476.

11. *Griggs v. Duke Power Co,* 401 U.S. 424 (1971).

12. Ibid. at p. 430.

13. *Watson v. Fort Worth Bank & Trust,* 487 U.S. 977, 108 S. Ct. 2777, 101 L. Ed. 2d 827, 1988 U.S. LEXIS 3035 (1988).

14. *Adarand v. Pena,* 115 S.Ct. 2097 (1995).

15. *City of Richmond v. J. A. Croson Co.,* 488 U.S. 469 (1989).

16. See http://www.eeoc.gov/initiatives/e-race/index.html (accessed August 1, 2008).

The Civil Rights Act of 1991, the Glass Ceiling Act, and the Pregnancy Discrimination Act

> Yes, I will bring the understanding of a woman to the Court, but I doubt that alone will affect my decisions. I think the important thing about my appointment is not that I will decide cases as a woman, but that I am a woman who will get to decide cases.
>
> Justice Sandra Day O'Connor[1]

INTRODUCTION

This chapter describes the provisions of two significant amendments to the Civil Rights Act of 1964—the Civil Rights Act of 1991, which affects all forms of discrimination against protected classes and includes the Glass Ceiling Act, and the Pregnancy Discrimination Act of 1978.

THE CIVIL RIGHTS ACT OF 1991

Twenty-seven years after the Civil Rights Act went into effect, Congress revisited the issues of employment discrimination. Among other things, Congress disagreed with the U.S. Supreme Court's interpretations of the act and amended the law accordingly. Two cases in particular aroused congressional concern: the *Hopkins v. Price Waterhouse* case[2] and the *Wards Cove Packing Co. v. Atonio* case. *Hopkins* was a mixed motive case in which the defendant employer had both legitimate and illegitimate reasons for not promoting Hopkins to partner. *Wards Cove* (see Case for Discussion 9-1) was a disparate impact case in which the plaintiffs sought relief for discriminatory work situations. Because, among other things, plaintiffs could not point out clearly the practices that led to the adverse impact, the plaintiffs lost the case. In the 1991 amendments to the Civil Rights Act of 1964, Congress specified the analysis that was to apply to mixed motive and disparate impact cases.

The Civil Rights Act of 1991 and Mixed Motive Cases

The U.S. Supreme Court took up the *Hopkins v. Price Waterhouse* case to resolve discrepancies in the federal appellate courts' interpretations of the law when employers had both legitimate and illegitimate reasons for taking actions against employees.

At least three distinct positions could have been taken in cases such as *Hopkins:*

1. The position taken by the dissenting judges in *Hopkins*—that when the employer demonstrates a credible legitimate reason for its action, the employer is not liable.
2. The position taken by the Court in *Hopkins*—that when there is clear evidence of a discriminatory motive, the employer is not liable if it can demonstrate by a preponderance of the evidence that it would have made the same decision in the absence of the discriminatory motive.
3. The position taken by Congress in the Civil Rights Act of 1991—that in mixed motive cases, "[A]n unlawful employment practice is established when the complaining party demonstrates that race, color, religion, sex, or national origin was a motivating factor for any employment practice, even though other factors also motivated the practice"[3]. In such a case the court may grant declaratory relief, injunctive relief, and attorney's fees and costs directly associated with the plaintiff's claim[4].

The Court in *Hopkins* distinguished mixed motive cases from those in which a plaintiff has merely established a presumption of discrimination, as opposed to those presenting clear evidence of discrimination. Although this distinction benefits employee–plaintiffs, it nevertheless permits employers to engage in discriminatory action as long as they can establish that adverse employment decisions would have been made even in the absence of a discriminatory motive. The Civil Rights Act of 1991 closed the door on that possibility.

The Civil Rights Act of 1991 and Disparate Impact Cases

In Chapter 7 the case of *Griggs v. Duke Power* indicated that the U.S. Supreme Court recognizes what has become known as the *disparate impact case*— where a plaintiff establishes illegal discrimination, not on the basis of intentional discriminatory motives, but on the basis of statistical evidence that an employer practice has an adverse impact on a protected class, and the practice is not job-related. After *Griggs,* but before the 1991 act, there was disagreement about how a disparate impact case should be analyzed and decided. The

U.S. Supreme Court took up the case of *Wards Cove v. Atonio* to settle the matter. However, Congress was not satisfied with the Court's decision in *Wards Cove.*

In the *Wards Cove* case (involving the protected classes of race and national origin) the Supreme Court makes several references to the *Watson v. Fort Worth Bank* case (involving race and sex discrimination). The *Watson* case is presented for discussion in Chapter 8. Note that cases brought under Title VII of the Civil Rights Act are analyzed in a similar manner by the courts, but there are a few differences, depending on the protected class at issue.

Case for Discussion 9-1

WARDS COVE PACKING CO. V. ATONIO, 490 U.S. 642 (1989)[5]

Facts

Title VII of the Civil Rights Act of 1964, 78 Stat. 253, as amended, makes it an unfair employment practice for an employer to discriminate against any individual with respect to hiring or the terms and condition of employment because of the individual's race, color, religion, sex, or national origin; or to limit, segregate, or classify employees in ways that would adversely affect any employee because of the employee's race, color, religion, sex, or national origin. *Griggs v. Duke Power Co.,* 401 U.S. 424, 431 (1971), construed Title VII to proscribe "not only overt discrimination but also practices that are fair in form but discriminatory in practice." Under this basis for liability, which is known as the "disparate impact" theory and which is involved in this case, a facially neutral employment practice may be deemed violative of Title VII without evidence of the employer's subjective intent to discriminate that is required in a "disparate treatment" case. The claims before us are disparate impact claims, involving the employment practices of petitioners, two companies that operate salmon canneries in remote and widely separated areas of Alaska. The canneries operate only during the salmon runs in the summer months. . . . In May or June of each year . . . workers arrive and prepare the equipment and facilities for the canning operation. Most of these workers possess a variety of skills. When salmon runs are about to begin, the workers who will operate the cannery lines arrive, remain as long as there are fish to can, and then depart. . . .

Jobs at the canneries are of two general types: "cannery jobs" . . . which are unskilled positions; and "noncannery jobs," which fall into a variety of classifications. Most noncannery jobs are classified as skilled positions.

Cannery jobs are filled predominantly by nonwhites. . . . Noncannery jobs are filled with predominantly white workers, who are hired during the winter months from the companies' offices in Washington and Oregon. Virtually all of the noncannery jobs pay more than cannery positions. The predominantly white noncannery workers and the predominantly nonwhite cannery employees live in separate dormitories and eat in separate mess halls.

In 1974 respondents, a class of nonwhite cannery workers who were (or had been) employed at the canneries, brought this Title VII action against petitioners. Respondents alleged that a variety of petitioners' hiring/promotion practices—e.g., nepotism, a rehire preference, a lack of objective hiring criteria, separate hiring channels, a practice of not promoting from within—were responsible for the racial stratification of the workforce and had denied them and other nonwhites employment as noncannery workers on the basis of race. Respondents also complained of petitioners' racially segregated housing and dining facilities. . . .

The district court . . . rejected all of respondents' disparate treatment claims. It also rejected the disparate impact challenges involving the subjective employment criteria . . . on the ground that those criteria were not subject to attack under a disparate impact theory. Petitioners' "objective" employment practices . . . were rejected for failure of proof.

The court of appeals agreed to hear the case . . . to settle an intracircuit conflict over the question whether subjective hiring practices could be analyzed under a disparate impact model; the court of appeals held—as this Court . . . ruled in *Watson v. Fort Worth Bank & Trust,* 487 U.S. 977(1988)—that disparate impact analysis could be applied to subjective hiring practices. The Ninth Circuit also concluded that in such a case, "[o]nce the plaintiff class has shown disparate impact caused by specific, identifiable employment practices or criteria, the burden shifts to the employer" to "prove the business necessity" of the challenged practice. . . .

***

Statistical analysis in disparate impact cases:

[T]he comparison between the racial composition of the cannery workforce and that of the noncannery workforce . . . was flawed for several reasons. Most obviously, with respect to the skilled noncannery jobs at issue here, the cannery workforce in no way reflected "the pool of *qualified* job applicants" or the "*qualified* population in the labor force." Measuring alleged discrimination in the selection of accountants, managers, boat captains, electricians, doctors, and engineers—and the long list of other "skilled" noncannery positions found to exist by the district court—by comparing the number of nonwhites occupying these jobs to the number of nonwhites filling cannery worker positions is nonsensical. If the absence of minorities holding such skilled positions is due to a dearth of qualified nonwhite applicants (for reasons that are not petitioners' fault), petitioners' selection methods or employment practices cannot be said to have had a "disparate impact" on nonwhites.

***

Since the statistical disparity relied on by the court of appeals did not suffice to make out a prima facie case, any inquiry by us into whether the specific challenged employment practices of petitioners caused that disparity is pretermitted, as is any inquiry into whether the disparate impact that any employment practice may have had was justified by business considerations. Disparate impact causation and justification:

. . . The law in this respect was correctly stated by Justice O'Connor's opinion last term in *Watson v. Fort Worth Bank & Trust:*

> [W]e note that the plaintiff's burden in establishing a prima facie case goes beyond the need to show that there are statistical disparities in the employer's workforce. The plaintiff must begin by identifying the specific employment practice that is challenged. . . . Especially in cases where an employer combines subjective criteria with the use of more rigid standardized rules or tests, the plaintiff is in our view responsible for isolating and identifying the specific employment practices that are allegedly responsible for any observed statistical disparities. . . .

Here respondents have alleged that several "objective" employment practices (e.g., nepotism, separate hiring channels, rehire preferences), as well as the use of "subjective decision making" to select noncannery workers, have had a disparate impact on nonwhites. . . . Respondents will . . . have to demonstrate that the disparity they complain of is the result of one or more of the employment practices that they are attacking here, specifically showing that each challenged practice has a significantly disparate impact on employment opportunities for whites and nonwhites. . . .

***

Decision

Consequently, on remand, the courts below are instructed to require, as part of respondents' prima facie case, a demonstration that specific elements of the petitioners' hiring process have a significantly disparate impact on nonwhites.

Dissent

JUSTICE BLACKMUN, joined by JUSTICE BRENNAN and JUSTICE MARSHALL

. . . Today a bare majority of the Court takes three major strides backward in the battle against race discrimination. It reaches out to make last term's plurality opinion in *Watson v. Fort Worth Bank & Trust* the law, thereby upsetting the longstanding distribution of burdens of proof in Title VII disparate impact cases. It bars the use of internal workforce comparisons in the making of a prima facie case of discrimination, even where the structure of the industry in question renders any other statistical comparison meaningless. . . .

Dissent

JUSTICE STEVENS, joined by JUSTICE BRENNAN, JUSTICE MARSHALL, and JUSTICE BLACKMUN

The majority's opinion begins with recognition of the settled rule that "a facially neutral employment practice may be deemed violative of Title VII without evidence of the employer's subjective intent to discriminate that is required in a 'disparate treatment' case." It then departs from the body of law engendered by this disparate impact theory, reformulating the order of proof and the weight of the parties' burdens. Why the Court undertakes these unwise changes . . . is a mystery to me.

Questions for Discussion

1. In the *Watkins v. Fort Worth Bank & Trust* case the U.S. Supreme Court stated that a disparate impact analysis can be applied in situations involving only subjective employment criteria. In other words, objective criteria such as the requirement of a high school diploma and passing of a particular aptitude test (such as that in *Griggs v. Duke Power*) are not a necessary element of a disparate impact claim. For example, the *Watkins* plaintiff could argue that personal interviews conducted by all-white personnel with no proper training caused a disparate impact on black applicants. The plaintiff could use this information to statistically link this practice with the percentage of qualified blacks who applied for positions and the percentage of blacks in the employer's workplace to prove discrimination (even though there may be no *intent* to discriminate). How difficult would it be for the plaintiffs in *Wards Cove* to link the stated practices to the disparate impact?

2. Compare the *Watkins* facts with the *Wards Cove* facts. In light of *Watkins,* was *Wards Cove* accurately decided? What would the plaintiffs in *Wards Cove* have to put in evidence to win a disparate impact case?

3. In the dissenting opinion, the judge pointed out that precedent required employers in disparate impact cases to demonstrate that the practice in question was "essential" for a good business necessity justification. What practices did the plaintiffs in *Wards Cove* single out as having a disparate impact? Which of these could the employer justify on business necessity grounds? How essential were those practices? What could the employer do to make it more likely that nonwhite candidates would eventually work in the better-paying noncannery positions?

How the Civil Rights Act of 1991 Changes the Disparate Impact Case

After *Wards Cove,* Congress changed the law by adding the following sections:

An unlawful employment practice based on disparate impact is established under this title only if—

- A complaining party demonstrates that a respondent uses a particular employment practice that causes a disparate impact on the basis of race, color, religion, sex, or national origin and the respondent fails to demonstrate that the challenged practice is job related for the position in question and consistent with business necessity; or

- The complaining party makes the demonstration . . . with respect to an alternative employment practice and the respondent refuses to adopt such alternative employment practice.

With respect to demonstrating that a particular employment practice causes a disparate impact . . . , the complaining party shall demonstrate that each particular challenged employment practice causes a disparate impact, *except that if the complaining party can demonstrate to the court that the elements of a respondent's decision-making process are not capable of separation for analysis, the decision-making process may be analyzed as one employment practice.*[6] [Emphasis added.]

After *Watkins, Wards Cove,* and the Civil Rights Act of 1991, what should employers do to avoid challenges to their practices with regard to the number of minorities in their workforce?

Management **Perspective**

amicus curiae brief
A document (also known as a "friend of the court" brief) filed by a nonparty who has an interest in a case. It supports one of the parties in the case.

Using subjective criteria in employment decision making can pose problems when trying to establish the employer's rationale for denying a promotion, failing to hire, or terminating an employee. At the same time, subjective decision making is often a valid basis for making these decisions. If employers could validate the subjective criteria, as they can the objective criteria, employers might be in a better defensive position when charged with illegal discrimination.

The American Psychological Association filed an **amicus curiae brief** in the *Watson v. Fort Worth Bank & Trust* case and indicated, among other things, that "subjective systems can be validated by procedures generally accepted by the scientific community"[7]. In a recent paper, "Disparate Impact and Subjective Human Resource Decision Systems: *Watson v. Fort Worth Bank*"[8], Dr. Becker drew from the APA's brief and made the case that selection procedures based on subjective practices, such as interviews and supervisor ratings, can be measured for validity and reliability just like objective criteria such as IQ and diploma requirements.

The validation and reliability of interviewing and/or rating candidates or employees rests on the question of whether the evaluator (the interviewer or supervisor) is biased by irrelevant factors or characteristics of the person at issue[9]. "Selection procedures or devices are validated for a particular job when they have been demonstrated scientifically to make reliable and meaningful distinctions between individuals on the basis of their ability to perform particular tasks with competence or to function successfully in a particular job"[10]. Interview questions must be linked to job analysis and performance criterion data[11]. The validity of interviewers themselves must also be established[12]. This can be accomplished through the use of a structured interview guide and interviewer training, and the training should be done with applicants of a different gender and race than the interviewer[13]. "Biases to which interviews are typically subject include the 'halo effect,' stereotyping, and the 'similar to me' phenomenon"[14]. The paper also includes analysis of rating practices and how those subjective processes can be validated.

(Continued)

Dr. Becker concludes her paper with a checklist for human resource managers, titled "Protocol for the Defense of Subjective Assessment Systems." The first of these protocols is as follows:

I. General Criteria for the Defense of Subjective Assessment Systems
   A. Was the subjective assessment system used by the employer for personnel decisions, validated?
   B. Was each of the subjective assessment devices used, validated?
      1. Do the assessment devices used reflect a representative sample of job performance or job-required knowledge?
      2. Are the assessment devices used predictive of job performance?
      3. Do the assessment devices used identify personal or behavioral characteristics significantly correlated with successful job performance?
   C. Was a job analysis conducted for the position for which applicants will be hired and/or to which applicants will be promoted?
   D. Were the knowledge, skills, and abilities required for satisfactory performance in the job identified through job analysis?
   E. Even if local validation studies of the subjective assessment devices used by the employer were not conducted for cost reasons, were subjective assessment devices used that had been validated for similar jobs?
   F. Was an assessment skills center used to evaluate the ability of the candidate to perform managerial work?[15]

The Civil Rights Act of 1991 and Expatriate Employees

The question of whether the Civil Rights Act of 1964 prohibits U.S. companies from discriminating against employees who work for them in foreign countries was addressed by the 1991 U.S. Supreme Court in *EEOC v. Arabian American Oil Co.*[16]. Section 702 of the Civil Rights Act, Title VII, known as the alien exemption clause[17], states that Title VII "shall not apply to an employer with respect to the employment of aliens outside any State." This clause, however, has been the subject of differing interpretations. Does the provision support an inference that Title VII is to be given no extraterritorial effect outside the country—even to Americans working abroad for American companies? After looking at Title VII's language, the Court decided that Congress had not clearly provided for overseas enforcement. As a direct result of this conclusion by the Supreme Court, Congress amended the Civil Rights Act in 1991 to specifically extend the application of Title VII beyond U.S. borders by changing the definition of *employee* as follows:

> *Definition of Employee.* The Civil Rights Act of 1964 and the Americans with Disabilities Act of 1990 are each amended by adding at the end the following: "With respect to employment in a foreign country, such term includes an individual who is a citizen of the United States"[18]. This amendment was necessary to clarify whether these laws protected U.S. citizens working abroad for U.S. companies.

The Civil Rights Act of 1991: Expanded Remedies and the Right to Jury Trial

Before the passage of the Civil Rights Act of 1991, plaintiffs were restricted to equitable damages—that is, reinstatement, injunctive relief, and so on. In other words, they could not obtain money damages in compensation for the harm done. In a big boost to plaintiff–employees who face workplace discrimination, Congress in 1991 provided that the complaining party in a disparate treatment case may recover compensatory and punitive damages as well as the other forms of relief provided by the act. Moreover, plaintiffs can now request that a case be tried before a jury—a major benefit to employees. The damage awards are, however, limited, as indicated in the following section of the law:

> *Limitations.* The sum of the amount of compensatory damages awarded under this section for future pecuniary losses, emotional pain, suffering, inconvenience, mental anguish, loss of enjoyment of life, and other nonpecuniary losses, and the amount of punitive damages awarded under this section, shall not exceed, for each complaining party—
>
> (A) in the case of a respondent who has more than 14 and fewer than 101 employees in each of 20 or more calendar weeks in the current or preceding calendar year, $50,000;
>
> (B) in the case of a respondent who has more than 100 and fewer than 201 employees in each of 20 or more calendar weeks in the current or preceding calendar year, $100,000; and
>
> (C) in the case of a respondent who has more than 200 and fewer than 501 employees in each of 20 or more calendar weeks in the current or preceding calendar year, $200,000; and
>
> (D) in the case of a respondent who has more than 500 employees in each of 20 or more calendar weeks in the current or preceding calendar year, $300,000[19].

The Civil Rights Act of 1991: The Glass Ceiling Act

The Glass Ceiling Act is part of the Civil Rights Act of 1991 amending the Civil Rights Act of 1964. The purposes of the Glass Ceiling Act are as follows:

SEC. 202. FINDINGS AND PURPOSE.

(a) FINDINGS: Congress finds that—
(1) despite a dramatically growing presence in the workplace, women and minorities remain underrepresented in management and decision-making positions in business;
(2) artificial barriers exist to the advancement of women and minorities in the workplace;
(3) United States corporations are increasingly relying on women and minorities to meet employment requirements and are increasingly aware of the advantages derived from a diverse workforce;

(4) the "Glass Ceiling Initiative" undertaken by the Department of Labor, including the release of the report titled "Report on the Glass Ceiling Initiative," has been instrumental in raising public awareness of—
  (A) the underrepresentation of women and minorities at the management and decision-making levels in the United States workforce;
  (B) the underrepresentation of women and minorities in line functions in the United States workforce;
  (C) the lack of access for qualified women and minorities to credential-building developmental opportunities; and
  (D) the desirability of eliminating artificial barriers to the advancement of women and minorities to such levels;

(5) the establishment of a commission to examine issues raised by the Glass Ceiling Initiative would help—
  (A) focus greater attention on the importance of eliminating artificial barriers to the advancement of women and minorities to management and decision-making positions in business; and
  (B) promote workforce diversity;

(6) a comprehensive study that includes analysis of the manner in which management and decision-making positions are filled, the developmental and skill-enhancing practices used to foster the necessary qualifications for advancement, and the compensation programs and reward structures utilized in the corporate sector would assist in the establishment of practices and policies promoting opportunities for, and eliminating artificial barriers to, the advancement of women and minorities to management and decision making positions; and

(7) a national award recognizing employers whose practices and policies promote opportunities for, and eliminate artificial barriers to, the advancement of women and minorities will foster the advancement of women and minorities into higher-level positions by—
  (A) helping to encourage United States companies to modify practices and policies to promote opportunities for, and eliminate artificial barriers to, the upward mobility of women and minorities; and
  (B) providing specific guidance for other United States employers that wish to learn how to revise practices and policies to improve the access and employment opportunities of women and minorities.

(b) PURPOSE: The purpose of this title is to establish—
  (1) a Glass Ceiling Commission to study—
    (A) the manner in which business fills management and decision-making positions;
    (B) the developmental and skill-enhancing practices used to foster the necessary qualifications for advancement into such positions; and
    (C) the compensation programs and reward structures currently utilized in the workplace; and
  (2) an annual award for excellence in promoting a more diverse skilled workforce at the management and decision-making levels in business.

SEC. 203. ESTABLISHMENT OF GLASS CEILING COMMISSION.

(a) IN GENERAL- There is established a Glass Ceiling Commission (referred to in this title as the "Commission"), to conduct a study and prepare recommendations . . .[20]

Evidence of Women's Progress

The Glass Ceiling Commission conducted its study and disseminated its results. Has progress been made? Some argue that women are still disproportionately absent from the ranks of CEOs and other chief executive positions in U.S. businesses. Statistics support this. However, other studies show marked differences in the extent to which women have improved themselves educationally and the types of positions they pursue compared to decades ago.

Figure 9.1 shows that women have moved away from traditionally female occupations and into fields where they formerly had far fewer numbers. "In 1972,

FIGURE 9.1
Gender No Longer Occupational Destiny

Source: Bureau of Labor Statistics, Current Population Survey, Employment and Earnings

(a) **Women Filling Ranks of Higher-Paying Occupations. . .**			
	Women's share of employment		Percentage point gain
	1972	**2005**	
Accountants	21.7	61.9	40.2
Designers	18.2	55.0	36.8
Pharmacists	12.7	48.3	35.6
Public relations specialists	29.9	61.4	31.5
Psychologists	38.0	67.3	29.3
Advertising agents and sales	22.7	50.2	27.5
Lawyers	4.0	30.2	26.2
Chemists	10.1	35.3	25.2
Biological scientists	25.0	48.7	23.7
Photographers	15.6	39.0	23.4
Postsecondary teachers	22.0	44.4	22.4
Physicians and surgeons	10.1	32.3	22.2
Architects	3.0	24.4	21.4
Dentists	1.9	22.5	20.6
Real estate agents	36.7	57.1	20.4
Clergy	1.6	15.5	13.9
Computer programmers	19.9	28.4	8.5

(b) **. . .and Leaving Those Once Considered "Women's Work"**			
	Women's share of Employment		Percentage point gain
Restaurant servers	91.8	71.8	−20.0
Cooks	62.2	42.3	−19.9
Telephone operators	96.7	78.0	−18.7
Tailors, dressmakers, sewers	92.3	79.3	−13.0
Private household cleaners, servants	97.2	85.9	−11.3
Cashiers	86.6	75.9	−10.7
Models and product promoters	93.8	85.9	−7.9
Laundry and dry-cleaning workers	69.7	62.8	−6.9
Registered nurses	97.6	92.3	−5.3
Receptionists	97.0	92.4	−4.6
Elementary school teachers	85.1	82.2	−2.9
Secretaries	99.1	97.3	−1.8
Typists and word processors	96.1	95.0	−1.1

women accounted for just 1.9 percent of dentists, 3 percent of architects, and 4 percent of lawyers. Three decades later, their shares have risen to 22.5 percent of dentists, 24.4 percent of architects, and 30 percent of lawyers" [21].

In education, women have outnumbered men in receipt of bachelor's degrees, at 57.5 percent of diplomas granted in 2004 in the United States. At the masters level, women rose to 59 percent of degrees granted. Women PhD recipients went from 29 percent in 1950 to 47.7 percent.

"Women have also made great strides in a handful of disciplines that require additional education and lead to high-paying and prestigious occupations. They earn three-quarters of veterinary medicine degrees and two-thirds of pharmacy degrees. Women make up nearly half the graduates in law and medicine, and they're receiving more than 40 percent of the MBAs and dentistry degrees. In the early 1970s, women accounted for less than 20 percent of the pharmacy graduates and less than 10 percent of the graduates in the other fields" [22].

THE PREGNANCY DISCRIMINATION ACT OF 1978

Fourteen years after Congress prohibited discrimination in the workplace on the basis of sex, it clarified the meaning of those words by amending the Civil Rights Act of 1964 as follows:

> Section 701 of the Civil Rights Act of 1964 is amended by adding at the end thereof the following new subsection:
>
> "(k) The terms 'because of sex' or 'on the basis of sex' include, but are not limited to, because of or on the basis of pregnancy, childbirth, or related medical conditions; and women affected by pregnancy, childbirth, or related medical conditions shall be treated the same for all employment-related purposes, including receipt of benefits under fringe benefit programs, as other persons not so affected but similar in their ability or inability to work, and nothing in section 703(h) of this title shall be interpreted to permit otherwise. This subsection shall not require an employer to pay for health insurance benefits for abortion, except where the life of the mother would be endangered if the fetus were carried to term, or except where medical complications have arisen from an abortion: provided, that nothing herein shall preclude an employer from providing abortion benefits or otherwise affect bargaining agreements in regard to abortion." [23]

It would be another 15 years before Congress passed a major piece of legislation to further recognize the particular needs of working women—the Family and Medical Leave Act of 1993.

Statistics on Pregnancy Discrimination Charges: EEOC

In fiscal year 2006 the EEOC received 4,901 charges of pregnancy-based discrimination. The EEOC resolved 4,629 pregnancy discrimination charges in FY 2006 and recovered $10.4 million in monetary benefits for

FIGURE 9.2   U.S. EEOC and FEPA Pregnancy Discrimination Charges: Fiscal Year 1997 through Fiscal Year 2006

	FY 1997	FY 1998	FY 1999	FY 2000	FY 2001	FY 2002	FY 2003	FY 2004	FY 2005	FY 2006
Receipts	3,977	4,219	4,166	4,160	4,287	4,714	4,649	4,887	4,730	4,901
Resolutions	4,595	4,467	4,343	4,480	4,280	4,778	4,847	4,877	4,625	4,629
Resolutions by Type										
Settlements	395	424	505	602	518	607	685	756	656	650
	8.6%	9.5%	11.6%	13.4%	12.1%	12.7%	14.1%	15.5%	14.2%	14.0%
Withdrawals with Benefits	379	328	359	322	327	408	429	420	413	426
	8.2%	7.3%	8.3%	7.2%	7.6%	8.5%	8.9%	8.6%	8.9%	9.2%
Administrative Closures	1,110	1,027	902	824	764	846	901	787	765	790
	24.2%	23.0%	20.8%	18.4%	17.9%	17.7%	18.6%	16.1%	16.5%	17.1%
No Reasonable Cause	2,432	2,534	2,389	2,452	2,373	2,634	2,629	2,723	2,570	2,574
	52.9%	56.7%	55.0%	54.7%	55.4%	55.1%	54.2%	55.8%	55.6%	55.6%
Reasonable Cause	279	154	188	280	298	283	203	191	221	189
	6.1%	3.4%	4.3%	6.3%	7.0%	5.9%	4.2%	3.9%	4.8%	4.1%
Successful Conciliations	71	66	81	110	123	126	75	87	92	74
	1.5%	1.5%	1.9%	2.5%	2.9%	2.6%	1.5%	1.8%	2.0%	1.6%
Unsuccessful Conciliations	208	88	107	170	175	157	128	104	129	115
	4.5%	2.0%	2.5%	3.8%	4.1%	3.3%	2.6%	2.1%	2.8%	2.5%
Merit Resolutions	1,053	906	1,052	1,204	1,143	1,298	1,317	1,367	1,290	1,265
	22.9%	20.3%	24.2%	26.9%	26.7%	27.2%	27.2%	28.0%	27.9%	27.3%
Monetary Benefits (Millions)*	$5.6	$5.3	$6.7	$20.6	$7.5	$10.0	$12.4	$11.7	$11.8	$10.4

*Does not include monetary benefits obtained through litigation.

   This chart represents the total number of charge receipts filed and resolved under Title VII alleging pregnancy discrimination as an issue. The data in the pregnancy discrimination table reflect charges filed with EEOC and state and local Fair Employment Practices Agencies (FEPAs) around the country that have a work-sharing agreement with the commission.

   The EEOC's total workload includes charges carried over from previous fiscal years, new charge receipts, and charges transferred to the EEOC from FEPAs. Resolution of charges each year may therefore exceed receipts for that year because the workload being resolved is drawn from a combination of pending cases, new receipts, and FEPA transfer charges. The total of individual percentages may not always sum to 100 percent due to rounding.

   The data are compiled by the Office of Research, Information, and Planning from the EEOC's national database.

This page was last modified on January 31, 2007.

charging parties and other aggrieved individuals, not including monetary benefits obtained through litigation. (See the EEOC Web site at www. EEOC.gov.)

   Figure 9.2[24] shows the number of pregnancy discrimination charges filed, conciliated, and otherwise resolved from the years 1997 to 2006.

The EEOC Takes Pregnancy Discrimination Seriously

The EEOC posted on its Web site the following article titled "Expecting Mother Forced to Choose between Parenthood and Livelihood, Suit Says"[25]. The case is *EEOC v. John Harvard's Brew House,* Civil Action No.03- CV-3800, U.S. District Court for Eastern District of New York (2003).

> The U.S. Equal Employment Opportunity Commission (EEOC) filed a pregnancy discrimination lawsuit in federal district court against John Harvard's Brew House, a restaurant and brewery business operating in nine states with a local branch in Lake Grove, Long Island.
>
> The EEOC's suit charged that John Harvard's Brew House discriminated against Jennifer James once she informed its management that she was pregnant. Ms. James' career had advanced rapidly from a starting position of server, to supervisor, and to manager-in-training. However, as soon as she informed the company of her pregnancy, her career abruptly ended. She was told to "consider her options." When she insisted on continuing with her pregnancy, her management training was discontinued and she was ultimately terminated from her employment in August 2001.
>
> EEOC filed the lawsuit after its efforts to voluntarily conciliate the matter without litigation proved futile. The suit seeks monetary relief, an order requiring the company to implement policies and procedures against discrimination, and a permanent injunction against discrimination.
>
> "The EEOC takes very seriously allegations of pregnancy discrimination," said Katherine Bissell, the EEOC's regional attorney in New York. "No employee should ever be forced to choose between parenthood and a livelihood. The EEOC will continue to vigorously pursue such cases."
>
> Spencer H. Lewis, EEOC's New York district director, added, "Employers should be aware that they cannot discriminate based on pregnancy or sex. Employment decisions motivated by sex-based stereotypes cannot be sanctioned."

Case for Discussion 9-2

CALIFORNIA FEDERAL SAVINGS & LOAN ASSN. ET AL. V. GUERRA, DIRECTOR, DEPARTMENT OF FAIR EMPLOYMENT AND HOUSING, ET AL., 479 U.S. 272 (1987)[26]

A California statute required the reinstatement of women who had taken a reasonable pregnancy disability leave. The law was challenged by various employers and organizations, claiming that Title VII of the Civil Rights Act of 1964, as amended by the Pregnancy Discrimination Act of 1978, preempted the state statute.

Under the U.S. Constitution, federal laws are "supreme" under the Supremacy Clause. That is, they trump any state laws that conflict with the federal law. This principle undergirds the Guerra case.

Facts

California's Fair Employment and Housing Act (FEHA) is a comprehensive statute that prohibits discrimination in employment and housing. In September 1978 California amended the FEHA to proscribe certain forms of employment discrimination on the basis of pregnancy. It requires employers to provide female employees an unpaid pregnancy disability leave of up to four months. Respondent Fair Employment and Housing Commission, the state agency authorized to interpret the FEHA, has construed the law to require California employers to reinstate an employee returning from such pregnancy leave to the job she previously held, unless it is no longer available due to business necessity. In the latter case, the employer must make a reasonable, good-faith effort to place the employee in a substantially similar job. The statute does not compel employers to provide paid leave to pregnant employees. Accordingly, the only benefit pregnant workers actually derive is a qualified right to reinstatement.

***

Lillian Garland was employed by Cal Fed as a receptionist for several years. In January 1982 she took a pregnancy disability leave. When she was able to return to work in April of that year, Garland notified Cal Fed but was informed that her job had been filled and that there were no receptionist or similar positions available. Garland filed a complaint with respondent Department of Fair Employment and Housing, which issued an administrative accusation against Cal Fed on her behalf. Respondent charged Cal Fed with violating FEHA. Prior to the scheduled hearing before respondent Fair Employment and Housing Commission, Cal Fed, joined by petitioners Merchants and Manufacturers Association and the California Chamber of Commerce, brought this action in the United States District Court for the Central District of California. They sought a declaration that [the law] is inconsistent with and preempted by Title VII and an injunction against enforcement of the section. The district court granted petitioners' motion for summary judgment. Citing *Newport News Shipbuilding & Dry Dock Co. v. EEOC,* 462 U.S. 669 (1983), the court stated that "California employers who comply with state law are subject to reverse discrimination suits under Title VII brought by temporarily disabled males who do not receive the same treatment as female employees disabled by pregnancy. . . ." On this basis, the district court held that "California state law and the policies of interpretation and enforcement . . . which require preferential treatment of female employees disabled by pregnancy, childbirth, or related medical conditions are preempted by Title VII and are null, void, invalid, and inoperative under the Supremacy Clause of the United States Constitution."

***

Decision of Court of Appeals

The court held that in enacting the PDA Congress intended "to construct a floor beneath which pregnancy disability benefits may not drop—not a ceiling above which they may not rise." Because it found that the California statute furthers the goal of equal employment opportunity for women, the court of appeals concluded, "Title VII does not preempt a state law that guarantees pregnant women a certain number of pregnancy disability leave days, because this is neither inconsistent with, nor unlawful under, Title VII."

Decision of Supreme Court

The Court affirmed the court of appeals and upheld the California statute. The California law is not preempted by the federal Pregnancy Discrimination Act.

Question for Discussion

The decision in this case concerned California state law that gives pregnant women greater rights than are provided by federal law with regard to pregnancy discrimination. This case was tried and decided before Congress passed the Family and Medical Leave Act. What are the implications of this decision for state laws that mandate paid or unpaid leave for illness, childbirth, or related reasons?

Global **Perspective**   **Attitudinal Factors That Contribute to a Glass Ceiling**

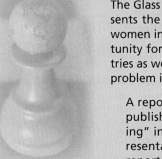

The Glass Ceiling Act passed by Congress in the Civil Rights Act of 1991 represents the determination of the United States to improve opportunities for women in the higher ranks of corporate America. Advocates for equal opportunity for women in senior positions have taken up the issue in other countries as well. The following excerpt lists some possible attitudinal roots of the problem in Ireland[27]:

> A report by the Irish Business and Employers Confederation (IBEC), published in March 2002, concluded that there existed a "glass ceiling" in Ireland's workplaces, evidenced by a low level of female representation in senior management positions. This "glass ceiling," the report argued, is created by a number of structural and attitudinal barriers. The attitudinal factors contributing to a "glass ceiling" include the following:
>
> - Characteristics considered to be "masculine" (for example, being forceful, aggressive, independent, objective, or competitive) are generally regarded as traits required for management, rather than so-called feminine characteristics (such as being cooperative, flexible, subjective, intuitive, or emotional), which can be viewed as ineffective management traits.
> - Women's tendency to move into support or nonstrategic functions such as human resources and administration at junior management levels rather than into line management functions that lead to more senior positions.

- Perceptions of the social and occupational roles of men and women influence appointment and promotional decisions.
- The perceived risk of placing women in nontraditional roles.
- Occupational socialization, whereby applicants themselves frequently prepare and apply for jobs along gender lines; that is, women may limit their applications to what are perceived as "female" type positions.
- Women "select themselves out" of some training initiatives and promotional opportunities because of family commitments.
- Women do not promote themselves.

Summary

The Civil Rights Act of 1991 was passed, in part, to counteract the effects of court decisions that Congress believed were misinterpretations of the objectives of the Civil Rights Act of 1964—specifically the mixed motive case of *Hopkins v. Price Waterhouse* and the disparate impact case of *Wards Cove v. Atonio*. In addition, Congress included the Glass Ceiling Act in this 1991 legislation.

Other major provisions of the 1991 act were these:

- Judicial remedies: The act expanded the judicial remedies available to plaintiffs. Whereas the Civil Rights Act of 1964 allowed only equitable remedies such as injunctions and reinstatement of the employee, the 1991 act allowed recovery for compensatory damages and, more significantly, punitive damages in egregious cases. Congress, however, set limits on these remedies.
- Jury trial: Perhaps more damaging to employers was the provision allowing jury trials in discrimination cases.
- Application to expatriates: The 1991 act clarified that these laws apply to American citizens working abroad for U.S. companies.

The Pregnancy Discrimination Act of 1978 made it explicit that the terms *because of sex* or *on the basis of sex* include pregnancy, childbirth, and other related medical conditions and that women so affected must be treated the same as other employees.

Questions

1. Gwen J. was employed by the Atlantic City Hilton Casino when she became pregnant. On the advice of her doctor she requested leave beginning October 5, 1997. Later she requested an extension of the leave through February 1998. Both requests were approved. Hilton's policy was to grant medical leaves of absence for no more than 26 weeks total within a 12-month period. Because of medical complications, Gwen's doctor had her request an extension of leave for the duration of the pregnancy. Hilton

221

informed Gwen that her maximum leave would be reached on April 1, 1998, and if she did not return to work after that date, her employment would be terminated. When Gwen was fired for not returning to work on April 2, she sued Hilton for gender discrimination in violation of state law (NJ Law against Discrimination), wrongful termination in violation of public policy, and intentional infliction of emotional distress. The trial court found Hilton's leave policy to be per se discriminatory because pregnancy and its complications are unique to women. Hilton appealed.

a. Analyze this case and make a decision. What is the rationale for your decision?

b. How much leave is Gwen entitled to when you consider FMLA and NJ family leave law together?

2. Paula A. was employed from December 22, 1981, until December 6, 1982, as a nurse's assistant at Grandview Care Center's nursing home. She learned she was pregnant in the fall of 1982. Because of pregnancy complications she had to stay home from work on a few occasions. In a previous pregnancy she had experienced a premature birth and the death of her child. Grandview's policy for leaves allowed three months of unpaid leave for maternity leave, and unpaid leave of absence for illness with no limitation of time if the leave request was the result of a doctor's recommendation and the employer approved it. On November 30, after taking a one-week sick leave on the advice of her doctor, Paula made a written request for a six-month leave. She was told the company policy limited maternity leave to three months. Paula's pregnancy-related illness caused her to miss the next three days of work. On December 6 she was told to resign or be fired for having violated company policy stating that an employee could be fired for failing to report to work for three days without calling in. Although standard policy was to act on leave requests the day after receipt of the request, Paula's request was not acted upon. Paula resigned and filed a charge of sex discrimination with the EEOC. Suit was filed against Grandview. The trial court held for Paula and ordered reinstatement. Grandview reinstated Paula on June 14, 1985, and appealed the decision.

a. How should the appellate court decide the case? Explain your reasoning.

b. Why did Paula not sue under the Pregnancy Discrimination Act?

c. How could this action have been prevented?

3. Cynthia E. began working for Oshkosh B'Gosh, a manufacturer of children's clothing, in October 1992. In the employee handbook, which Cynthia acknowledged she received, the absenteeism policy is explained. Points (one per hour) are given due to tardiness, absence, and "leaving early." If an employee is out sick for four consecutive days, it is considered one "occurrence" for which eight points are assessed. Employees who miss no days in any 12-month period are rewarded with eight points. FMLA leave and

other stated exceptions are not counted in the points system. When an employee reaches more than 80 points within any 12-month period, he or she may be terminated. A process is in place to notify and counsel an employee when certain point levels are reached: 30 points, 45 points, 70 points, and 80 points. Cynthia reached 30 points at the end of April 1993, 45 points at the end of May 1993, 60 points on July 27, 1993, and 70 by the end of November 1993. In December 1993, and January 1994, Cynthia accumulated 12.5 points for absenteeism. She had received the requisite notifications and counseling along the way as prescribed in the handbook and was fired on January 12, 1994, for excessive absenteeism. She challenged the discharge as a violation of FMLA.

a. What must Cynthia prove to prevail in this case?

b. State the pros and cons of the employer's absenteeism policy.

4. In 1983 Ariana H. accepted a position with Pantzer Management Company as assistant controller. Martin F. was hired in 1985 as controller. When the owner of the company first interviewed Ariana, he asked whether she had plans to marry and have children within five years of being married. He had asked other female job candidates the same question. When Ariana announced her engagement to marry in 1984, the owner asked her to polish some silver for him for the practice. (He denied saying this.) Ariana received favorable performance reviews and bonuses several times along with words of praise for her competence, patience, and fairness in dealing with others. Some time later Martin F. had to fill a staff position and remarked that he wanted to hire a male for that position, that they really would not consider a female at that time . . . that the biological clock was ticking to have children. This issue was discussed at an executive meeting, and all but Ariana agreed with Martin. In January 1987 Ariana told Martin and others that she was pregnant and that she planned to take at least three months' maternity leave. They expressed happiness for her and assured her that her job would be waiting for her. Ariana gave birth on July 26, 1987. While on leave, she received a memo stating that on August 12 another employee had been promoted to her position. She immediately called and was told by Martin that they felt the need to promote this person. She called a week later and discovered that her desk had been taken over with access to all her personal belongings. She met with Martin and the owner in October and was told that she would retain her title. However, her new job, working on special projects, would take little time and was "practically nothing" compared to her former responsibilities. When Ariana returned, things went from bad to worse. She felt that others had a bad attitude toward her, and Martin felt that she was the one with the bad attitude. Ariana and Martin had a heated verbal exchange that led to her discharge.

Pantzer's policy on maternity leave was to grant 28 days with pay and an indefinite length of time for unpaid leave. However, the employee had to specify the date of return. For sick leave, there was no corresponding requirement to specify the time of return to work. Four employees had taken sick leave, one for months, and all four were returned to the same positions at work.

a. What is the likely outcome of the case?

b. If Ariana wins the case, will she be awarded punitive damages?

c. On what basis would a court award punitive damages?

References

1. *Sandra Day O'Connor Quotes* from www.womenshistory.about.com/od/quotes/a/s/_d_oconnor.htm (accessed March 5, 2008).

2. *Hopkins v. Price Waterhouse,* 109 S. Ct. 1775 (1989).

3. 42 U.S.C. 2000e, Sec. 703(m).

4. 42 U.S.C. 2000e, Sec. 706(g).

5. *Wards* Cove *Packing Co. v. Atonio,* 490 U.S. 642 (1989).

6. 42 U.S.C. 2000e, Sec. 703(k)(1)(A).

7. APA Amicus Brief at p. 6 and n. 1.

8. P. Alexander, "Disparate Impact and Subjective Human Resource Decision Systems: *Watson v. Fort Worth Bank*" (unpublished manuscript).

9. Id. at p. 11.

10. APA Amicus Brief at p. 11 and n. 15, and Becker at p. 11.

11. APA Amicus Brief at p. 14 and n. 24, and Becker at p. 14.

12. APA Amicus Brief at p. 15, and Becker at p. 15.

13. Ibid.

14. APA Amicus Brief at p. 14, and Becker at p. 13.

15. Becker at pp. 20–21.

16. *EEOC v. Arabian American Oil Co. et al.,* 499 U.S. 244, 111 S. Ct. 1227, 113 L.Ed.2d 274 (1991).

17. 42 U.S.C. 2000e-1.

18. Public Law 102-166—Nov. 21, 1991, 102d Congress, Sec. 109.

19. Public Law 102-166—Nov. 21, 1991, 102d Congress, Sec. 102.

20. Public Law 102-166—Nov. 21, 1991, 102d Congress, Title II, Sec. 202.

21. W. M. Cox and R. Alm, "Women at Work: A Progress Report"*Economic Letter—Insights from the Federal Reserve Bank of Dallas* 2, no. 5 (May 2007). See also www.dallasfed.org.

22. Ibid.

23. 42 U.S.C. 2000e, Sec. 701(k).

24. See www.eeoc.gov/stats/pregnanc.html (accessed July 25, 2007).

25. *EEOC v. John Harvard's Brew House,* Civil Action No.03- CV-3800, U.S. District Court for Eastern District of New York (2003). See also www.eeoc.gov/press/8-06-03.html (accessed July 25, 2007).

26. *California Federal Savings & Loan Assn. et al. v. Guerra, Director, Department of Fair Employment and Housing, et al.,* 479 U.S. 272 (1987).

27. "Report Finds 'Glass Ceiling' Obstructs Women in Management." See http://eurofound.europa.eu/eiro/2002/04/feature/ie0204204f.htm (accessed March 30, 2008).

Chapter Ten

Sex Discrimination, the Equal Pay Act, and the Civil Rights Act

There are Kingdoms in which the heart should reign supreme. That kingdom belongs to woman. . . . I would not, and I say it deliberately, degrade woman by giving her the right of suffrage. I mean the word in its full signification, because I believe that woman as she is to-day, the queen of home and of hearts, is above the political collisions of this world, and should always be kept above them.

Senator Henry W. Blair during the
congressional debate on woman suffrage in 1886[1]

INTRODUCTION

Times have changed dramatically since the chapter-opening sentiments were expressed. Women have been not only allowed to vote but also to work in all occupations, many of which were formerly the exclusive province of men. Although the legal barriers have come down, stereotyping continues to linger. As discussed in previous chapters, in 1964 Congress passed the Civil Rights Act.

Laws prohibiting sex discrimination in the workplace protect women from ingrained cultural biases that limit their ability to obtain and retain positions at pay scales equivalent to those enjoyed by men, and help them break through the "glass ceiling" to rise to top levels of management. Five major federal statutory laws help level the playing field for women in the workplace: the Equal Pay Act of 1963 (an amendment to the Fair Labor Standards Act), Title VII of the Civil Rights Act of 1964, the Pregnancy Discrimination Act of 1978 (an amendment to the Civil Rights Act of 1964), the Civil Rights Act of 1991 (an amendment to the Civil Rights Act that includes the Glass Ceiling Act), and the Family and Medical Leave Act of 1993.

The Civil Rights Act of 1991, the Glass Ceiling Act, and the Pregnancy Discrimination Act have been discussed in Chapter 9. This chapter describes the Civil Rights Act of 1964 and the Equal Pay Act of 1963. The Family and Medical Leave Act of 1993 will be the subject of Chapter 15, along with comparisons of the FMLA with state workers' compensation laws and the Americans with Disabilities Act.

UNINTENDED CONSEQUENCES

Although the objectives of most laws are fairly clear, what is less clear is how to interpret statutory language in situations not envisioned by the writers and supporters of those laws. Many complex issues have arisen under the umbrella of sex discrimination. As is the case with most legislation, there have been a number of unintended consequences and questions for interpretation. For example, is it a violation of the Civil Rights Act when a female supervisor discriminates against a male? When a male supervisor discriminates against a male employee who happens to be gay? When a supervisor discriminates against a male employee who has a sex change operation and is now a woman? These are just a few of many unforeseen issues that have arisen under these laws.

THE EQUAL PAY ACT OF 1963

The Equal Pay Act of 1963 (EPA) is an amendment to the Fair Labor Standards Act of 1938 (FLSA). The FLSA established minimum wages and time and a half for overtime, among other things. The crucial language of the EPA is as follows[2]:

> SEC. 206. *[Section 6]*
>
> (d) (1) No employer having employees subject to any provisions of this section shall discriminate, within any establishment in which such employees are employed, between employees on the basis of sex by paying wages to employees in such establishment at a rate less than the rate at which he pays wages to employees of the opposite sex in such establishment for equal work on jobs the performance of which requires equal skill, effort, and responsibility, and which are performed under similar working conditions, except where such payment is made pursuant to (i) a seniority system; (ii) a merit system; (iii) a system which measures earnings by quantity or quality of production; or (iv) a differential based on any other factor other than sex: *Provided,* That an employer who is paying a wage rate differential in violation of this subsection shall not, in order to comply with the provisions of this subsection, reduce the wage rate of any employee.

The EPA, however, has had limited success in raising pay for most women in the workforce because the only beneficiaries of this law have been women who work alongside men, doing the same jobs in the same company. For women working in careers dominated by females—often in jobs with traditionally lower pay, such as administrative assistants, clerical workers, nurses, or elementary school teachers—the law has had no impact. For example, a secretary doing high-level administrative work for ABC Company might be paid less than a custodial engineer working for the same company; the EPA would not help that secretary change the pay inequity.

Continuing Wage Gap

Many studies have shown that the wage gap between men and women continues to exist. In fact, a study of management positions in industries that employ over 70 percent of the workforce showed that women managers consistently made less than their male counterparts in 7 of the 10 industries surveyed, and this pay gap *increased* between 1995 and 2000. The report was issued in 2001 by the U.S. General Accounting Office (now the Government Accountability Office)[3].

EPA Remedies

Remedies under the EPA are limited to back pay. Punitive damages are not provided in the statute. However, a bill passed by the House of Representatives in July of 2008 and currently before the Senate—the Paycheck Fairness Act—will change the remedy provisions of the EPA. Among other things, this law will allow the same compensatory and punitive damages for wage discrimination based on sex as are available for wage discrimination based on race or national origin.

The EPA and the Civil Rights Act

The limitations of the EPA have led some people to take wage discrimination claims to court under a different law. In one prominent case, female prison guards, earning less than their male counterparts in the same prison, sought relief by arguing their case under Title VII of the Civil Rights Act of 1964. The work of the female guards and male guards was somewhat similar, but not the same in all respects, thereby precluding a claim under the EPA. If the case had been brought under the EPA, the chance of success would have been negligible. In *Washington County v. Gunther* (see Case for Discussion 10-1) the U.S. Supreme Court was asked to decide whether the women's claim of wage discrimination was preempted by the language of the EPA. Was the pay inequity claim one that can be brought only under the Equal Pay Act, or can it be brought under the broad claim of sex discrimination under the Civil Rights Act? Furthermore, if brought under the Civil Rights Act, to what extent do the EPA provisions preempt the provisions of the Civil Rights Act, given the language of this amendment (known as the Bennett Amendment)? ". . . [I]t shall not be an unlawful employment practice for any employer to differentiate upon the basis of sex in determining the amount of its employees' wages if such differentiation is 'authorized' by the Equal Pay Act of 1963."

Case for Discussion 10-1

COUNTY OF WASHINGTON V. GUNTHER, 452 US 161, 452 US 161 (1981)[4]

Facts

The plaintiffs were four women who were employed to guard female prisoners and to perform other services in the jail, such as clerical tasks. They argued that their pay was lower than the pay of male guards in the same prison. The suit arose after the county eliminated the female section of the jail and transferred some of the female guards to another jail in the county. The remaining guards, the plaintiffs, were discharged and claimed, among other things, that the discrepancy in their pay was the result of intentional sex discrimination and they were entitled to back pay.

After trial, the district court found that the male guards supervised more than 10 times as many prisoners per guard as did the female guards, and that the females devoted much of their time to less valuable clerical duties. It therefore held that respondents' jobs were not substantially equal to those of the male guards, and that respondents were thus not entitled to equal pay.

We emphasize at the outset the narrowness of the question before us in this case. Respondents' claim is not based on the controversial concept of "comparable worth," under which plaintiffs might claim increased compensation on the basis of a comparison of the intrinsic worth or difficulty of their job with that of other jobs in the same organization or community. Rather, respondents seek to prove, by direct evidence, that their wages were depressed because of intentional sex discrimination, consisting of setting the wage scale for female guards, but not for male guards, at a level lower than its own survey of outside markets and the worth of the jobs warranted. The narrow question in this case is whether such a claim is precluded by the last sentence of 703(h) of Title VII, called the "Bennett Amendment." That sentence provides that it shall not be an unlawful employment practice for any employer to differentiate upon the basis of sex in determining the amount of its employees' wages if such differentiation is "authorized" by the Equal Pay Act of 1963.

***

Under petitioners' reading of the Bennett Amendment, only those sex-based wage discrimination claims that satisfy the "equal work" standard of the Equal Pay Act could be brought under Title VII. In practical terms, this means that a woman who is discriminatorily underpaid could obtain no relief—no matter how egregious the discrimination might be—unless her employer also employed a man in an equal job in the same establishment, at a higher rate of pay. Thus if an employer hired a woman for a unique position in the company and then admitted that her salary would have been higher had she been male, the woman would be unable to obtain legal redress under petitioners' interpretation. Similarly, if an employer used a transparently sex-biased system for wage determination, women holding jobs not equal to those held by men would be denied the right to prove that the system is a pretext for discrimination. . . .

Petitioners argue strenuously that the approach of the court of appeals places "the pay structure of virtually every employer and the entire economy . . . at risk and subject to scrutiny by the federal courts." They raise the specter that "Title VII plaintiffs could draw any type of comparison imaginable concerning job duties and pay between any job predominantly performed by women and any job predominantly performed by men." But whatever the merit of petitioners' arguments in other contexts, they are inapplicable here, for claims based on the type of job comparisons petitioners describe are manifestly different from respondents' claim. Respondents contend that the County of Washington evaluated the worth of their jobs; that the county determined that they should be paid approximately 95 percent as much as the male correctional officers; that it paid them only about 70 percent as much, while paying the male officers the full evaluated worth of their jobs; and that the failure of the county to pay respondents the full evaluated worth of their jobs can be proved to be attributable to intentional sex discrimination. Thus, respondents' suit does not require a court to make its own subjective assessment of the value of the male and female guard jobs, or to attempt by statistical technique or other method to quantify the effect of sex discrimination on the wage rates.

Decision

Essentially, the Court ruled that Title VII can be used to argue sex discrimination—regarding wages—even in circumstances in which the jobs of the women and the men are different. The language of the Equal Pay Act does not preclude such actions.

Questions for Discussion

1. Based on the excerpt given here, what is the Supreme Court's position regarding the female guards' claim?
2. What essential question was the Court addressing?
3. If the county had not evaluated the worth of the various positions in its system, what impact would that have had on the outcome of the case?
4. If women teachers in a public elementary school were hired at lower salaries than those offered to male teachers and there were no differences in qualifications for the positions, and no differences in the experience or qualifications of the individuals hired, what are the chances that the women teachers would be successful in arguing intentional sex discrimination under the Civil Rights Act? Under the Equal Pay Act?
5. What difference does it make whether a case is brought under the Civil Rights Act or under the EPA?
6. From a management perspective, what lessons can be derived from the *Gunther* case?

COMPARABLE WORTH THEORY

Compensation that recognizes comparable worth is *not* a requirement of U.S. law. Nonetheless, since the ruling in *Gunther,* some states and organizations have installed comparable worth strategies in their workforces. To undertake a *comparable worth* strategy, a comprehensive survey is conducted of all the occupations and positions of the enterprise. Point values are assigned to numerous aspects of the skill levels required, the value of the work, the degree of effort needed, and so on. Finally the points are summed, and all people in positions that have the same point value are to be paid the same. Naturally other factors such as length of time working with the entity would mediate such pay decisions. Opponents of this theory argue that market forces of supply and demand should be the dominant influence in pay decisions.

Global **Perspective**

Canada's Comparable Worth Doctrine

The law of Canada states that it is a discriminatory practice for an employer to establish or maintain differences in wages between male and female employees employed in the same establishment who are performing work of equal value[5]. Note the difference between that language and the language of the EPA. The Canadian requirement is often referred to as the *comparable worth doctrine*. What has happened since the law of comparable worth went into effect in Canada in 1976?

The following excerpts are taken from a 2004 law review article by Beth Bilson, Chair of Canada's Pay Equity Task Force[6]:

A differential in the wages of men and women has long been an endemic phenomenon in industrialized countries, including Canada. Though this gender wage gap has varied somewhat in size over time, it has proved stubbornly resistant to elimination, and has continued to hover at around 25 percent in most countries. In Canada, the ratio of women's wages in comparison to men's wages is currently calculated to be approximately 70.8 percent for full-time, full-year employees.

The factors that contribute to the gender wage gap are not completely understood, and such considerations as educational attainment, workforce experience, and family commitments have been raised as possible explanations for the continuing difference in wages. When all of these factors are taken into account, however, there still remains a portion of the wage gap that cannot be explained in any of these ways and that has been acknowledged as a manifestation of discrimination against women.

In the first half of the 20th century, those concerned with gender discrimination tended to focus on the practice of paying women a lower wage for doing the same work as men. Grounded in the premise that men, as breadwinners, required higher wages, and that the presence of women in the workforce threatened the employment of husbands and fathers, the payment of "women's rates" was relatively common. Even where a separate rate was not specifically attached to a job, the wages of women were often lower. Forms of equal pay legislation that were meant to address this kind of discrimination were grounded in the principle of "equal pay for equal work" and usually took the form of provisions in labor standards legislation that were enforced through an inspection system.

By mid-century, many supporters of gender equality concluded that the principle of equal pay for equal work failed to capture the systemic aspect of wage discrimination. These supporters urged the adoption of the principle of "equal pay for work of equal value," an idea that would encourage the analysis of basic assumptions and habits that had built up around the assessment of the work performed by men and women. Underlying this principle is a recognition that men and women are segregated to a marked degree in different jobs; only by examining carefully the actual work done by people doing those different jobs does it become possible to decide whether work is being given a lower value because it is being done by women.

The International Labor Organization lent its support to this principle in Convention No. 100, which was titled the Convention Concerning Equal Remuneration for Men and Women Workers for Work of Equal Value, adopted in 1951. Article 2.1 of Convention No. 100 reads as follows: "Each Member shall, by means appropriate to the methods in operation for determining rates of remuneration, promote and, in so far as it is consistent with such methods, ensure the application to all workers of the principle of equal remuneration for men and women workers for work of equal value."

The international commitment made in ratifying Convention No. 100 was confirmed by the Canadian government as, on a number of subsequent occasions, Canada became a signatory to international covenants reinforcing the principle of equal pay for work of equal value.

The principle of equal pay for work of equal value, generally referred to as pay equity, first took legislative form in Canada in the 1970s. It should be noted that the platform for legislative action on this issue was not labor standards legislation, but human rights legislation. Indeed, the earliest provision of this type was Article 19 of the Charter of Human Rights and Freedoms of Quebec, passed in 1975. Article 19 purported to address wage discrimination based on a number of prohibited grounds in addition to sex. The implication of this choice was that the concept of equal pay for work of equal value should be placed within the framework of fundamental rights rather than treated as simply another employment-related issue.

Case for Discussion 10-2

SIMENS V. ASHCROFT, (2003), APPEAL NO. 01A21778 AGENCY NO. F-99-5333 U.S. EQUAL EMPLOYMENT OPPORTUNITY COMMISSION[7]

Facts

Simens was employed by the Department of Justice's Federal Bureau of Investigation when she was nominated and approved to serve as the agency's representative on the President's Commission for Critical Infrastructure Protection (PCCIP). The male whom she replaced in that position had been paid at the senior executive service (SES) level. When she realized that her pay was not raised to the SES level, she made repeated requests for that compensation. The agency gave several reasons for its denial to do so. Among them was the following: It would jeopardize her law enforcement retirement because this position was not a law enforcement role, and the agency was unwilling to allocate any new SES slot to the PCCIP because of mission-critical priorities.

In the words of the decision, "[T]o establish an inference that the agency violated the EPA, complainant must first carry her burden of showing us that the agency paid this male predecessor more than it paid her for performing a job requiring 'equal skill, effort, and responsibility' under 'similar working conditions.' Cf. EEOC Compliance Manual, Section 10: Compensation Discrimination, at 24 (Dec. 5, 2000) . . . (noting that in order to establish a prima facie case under the EPA, a complainant must demonstrate that he or she (1) receives a lower wage than paid to an employee of the opposite sex in the same establishment; and (2) the employees perform substantially equal work (in terms of skill, effort, and responsibility) under similar working conditions)."

To escape liability at this point, the agency would have to give evidence that the wage disparity was based on one of the four defenses in the statute. In other words, the agency must show that sex played no part in the compensation differential. The agency could argue that the difference in pay was based on a bona fide seniority system, a merit system, a system that measures earnings by quantity or quality of production, or any other factor other than sex.

Decision

In the words of the EEOC, "We think the agency met this affirmative defense by showing that the pay disparity between complainant and her predecessor was based on a 'factor other than sex'—namely, that her predecessor already occupied an SES position before he was appointed to PCCIP, and that his appointment thus did not require placement in an SL post (potentially raising retirement benefit issues) or compel creation of a new SES position. According to the agency, elevating complainant to SL or SES status would have caused both of these problems, and the agency thus did not promote her. This gender-neutral explanation has not been rebutted by complainant and suffices to convince us that the agency did not violate the EPA on these facts."

Questions for Discussion

1. What kind of evidence would be needed to rebut the defenses of the agency?
2. How difficult is it to come up with a defense for wage discrimination under the affirmative defense of "any other factor other than sex"?
3. If a male applicant and a female applicant are fully qualified for a position, but the male has a PhD (not a requirement for the job and in an unrelated field), would a company be in a good position to defend hiring the male?
4. What are the four defenses recognized in the EPA that would defeat a plaintiff's claim of wage discrimination based on sex?

THE CIVIL RIGHTS ACT OF 1964

The Civil Rights Act is a comprehensive federal statute aimed at reducing discrimination in public accommodations and employment situations. The portion of the act that covers employment is Title VII; employers of 15 or more workers must comply with its provisions. The initial focus of the bills that led up to the passage of this groundbreaking federal law was prejudicial treatment of people based on race and color. Other prohibited classifications under this law are national origin, religion, and sex. The decision to include prohibition of discrimination based on sex has an interesting history. There is some controversy concerning whether Congressman Howard W. Smith's last-minute move to amend the law by adding the word *sex* was done, ironically, in an attempt to defeat passage of the bill rather than in a genuine effort to promote the interests of women. Some believe he intended to defeat the bill; however, research supports a different conclusion, recognizing his significant efforts to address sex discrimination in the drive for an Equal Rights Amendment to the Constitution. Congressman Smith was a known supporter of that effort[8].

Disparate Treatment and Disparate Impact Cases

As noted in Chapter 7, cases of discrimination in the workplace, based on the Civil Rights Act, can be argued under either a disparate treatment or disparate impact analysis. When an employee believes that her boss fired her on the basis of her gender, she must produce evidence that the firing was based on illegal discrimination using the disparate treatment analysis. If she can prove, for example, that there were supervisory comments such as "you women have no common sense and are too emotional" or "women should be at home raising children," her claim of discriminatory motive is supported, and a judge or jury could therefore believe that the termination was prompted by discrimination.

Words that company personnel use can come back to haunt them as potent evidence of discriminatory intent.

On the other hand, if a woman has been overlooked for promotion in favor of a man, and there is no concrete evidence of discriminatory motive, but she can prove statistically that women in that company have little chance of success, her case might better be argued under a disparate impact analysis. To succeed she must present evidence that the employer uses criteria for decision making (whether for hiring, promotion, or other use) that have a disproportionately greater negative impact on women.

In a disparate impact case the focus would be on the policies and practices of the company that led to an adverse impact on a statutorily protected class (such as race, national origin, or sex). The plaintiff's statistics must show the percentage of employees in the protected class (in this case females) working for the company as compared to the percentage of qualified females in the relevant labor market. If the statistics support her position, the company is unfairly (although unintentionally) limiting the opportunities of women. Remember: It is unnecessary to prove discriminatory intent in a disparate impact case.

Defenses

When a plaintiff–employee successfully proves a disparate treatment case, an employer has one defense—the employer must credibly show that there is a *bona fide occupational qualification (BFOQ)* that warrants the discriminatory treatment. In other words, when the issue is sex discrimination the employer must have a genuine rationale for favoring a male over a female or vice versa. For example, to be a candidate for a female modeling job, the person must be a woman—that is a BFOQ for the position. *Note:* The BFOQ defense is not available when the discrimination at issue is based on race.

An employer facing a disparate impact case can defend itself by producing evidence that the practices or policies that have an adverse impact on a protected class are necessary to the business and are job-related.

The Prima Facie Case

Over time the courts have fashioned what is known as the *prima facie case* for alleged discrimination under the EPA, the Civil Rights Act, the Age Discrimination in Employment Act, or other laws. When certain facts have been alleged by a plaintiff–employee, there is a presumption that illegal discrimination has taken place. For example, in a case alleging failure to hire based on discrimination, the facts that must be in evidence to establish a presumption of discrimination are as follows[9]:

- The plaintiff is in a protected class (for most sex discrimination cases, this would be female).
- The plaintiff applied and was qualified for the position.
- The plaintiff was not hired.
- The position remained open, and the employer continued to seek applicants.

Once a plaintiff has established a prima facie case, the burden of proof passes to the defendant, who must give evidence of a legitimate, nondiscriminatory reason for its decision not to hire (or to terminate, or other negative decision). If such evidence is provided, and a jury is not convinced of its veracity, the plaintiff might win. Likewise, if the plaintiff counters with evidence that the defendant's reasons are merely a pretext for discrimination and that the decision was actually motivated by illegal discrimination, the jury is likely to decide for the plaintiff. Basically the plaintiff has the ultimate burden of proving disparate treatment discrimination.

As stated in a previous chapter, the prima facie case differs for a disparate impact case. In a disparate impact case, the plaintiff must prove the following:

- There is a statistical imbalance of members of a particular protected class in the workplace when comparing the percentage of that class in the workplace with the percentage of qualified class members in the relevant labor market.
- One or more practices or policies of the employer is causing the imbalance.

Once the plaintiff has established this presumption of illegal discrimination, the defendant must prove a business necessity for the complained-of practice or policy. Failure to convince the fact finder of such business necessity can lead to a decision for the plaintiff on the grounds that the reason given was a pretext for actual discrimination.

Case for Discussion 10-3

PRICE WATERHOUSE V. HOPKINS, 109 S.CT. 1775 (1989)[10]

Facts

Ann Hopkins had worked at Price Waterhouse's Office of Government Services in Washington, DC, for five years when the partners in that office proposed her as a candidate for partnership. Of the 662 partners at the firm at that time, 7 were women. Of the 88 people proposed for partnership that year, only 1—Hopkins—was a woman.

. . . Judge Gesell specifically found that Hopkins had "played a key role in Price Waterhouse's successful effort to win a multimillion dollar contract with the Department of State. Indeed, none of the other partnership candidates at Price Waterhouse that year had a comparable record in terms of successfully securing major contracts for the partnership."

The partners in Hopkins's office praised her character as well as her accomplishments, describing her in their joint statement as "an outstanding professional" who had a "deft touch," a "strong character, independence, and integrity." Clients appear to have agreed with these assessments. At trial, one official from the State Department described her as "extremely competent, intelligent," "strong and forthright, very productive, energetic, and creative." Another high-ranking official praised Hopkins's decisiveness, broadminded-ness, and "intellectual clarity"; she was, in his words, "a stimulating conversationalist."

On too many occasions, however, Hopkins's aggressiveness apparently spilled over into abrasiveness. Staff members seem to have borne the brunt of Hopkins's brusqueness. Long before her bid for partnership, partners evaluating her work had counseled her to improve her relations with staff members. Although later evaluations indicated an improvement, Hopkins's perceived shortcomings in this important area eventually doomed her bid for partnership. Virtually all of the partners' negative remarks about Hopkins— even those of partners supporting her—had to do with her "interpersonal skills." Both "[s]upporters and opponents of her candidacy," stressed Judge Gesell, "indicated that she was sometimes overly aggressive, unduly harsh, difficult to work with, and impatient with staff."

There were clear signs, though, that some of the partners reacted negatively to Hopkins's personality because she was a woman. One partner described her as "macho"; another suggested that she "overcompensated for being a woman"; a third advised her to take "a course at charm school." Several partners criticized her use of profanity; in response, one partner suggested that those partners objected to her swearing only "because it's a lady using foul language." Another supporter explained that Hopkins "ha[d] matured from a tough-talking somewhat masculine hard-nosed manager to an authoritative, formidable, but much more appealing lady candidate." But it was the man who, as Judge Gesell found, bore responsibility for explaining to Hopkins the reasons for the Policy Board's decision to place her candidacy on hold who delivered the *coup de grace:* in order to improve her chances for partnership, Thomas Beyer advised, Hopkins should "walk more femininely, talk more femininely, dress more femininely, wear makeup, have her hair styled, and wear jewelry."

Dr. Susan Fiske, a social psychologist and Associate Professor of Psychology at Carnegie-Mellon University, testified at trial that the partnership selection process at Price Waterhouse was likely influenced by sex stereotyping. . . .

In previous years, other female candidates for partnership also had been evaluated in sex-based terms. As a general matter, Judge Gesell concluded, "candidates were viewed favorably if partners believed they maintained their femininity while becoming effective professional managers"; in this environment, "to be identified as a 'women's libber' was regarded as a negative comment." In fact, the judge found that in previous years "one partner repeatedly commented that he could not consider any woman seriously as a partnership candidate and believed that women were not even capable of functioning as senior managers—yet the firm took no action to discourage his comments and recorded his vote in the overall summary of the evaluations." . . .

The judge went on to decide . . . that some of the partners' remarks about Hopkins stemmed from an impermissibly cabined view of the proper behavior of women, and that Price Waterhouse had done nothing to disavow reliance on such comments. He held that Price Waterhouse had unlawfully discriminated against Hopkins on the basis of sex by consciously giving credence and effect to partners' comments that resulted from sex stereotyping. . . .

We need not leave our common sense at the doorstep when we interpret a statute. It is difficult for us to imagine that, in the simple words "because of," Congress meant to obligate a plaintiff to identify the precise causal role played by legitimate and illegitimate motivations in the employment decision she challenges. We conclude, instead, that Congress meant to obligate her to prove that the employer relied upon sex-based considerations in coming to its decision.

. . .

To say that an employer may not take gender into account is not, however, the end of the matter, for that describes only one aspect of Title VII. The other important aspect of the statute is its preservation of an employer's remaining freedom of choice. . . . The statute's maintenance of employer prerogatives is evident from the statute itself and from its history, both in Congress and in this Court.

To begin with, the existence of the BFOQ exception shows Congress's unwillingness to require employers to change the very nature of their operations in response to the statute. And our emphasis on "business necessity" in disparate impact cases, . . . and on "legitimate, nondiscriminatory reason[s]" in disparate treatment cases, ...results from our awareness of Title VII's balance between employee rights and employer prerogatives.

. . .

Decision

We hold that when a plaintiff in a Title VII case proves that her gender played a motivating part in an employment decision, the defendant may avoid a finding of liability only by proving by a preponderance of the evidence that it would have made the same decision even if it had not taken the plaintiff's gender into account. Because the courts below erred by deciding that the defendant must make this proof by clear and convincing evidence, we reverse the court of appeals' judgment against Price Waterhouse on liability and remand the case to that court for further proceedings.

Questions for Discussion

1. Why was this case analyzed as a disparate treatment case?
2. What was the major question before the Court?

3. Do you agree with the Court on the issue of the extent to which the employer bears the burden of proof in a mixed motive case? What impact did the Civil Rights Act of 1991 have on this issue?

4. If there is clear evidence that illegal discrimination entered the reasoning for an employee's dismissal, should it matter whether the employee was a good, bad, or moderately competent employee? Or that the employee had clearly violated company rules? Or that the employee embezzled money from the employer?

SEXUAL HARASSMENT

After a statute has been passed by Congress, it is open to interpretation by the courts. There was nothing in the express language of the Civil Rights Act regarding disparate treatment and disparate impact. Likewise, nothing in the explicit wording of the statute discussed sexual harassment, let alone a distinction between hostile environment harassment and quid pro quo sexual harassment.

One of the first ambiguities that had to be resolved under the Civil Rights Act was whether sexual harassment was a form of illegal sex discrimination. After several unsuccessful attempts by harassment victims to have it labeled as such, the courts began to declare that sexual harassment was indeed a form of sex discrimination. Over the years court decisions have divided these cases into two distinct types: quid pro quo harassment and hostile environment harassment.

Quid Pro Quo Harassment

Quid pro quo sexual harassment occurs when an employee is asked for sexual favors in exchange for favorable treatment in the workplace. In some cases this illegal discrimination might take the form of retaliation for not "going along," or not being promoted as a result of ignoring such requests, or not being hired because the candidate rebuffed such advances. *Quid pro quo* indicates an exchange: favorable treatment in exchange for sexual favors. When such requests emanate from supervisors, the courts have dealt harshly with the defendant company, finding **strict liability.** The supervisor is the agent of the company, and his or her actions are imputed to the company. The fact that a company has a sexual harassment policy in place might not protect the company from a finding of liability.

The prima facie case for establishing quid pro quo sexual harassment includes the following elements:

- The plaintiff belongs to a protected class.
- The plaintiff was subjected to unwelcome sexual harassment.
- The harassment was based on sex.
- As a result of the plaintiff's refusal to submit to the sexual demand of a supervisor, an adverse tangible employment action was taken against the plaintiff.

strict liability
An employer's normal defenses will not suffice. In other words, the employer cannot claim that it is not liable because it had no knowledge of the harassment or that a harassment policy existed and was not utilized. (Such defenses might be available if the harassment was done by a fellow worker or a customer.)

Hostile Environment Harassment

Cases in which there are no overt sexual requests or no denial of favorable treatment by the company (that is, the employee has not been denied a promotion or hiring) may nevertheless involve illegal sexual harassment. In such situations the employee must prove that actions of a sexual nature or with sexual overtones by either supervisory personnel or others seriously affect the employee's ability to perform the job functions. In other words, the behavior has created a *hostile environment*. The employer can raise defenses to this claim, such as lack of knowledge of the behavior, an effective sexual harassment policy, or failure of the employee to use the procedures available to deal with these situations.

The prima facie case for sexual harassment of the hostile environment type includes the following:

- The plaintiff belongs to a protected class.
- The plaintiff was subjected to unwelcome sexual harassment.
- The harassment was based on sex.
- The harassment was so severe or pervasive that it affected the plaintiff's terms, conditions, or privileges of employment. (Essentially, if the harassment makes it difficult or impossible to perform the functions of the job, it is likely to be regarded as creating a hostile environment for the plaintiff.)

Case for Discussion 10-4

The first major case involving sexual harassment discrimination that went to the U.S. Supreme Court was the *Meritor* case, decided in 1986. The *Meritor* case discusses, among other things, consensual sexual relations with a supervisor, the liability of an employer when it claims no knowledge of the harassment, quid pro quo and hostile environment harassment, and the defense of having a grievance procedure that was not used by the employee–plaintiff.

MERITOR SAVINGS BANK V. VINSON, 106 S.CT. 2399 (1986)[11]

This case presents important questions concerning claims of workplace sexual harassment brought under Title VII of the Civil Rights Act of 1964, 78 Stat. 253, as amended, 42 U. S. C. § 2000e et seq.

Facts

In 1974 respondent M. Vinson met Sidney Taylor, a vice president of what is now petitioner Meritor Savings Bank (bank) and manager of one of its branch offices. When respondent asked whether she might obtain employment at the bank, Taylor gave her an application, which she completed and returned the next day; later that same day Taylor called her to say that she had been hired. With Taylor as her supervisor, respondent started as a teller trainee and thereafter was promoted to teller, head teller, and assistant branch manager. She worked at the same branch for four years, and it is undisputed that her advancement there was based on merit alone. In September 1978 respondent notified Taylor that she was taking sick leave for an indefinite period. On November 1, 1978, the bank discharged her for excessive use of that leave.

Respondent brought this action against Taylor and the bank, claiming that during her four years at the bank she had "constantly been subjected to sexual harassment" by Taylor in violation of Title VII. She sought injunctive relief, compensatory and punitive damages against Taylor and the bank, and attorney's fees.

At the 11-day bench trial, the parties presented conflicting testimony about Taylor's behavior during respondent's employment. Respondent testified that during her probationary period as a teller trainee, Taylor treated her in a fatherly way and made no sexual advances. Shortly thereafter, however, he invited her out to dinner and, during the course of the meal, suggested that they go to a motel to have sexual relations. At first she refused, but out of what she described as fear of losing her job she eventually agreed. According to respondent, Taylor thereafter made repeated demands upon her for sexual favors, usually at the branch, both during and after business hours; she estimated that over the next several years she had intercourse with him some 40 or 50 times. In addition, respondent testified that Taylor fondled her in front of other employees, followed her into the women's restroom when she went there alone, exposed himself to her, and even forcibly raped her on several occasions. These activities ceased after 1977, respondent stated, when she started going with a steady boyfriend.

. . .

Finally, respondent testified that because she was afraid of Taylor she never reported his harassment to any of his supervisors and never attempted to use the bank's complaint procedure.

Taylor denied respondent's allegations of sexual activity, testifying that he never fondled her, never made suggestive remarks to her, never engaged in sexual intercourse with her, and never asked her to do so. He contended instead that respondent made her accusations in response to a business-related dispute. The bank also denied respondent's allegations and asserted that any sexual harassment by Taylor was unknown to the bank and engaged in without its consent or approval.

The district court . . . ultimately found that respondent "was not the victim of sexual harassment and was not the victim of sexual discrimination" while employed at the bank. The Court of Appeals for the District of Columbia Circuit reversed.

***

In defining "sexual harassment," the [EEOC] Guidelines first describe the kinds of workplace conduct that may be actionable under Title VII. These include "[unwelcome] sexual advances, requests for sexual favors, and other verbal or physical conduct of a sexual nature." Relevant to the charges at issue in this case, the Guidelines provide that such sexual misconduct constitutes prohibited "sexual harassment," whether or not it is directly linked to the grant or denial of an economic quid pro quo, where "such conduct has the purpose or effect of unreasonably interfering with an individual's work performance or creating an intimidating, hostile, or offensive working environment."

. . .

Respondent's allegations in this case—which include not only pervasive harassment but also criminal conduct of the most serious nature—are plainly sufficient to state a claim for "hostile environment" sexual harassment.

. . .

[T]he fact that sex-related conduct was "voluntary," in the sense that the complainant was not forced to participate against her will, is not a defense to a sexual harassment suit brought under Title VII. The gravamen of any sexual harassment claim is that the alleged sexual advances were "unwelcome." While the question whether particular conduct was indeed unwelcome presents difficult problems of proof and turns largely on credibility determinations committed to the trier of fact, the district court in this case erroneously focused on the "voluntariness" of respondent's participation in the claimed sexual episodes. The correct inquiry is whether respondent by her conduct indicated that the alleged sexual advances were unwelcome, not whether her actual participation in sexual intercourse was voluntary.

. . .

Finding that "the bank was without notice" of Taylor's alleged conduct, and that notice to Taylor was not the equivalent of notice to the bank, the [trial] court concluded that the bank therefore could not be held liable for Taylor's alleged actions. The court of appeals took the opposite view, holding that an employer is strictly liable for a hostile environment created by a supervisor's sexual advances, even though the employer neither knew nor reasonably could have known of the alleged misconduct. . . .

. . . We do not know at this stage whether Taylor made any sexual advances toward respondent at all, let alone whether those advances were unwelcome, whether they were sufficiently pervasive to constitute a condition of employment, or whether they were "so pervasive and so long continuing . . . that the employer must have become conscious of [them]" . . .

We therefore decline the parties' invitation to issue a definitive rule on employer liability, but we do agree with the EEOC that Congress wanted courts to look to agency principles for guidance in this area.

. . .

Finally, we reject petitioner's view that the mere existence of a grievance procedure and a policy against discrimination, coupled with respondent's failure to invoke that procedure, must insulate petitioner from liability. While those facts are plainly relevant, the situation before us demonstrates why they are not necessarily dispositive. Petitioner's general nondiscrimination policy did not address sexual harassment in particular, and thus did not alert employees to their employer's interest in correcting that form of discrimination. Moreover, the bank's grievance procedure apparently required an employee to complain first to her supervisor, in this case Taylor. Since Taylor was the alleged perpetrator, it is not altogether surprising that respondent failed to invoke the procedure and report her grievance to him. Petitioner's contention that respondent's failure should insulate it from liability might be substantially stronger if its procedures were better calculated to encourage victims of harassment to come forward.

. . .

Decision

In sum, we hold that a claim of "hostile environment" sex discrimination is actionable under Title VII, that the district court's findings were insufficient to dispose of respondent's hostile environment claim, and that the district court did not err in admitting testimony about respondent's sexually provocative speech and dress. As to employer liability, we conclude that the court of appeals was wrong to entirely disregard agency principles and impose absolute liability on employers for the acts of their supervisors, regardless of the circumstances of a particular case.

Accordingly, the judgment of the court of appeals reversing the judgment of the district court is affirmed, and the case is remanded for further proceedings consistent with this opinion.

Questions for Discussion

1. State clearly the differences between a hostile environment case and a quid pro quo case. Under which category does the *Meritor* case best fit?
2. Why was the case not decided on a quid pro quo basis?
3. What are the lessons of *Meritor* for today's managers?

Case for Discussion 10-5

Later U.S. Supreme Court Cases on Hostile Environment Harassment

In the following cases the U.S. Supreme Court discussed possible defenses that an employer can raise in hostile environment sex discrimination cases. The decisions are significant for employers who want to know how to avoid being charged with violations of the Civil Rights Act for sexual harassment.

BURLINGTON INDUSTRIES, INC. V. ELLERTH, 118 S. CT. 2257 (1998)[12]

FARAGHER V. CITY OF BOCA RATON, 118 S. CT. 2275 (1998)[13]

In these cases, decided on the same day, the plaintiffs sought damages for sexual harassment by immediate supervisors in situations that did not involve adverse tangible employment actions, such as discharge or demotion. In other words, the cases were of the hostile environment harassment type.

Normally sexual harassment or requests for favors by a supervisor are grounds for a quid pro quo argument in which the employer would be held strictly and vicariously liable with no defense available. However, in *Burlington* and *Faragher* no adverse employment action was taken against the plaintiffs; therefore, the sexual harassment in each case could be labeled only as a hostile environment situation.

It was established in these hostile environment cases that employers could avoid liability, either partially or entirely, by proving two things: (1) They exercised reasonable care to prevent and promptly correct any sexually harassing behavior and (2) the plaintiff unreasonably failed to take advantage of any preventive or corrective opportunities provided by the employer.

Excerpts from *Burlington*

An employer is subject to vicarious liability to a victimized employee for an actionable hostile environment created by a supervisor with immediate (or successively higher) authority over the employee. When no tangible employment action is taken, a defending employer may raise an affirmative defense to liability or damages, subject to proof by a preponderance of the evidence. The defense comprises two necessary elements: (a) that the employer exercised reasonable care to prevent and correct promptly any sexually harassing behavior, and (b) that the plaintiff employee unreasonably failed to take advantage of any preventive or corrective opportunities provided by the employer or to avoid harm otherwise. While proof that an employer had promulgated an anti-harassment policy with complaint procedure is not necessary in every instance as a matter of law, the need for a stated policy suitable to the employment circumstances may appropriately be addressed in any case when litigating the first element of the defense. And while proof that an employee failed to fulfill the corresponding obligation of reasonable care to avoid harm is not limited to showing any unreasonable failure to use any complaint procedure provided by the employer, a demonstration of such failure will normally suffice to satisfy the employer's burden under the second element of the defense. No affirmative defense is available, however, when the supervisor's harassment culminates in a tangible employment action, such as discharge, demotion, or undesirable reassignment.

Relying on existing case law which held out the promise of vicarious liability for all quid pro quo claims, Ellerth focused all her attention in the Court of Appeals on proving her claim fit within that category. Given our explanation that the labels quid pro quo and hostile work environment are not controlling for purposes of establishing employer liability, Ellerth should have an adequate opportunity to prove she has a claim for which Burlington is liable.

Although Ellerth has not alleged she suffered a tangible employment action at the hands of Slowik, which would deprive Burlington of the availability of the affirmative defense, this is not dispositive. In light of our decision, Burlington is still subject to vicarious liability for Slowik's activity, but Burlington should have an opportunity to assert and prove the affirmative defense to liability.

Decision

For these reasons, we will affirm the judgment of the Court of Appeals, reversing the grant of summary judgment against Ellerth. On remand, the District Court will have the opportunity to decide whether it would be appropriate to allow Ellerth to amend her pleading or supplement her discovery.

Questions for Discussion

1. Under what circumstances, if any, should an employer be subject to liability for sexual harassment discrimination when that employer has a sexual harassment policy in place?

2. Is your answer the same if the sexual harassment claims are of the quid pro quo type?

3. What did the U.S. Supreme Court clarify in *Burlington* and *Faragher?*

Note: In cases interpreting and applying Title VII, the courts must follow the precedent (the reasoning and logic) of prior decisions—particularly the opinions of the U.S. Supreme Court. It is worth noting that although the courts tend to follow the precedent of Title VII cases (whether the cases are based on sex discrimination, race discrimination, or another category), the defenses provided in the *Burlington* and *Faragher* cases have not yet been recognized by the Supreme Court in cases involving harassment in *race* discrimination suits. It remains to be seen how this will evolve.

Management **Perspective**

Employers are well aware of the need for training to avoid the pitfalls of discriminatory behavior on the part of employees and managers. The costs of defending such legal actions encompass not only attorney fees but also the lost time for retrieval of documents and records, the time away from the job to testify, the emotional toll on all involved, and the negative effects on worker morale. How well this training is done, how often it is done, when it is done, and by whom it is done are just a few questions that must be answered by those managing the human resources of the company. A prominent example of the precautions that must be taken in antiharassment and antidiscrimination training was provided in a 1992 federal appellate case from California, *Stender v. Lucky Stores, Inc.*[14]. In an article advocating the need for adequate training, an attorney referred to that case and stated the following[15]:

> A cruel irony for some employers that have provided harassment or discrimination prevention training is that the training itself, or the conduct of participants during the training, has sometimes been used as evidence against the employer in a subsequent lawsuit. As a result, employers need to ensure that the trainer is cognizant of the types of training methodologies that are legally risky.
>
> For example, some trainers encourage participants to explore and express their internal or societal biases and prejudices. This seems like a good training technique—but the expressions of these biases can come back to haunt the employer in a future lawsuit. In *Stender v. Lucky Stores, Inc.,* the company hired an attorney to provide training to its managers on sexual harassment and sex discrimination in promotion. The trainer asked the participants to volunteer a stereotype that they had heard in the workplace about women. Notes from the training recorded comments from managers such as that "women do not want to work late shifts, that men do not want to compete with women or have a woman as their boss, that a woman's income is a second income in a household, that men resent the promotion of women, that black women are aggressive, that women who are promoted frequently step down, and that women do not have the drive to get ahead."
>
> In a class action lawsuit filed against the company by several female employees, the plaintiffs sought discovery of these notes. Despite the company's objections that the notes were protected by the attorney–client privilege and that disclosing the notes would discourage open and frank discussions in future EEO trainings, the court ordered the company to disclose the notes. The court also concluded that the comments were not just portrayals of social stereotypes, but reflections of what many of the employer's managers believed. Thus the court ruled that the notes constituted "evidence of discriminatory attitudes and stereotyping of women" by the company's managers. After the court's ruling, the company settled the lawsuit for approximately $107 million.

ADVICE REGARDING HARASSMENT AND DISCRIMINATION PREVENTION TRAINING

In the same article the author provided the following advice on training:

- The training should cover not just sexual harassment but all types of illegal harassment. There is consensus among federal appellate courts that the liability standards developed for sexual harassment cases apply to all types of harassment. Training should be provided for all employees, not just supervisors, shortly after they are hired.
- The training should be provided periodically. . . . It should not be simply a one-time event. EEOC guidelines indicate that employees should receive periodic

(Continued)

training on the topic. Courts' interpretations of the laws continually change, and employees need to be kept up-to-date and refreshed on this topic.

- The trainer must be expert in harassment and discrimination law, and training must be legally accurate. Years ago many employers thought of harassment prevention training in the same way they thought of other basic employee training: Any good trainer could provide adequate training on the topic. Courts, however, have now made clear that employers must ensure that the person(s) who provide prevention training must

  Completely understand the complex body of harassment and discrimination laws.

  Keep up-to-date with new cases that constantly change the interpretations of these laws.

- The training should be of a substantial length and effective. . . . Not just any training will do. Instead employers must show that their harassment prevention training is substantial, and that employees understand their responsibilities. For example, in *Wagner v. Dillard Dept. Stores,* 85 Fair Empl. Prac. Cas. (BNA) 295 (M.D.N.C. 2000), the court upheld a $150,000 punitive damages award in a pregnancy discrimination case because the employer's efforts to educate managers about discrimination was limited to posting the policy on a bulletin board and showing employees a 10-minute video with handouts.

- The training should not have a posttest that allows participants to fail. . . . At what level do you set the pass rate? If an employee fails the test, what do you do? Do you train him again? What if two months later he harasses a co-worker? Have you just given the plaintiff's attorney evidence that you knew that the employee did not understand the harassment laws or your policy but you did nothing? . . . An online harassment prevention program . . . could allow an employer to ensure that each employee understands the topic but not allow an employee to fail a test. (The online program can keep giving the employee feedback and new questions until the employee demonstrates understanding of the material.)

- The training should not constitute evidence of harassment or discrimination itself. . . . [E]mployers need to ensure that the trainer is cognizant of the types of training methodologies that are legally risky.

Same-Sex Harassment, Discrimination Based on Sexual Orientation, and Discrimination Based on Gender Identity

Although several states have statutes that either explicitly prohibit discrimination on the basis of sexual orientation or have been interpreted to cover such a classification, Title VII has not yet been interpreted to bring this category within the meaning of sex discrimination. It has nevertheless been the subject of discussion in court cases as well in Congress.

There has also been discussion of discrimination based on gender identity. The term *gender identity* means the gender-related identity, appearance, mannerisms, or other gender-related characteristics of an individual, without regard to the individual's designated sex at birth.

The U.S. Supreme Court, in the *Oncale* case (see Case for Discussion 10-6), found that male harassment of a male (same-sex harassment) is actionable on sex discrimination grounds under Title VII because it involves harassment based on sex. On the other hand, the 1979 *DeSantis* case illustrates the belief that homosexuality is not a protected classification under that law.

Case for Discussion 10-6

ONCALE V. SUNDOWNER OFFSHORE SERVICES, 118 S. CT. 998 (1998)[16]

The following excerpts from the *Oncale* case express the U.S. Supreme Court's reasoning and logic about sexual harassment, in particular hostile environment harassment.

Facts

Oncale was working for respondent Sundowner Offshore Services on a Chevron U.S.A., Inc., oil platform in the Gulf of Mexico. He was employed as a roustabout on an eight-man crew that included respondents John Lyons, Danny Pippen, and Brandon Johnson. Lyons, the crane operator, and Pippen, the driller, had supervisory authority. On several occasions Oncale was forcibly subjected to sex-related, humiliating actions against him by Lyons, Pippen, and Johnson in the presence of the rest of the crew. Pippen and Lyons also physically assaulted Oncale in a sexual manner, and Lyons threatened him with rape. Oncale's complaints to supervisory personnel produced no remedial action; in fact, the company's safety compliance clerk, Valent Hohen, told Oncale that Lyons and Pippen "picked [on] him all the time too," and called him a name suggesting homosexuality. Oncale eventually quit, asking that his pink slip reflect that he "voluntarily left due to sexual harassment and verbal abuse."

When asked at his deposition why he left Sundowner, Oncale stated, "I felt that if I didn't leave my job, that I would be raped or forced to have sex." Oncale filed a complaint against Sundowner in the United States District Court for the Eastern District of Louisiana, alleging that he was discriminated against in his employment because of his sex.

***

We see no justification in the statutory language or our precedents for a categorical rule excluding same-sex harassment claims from the coverage of Title VII. As some courts have observed, male-on-male sexual harassment in the workplace was assuredly not the principal evil Congress was concerned with when it enacted Title VII. But statutory prohibitions often go beyond the principal evil to cover reasonably comparable evils, and it is ultimately the provisions of our laws rather than the principal concerns of our legislators by which we are governed. Title VII prohibits "discriminat[ion] . . . because of . . . sex" in the "terms" or "conditions" of employment. Our holding that this includes sexual harassment must extend to sexual harassment of any kind that meets the statutory requirements.

***

Courts and juries have found the inference of discrimination easy to draw in most male–female sexual harassment situations because the challenged conduct typically involves explicit or implicit proposals of sexual activity; it is reasonable to assume those proposals would not have been made to someone of the same sex. The same chain of inference would be available to a plaintiff alleging same-sex harassment, if there were credible evidence that the harasser was homosexual. But harassing conduct need not be motivated by sexual desire to support an inference of discrimination on the basis of sex. A trier of fact might reasonably find such discrimination, for example, if a female victim is harassed in such sex-specific and derogatory terms by another woman as to make it clear that the harasser is motivated by general hostility to the presence of women in the workplace. A same-sex harassment plaintiff may also, of course, offer direct comparative evidence about how the alleged harasser treated members of both sexes in a mixed-sex workplace. Whatever evidentiary route the plaintiff chooses to follow, he or she must always prove that the conduct at issue was not merely tinged with offensive sexual connotations, but actually constituted "*discrimination . . . because of . . . sex.*"

And there is another requirement that prevents Title VII from expanding into a general civility code: As we emphasized in *Meritor* and *Harris,* the statute does not reach genuine but innocuous differences in the ways men and women routinely interact with members of the same sex and of the opposite sex. The prohibition of harassment on the basis of sex requires neither asexuality nor androgyny in the workplace; it forbids only behavior so objectively offensive as to alter the "conditions" of the victim's employment. "Conduct that is not severe or pervasive enough to create an objectively hostile or abusive work environment—an environment that a reasonable person would find hostile or abusive—is beyond Title VII's purview." We have always regarded that requirement as crucial, and as sufficient to ensure that courts and juries do not mistake ordinary socializing in the workplace—such as male-on-male horseplay or intersexual flirtation—for discriminatory "conditions of employment."

***

Decision

Because we conclude that sex discrimination consisting of same-sex sexual harassment is actionable under Title VII, the judgment of the Court of Appeals for the Fifth Circuit is reversed, and the case is remanded for further proceedings consistent with this opinion.

Questions for Discussion

1. To discourage sexual harassment in the workplace, some companies establish policies forbidding dating between employees. In light of the *Oncale* decision, should this be extended to homosexual dating?
2. To what extent should companies include homosexuality in their policies?

Case for Discussion 10-7

The court in *DeSantis v. Pacific Telephone* addressed a different issue: whether Title VII prohibits discrimination based on homosexuality.

DESANTIS V. PACIFIC TELEPHONE AND TELEGRAPH CO., INC., 608 F.2D 327 (1979)[17]

Male and female homosexuals claimed they were illegally discriminated against under Title VII by their employers based on their homosexuality.

Excerpt from DeSantis:

DeSantis, Boyle, and Simard, all males, claimed that Pacific Telephone & Telegraph Co. (PT&T) impermissibly discriminated against them because of their homosexuality. DeSantis alleged that he was not hired when a PT&T supervisor concluded that he was a homosexual. According to appellants' brief, "BOYLE was continually harassed by his co-workers and had to quit to preserve his health after only three months because his supervisors did nothing to alleviate this condition." Finally, "SIMARD was forced to quit under similar conditions after almost four years of employment with PT&T, but he was harassed by his supervisors (as well). . . . In addition, his personnel file has been marked as not eligible for rehire, and his applications for employment were rejected by PT&T in 1974 and 1976." Appellants DeSantis, Boyle, and Simard also alleged that PT&T officials have publicly stated that they would not hire homosexuals.

Decision

Both the trial court and the federal appellate court held that sex discrimination under Title VII does not apply here and should not be judicially extended to include homosexuality.

Question for Discussion

DeSantis was decided in 1979. In light of the 1998 Oncale decision, would this case be decided differently today? Why or why not?

THE EMPLOYMENT NONDISCRIMINATION ACT (ENDA): PROPOSED LEGISLATION

In the absence of antidiscrimination protection for homosexuals at the federal level, a bill has been proposed to Congress. The popular name for this proposed legislation is the Employment Non-Discrimination Act (ENDA). "The central edict of ENDA is contained in Section 4 of the Act, which prohibits employers and other covered entities from 'subjecting an individual to a different standard or treatment on the basis of sexual orientation.'"[18] As of August 2, 2008 Congress had not passed this legislation.

Summary

Five major federal statutes establish and bolster the rights of women in the workplace: the Equal Pay Act of 1963 (an amendment to the Fair Labor Standards Act); the Civil Rights Act of 1964; the Pregnancy Discrimination Act of 1978 (an amendment to the Civil Rights Act); the Civil Rights Act of 1991, including the Glass Ceiling Act (an the amendment to the Civil Rights Act of 1964); and the Family and Medical Leave Act of 1993.

The Equal Pay Act requires employers to pay equal wages to men and women who work in the same company for "equal work on jobs the performance of which requires equal skill, effort, and responsibility, and which are performed under similar working conditions." Exceptions to those requirements occur (1) when there is a good-faith seniority system in place, (2) when pay is based on merit, (3) when pay is based on quantity or quality of production, or (4) when pay is based on any other factor other than sex.

The comparable worth theory, not generally adopted in the U.S., was developed to circumvent the limiting factor of the EPA—that comparisons between wages of men and women must be made within a company where men and women are doing the same work. A comparable worth argument would be made under the Civil Rights Act rather than under the EPA. The use of comparable worth evidence involves extensive evaluation of every position within a company, assigning point values to those positions on the basis of criteria indicating the levels of skill, effort, and responsibility needed to perform those jobs. Pay would be based on the summed point totals of the positions. In this method, for example, the point total for a secretary's position might be equal to the point total for a midlevel manager's position, and the pay would therefore be required to be the same.

Sex discrimination under the Civil Rights Act of 1964 has been interpreted by the courts to include two distinct types: disparate treatment and disparate impact. In a disparate treatment case the plaintiff carries the burden of proving intentional discrimination. This can be presumed after the plaintiff establishes a prima facie case. In a disparate impact case it is not necessary for the plaintiff to prove intentional discrimination. Rather, the plaintiff must prove that an employer's practice or policy is causing an adverse impact on a protected class (such as women) and that statistical evidence bears this out.

Sexual harassment is considered a form of sex discrimination, although nothing in any statute directly addresses it. The courts have defined two types of sexual harassment: quid pro quo harassment and hostile environment harassment. In a quid pro quo case, the plaintiff is asserting that the employer (by its agent) has made a condition of employment contingent on sexual favors. When a supervisor is found to have requested sexual favors and adverse tangible employment action has resulted from the employee's denial of such favors, the employer is held to be strictly liable—that is, no defense can be made to avoid liability on the part of the employer. In a hostile environment case, the plaintiff alleges that conditions at work involving sexual characteristics (conversations, pictures, actions, and so on) are so pervasive or so serious as to substantially affect his or her ability to perform the job. In a hostile environment case an employer can raise the defenses of (1) having an effective sexual harassment policy in place and (2) evidence that the plaintiff did not use procedures set up to protect employees from continued harassment.

Questions

1. Between 1980 and 1994 United Airlines required female flight attendants to weigh between 14 and 25 pounds less than their male colleagues of the same height and age. For example, the maximum weight for a 5′7″, 30-year-old woman was 142 pounds, whereas a man of the same height and age could weigh up to 161 pounds. A 5′11″, 50-year-old woman could weigh up to 162 pounds, whereas the weight limit for a man of the same height and age was 185 pounds. United's weight table for men during this period was based on a table of desirable weights and heights published by the Metropolitan Life Insurance Company ("MetLife"). The comparable weight table for women was based on a table of maximum weights established by Continental Air Lines ("Continental"). A comparison of United's MetLife-derived limits for men to the Continental-derived weight limits for women revealed that United generally limited men to maximum weights corresponding to large body frames for men on the MetLife charts but generally limited women to maximum weights corresponding to medium body frames for women on the MetLife charts.

   The 13 named plaintiffs worked for United as flight attendants while United's 1980–1994 weight policy was in effect. The named plaintiffs attempted to lose weight by various means, including severely restricting their caloric intake, using diuretics, and purging. Ultimately, however, plaintiffs were each disciplined and/or terminated for failing to comply with United's maximum weight requirements. In 1992 plaintiffs filed an employment discrimination action.

   In 1995 United offered to reinstate many class and subclass members who had been terminated under the weight policy. United did not require individuals accepting reinstatement to waive any potential claims against it arising from earlier discipline or termination.

   a. Was United's weight limit policy prior to 1994 a violation of Title VII? Why or why not?

   b. To successfully defend itself against the discrimination charge, what evidence must United provide?

2. Mary D., who had been working for California's Department of Health Services since 1992, was transferred to a different branch under the supervision of Paul S. in 1995. She claims that Paul sexually harassed her from early 1996 to late 1997, and his behavior included inappropriate comments and unwelcome physical touching. Under oath she stated that on one occasion he told her he would overlook her attendance problems if she would let him touch her vagina and then proceeded to grab her crotch. This was related to a coworker in 1996 but not formally reported to management

until November 1997. After investigation, disciplinary action took place and Paul retired. Mary brought a legal action in state court against Paul and the Health Department under California's Fair Employment and Housing Act. The DHS moved for summary judgment.

Should the court rule in its favor? Why or why not?

3. Indian Head Casino employed Maura P. as a warehouse worker and heavy equipment operator. She was the only woman in this job and in her local Teamsters bargaining unit.

Maura experienced a number of problems with management and her co-workers that led to an escalating series of disciplinary sanctions, including informal rebukes, a denial of privileges, and suspension. The casino finally terminated her after she was involved in a physical altercation in a warehouse elevator with a fellow Teamsters member. The casino disciplined both employees because the facts surrounding the incident were in dispute, but Maura's fellow worker, who had a clean disciplinary record, received only a five-day suspension.

Maura subsequently filed a lawsuit against the casino, asserting claims of sex discrimination and sexual harassment under Title VII. The court dismissed the sexual harassment claim but allowed the claim for sex discrimination to go to the jury. At trial, Maura presented evidence that (1) she was singled out for "intense 'stalking'" by one of her supervisors, (2) she received harsher discipline than men for the same conduct, (3) she was treated less favorably than men in the assignment of overtime, and (4) supervisors repeatedly "stacked" her disciplinary record and "frequently used or tolerated" sex-based slurs against her.

What should the court decide? Analyze the case and come to a decision. Indicate the reasons for your answer.

4. Phillips Modern was owned and operated by Scott Phillips, whose wife Lori was also involved with the company. Tenge worked for the company as a secretary and eventually became the highest-paid employee. Tenge was an at-will employee. Around 2002 Lori began to believe that Scott and Tenge were involved in a romantic relationship.

Tenge admitted to two instances of touching that occurred in Lori's presence. Tenge agreed that this was physical contact that was suggestive and of a risqué nature, and that Lori could have suspected the two had an intimate relationship.

Tenge also testified that she wrote notes of a sexual or intimate nature to Scott some 5–10 times. She stated that she put these notes in a location where other people could see them, even though she was not getting along with Lori and she knew that Lori might have the power to fire her. Indeed, Lori found one of these notes in the company dumpster, pieced it together, and reacted by terminating Tenge's employment in November 2002. Scott ultimately dismissed her on February 17, 2003, saying that his wife was "making me choose between my best employee or her and the kids."

Is Phillips Modern liable for violation of Title VII? Why or why not? What additional factors would influence your decision?

5. Plaintiff Darlene Jespersen worked successfully as a bartender at Harrah's for 20 years and compiled what by all accounts was an exemplary record. During Jespersen's entire tenure with Harrah's, the company maintained a policy encouraging female beverage servers to wear makeup.

In February 2000 Harrah's implemented a "Beverage Department Image Transformation" program at 20 Harrah's locations. The program stated,

---

Beverage bartenders and barbacks will adhere to these additional guidelines:

Overall Guidelines (applied equally to male/female):
Appearance:

- Must maintain personal best image portrayed at time of hire.
- Jewelry, if issued, must be worn. Otherwise, tasteful and simple jewelry is permitted; no large chokers, chains, or bracelets.
- No faddish hairstyles or unnatural colors are permitted.

Males:

- Hair must not extend below top of shirt collar. Ponytails are prohibited.
- Hands and fingernails must be clean and nails neatly trimmed at all times. No colored polish is permitted.
- Eye and facial makeup is not permitted.
- Shoes will be solid black leather or leather type with rubber (nonskid) soles.

Females:

- Hair must be teased, curled, or styled every day you work. Hair must be worn down at all times, no exceptions.
- Stockings are to be of nude or natural color consistent with employee's skin tone. No runs.
- Nail polish can be clear, white, pink, or red color only. No exotic nail art or length.
- Shoes will be solid black leather or leather type with rubber (nonskid) soles.
- Makeup (face powder, blush, and mascara) must be worn and applied neatly in complementary colors. Lip color must be worn at all times.

Jespersen did not wear makeup on or off the job, and in her deposition stated that wearing it would conflict with her self-image. It is not disputed that she found the makeup requirement offensive and felt so uncomfortable wearing makeup that she found it interfered with her ability to perform as a bartender. Unwilling to wear the makeup, and not qualifying for any open positions at the casino with a similar compensation scale, Jespersen left her employment with Harrah's.

Was Harrah's grooming policy illegally discriminatory? Why or why not?

6. For each of the previous problems, state how different management styles might have prevented legal action. Using the Internet, find policies, practices, and training programs that relate to sex discrimination and sexual harassment. Evaluate those efforts in light of the cases described here.

References

1. Spoken by Senator Henry W. Blair during the congressional debate on woman suffrage in 1886. From H. W. Blair, J. E. Brown, J. N. Dolph, G. G. Vest, and Geo. F. Hoar, *The Project Gutenberg EBook of Debate on Woman Suffrage in the Senate of the United States, 2d Session, 49th Congress, December 8, 1886, and January 25, 1887.* See also http://www.gutenberg.org/files/11114/11114.txt.

2. 29 U.S.C. 206(d). The Equal Pay Act is part of the Fair Labor Standards Act, 29 U.S.C. 201 et. seq.

3. See www.gao.gov/new.items/d02156.pdf, U.S. General Accounting Office, Women in Management: Analysis of Selected Data from the Current Population Survey 18-19, GAO-02-156 (October 2001) (accessed July 13, 2007).

4. *County of Washington v. Gunther,* 452 US 161, 452 US 161(1981).

5. 11 S.C. 1976-77, c. 33. Section 11(1)

6. B. Bilson, *A Colloquy on Employment and Labour Law and Policy for New Millennium: Promises and Paradoxes: The Ravages of Time: The Work of the Federal Pay Equity Task Force and Section 11 of the Canadian Human Rights Act, Sask. L. Rev.* 67, p. 525. Copyright (c) 2004 Saskatchewan Law Review Saskatchewan Law Review (Beth Bilson, College of Law, University of Saskatchewan; Chair, Pay Equity Task Force. This paper was drafted prior to the release of the final report of the Pay Equity Task Force.)

7. *Simens v. Ashcroft (2003),* Appeal No. 01A21778 Agency No. F-99-5333 U.S. Equal Employment Opportunity Commission.

8. J. Freeman, "How 'Sex' Got Into Title VII: Persistent Opportunism as a Maker of Public Policy." A slightly different version was published in *Law and Inequality: A Journal of Theory and Practice* 9, no. 2 (March 1991), pp. 163–184.

9. As established in the *McDonnell Douglas* case, 411 U.S. 792, at 802 (1973).

10. *Price Waterhouse v. Hopkins,* 109 S. Ct. 1775 (1989).

11. *Meritor Savings Bank v. Vinson,* 106 S. Ct. 2399 (1986).

12. *Burlington Industries, Inc. v. Ellerth,* 118 S. Ct. 2257 (1998).

13. *Faragher v. City of Boca Raton,* 118 S. Ct. 2275 (1998).

14. *Stender v. Lucky Stores, Inc.,* 803 F. Supp. 259 (N.D. Cal. 1992).

15. The quoted material first appeared in "Harassment and Discrimination Training: What the Law Requires," by Michael W. Johnson, co-President of the Brightline Learning Division of Global Compliance Services, Inc., which appears at the following URL: http://www4.globalcompliance.com/images/Brightline/PDFs/Harassment%20&%20Discrimination%20Training—What%20the%20Law%20Requires.pdf. M.W. Johnson, "Harassment and Discrimination Prevention Training: What the Law Requires," presented to the Chicago Bar Association's Labor and Employment Law Section on May 5, 2003. Copyright 2003 Brightline Compliance, LLC. See www.brightline compliance.com/training/law-of-training.html (accessed July 24, 2007). The information about the settlement is from F. D. Blau, and L. M. Kahn, "Gender Differences in Pay," NBER Working Paper No. W7732 (June 2000). See also http://ssrn.com/abstract=232114 (accessed July 24, 2007).

16. *Oncale v. Sundowner Offshore Services,* 118 S. Ct. 998 (1998).

17. *DeSantis v. Pacific Telephone and Telegraph Co., Inc.,* 608 F.2d 327 (1979).

18. K. A. Kovach, and P. E. Millspaugh, "Employment Nondiscrimination Act: On the Cutting Edge of Public Policy—Gay Rights Legislation," *Business Horizons,* July–August 1996, pp. 65–73.

Bibliography

Portions of this chapter were printed first in the *Journal of Global Competition.* R. Twomey, "Women in the World's Labor Market: The Issue of Pay Equity," *Journal of Global Competition,* Vol. 12(1), 2004.

Reaching for Equal Opportunity Based on Religion, National Origin, Age, and Disability

11. Religious Discrimination

12. National Origin Discrimination and Immigration Issues

13. Age Discrimination

14. Disability Discrimination

Religious Discrimination

> Each religion, by the help of more or less myth which it takes more or less seriously, proposes some method of fortifying the human soul and enabling it to make its peace with its destiny.
>
> George Santayana (1863–1952)[1]

INTRODUCTION

accommodation
The requirement of accommodation arises from two federal statutes—the Civil Rights Act with regard to religious discrimination and the Americans with Disabilities Act. Employers must take into consideration the needs of employees and make whatever reasonable changes and modifications are necessary to make it possible for employees to continue to work for the employer. The courts recognize the corresponding burden on the employer, and determinations of what constitutes a reasonable accommodation are made case by case.

Previous chapters covered the protected classes of sex, race, and color. The remaining protected classes under the Civil Rights Act encompass national origin and religion. This chapter explores the prohibition of discrimination against employees, or potential employees, on the basis of their religious beliefs.

The Civil Rights Act of 1964 not only prohibits discrimination on the basis of creed or religion, but also requires **accommodation** of an employee's religious beliefs. The accommodation should not result in more than a minimal burden on the company. This accommodation requirement is similar to, but not as restrictive as, the accommodation requirement of the Americans with Disabilities Act covered in Chapter 14.

In analyzing a case based on religious discrimination, courts consider three factors:

- Whether an employee is within a protected class—that is, whether the employee's belief comes within the protection of the law.
- Whether an employee has requested and been denied an accommodation that is reasonable.
- Whether an employer's adverse action was motivated by illegal bias.

It is not always an *employee's* religious belief that can trigger a discrimination charge. An employer might introduce activities that constitute religious practices or border on religious beliefs. In so doing a company exposes itself to possible legal problems. For example, training for personal development that uses meditation, guided visualization, self–hypnosis, or any techniques that employees may claim are prohibited by their religion could result in legal entanglements if such cases are not properly managed. In fact, the EEOC has issued a policy guidance on this type of training program:

> Although the courts and the Commission have not addressed the particular conflicts raised by the "new age" training programs, this issue can be resolved under the traditional Title VII theory of religious accommodation. While there may be some disagreement over whether the training programs themselves are religious, an employee need only demonstrate that participation in the programs in some manner conflicts with his/her personal religious beliefs.[2]

WHAT CONSTITUTES AN EMPLOYEE'S RELIGION OR BELIEF?

Religion is defined in the Civil Rights Act as including "all aspects of religious observance and practice, as well as belief, unless an employer demonstrates that he is unable to reasonably accommodate to an employee's . . . religious observance or practice without undue hardship on the conduct of the employer's business."[3]

It was left to the courts to flesh out exactly what the words of the statute mean, and many courts have interpreted it broadly. The Equal Employment Opportunity Commission (EEOC) takes the position that a protected belief includes "moral or ethical beliefs as to what is right and wrong which are sincerely held with the strength of traditional religious views. . . . The fact that no religious group espouses such beliefs or the fact that the religious group to which the individual professes to belong may not accept such belief will not determine whether the belief is a religious belief of the employee. . . ."[4] Needless to say, this presents a problem for an employer who wishes to respect an employee's beliefs but who finds it difficult to recognize or understand those beliefs. Management faces the challenge of carefully dealing with requests for religious accommodation and of respectfully considering each employee's request. Making light of such a request, denigrating an employee's belief, or responding in any way less than seriously can easily create legal trouble for an employer.

Employers are advised to establish consistent rules for all such requests. For example, employers could honor requests for time off for religiously affiliated reasons but limit such time off to a set number of days in a year or a month—and then be sure to apply the rule consistently to all employees. With regard to the wearing of religious garb, an employer could establish a reasonable and justifiable requirement for uniformity when appropriate—such as for meter readers who represent a company while making home visits. In such a case an employer can argue that granting an employee's request to wear a religious head scarf, for example, is not a reasonable accommodation. In the absence of consistently applied and justifiable rules, an employer risks vulnerability to charges of religious discrimination.

WHAT CONSTITUTES REASONABLE ACCOMMODATION FOR RELIGION?

Legal problems can be avoided by honestly evaluating a requested accommodation to determine whether it is reasonable and whether it presents more than a minimal burden on the company. An employer has no obligation to accommodate an employee who does not make his or her religious needs known and does not request an accommodation.

Inherently reasonable accommodations, according to the EEOC, include voluntary swapping of time between workers, allowing flexible hours, and making lateral switches in job assignments[5].

When an employer makes a good-faith effort to accommodate an employee's request, courts generally support the employer when none of the attempted accommodations proves satisfactory. The employer should consider several possible accommodations and would be wise to try more than one if the first is not workable. In determining whether an accommodation constitutes an undue hardship for an employer, the EEOC looks at the cost of the accommodation "in relation to the size and operating cost of the employer"[6]. The employer should be prepared to state the actual cost of the proposed accommodation and, if it believes that the cost is burdensome, make its case with evidence showing that given the size and resources of the company, the cost is not justifiable.

Case for Discussion 11-1

The *Trans World Airlines* case is a seminal case on the issues raised by the religious discrimination prohibitions of Title VII. It points out, among other things, how the Court balances the needs of employers against those of employees. It sets out parameters for courts to consider when determining whether an accommodation is reasonable (what constitutes an undue burden). Finally, it provides insights about conflicting federal priorities—workers' rights to collective bargaining and the rights granted by Title VII.

TRANS WORLD AIRLINES, INC. V. HARDISON ET AL., 432 U.S. 63 (1977)[7]

Facts

[R]espondent Hardison was hired by TWA to work as a clerk in the Stores Department at its Kansas City base. Because of its essential role in the Kansas City operation, the Stores Department must operate 24 hours per day, 365 days per year; and whenever an employee's job in that department is not filled, an employee must be shifted from another department, or a supervisor must cover the job, even if the work in other areas may suffer.

Hardison . . . was subject to a seniority system contained in a collective bargaining agreement. . . . The most senior employees have first choice for job and shift assignments, and the most junior employees are required to work when the union steward is unable to find enough people willing to work at a particular time or in a particular job to fill TWA's needs.

In the spring of 1968 Hardison began to study the religion known as the Worldwide Church of God. One of the tenets of that religion is that one must observe the Sabbath by refraining from performing any work from sunset on Friday until sunset on Saturday . . . [and] on certain specified religious holidays.

When Hardison informed Everett Kussman, the manager of the Stores Department, of his religious conviction regarding observance of the Sabbath, Kussman agreed that the union steward should seek a job swap for Hardison or a change of days off; that Hardison would have his religious holidays off whenever possible if Hardison agreed to work the traditional holidays when asked; and that Kussman would try to find Hardison another job that would be more compatible with his religious beliefs. The problem was temporarily solved when Hardison transferred to the 11 p.m.–7 a.m. shift. Working this shift permitted Hardison to observe his Sabbath.

The problem soon reappeared when Hardison bid for and received a transfer from Building 1 to Building 2, where he would work the day shift. The two buildings had entirely separate seniority lists; and while in Building 1 Hardison had sufficient seniority to observe the Sabbath regularly, he was second from the bottom on the Building 2 seniority list.

In Building 2 Hardison was asked to work Saturdays when a fellow employee went on vacation. TWA agreed to permit the union to seek a change of work assignments for Hardison, but the union was not willing to violate the seniority provisions . . . and Hardison had insufficient seniority to bid for a shift having Saturdays off.

A proposal that Hardison work only four days a week was rejected by the company. Hardison's job was essential, and on weekends he was the only available person on his shift to perform it. To leave the position empty would have impaired supply shop functions, which were critical to airline operations; to fill Hardison's position with a supervisor or an employee from another area would simply have undermanned another operation; and to employ someone not regularly assigned to work Saturdays would have required TWA to pay premium wages.

When an accommodation was not reached, Hardison refused to report for work on Saturdays. A transfer to the twilight shift proved unavailing because that schedule still required Hardison to work past sundown on Fridays. After a hearing, Hardison was discharged on grounds of insubordination for refusing to work during his designated shift.

Hardison . . . brought this action for injunctive relief in the United States District Court against TWA . . . claiming that his discharge by TWA constituted religious discrimination. . . . The district court ruled in favor of the defendants. . . . The court of appeals reversed the judgment for TWA [and] held that TWA had not satisfied its duty to accommodate. . . .

***

In 1967 the EEOC amended its guidelines to require employers "to make reasonable accommodations to the religious needs of employees and prospective employees where such accommodations can be made without undue hardship on the conduct of the employer's business."

***

We disagree with the court of appeals in all relevant respects. It is our view that TWA made reasonable efforts to accommodate and that each of the court of appeals' suggested alternatives would have been an undue hardship within the meaning of the statute as construed by the EEOC guidelines.

***

We are also convinced, contrary to the court of appeals, that TWA itself cannot be faulted for having failed to work out a shift or job swap for Hardison. Both the union and TWA had agreed to the seniority system; the union was unwilling to entertain a variance over the objections of men senior to Hardison; and for TWA to have arranged unilaterally for a swap would have amounted to a breach of the collective bargaining agreement.

***

Without a clear and express indication from Congress, we cannot agree with Hardison and the EEOC that an agreed-upon seniority system must give way when necessary to accommodate religious observances. The issue is important and warrants some discussion.

***

Our conclusion is supported by the fact that seniority systems are afforded special treatment under Title VII itself. Section 703(h) provides in pertinent part,

> Notwithstanding any other provision of this subchapter, it shall not be an unlawful employment practice for an employer to apply different standards of compensation, or different terms, conditions, or privileges of employment pursuant to a bona fide seniority or merit system . . . provided that such differences are not the result of an intention to discriminate because of race, color, religion, sex, or national origin. . . . 42 U.S.C. § 2000e-2(h).

***

Decision

The Court reversed the decision of the court of appeals and held in favor of TWA.

Dissent

MR. JUSTICE MARSHALL, joined by MR. JUSTICE BRENNAN

***

Today's decision deals a fatal blow to all efforts under Title VII to accommodate work requirements to religious practices. The Court holds, in essence, that although the EEOC regulations and the Act state that an employer must make reasonable adjustments in his work demands to take account of religious observances, the regulation and Act do not really mean what they say. An employer, the Court concludes, need not grant even the most minor special privilege to religious observers to enable them to follow their faith. As a question of social policy, this result is deeply troubling, for a society that truly values religious pluralism cannot compel adherents of minority religions to make the cruel choice of surrendering their religion or their job. And as a matter of law today's result is intolerable, for the Court adopts the very position that Congress expressly rejected in 1972, as if we were free to disregard congressional choices that a majority of this Court thinks unwise. I therefore dissent.

Questions for Discussion

1. In balancing the interests of employer and employee, do you believe the *TWA* decision shows a bias in favor of employers?
2. If the decision favored Hardison, what argument would employers make regarding the ultimate consequences?
3. Do you find the dissenting opinion persuasive? Explain why or why not.

Case for Discussion 11-2

Prima Facie Case

MANN V. FRANK, U.S. POSTAL SERVICE, 7 F.3D 1365 (1993)[8]

Facts

Mann is a Seventh Day Adventist. Her religious beliefs prohibit work from sundown Friday to sundown Saturday. The terms and conditions of Mann's employment are determined in part by a national collective bargaining agreement between the Postal Service and the American Postal Workers Union, AFL-CIO. Under the collective bargaining agreement applicable to Mann, regular shift assignments at the Postal Service are determined by seniority. The overtime provisions of the collective bargaining agreement state that employees desiring to work overtime shall place their names on an overtime desired list (ODL). When the need for overtime arises, employees possessing the requisite skills who have listed their names on the ODL are selected in order of their seniority on a rotating basis. The collective bargaining agreement further provides that employees not on the ODL may be required to work overtime only if all available employees on the ODL have been utilized. In such a case, overtime is assigned in order of reverse seniority, with the first overtime shift assigned to the most junior employee. There is no requirement that employees sign the ODL, and employees are not disciplined for not signing the ODL.

***

During the week of November 11, 1985, postal supervisor Robert Zajic detected the need for overtime during the Friday night–Saturday morning shift to prevent mail delay. According to the collective bargaining agreement, Mann was required to work this overtime shift because her name, in contrast to Higgins, was listed on the ODL. Zajic, knowing of Mann's religious constraints, asked Higgins to cover the overtime shift, but Higgins declined. Higgins claimed that she could not be forced to work until the ODL had been exhausted, and if she were forced to work before the ODL was utilized, she would file a grievance against the Postal Service for violating the terms of the collective bargaining agreement. Mann was instructed to work the overtime shift. Mann failed to report to work and instead phoned in reporting car trouble. Mann was unable to provide satisfactory documentation to the Postal Service to substantiate her claim of car trouble and failed to provide an alternative explanation for her absence. Consequently, Mann was charged absent without leave (AWOL) and suspended for seven days without pay. Mann subsequently removed her name from the ODL. She has not been asked to work on her Sabbath since removing her name from the ODL.

Mann brought suit against the Postal Service in district court under Title VII of the Civil Rights Act of 1964. She alleged she was discriminated against on the basis of religion. The district court entered judgment for the Postal Service after a bench trial. The district court found that the Postal Service had made reasonable accommodations for Mann's religious beliefs in the form of the collective bargaining agreement's seniority system and the voluntary ODL. The district court found that Mann's requested accommodations would result in undue hardship on the Postal Service. The district court further determined that Mann had not been subjected to disparate treatment because of her religious beliefs.

***

First, reasonably accommodating Mann would have compromised Higgins's contractual rights as secured by the collective bargaining agreement. The collective bargaining agreement provides a neutral seniority system for awarding shift assignments and a voluntary, seniority-based policy for assigning overtime work shifts (the ODL). The record showed that any further efforts by the

Postal Service to reasonably accommodate Mann would have violated the terms of the collective bargaining agreement and contravened the procedures for assigning overtime shifts pursuant to the ODL. The record showed that the Postal Service approached both Higgins and the union steward in an effort to reasonably accommodate Mann. Higgins was not willing to work overtime in place of Mann, and the union was not willing to waive the filing of a grievance if Higgins had been forced to work overtime in Mann's place. The Postal Service's efforts satisfied Title VII's reasonable accommodation provision.

Second, the seniority system and the voluntary ODL in the collective bargaining agreement themselves represented significant accommodations to Mann's religious needs. Hardison held that the seniority system in place at TWA established a neutral vehicle for minimizing occasions when an employee would be scheduled to work a Sabbath day, and, as such, the seniority system itself constituted a significant accommodation to the religious needs of employees. In the instant case, the seniority system and the voluntary ODL represented a nondiscriminatory vehicle for minimizing the number of occasions when an employee would be called upon to work an overtime shift on a day that he or she preferred to have off.

Undue Hardship

Hardison held that any accommodation involving more than de minimis costs to the employer constitutes undue hardship. The district court found that Mann's suggested accommodations would have resulted in more than de minimis costs to the Postal Service. Substantial evidence supported the district court's findings that the accommodation alternatives proposed by Mann would have caused the Postal Service undue hardship.

Mann's suggested accommodations included requiring another employee not listed on the ODL to work overtime in Mann's place, requiring employees already working the shift in question to increase their work rotations to absorb the effects of Mann's absence, or doing without Mann entirely. Compelling Higgins to work involuntarily in Mann's place would have contravened the seniority and ODL provisions of the collective bargaining agreement and deprived Higgins of her contractual rights. This proposed accommodation constitutes undue hardship.

Disparate Treatment

Mann also argues that the Postal Service subjected her to disparate treatment because of her religion in violation of Title VII. Mann alleges three instances of disparate treatment: (1) Mann was excused from working overtime while in a different section, but was denied such an allowance once she transferred to pay section 218; (2) the Postal Service excused a Seventh Day Adventist co-worker from working overtime on his Sabbath but refused to excuse Mann on the day in question; (3) the Postal Service excused employees from working overtime for secular reasons but refused her requests to be excused for religious reasons. As the district court properly found, each of these claims must fail.

Prima Facie Case of Religious Discrimination

A disparate treatment case based on religion requires a plaintiff to show that she is, or was, treated less favorably than others because of her religious beliefs. *International Brotherhood of Teamsters v. United States,* 431 U.S. 324, 335 n.15 (1977). In a disparate treatment case, the plaintiff must prove that she is a member of a protected class and must compare her treatment to that of a similarly situated member of a nonprotected class.

***

The district court properly determined that Mann's first claim of disparate treatment could not succeed because Mann sought to compare herself with herself. Rather than supporting a claim of disparate treatment, the fact that the Postal Service excused Mann from working on her Sabbath before she transferred into pay section 218 supports the finding that the Postal Service made efforts in the past to reasonably accommodate Mann's religious needs. The different duties performed by employees in pay section 218 required specialized knowledge and made it more difficult to excuse Mann from her shift.

Mann's second claim of disparate treatment is as unique as her first. Mann, comparing herself to another Postal Service employee who was also a Seventh Day Adventist, claimed that she had been treated less favorably than her coworker. Mann cannot state a prima facie case of disparate treatment on the basis of religion by comparing her treatment to that of a member of the same protected class.

As her third claim, Mann contended that the Postal Service excused employees from working overtime for secular reasons but refused her requests to be excused for religious reasons. The evidence produced at trial showed that the Postal Service excused employees only for secular reasons which were nonrecurring occasions such as birthdays and anniversaries, but would not excuse a repeated and regular weekly absence such as the Sabbath exemption which Mann sought.

Decision

For the reasons stated above, we affirm the judgment of the district court.

The court held in favor of the Postal Service on the disparate treatment claim, holding that the accommodations requested posed an undue burden on the employer.

Question for Discussion

collective bargaining agreement
The resulting contract signed by a labor union and management pertaining to the terms and conditions of employment for all the employees in the contracting organization.

One of the benefits of a **collective bargaining agreement** is that the rights of the workers are spelled out clearly in a comprehensive and detailed written contract. Assume that there was no collective bargaining agreement. How difficult would it be for the employer to defend itself in this case?

THE WORKPLACE RELIGIOUS FREEDOM ACT

In response to *Hardison* and other court opinions dealing with the reasonable accommodation requirement for religious purposes, a bill known as the Workplace Religious Freedom Act was introduced in Congress. Although it has not been enacted into law, advocates continue to hope that Congress will consider and pass this bill in the future. In the words of the sponsor,

> The Workplace Religious Freedom Act is necessary to reestablish the intent of Congress that only real hardship is reason for an employer not to provide a reasonable accommodation for an employee. My bill would define "undue hardship" as a "significant difficulty or expense," similar to the definition used in the Americans with Disabilities Act. The bill establishes several criteria for determining what constitutes a significant difficulty or expense, including the costs of providing such an accommodation, the size of the employer (in terms of financial resources and number of employees), and the geographic separateness or administrative or fiscal relationship of an employer's multiple facilities. I believe the proposed new definitions of "reasonable accommodation" and "undue hardship" strike the appropriate balance between employer and employee rights as they relate to religious liberty in the workplace.
>
> To clarify the rights of employers . . ., the legislation states that an employee must be able to perform the "essential functions" of his or her job "with or without reasonable accommodation." This provision ensures that an employee cannot request an accommodation that would make it impossible to fulfill the core requirements of a job. The "essential functions" term cannot, however, be interpreted to include practices such as wearing religious clothing, taking time off for religious observances, or "other practices that may have a temporary or tangential impact on the ability to perform job functions." Those practices may not be considered an "essential function" of a job under this legislation, unless an accommodation for those practices is believed to be an "undue hardship" on the employer.

> . . .

> The state of New York passed a law similar to WRFA in 2002 that, by all reports, has not resulted in the dire predictions anticipated by critics on both the right and left. According to Attorney General Eliot Spitzer, New York's law has not been overly burdensome on businesses or resulted in an increase in litigation; nor has it resulted in the infringement of a woman's ability to have an abortion or purchase birth control as the ACLU has predicted.[9]

Opponents' Position on WRFA

The ACLU has gone on record to oppose passage of the WRFA. Its major concern is that in making it more difficult for employers to refuse to accommodate employees' religious rights, the civil rights of others are at risk. For example, if an employee refuses on religious grounds to perform an abortion in a public hospital, the rights of the patient requesting the abortion will be thwarted. Another example is an employee who proselytizes his religion to mental health patients in a public facility, thereby infringing on the religious freedom of others. The ACLU gives several other examples of the potential harm that WRFA could cause if passed.[10]

THE MINISTERIAL EXCEPTION

When the employer itself is a religious organization, the law permits an exception to the restrictions of Title VII. In other words, a religious organization can legally require that a job candidate be a member of a particular religion. According to 42 U.S.C. § 2000 e-1(a), the law does not apply to institutions "with respect to the employment of individuals of a particular religion to perform work connected with the carrying on by such (an institution) of its activities." Also, under Section 703 of the law, religious educational organizations are exempted, allowing them to "hire . . . employees of a particular religion if such organization is, in whole or in substantial part, owned, supported, controlled, or managed by a particular religion . . ." or if its program is "directed toward the propagation of a particular religion."[11]

The ministerial exception to Title VII has its roots in the First Amendment of the U.S. Constitution, which provides that "Congress shall make no law respecting an establishment of religion, or prohibiting the free exercise thereof. . . ." Accordingly, the government (whether legislative, judicial, or executive) cannot interfere in the activities, decisions, and policies of religious institutions. To do so could be interpreted as a form of "establishment" of religion. Therefore, when an employee of a church makes a claim of religious discrimination, she is likely to fail in court. When a court (an arm of the government) interferes in the policies of a church by its ruling, it ostensibly acts unconstitutionally. It is less clear whether an employee would be successful bringing a sex, race, or national origin discrimination case against a religious organization. If the employee in question is a minister or someone in such a position within a religious organization, the courts have held that the First Amendment requires a "hands off" approach. In other words, such matters will not be decided in the civil courts; they are part of the ecclesiastical affairs of the religious institution, and the Constitution prohibits interference. If the employee holds a position not directly related to the religious functions of the institution, the matter is less clear.

In a case involving a nonprofit gymnasium that was open to the public but affiliated with a religious organization, an employee who was terminated for not abiding by the religious requirements of the church brought a Title VII action for religious discrimination. The U.S. Supreme Court in *Church of Jesus Christ of Latter-Day Saints v. Amos,* 483 U.S. 327 (1987) held that the not-for-profit employer was exempt from the law's requirements and stated that Title VII's ministerial exemption was constitutional. A distinction was made between for-profit and not-for-profit religiously affiliated organizations, cautioning that if an employer operates for profit, it likely would not be treated the same as in the *Amos* case.

Case for Discussion 11-3

MCCLURE V. THE SALVATION ARMY, 460 F.2D 553 (1972)[12]

Facts

In this federal appellate case Mrs. McClure, an ordained minister for the Salvation Army, brought suit against the church for sex discrimination under the Civil Rights Act. Specifically, she alleged that she had received a lower salary and fewer benefits than that accorded similarly situated male church officers, and that she had been discharged because of her complaints to her superiors and to the EEOC with regard to these practices.

The Salvation Army moved to dismiss because it claimed it was not subject to the provisions of Title VII by reason of § 702. Also, since it is a church, application of the provisions of Title VII to the Salvation Army under the circumstances presented by this action would constitute a violation of the First Amendment of the Constitution of the United States.

The Title VII Issue

Section 702 of Title VII, 42 U.S.C. § 2000e-1, reads as follows:

> This subchapter shall not apply to an employer with respect to the employment of aliens outside any state, or to a religious corporation, association, or society, with respect to the employment of individuals of a particular religion to perform work connected with the carrying on by such corporation, association, or society of its religious activities or to an educational institution with respect to the employment of individuals to perform work connected with the educational activities of such institution.

Mrs. McClure and the EEOC contend that the exemption permits a religious organization to discriminate only on the basis of religion. They contend that the section was intended to allow a religious organization to employ persons of a particular faith to perform work connected with the carrying on of their religious activities without otherwise violating the provisions of Title VII. Both the language and the legislative history of the section support this contention. The original House version of § 702 provided a religious organization with a blanket exemption from the provisions of Title VII. This version reads as follows: "This title shall not apply to . . . a religious corporation, association, or society."

Subsequently an amendment was proposed: "Section 704 formerly Section 703 and later renumbered as Section 702 has been amended to limit the general exemption of religious groups to those practices relating to the employment of individuals of a particular religion to perform work connected with the employer's religious activities. . . ."

The language and the legislative history of § 702 compel the conclusion that Congress did not intend that a religious organization be exempted from liability for discriminating against its employees on the basis of race, color, sex, or national origin with respect to their compensation, terms, conditions, or privileges of employment.

***

The Constitutional Issue

Does the application of the provisions of Title VII to the relationship between the Salvation Army and Mrs. McClure (a church and its minister) violate either of the religion clauses of the First Amendment?

The Supreme Court has many times recognized that the First Amendment has built a "wall of separation" between church and state. Though that "wall of separation" between permissible and impermissible intrusion of the state into matters of religion may blur, or become indistinct, or vary, it does and must remain high and impregnable. . . .

***

The relationship between an organized church and its ministers is its life-blood. The minister is the chief instrument by which the church seeks to fulfill its purpose. Matters touching this relationship must necessarily be recognized as of prime ecclesiastical concern. Just as the initial function of selecting a minister is a matter of church administration and government, so are the functions which accompany such a selection. It is unavoidably true that these include the determination of a minister's salary, his place of assignment, and the duty he is to perform in the furtherance of the religious mission of the church.

***

An application of the provisions of Title VII to the employment relationship which exists between the Salvation Army and Mrs. McClure, a church and its minister, would involve an investigation and review of these practices and decisions and would, as a result, cause the state to intrude upon matters of church administration and government which have so many times before been proclaimed to be matters of a singular ecclesiastical concern. Control of strictly ecclesiastical matters could easily pass from the church to the state. The church would then be without the power to decide for itself, free from state interference, matters of church administration and government.

***

Decision

The Court affirmed the lower court and held in favor of the defendant, the Salvation Army.

Questions for Discussion

1. Does the *McClure* case mean that any and all employment decisions made by a religious organization are exempt from application of the Civil Rights Act?

2. Under what circumstances do you believe a court would hold a religious organization to the provisions of the Civil Rights Act?
3. Does the ministerial exception apply only to ministers (or people working in such a capacity)? Could it apply when the employee is a layperson? Under what circumstances?

PUBLIC SECTOR RELIGIOUS DISCRIMINATION

When the government is the employer or the party that is negatively impacting a citizen on the basis of his or her religious beliefs, the First Amendment guarantee of freedom of religion is at issue. The U.S. Supreme Court made a 1990 decision that involved a denial of unemployment benefits to two individuals who had been fired from a private sector position as counselors because of illegal ingestion of peyote. The state of Oregon made it a crime to possess peyote. The employees, Smith and Black, argued that their use of peyote occurred in conjunction with their Native American religious practices, and therefore the terminations were a violation of their constitutional rights. The case was *Employment Division v. Smith* (1990)[13]. In deciding against the plaintiffs, Black and Smith, the Court held that the First Amendment's protection of the free exercise of religion does not allow a person to flout the law by reasoning that the law contravenes their religious beliefs. The Court stated, "To permit this would be to make the professed doctrines of religious belief superior to the law of the land, and in effect to permit every citizen to become a law unto himself." By the same logic, religious beliefs do not excuse people from obeying a number of valid and generally applicable laws such as child labor laws, Sunday closing laws, the Selective Service, payment of taxes, and others.

Management **Perspective**

A good source of information about religious discrimination in the workplace is the EEOC Web site at www.eeoc.gov/types/religion.html. The following information, and more, will be found there.

Incidents of religious discrimination remain a concern in American workplaces. In Fiscal Year 2006, EEOC received 2,541 charges of religious discrimination. EEOC resolved 2,387 religious discrimination charges and recovered $5.7 million in monetary benefits for charging parties and other aggrieved individuals (not including monetary benefits obtained through litigation)[14].

(Continued)

Societal factors, of course, influence the number of cases that arise in the area of discrimination, and with regard to religious and national origin discrimination, a contributing factor was the 9/11 set of terrorist attacks of 2001. Attesting to the fact that those events increased the number of charges filed by people who are Muslim, Arab, South Asian, or Sikh, the EEOC provided examples of such charges along with advice about how to handle such cases. The following is taken from the EEOC's fact sheet[15]:

HIRING AND OTHER EMPLOYMENT DECISIONS

Narinder, a South Asian man who wears a Sikh turban, applies for a position as a cashier at XYZ Discount Goods. XYZ fears Narinder's religious attire will make customers uncomfortable. What should XYZ do?

XYZ should not deny Narinder the job due to notions of customer preferences about religious attire. That would be unlawful. It would be the same as refusing to hire Narinder because he is a Sikh.

XYZ Discount Goods should also consider proactive measures for preventing discrimination in hiring and other employment decisions. XYZ could remind its managers and employees that discrimination based on religion or national origin is not tolerated by the company in any aspect of employment, including hiring. XYZ could also adopt objective standards for selecting new employees. It is important to hire people based on their qualifications rather than on perceptions about their religion, race, or national origin.

HARASSMENT

Muhammad, who is Arab American, works for XYZ Motors, a large used car business. Muhammad meets with his manager and complains that Bill, one of his coworkers, regularly calls him names like "camel jockey," "the local terrorist," and "the ayatollah" and has intentionally embarrassed him in front of customers by claiming that he is incompetent. How should the supervisor respond?

Managers and supervisors who learn about objectionable workplace conduct based on religion or national origin are responsible for taking steps to correct the conduct by anyone under their control. Muhammad's manager should relay Muhammad's complaint to the appropriate manager if he does not supervise Bill. If XYZ Motors then determines that Bill has harassed Muhammad, it should take disciplinary action against Bill that is significant enough to ensure that the harassment does not continue.

Workplace harassment and its costs are often preventable. Clear and effective policies prohibiting ethnic and religious slurs, and related offensive conduct, are needed. Confidential complaint mechanisms for promptly reporting harassment are critical, and these policies should be written to encourage victims and witnesses to come forward. When harassment is reported, the focus should be on action to end the harassment and correct its effects on the complaining employee.

RELIGIOUS ACCOMMODATION

Three of the 10 Muslim employees in XYZ's 30-person template design division approach their supervisor and ask that they be allowed to use a conference room in an adjacent building for prayer. Until making the request, these employees prayed at their workstations. What should XYZ do?

XYZ should work closely with the employees to find an appropriate accommodation that meets their religious needs without causing an undue hardship for XYZ. Whether a reasonable accommodation would impose undue hardship and therefore not be required depends on the particulars of the business and the requested accommodation.

When the room is needed for business purposes, XYZ can deny its use for personal religious purposes. However, allowing the employees to use the conference room for prayers likely would not impose an undue hardship on XYZ in many other circumstances.

Similarly, prayer often can be performed during breaks, so that providing sufficient time during work hours for prayer would not result in an undue hardship. If going to another building for prayer takes longer than the allotted break periods, the employees still can be accommodated if the nature of the template design division's work makes flexible scheduling feasible. XYZ can require employees to make up any work time missed for religious observance.

In evaluating undue hardship, XYZ should consider only whether it can accommodate the three employees who made the request. If XYZ can accommodate three employees, it should do so. Because individual religious practices vary among members of the same religion, XYZ should not deny the requested accommodation based on speculation that the other Muslim employees may seek the same accommodation. If other employees subsequently request the same accommodation and granting it to all of the requesters would cause undue hardship, XYZ can make an appropriate adjustment at that time. For example, if accommodating five employees would not cause an undue hardship but accommodating six would impose such hardship, the sixth request could be denied.

Like employees of other religions, Muslim employees may need accommodations such as time off for religious holidays or exceptions to dress and grooming codes.

TEMPORARY ASSIGNMENTS

Susan is an experienced clerical worker who wears a hijab (head scarf) in conformance with her Muslim beliefs. XYZ Temps places Susan in a long-term assignment with one of its clients. The client contacts XYZ and requests that it notify Susan that she must remove her hijab while working at the front desk, or that XYZ assign another person to Susan's position. According to the client, Susan's religious attire violates its dress code and presents the "wrong image." Should XYZ comply with its client's request?

(Continued)

XYZ Temps may not comply with this client request without violating Title VII. The client would also violate Title VII if it made Susan remove her hijab or changed her duties to keep her out of public view. Therefore, XYZ should strongly advise against this course of action. Notions about customer preference, real or perceived, do not establish undue hardship, so the client should make an exception to its dress code to let Susan wear her hijab during front desk duty as a religious accommodation. If the client does not withdraw the request, XYZ should place Susan in another assignment at the same rate of pay and decline to assign another worker to the client.

BACKGROUND INVESTIGATIONS

Anwar, who was born in Egypt, applies for a position as a security guard with XYZ Corp., which contracts to provide security services at government office buildings. Can XYZ require Muhammad to undergo a background investigation before he is hired?

XYZ may require Anwar to undergo the same preemployment security checks that apply to other applicants for the same position. As with its other employment practices, XYZ may not perform background investigations or other screening procedures in a discriminatory manner. In addition, XYZ may require a security clearance pursuant to a federal statute or executive order. Security clearance determinations for positions subject to national security requirements under a federal statute or an executive order are not subject to review under the equal employment opportunity statutes.

Global **Perspective**

Religious Freedom in Singapore[16]

The following excerpts from a Singapore case reflect an opinion different from American courts regarding the protection of religious beliefs of employees. The appellant in the case was a teacher in the Singapore school system. The respondent was the ITE.

***

As is the practice in Singapore schools, teachers and students take the national pledge and sing the national anthem during the school assembly. In 1988 the Ministry of Education introduced a new mode for taking the national pledge, which required the right clenched fist to be placed over the left chest. The ITE . . . promptly enforced this new mode in the school through a circular distributed to students and staff. . . .

Throughout his employment, the appellant's practice was to be present at morning assembly. However, he did not take the national pledge or sing the national anthem. As a Jehovah's Witness, he believed that taking the national pledge or singing the national anthem were acts of worship which should be reserved exclusively for God and not for country. . . . The new mode made it obvious that the appellant was not participating in the pledge and anthem ceremony, since the appellant's right fist was not raised when the pledge was taken.

. . . On 2 January 1991, a letter was sent to the appellant, reminding him that it was a standing policy for all training staff on duty during the first period of the day to be present at the morning assembly and to take the national pledge. . . . The letter warned him that noncompliance with the 1988 circular may lead to disciplinary action. The appellant did not change his position.

***

On 6 April 1994 the appellant was informed that disciplinary proceedings had been instituted against him. The appellant was charged with misconduct for refusing to take the national pledge and sing the national anthem. The appellant was brought before a committee of inquiry. . . . Following the disciplinary proceedings, the plaintiff was dismissed by the ITE with effect from 1 November 1994.

***

ARGUMENTS ON CONSTITUTIONAL AND CONTRACTUAL ISSUES

The appellant's main contention was that the ITE's policy requiring participation in the pledge and anthem ceremony was unconstitutional. . . . Counsel for the ITE submitted that the dismissal was fair. He said that good teachers were required to be good role models . . . that the appellant's refusal to participate in the pledge and anthem ceremony made him unfit to be a good role model for students. . . .

TRIAL JUDGE'S FINDINGS ON CONSTITUTIONAL AND CONTRACTUAL ISSUES

. . . [T]he trial judge examined whether the appellant breached his contract of employment. This was a purely contractual analysis, without reference to constitutional rights. He raised common law principles that a servant must obey the master's orders, and he examined the degree of misconduct which would justify dismissal. Reading the ITE 1988 circular as falling within the contract of employment, he found that the appellant was in breach of the employment contract in refusing to take the national pledge or sing the national anthem in accordance with the 1988 circular.

***

(Continued)

The trial judge held that the state's interest in the education system must prevail over that of the individual. The trial judge held that the pledge and anthem ceremony was not a religious ceremony. In this case, the appellant's personal religious beliefs did not agree with the ITE's rules. Accordingly, the appellant's refusal to take the pledge and sing the anthem constituted misconduct contrary to the ITE's rules.

THE APPEAL

***

. . . [T]he protection of freedom of religion under our Constitution is premised on removing restrictions to one's choice of religious belief. This has been described as accommodative secularism. Obviously, not every conviction or belief, including those held with what ironically may best be described as religious fervor, qualifies as a religious belief. Indeed, we were inclined to agree with the view of the lower court . . . that such beliefs would best be philosophical choices rather than religious beliefs. In other words, although the pledge ceremony does not demand worship of the flag as a symbol, if a person held that understanding, that perception was a philosophical choice. It seemed clear to us that the appellant's interpretation of the pledge and anthem ceremony as a religious ceremony was a distortion of secular fact into religious belief. It is not accepted as a religious belief and is not entitled to protection under the Constitution of Singapore.

Indeed, to accept the appellant's interpretation would rob the Constitution of any operative effect. How can the same Constitution guarantee religious freedom if, by asking citizens to pledge their allegiance to country, it is (as the appellant suggests) coercing participation in a religious ceremony? This excruciatingly absurd interpretation cannot have been what was envisaged by the authors of the Constitution. Not only did the plaintiff fail to prove the unconstitutionality of the policy; but the irresistible conclusion for this court was that, in the present case, there was no valid religious belief protected by the Constitution.

***

CONCLUSION

In the circumstances, we find no good reason to overturn the decision below that the dismissal of the appellant for misconduct was fair. The appeal is dismissed, with costs to the respondent.

Summary

Title VII of the Civil Rights Act of 1964 prohibits religious discrimination in the workplace. Employees who claim that their work requirements interfere with their religious beliefs must be accommodated by their employers.

Whether an accommodation is reasonable and therefore obligatory depends on the extent to which it presents a hardship for the employer. Accommodations that pose an undue burden are not reasonable.

The Workplace Religious Freedom Act was proposed to Congress in 2004 to clarify what is meant by accommodation in the context of religious discrimination under Title VII. The concern by proponents of that bill is that without such clarification, religious freedom is endangered. Students should note that as of August, 2008, this bill has not been passed into law by Congress.

The ministerial exception to the provisions of Title VII applies to religious organizations and allows them to hire and fire people based on their religious beliefs. The extent to which the ministerial exception applies to other forms of discrimination by religious organizations is not clear. Decisions are made on a case-by-case basis, and such factors as the nature of the position involved, the role that the employee plays in the organization, and whether the organization is a for-profit or nonprofit entity will affect the outcome.

Questions

1. Natalie B. alleges that her employer, Costco Wholesale Corp. (Costco), failed to offer her a reasonable accommodation after she alerted it to a conflict between the "no facial jewelry" provision of its dress code and her religious practice as a member of the Church of Body Modification (CBM). She argues that this failure amounts to religious discrimination in violation of Title VII. The district court granted summary judgment for Costco, concluding that Costco reasonably accommodated Natalie by offering to reinstate her if she either covered her facial piercing with a bandage or replaced it with a clear retainer.

   Before her first day of work, Natalie received a copy of the Costco employment agreement, which included the employee dress code. When she was hired, Natalie had multiple earrings and four tattoos, but no facial piercings.

   Natalie moved from her position as a front-end assistant to the deli department in September 1997. In 1998 Costco revised its dress code to prohibit food handlers, including deli employees, from wearing any jewelry. Natalie's supervisor instructed her to remove her earrings pursuant to the revised code, but Natalie refused. Instead she requested to transfer to a front-end position, where she would be permitted to continue wearing her jewelry. Natalie did not indicate at the time that her insistence on wearing her earrings was based on a religious or spiritual belief.

   Costco approved Natalie's transfer back to a front-end position in June 1998 and promoted her to cashier soon thereafter. Over the ensuing two years, she engaged in various forms of body modification, including facial piercing and cutting. Although these practices were meaningful to Natalie, they were not motivated by a religious belief.

In March 2001 Costco further revised its dress code to prohibit all facial jewelry, aside from earrings, and disseminated the modified code to its employees. Natalie did not challenge the dress code or seek an accommodation, but rather continued uneventfully to wear her eyebrow piercing for several months.

Costco began enforcing its no facial jewelry policy in June 2001. On June 25, 2001, Natalie was informed that she would have to remove her facial piercings. She did not comply, returning to work the following day still wearing her piercings. When the supervisor reiterated the no facial jewelry policy, Natalie indicated for the first time that she was a member of the Church of Body Modification (CBM) and that her eyebrow piercing was part of her religion.

The CBM was established in 1999 and counts approximately 1,000 members who participate in such practices as piercing, tattooing, branding, cutting, and body manipulation. Among the goals espoused in the CBM's mission statement are for its members to "grow as individuals through body modification and its teachings," to "promote growth in mind, body, and spirit," and to be "confident role models in learning, teaching, and displaying body modification." The church's Web site, apparently its primary mode for reaching its adherents, did not state that members' body modifications had to be visible at all times or that temporarily removing body modifications would violate a religious tenet.

Natalie suggested that she be allowed to cover her eyebrow piercing with a flesh-colored bandage. Shevchuk rejected the suggestion and told Natalie that she had to remove the piercing or go home. She left. On July 14 Natalie received notice in the mail that she had been terminated for her unexcused absences resulting from noncompliance with the dress code. She claims that this was her first notice that Costco had decided not to grant her request for an accommodation that would reconcile the dress code with her religious requirement of displaying her facial jewelry at all times.

a. Is Natalie likely to win this religious discrimination suit? Why or why not?

b. Analyze this case using the cases discussed in this chapter as a guide. What factors weigh in favor of Natalie? What factors weigh in favor of Costco?

c. How would you evaluate the HR management practices of Costco with regard to their handling of Natalie? Have they concerned themselves adequately with their line managers? With the capabilities and competencies of their employees? With their customers' needs and wants? With their investors' needs and wants?

d. What would it take for Costco to enroll Natalie and other employees into the overall goals and objectives of the company? Would this be worth exploring? Does this fit within the role of the HR manager?

2. Courtney S. began her employment with the INS (Immigration and Naturalization Service) in 1987. After her conversion to the Jewish religion, she was the only Jewish agent in her office. There is no dispute that Courtney performed her duties in an acceptable manner before the events at issue herein.

   In August 1990 appellant was assigned to take a statement from a nonimmigrant alien, Rob G., who was in the United States on a B-2 or "visitor for pleasure" visa, valid through September 20, 1990. Rob is an Israeli citizen of the Jewish faith. Courtney shortly thereafter began a romantic relationship with Rob and informed her supervisor of the relationship. According to the supervisor, he informed Courtney that such relationships are strongly discouraged by INS policy, and she was advised to sever all nonofficial contact with Rob immediately because even the appearance of impropriety could have serious repercussions.

   Courtney did not sever the relationship. In fact, she later traveled to Israel with Rob. Courtney said that when she returned from Israel, she was removed from cases involving the Israeli community. Members of other ethnic groups were allowed, and even encouraged, to work cases involving their ethnic communities because of their knowledge and understanding of the different culture. The supervisor stated that Courtney was removed from Israeli cases on account of her failure to sever her nonofficial relationship with Rob. Later Courtney severed her relationship with Rob.

   In February 1991 Courtney entered a program of study for the purpose of converting to Judaism and began to wear a Star of David necklace to work. She informed her supervisors about her intention to convert, and subsequently she requested leave in July 1991 to undergo her formal conversion.

   During 1991 training for agents was announced on three occasions. The practice was for a supervisor to sign up for training those agents whom the training would benefit and then inform the agents. Courtney's supervisors did not sign her up for any of the three training courses; for two of the courses she was the only one of eight employees in her unit who was not signed up. She said that she was discriminated against based on religion in this regard; that prior to the start of her conversion process, she had always been permitted to attend training courses. The head of the training programs speculated that Courtney was not included in the training courses because of her by then "strained relationship" with her supervisor.

   On September 4, 1991, Courtney submitted a memorandum requesting 56 hours of leave without pay "due to the scheduled school closures for my daughter and religious considerations. . . ." Seven specific dates were given, and Courtney indicated that each was a religious holiday. She paper-clipped to the memorandum a Jewish religious school calendar that identified the holidays by name.

   In a memorandum dated September 16, 1991, Courtney requested Leave Without Pay (LWOP) for the month of October for familial reasons: Her young daughter was having difficulty adjusting to her new school. She was requesting LWOP because she "does not maintain an active caseload, and is currently without outstanding assignments. . . ." The district director denied the request "in the interest of maintaining continuity in the Investigations Program." He indicated that Courtney should use "intermittent periods of annual leave" instead. On September 20, 1991, Courtney tried to set up a meeting with the district director, which was denied. The district director advised her to submit any further information in writing. Courtney did not respond and missed a couple days of work. The record showed that she was then charged AWOL for the missed time. On September 27, 1991, she reported for work only to discover that her desk had been moved to an unknown location, and that all of her work files and papers had been removed from the desk and the desk was covered with computer equipment.

Courtney brought an action for religious discrimination. As evidence of discriminatory animus, Courtney submitted a comment by the assistant district director to a coworker during the Persian Gulf War, uttered with a sarcastic tone, "Those f--g Israelis will always get even," apparently in reference to the likelihood of Israeli involvement in the war following Scud missile attacks on Israel.

a. Does Courtney have a good case? What questions would you like to ask to determine your answer?

b. What could management have done differently to avoid this lawsuit?

c. What practices would you advise for this employer?

3. Fariba R. sued her former employer, Alamo Rent-A-Car, Inc. (Alamo), under Title VII for refusing to allow her to wear a head scarf at work. Because she insisted on wearing it, she was transferred to a lateral position (with the same pay and benefits) in which she would not deal with customers. Wearing a head scarf was mandated by her religion. The district court dismissed Fariba's complaint for failure to allege that she suffered an adverse employment action. Fariba appealed, arguing that Title VII religious discrimination claims do not require a showing of adverse employment action.

a. Should the appellate court uphold the decision of the trial court? Why or why not?

b. Did the company handle this matter as well as it could have?

c. Is it necessary for an employee to show an adverse employment action in order to be entitled to accommodation? What is the rationale for your answer?

4. Jessica C. was employed to teach English and religion at Ursuline, a Catholic private school in Wilmington, Delaware, that provides a college preparatory education for girls and young women from prekindergarten through grade 12. The school teaches religious principles of the Roman Catholic Church and indoctrinates its students according to those principles.

As Jessica has also acknowledged, its expectation is that the school's teachers will teach those religious principles and inculcate them in their students.

Jessica was fired after she lent her name to an advertisement in support of abortion rights.

The advertisement, which appeared on January 22, 2003, said the following:

> Thirty years ago today, the U.S. Supreme Court in *Roe v. Wade* guaranteed a woman's right to make her own reproductive choices. That right is under attack. We, the undersigned individuals and organizations, reaffirm our commitment to protecting that right. We believe that each woman should be able to continue to make her own reproductive choices, guided by her conscience, ethical beliefs, medical advice, and personal circumstances. We urge all Delawareans and elected officials at every level to be vigilant in the fight to ensure that women now and in the future have the right to choose.

Jessica asserted that she had a right to "speak out in protest in a democracy without retaliation by her employer or the loss of her job" and that she was a volunteer for Planned Parenthood, not in Planned Parenthood's medical office but as an assistant "with mailings and booth sitting at inner city health fairs handing out pamphlets that she thought were important." The principal stated that she would have to "consult elsewhere with someone from another level about plaintiff's continued employment, meaning consult with the Roman Catholic bishop and the diocese."

Two days later, on January 24, 2003, Jessica was again summoned to the principal's office, where she was told she was going to be fired but that she could resign instead if she wished. She was given the weekend to think it over. Jessica said it was illegal for them to fire her "for opposing practices of [Ursuline] which interfered with the legal right to an abortion."

What should the court decide? Support your answer.

5. Gerard F., Joel H., and Bob W. own and operate Basketballers and Health Club, Inc., a closely held, for-profit corporation. Basketballers operates seven sports and health club operations. Each provides recreational and exercise facilities as well as counseling regarding appropriate exercise programs for 18,000 members. Approximately 140 to 150 people are currently employed by the clubs. The parties agree that the clubs' facilities are excellent, described by some as the "Cadillac of the industry," and that membership dues are generally lower than those of the competition.

Gerard, Joel, and Bob are born-again Christians. Their fundamentalist religious convictions require them to act in accordance with the teachings of Jesus Christ and the will of God in their business as well as in their personal lives.

The owners permitted only born-again Christians to hold management positions, required managers to attend weekly Bible studies, and suggested that other personnel also attend.

One complainant, who was of the Jewish religious faith, alleges that she was forced to give up her membership in one of the clubs because they displayed fundamentalist Christian religious literature in the literature racks and on the walls of the sports club and otherwise engaged in conduct that was offensive to her.

Despite the discrimination allegations asserted in this case, Basketballers has employed, and continues to employ, married people, male and female unmarried people, and divorced males and females of various races. The Basketballers clubs have also employed, and continue to employ, people of various religious faiths—Jews, Roman Catholics, Protestants of various denominations, and others—so long as such other people are not offended by the owners' faith, are not antagonistic toward the Christian gospel, and will comply with management's work rules in a cheerful and obedient spirit.

Legal action was taken against the club owners for violating the state's civil rights laws prohibiting religious discrimination in employment.

a. Does this case involve a constitutional issue? Explain.

b. What would the owners' argument be?

c. If this case was based on the federal Civil Rights Act, how would the court decide? Support your answer.

d. Compare this case with the case in Question 4. How do the facts differ? Explain.

References

1. See *Famous Quotations Network* at www.famous-quotations.com/asp/cquotes. asp?Category=Religion+/+Faith (accessed on July 25, 2007).

2. See Training and Development Policy, EEOC Notice N-915.022, to be inserted in §628 of Volume II of the Compliance Manual, Religious Accommodation, after p. 628-20.

3. 42 U.S.C. § 2000e(j).

4. 29 C.F.R. § 1605.1.

5. 29 C.F.R. § 1605.2(d)(i–iii).

6. 29 C.F.R. § 1605.2(e).

7. *Trans World Airlines, Inc. v. Hardison et al.*, 432 U.S. 63, 97 S. Ct. 2264, 53 L. Ed. 2d 113 (1977).

8. *Mann v. Frank, U.S. Postal Service*, 7 F.3d 1365 (1993).

9. From the Committee on Education and the Workforce Hearings, Testimony of Congressman Mark Souder, Regarding H.R. 1445, the Workplace Religious Freedom Act Subcommittee on Employer–Employee Relations, November 10, 2005.

10. ACLU Letter to the House of Representatives on the Harmful Effects of the Workplace Religious Freedom Act (3/15/2005). See the ACLU Web site at www.aclu.org/religion/gen/16256leg20050315.html (accessed on July 25, 2007).

11. 42 U.S.C. § 2000e–2(e)(2).

12. *McClure v. The Salvation Army,* 460 F.2d 553 (1972).

13. *Employment Division v. Smith,* 494 U.S. 872 (1990).

14. Statistics from http://www.eeoc.gov/types/religion.html (accessed September 17, 2006).

15. See http://www.eeoc.gov/facts/backlash-employer.html (accessed September 17, 2006).

16. *Nappalli Peter Williams v. Institute of Technical Education*, 2 SLR 569 (1999), Civil Appeal No. 278 of 1998 (Singapore Law Reports).

Chapter Twelve

National Origin Discrimination and Immigration Issues

America needs to conduct this debate on immigration in a reasoned and respectful tone. Feelings run deep on this issue, and as we work it out, all of us need to keep some things in mind. We cannot build a unified country by inciting people to anger, or playing on anyone's fears, or exploiting the issue of immigration for political gain. We must always remember that real lives will be affected by our debates and decisions, and that every human being has dignity and value no matter what their citizenship papers say.[1]

President George W. Bush (2006)

INTRODUCTION

Many nations find themselves in a paradoxical dilemma of extolling guarantees of equality and justice for all while at the same time trying to preserve traditions, cultures, and jobs for their citizens in the face of rising tides of refugees, asylum seekers, and illegal aliens seeking economic opportunities. The picture is further complicated today by the ever-present threat of terrorism.

Many Americans take pride in the fact that the United States historically welcomed immigrants to its shores. Today there is tension in the country. One political group fights for tighter border controls to protect Americans from terrorists and illegal immigrants who drain resources from those who are here legally. Another group fights for the rights of illegal aliens who now number in the millions—people who readily find employment as unskilled laborers in businesses as well as private domains. The laws that impact immigration and immigrants are designed to address the multifaceted issues that arise in this context.

The Civil Rights Act of 1964 and its amendments prohibit discriminatory treatment of people on the basis of national origin. In this chapter we explore the nature of this protected class and the particular issues that arise in cases alleging such discrimination. First is a review of several laws that have an impact on national origin discrimination and how these laws affect the employment relationship.

THE GOVERNING STATUTES FOR NATIONAL ORIGIN ISSUES

The major statutory laws in the area of national origin discrimination are the Immigration and Nationality Act of 1952, the Immigration Reform and Control Act of 1986, and Title VII of the Civil Rights Act of 1964. These statutes, taken together, form the background for how employers are to handle and process people who emigrate to the United States, whether legally or otherwise. At times these laws place employers in awkward positions: They cannot discriminate against people on the basis of their national origin, yet they must be sure not to hire anyone who is not authorized to work in this country.

The Immigration and Nationality Act of 1952 (INA) was the first comprehensive federal law designed to restrict and control immigration to the United States, and its framework guides the current categorization of immigrants in such matters as quotas and reasons for exclusion and deportation. From janitorial help and agricultural workers to high-tech employees and top-level executives, many American companies employ a number of people from foreign countries. Most have direct authorization to work in this country; some are spouses or children of people who are authorized to work here; and some are illegal aliens. The question for employers is whether the people they hire have the right, under our immigration laws, to join their workforce.

The Immigration Reform and Control Act of 1986 (IRCA) is particularly significant to employers because it was passed to obtain the help of employers in enforcing the restrictions imposed by the Immigration and Nationality Act. It created an employer sanctions program to penalize employers for hiring unauthorized aliens. The objective was to remove incentives for illegal immigration by eliminating the job opportunities that draw illegal aliens to this country. Paradoxically it also amended the INA by adding Section 274B, which essentially makes it an unfair immigration-related employment practice to discriminate against a person because of his or her national origin. Employers of fewer than four workers are exempted from the provisions of this section. Those who are not permanent U.S. residents and those who are not authorized by either the IRCA or the INS to be employed in the—United States—that is, unauthorized aliens—are not protected under this section, and citizens may be favored over aliens if they are at least equally qualified for a position.

The Civil Rights Act of 1964, Title VII, is a comprehensive law prohibiting discrimination on the basis of race, color, creed, sex, and national origin by employers of 15 or more people. Citizens as well as aliens are protected by the prohibition against national origin discrimination. For example, a U.S. citizen for whom English is a second language could initiate action for national origin discrimination if his or her employer instituted an English-only rule in the workplace that applied in all situations, including break times. A court may find that such a policy violates Title VII if it is not necessary for the efficient operation of the business.

People who are immigrants, nonimmigrants, or permanent residents come under the umbrella term of *aliens*. The hiring, firing, and general treatment of these individuals is a sensitive area for employers. Aliens can be further subdivided into those authorized to work in this country and those who are not so authorized. We explore two topics in the remainder of this chapter: how employers can determine whether an alien is authorized to work, and how the courts determine whether an employer has violated the law regarding national origin discrimination. For each topic, legal provisions and related issues are presented.

EMPLOYERS MUST DETERMINE WHETHER AN ALIEN IS AUTHORIZED TO WORK IN THE UNITED STATES

Defining Terms

The first challenge for HR managers is to have some knowledge of the various categories of people with regard to immigration law. Here is a list of terms classifying people by citizenry and alien status:

- *U.S. citizen:*
  - An individual born in the United States and its territories (excluding children of accredited foreign diplomats).
  - An individual born abroad of U.S. citizen parent(s) (if both parents are citizens at the time of birth, or if one parent is a U.S. citizen who has satisfied certain U.S. residency requirements).
  - Any person naturalized as a U.S. citizen or who acquired U.S. citizenship by reason of the naturalization of one or both parents[2].
- *National of the U.S:* A citizen of the United States or a person, though not a citizen, who owes permanent allegiance to the United States (this applies to residents of certain territories)[3].
- *Alien:* Any person who is not a citizen or a national of the United States[4].
- *Immigrant:* Every alien except those who are eligible and fall within one of the nonimmigrant visa categories (the term *immigrant* is often used interchangeably with *permanent resident*)[5].
- *Nonimmigrant:* An alien admitted to the United States pursuant to a nonimmigrant visa; that is, those who seek entry for a specific purpose that can be accomplished during a temporary period[6].

- *Permanent resident:* A person who has been lawfully accorded the privilege of residing permanently in the United States as an immigrant in accordance with the immigration laws (individuals in this category are often referred to as possessing a *green card*)[7].

For all practical purposes, permanent residents have the same rights and privileges as American citizens with the exception that they are not entitled to vote and, in many cases, are ineligible to work for a state or federal government agency. They may remain in the United States as long as they wish and can work without any restrictions. As a general rule, permanent residents may have their status revoked and be deported only for engaging in certain types of conduct regarded as an "excludable act" under the immigration laws. Permanent resident status may also be abandoned voluntarily or through an extended absence from the United States[8].

As previously noted, under the provisions of the INA and the IRCA, employers face penalties if they hire unauthorized aliens. How can an employer ensure that an individual is, in fact, someone who has authorization to work in this country?

Here are two more lists. List #1 describes people who are authorized to work in the United States with no restriction as to location or type of work, and List #2 describes people who have been admitted to the country with authorization to work for a particular employer.

List #1: Aliens Who Are Authorized to Work in the United States with No Restrictions, No Location or Type of Employment[9].

Permanent residents: People who possess green cards pursuant to appropriate INS forms.

Legalized aliens: People admitted to the United States as lawful temporary residents pursuant to appropriate INS forms, such as special agricultural workers.

Refugees or refugee parolees: People who can establish such status by presenting an employment authorization document issued by the INS.

Asylees: People granted political asylum as evidenced by an employment authorization document issued by the INS.

Fiancées and dependent children: Nonimmigrant fiancées who can present a K visa, and children who can present an employment authorization document issued by the INS.

Parents and children of certain special immigrants: Parents (N-8) or dependent children (N-9) of aliens granted permanent residence as special immigrants by reason of their status as officers or employees of selected international organizations.

Trust territory residents: People admitted as citizens of the federated states of Micronesia or of the Marshall Islands as evidenced by an employment authorization document issued by the INS.

Suspension of deportation cases and withholding of deportation cases: People granted suspension or withholding of deportation as evidenced by an employment authorization document issued by the INS.

Voluntary departure: People who have been granted extended voluntary departure as members of certain nationality groups pursuant to a request made to the INS by the secretary of state. They must show employment authorization documents issued by the INS.

List #2: Aliens Who Are Authorized to Work in the United States for a Specific Employer[10].

Foreign government officials, employees of such officials, and foreign government officials in transit: People admitted pursuant to A-1, A-2, A-3, C-2, or C-3 visas. They are employed by their own foreign government entity in this country.

Crewmen: People admitted pursuant to D-1 or D-2 visas. They are employed by the transportation company for which they worked at the time of their arrival.

Treaty traders and treaty investors: People who possess E-1 or E-2 visas. They are employed by the treaty-qualifying company through whom they obtained that status.

Students: People holding F-1 visas. They may be employed under limited circumstances.

International organization representatives: People with G-1, G-2, G-3, or G-4 visas. They are employed by their sponsoring government.

Employees of international organization representative: People with G-5 visas.

Temporary workers or trainees: People with H-1, H-2A, H-2B, or H-3 visas. Prior to changes in the act in 2000, they could be employed only by the employer through whom they obtained that status.

Information media representative: Aliens admitted with I visas who are employed by a sponsoring news agency or bureau.

Exchange visitors: Aliens with J-1 visas who are employed by the exchange visitor program sponsor or other designee within U.S. Information Agency–approved guidelines.

Intracompany transferees: People admitted with L-1 visas who work for the employer through which this status was obtained.

NATO officials: Officers and personnel of nations of the NATO organization, admitted pursuant to a NATO visa (NATO-1 through NATO-6).

NATO attendants, servants, and personal employees: These people are admitted with NATO-7 visas and are employed by the sponsoring NATO alien.

Visa extension applicants: People who were admitted with certain types of visas whose visas have expired and who have applied for an extension in a timely manner. They can continue their employment with the same employer for a limited period of time.

Knowing the descriptions of people authorized to work in the United States is useful, but it does not provide the precise information an employer needs to efficiently and effectively screen applicants to determine their status. Furthermore, turning away people who are believed to be, appear to be, or act like aliens is almost certain to run afoul of the Civil Rights Act or the IRCA amendment to the INA, both of which prohibit discrimination against people on the basis of national origin. Next we present some of the guidelines provided by the Equal Employment Opportunity Commission to assist employers in establishing verification of employees—a procedure that must be followed in conjunction with completion of the required I-9 form, also known as the Immigration Eligibility Verification Form. This form must be completed for each employee.

EEOC Guidance Regarding Documentation Considered Sufficient to Establish Authorization to Work

Under provisions of the Immigration Reform and Control Act of 1986, employers are required by the U.S. Department of Justice to verify that all new employees are eligible to work in the United States. Employers must complete a Form I-9 (see Figure 12.1) for every employee, and they must review and keep records on their employees' legal status, including evidence of the documents presented by the employees to verify their authorized status. Basically employees must present original documentation establishing their authorization to work as well as original documentation establishing their identity. Documents that are acceptable for these purposes fall into three categories[11]: those that are acceptable to establish employment eligibility verification and fulfill requirements of both

FIGURE 12.1
The I-9 Form

The first category—documents that are acceptable to establish employment eligibility verification—includes the following:

United States passport (unexpired or expired).

Unexpired foreign passport with I-551 stamp or I-94 card.

Unexpired foreign passport with Form I-94 containing an endorsement of the alien's nonimmigrant status. (*Note:* If an I-94 is presented with an unexpired foreign passport, please complete second document information under List A. The passport information will be the first document recorded and the I-94 the second.)

Alien registration receipt card or permanent resident card (INS Form I-551).

Unexpired temporary resident card (INS Form I-688).

Unexpired employment authorization card (INS Form I-688A).

Unexpired employment authorization document issued by the INS that contains a photograph (INS Form I-766 or I-688B).

Alien registration receipt card or permanent resident card (INS Form I-551).

Unexpired temporary resident card (INS Form I-688).

Unexpired employment authorization card (INS Form I-688A).

Unexpired employment authorization document issued by the INS that contains a photograph (INS Form I-766 or I-688B).

work authorization and identity; those that are acceptable to establish identity only; and those that are acceptable for employment eligibility verification only.

The government has established a basic pilot program that electronically searches databases of Social Security and immigration information to verify worker eligibility status for employers. Currently there are about 6,000 employers in the pilot program. Efforts are under way to expand the pilot to a mandatory program for employers; that move would make it easier to monitor and punish employers who hire illegal aliens[12]. Pursuant to the IRCA, a fine of $10,000 would be assessed against violating companies. Some argue that such a system constitutes a form of harassment, that the information provided will be unreliable, and that it not only violates privacy rights but will also increase discrimination against all immigrants.

Specialized Visas

Commonly used business and employment visas[13] include the following:

B-1 visitors for business: Short-term, maximum of one year. Restrictions: no "local" employment (no payment of salary from U.S. sources); must intend to depart the United States at conclusion of authorized stay; sufficient ties to home country required for issuance.

H-1B specialty occupation visas: Temporary employment for degreed (or equivalent) aliens in professional or specialty occupations; maximum of six years. Restrictions: employer- and employment-specific—no other work in the United States allowed; labor condition application must be filed prior to submission of petition; employee normally needs at least an equivalent of a bachelor's degree to qualify; spouses and children may not work.

Developing Issues on Visas

H-1B Visas

Congress passed the American Competitiveness in the Twenty-First Century Act in 2000. A primary purpose of this act was to increase the number of H-1B visas available to U.S. businesses. The H-1B visa classification is available to people who qualify in a specialty occupation. According to INS regulations, a "specialty occupation" is one that requires theoretical and practical application of a body of highly specialized knowledge. The alien must have attained a U.S. bachelor's degree (or a foreign degree/work experience equivalent) in a field related to the specialty. If a license is required to perform the job, the person must have such a license. In some cases work experience in a related field may substitute for university education.[14]

In 1998 the number of temporary foreign high-tech workers let in with H-1B visas was increased from the 1998 number of 65,000 to 107,500 by 2001. This number was later further increased by the American Competitiveness statute of 2000 to 195,000 in the three years following passage of the act. The law also made it possible for employees to change employers upon a proper filing by a prospective employer[15].

L and E Visas

In January 2002 Congress passed two laws (HR 2278 and HR 2277) that granted work authorization to spouses of L (intracompany transferees) and E (treaty trader and treaty investor) nonimmigrant visa holders. They are now allowed to work based on their L or E "dependent" classification. Previously they were permitted entrance to the United States but could not work without obtaining their own work authorization visas[16].

9/11 Repercussions

One immigration concern arising from the 9/11/01 terrorist attacks in New York City and Pennsylvania led to the action of the Department of State in creating a new security clearance: the Visas Condor. Males between the ages of 16 and 45 from many Middle Eastern countries are subject to a 30-day wait before a nonimmigrant visa can be issued. No expedition is considered, and the 30 days begin only when the American consul sends the information to the Department of State for transmission to intelligence agencies[17].

NATIONAL ORIGIN DISCRIMINATION: CIVIL RIGHTS ACT (TITLE VII)

Issues that arise under Title VII's prohibition of national origin discrimination involve a variety of factors. Some turn on the question of whether a U.S. company operating through an affiliate abroad can be held liable for discrimination under Title VII. Others focus on a company's requirement of "English only" being spoken in a workplace. Still others raise concerns about whether unauthorized aliens are entitled to the same protection under U.S. laws as U.S. citizens. These and other issues are explored next.

Case for Discussion 12-1

The Prima Facie Case of National Origin Discrimination

PANLILIO V. DALLAS INDEPENDENT SCHOOL DISTRICT, 643 F.2D 315 (1981)[18]

The prima facie case for a national origin discrimination case was set out in this federal court opinion.

Facts

A Filipino woman applied for a teaching position and was rejected because her record showed she was too demanding of students and in her previous position had ignored rules involving corporal punishment of children. Panlilio brought a legal action against the district charging violation of Title VII's prohibition of discrimination on the basis of national origin. The trial court held that the defendant school district had a legitimate nondiscriminatory reason for its denial of her application.

As the district court noted, the principles announced in *McDonnell Douglas Corp. v. Green* govern disparate treatment cases under Title VII alleging discrimination on the basis of national origin. The plaintiff in a Title VII case must carry the initial burden under the statute of establishing a prima facie case of discrimination on the basis of national origin. This may be done by showing

1. that she is a person of foreign national origin;
2. that she applied and was qualified for a job for which the employer was seeking applicants;
3. that despite her qualifications she was rejected; and
4. that after her rejection the position remained open, and the employer continued to seek applicants from people of the plaintiff's qualifications.

If the plaintiff proves a prima facie case of unlawful discrimination, the burden then shifts to the employer to articulate some legitimate nondiscriminatory reason for the employment decision. This circuit held in *Turner v. Texas Instruments, Inc.*, 555 F.2d 1251, 1255 (5th Cir. 1977), that the employer, in meeting the burden imposed by the second prong of the *McDonnell Douglas* inquiry, must prove by a preponderance of the evidence that legitimate nondiscriminatory reasons existed for the employment decision challenged by the plaintiff.

Decision

The appellate court affirmed the trial court's ruling in favor of the school district, holding that the defendant had a legitimate, nondiscriminatory reason for its decision in rejecting Panlilio's application.

Questions for Discussion

The court relied on the *McDonnell Douglas* framework in analyzing this case. What if Panlilio had been hired and was harassed by coworkers, and that she attributed the harassment to national origin discrimination? Would the *McDonnell Douglas* framework still be applied by the court? Support your answer.

The Meaning of "National Origin"

The meaning of *national origin discrimination* has been refined by the courts over the years in their interpretations of the language of the Civil Rights Act and the Immigration Reform and Control Act.

One thing is clear: The protected class under national origin is not restricted to people who have immigrated to the United States from other countries. The EEOC defines national origin discrimination broadly as "including, but not limited to, the denial of equal employment opportunity because of an individual's, or his or her ancestor's, place of origin; or because an individual has the physical, cultural, or linguistic characteristics of a national origin group"[19].

Particular attention is given to charges of discrimination that are grounded in national origin considerations, such as these:

- Marriage to or association with people of a national origin group.
- Membership in or association with an organization identified with or seeking to promote the interests of national origin groups.
- Attendance or participation in schools, churches, temples, or mosques generally used by people of a national origin group.
- A person's name or spouse's name being associated with a national origin group.

English-Only Rules

The EEOC has issued guidelines regarding workplace English-only rules[20]. Guidelines do not rise to the force of law, but they are provided as an aid in compliance. It is up to the courts to determine whether the guidelines will eventually be enforced in a particular case, thereby establishing precedent. The guidelines on English-only rules are as follows:

Sec. 1606.7 Speak-English-only rules.

(a) When applied at all times. A rule requiring employees to speak only English at all times in the workplace is a burdensome term and condition of employment. The primary language of an individual is often an essential national origin characteristic. Prohibiting employees at all times, in the workplace, from speaking their primary language or the language they speak most comfortably, disadvantages an individual's employment opportunities on the basis of national origin. It may also create an atmosphere of inferiority, isolation, and intimidation based on national origin that could result in a discriminatory working environment. Therefore, the Commission will presume that such a rule violates Title VII and will closely scrutinize it.

(b) When applied only at certain times. An employer may have a rule requiring that employees speak only in English at certain times where the employer can show that the rule is justified by business necessity.

(c) Notice of the rule. It is common for individuals whose primary language is not English to inadvertently change from speaking English to speaking their primary language. Therefore, if an employer believes it has a business necessity for a speak-English-only rule at certain times, the employer should inform its employees of the general circumstances when speaking only in English is required and of the consequences of violating the rule. If an employer fails to effectively notify its employees of the rule and makes an adverse employment decision against an individual based on a violation of the rule, the Commission will consider the employer's application of the rule as evidence of discrimination on the basis of national origin.

In light of these EEOC guidelines, employers should ask the following questions about their own workplaces before establishing English-only rules:

Under what circumstances do employees speak in their native languages?
Are they only for employee-to-employee conversations, or are they used in circumstances that interfere with business relationships, such as in customer or supplier interactions? If employees have regular interactions with customers, an English-only rule would probably be considered reasonable.

Does use of a different language by some of the workers create tension and interfere with the ability of others to perform their work?
If the workforce consists of a culturally diverse population, and the workers must interact regularly to accomplish the tasks at hand, an English-only rule may be necessary to ensure smooth operations.

Does use of a different language affect employees' morale?
Employee morale can be negatively affected by allowing some employees to converse in a language other than English if the workplace is not well managed. Conversely, an inflexible English-only policy can have a negative effect on employee morale, and could be a violation of Title VII, if there are no legitimate business reasons for it.

Does use of a different language create concerns about safety?
A concern about safety in the workplace is a nondiscriminatory legitimate reason to institute an English-only rule. The nature of the business would determine whether this is in fact a legitimate business necessity.

Does use of a different language make the likelihood of harassment greater?
In an intense, highly interactive environment, misinterpretations of intentions, verbal and otherwise, can be exacerbated by allowing some workers to converse in another language. This could translate to greater possibilities of racial, ethnic, or sexual harassment.

If there are reasonable grounds for instituting an English-only rule, whether for all employees at all times or one that is more flexible and less pervasive, how should such a rule be communicated?

For all workers who are affected:

- The rule should be communicated both orally and in writing in all relevant languages.
- The rule should be clear and unambiguous.
- The consequences of violating the rule should be reasonable, developmental, and appropriate.
- The rule should be communicated periodically to existing as well as new employees.

THE EEOC REACHES A LANDMARK "ENGLISH-ONLY" SETTLEMENT[21]

A few years ago the EEOC announced the largest settlement ever for English-only violations under Title VII of the Civil Rights Act of 1964. The employer, Watlow Electric Manufacturing Co., was required to pay $192,500 under the terms of the settlement. Watlow was held to have discriminated against Hispanic workers on the basis of their national origin by firing them for refusing to speak only English on the job.

The EEOC chairwoman at the time, Ida L. Castro, said, "The Commission will continue to defend employees' civil rights when rules are implemented that arbitrarily penalize a single group based on their national origin. It is imperative for employers to be aware that blanket English-only policies, those requiring workers to speak English at all times with no exceptions, may be unlawful if they are not clearly justified by business necessity."

Watlow must also provide comprehensive training to its management personnel, post a notice at its plant detailing the outcome of the litigation, and maintain certain employment records for EEOC review.

The EEOC's attorney added, "Cases involving language issues, accent discrimination, and restrictive language policies or practices are a strategic enforcement priority for the Commission. The Commission will aggressively prosecute such cases in order to remedy employment discrimination and protect the public interest."

Between fiscal years 1996 and 1999, the number of charge filings alleging English-only violations more than tripled from 77 to 253 charges.

The Distinction between Citizenship and National Origin Discrimination

A federal appellate court in *Fortino v. Quasar Co.*[22] noted, "Title VII does not . . . forbid discrimination on grounds of citizenship." Distinctions between citizenship and national origin discrimination were explored in early U.S. Supreme Court cases. In *Espinoza v. Farah Manufacturing Co.*[23] the Court ruled that citizenship discrimination may violate national origin discrimination prohibitions, but only when it has "the purpose or effect of discriminating on the basis of national origin," as for example where it is one part of a wider scheme of unlawful national origin discrimination. A 1977 EEOC decision involving a British citizen applied the *Espinoza* rule and reasoning to a case in which a public educational institution had a practice of precluding all aliens from being granted tenure. Although the EEOC noted that this was unconstitutional under the Equal Protection Clause of the Fourteenth Amendment, it did not violate Title VII's prohibition against national origin discrimination. It reasoned that there was no evidence to indicate that the exclusion of noncitizens had a disproportionate adverse impact on people of British origin. Also, there was no evidence that the practice was enforced in a disparate manner, such as by granting tenure to aliens of other than British nationality[24].

In a federal district court case, a Rockwell International division operating in the United States maintained a policy against hiring aliens[25]. It generally was unconcerned with the national origin of any particular applicant. When it discovered that several employees had falsified their applications by claiming U.S. citizenship, it discharged them. The EEOC claimed that this constituted national origin discrimination. The court, however, held that the determining factor in Rockwell's hiring decision was citizenship status, not national origin, and discrimination based on citizenship status is permissible, as established by the U.S. Supreme Court in *Espinoza.*

Extraterritorial Application of Title VII

The issue of whether the provisions of Title VII extend to corporations outside the geographical confines of the United States has been explored in several legal actions, including the U.S. Supreme Court case of *EEOC v. Arabian American Oil Co* (1991) presented in Case for Discussion 12-2. The prohibitions against employment discrimination in Title VII apply to employers as defined in Section 701(b) of that law. The only exceptions to these prohibitions are those specifically enumerated in Sections 701, 702, and 703. None of these provisions specified clearly whether U.S. citizens employed outside the United States are protected by this statute. Ultimately the issue was clarified by Congress when it enacted the Civil Rights Act of 1991 providing that the act protects U.S. citizens working abroad for employers covered by this law.

The *Arabian American Oil* case describes the various factors that come into play in deciding whether a U.S. statute can be applied beyond the country's borders.

Case for Discussion 12-2

EEOC V. ARABIAN AMERICAN OIL CO., ET AL., 499 U.S. 244 (1991)[26]

In this U.S. Supreme Court decision the Court struggled with the question of whether the Civil Rights Act protects U.S. citizens who work outside U.S. borders. The Court provides insights into the rationale for and against extraterritorial application of U.S. law. Managers can learn from this opinion how the Court interprets statutory law by attempting to ascertain what Congress intended by its language.

Facts

Petitioner Boureslan is a naturalized U.S. citizen who was born in Lebanon. The respondents are two Delaware corporations (referred to as Aramco). Aramco's principal place of business is Dhahran, Saudi Arabia, and it is licensed to do business in Texas.

In 1979 Boureslan was hired by Aramco as a cost engineer in Houston. A year later he was transferred, at his request, to work for Aramco in Saudi Arabia.

Boureslan remained with Aramco in Saudi Arabia until he was discharged in 1984. After filing a charge of discrimination with the EEOC, he instituted this suit in the United States District Court for the Southern District of Texas against Aramco. He sought relief under both state law and Title VII of the Civil Rights Act of 1964, on the ground that he was harassed and ultimately discharged by respondents on account of his race, religion, and national origin.

Respondents filed a motion for summary judgment on the ground that the district court lacked subject matter jurisdiction over Boureslan's claim because the protections of Title VII do not extend to United States citizens employed abroad by American employers. The district court agreed and dismissed Boureslan's Title VII claim . . .

***

Both parties concede, as they must, that Congress has the authority to enforce its laws beyond the territorial boundaries of the United States. Whether Congress has in fact exercised that authority in this case is a matter of statutory construction. It is our task to determine whether Congress intended the protections of Title VII to apply to United States citizens employed by American employers outside of the United States.

***

Boureslan and the EEOC contend that the language of Title VII evinces a clearly expressed intent on behalf of Congress to legislate extraterritorially. They rely principally on two provisions of the statute. First, petitioners argue that the statute's definitions of the jurisdictional terms "employer" and "commerce" are sufficiently broad to include United States firms that employ American citizens overseas. Second, they maintain that the statute's "alien exemption" clause necessarily implies that Congress intended to protect American citizens from employment discrimination abroad. Petitioners also contend that we should defer to the EEOC's consistently held position that Title VII applies abroad. We conclude that petitioners' evidence . . . falls short of demonstrating the affirmative congressional intent required to extend the protections of Title VII beyond our territorial borders.

***

An employer is subject to Title VII if it has employed 15 or more employees for a specified period and is "engaged in an industry affecting commerce." . . . Petitioners argue that by its plain language, Title VII's "broad jurisdictional language" reveals Congress's intent to extend the statute's protections to employment discrimination anywhere in the world by a United States employer who affects trade "between a state and any place outside thereof.". . .

***

Petitioners argue that Title VII's "alien exemption provision" "clearly manifests an intention" by Congress to protect United States citizens with respect to their employment outside of the United States. The alien exemption provision says that the statute "shall not apply to an employer with respect to the employment of aliens outside any state." Petitioners contend that from this language a negative inference should be drawn that Congress intended Title VII to cover United States *citizens* working abroad for United States employers. There is "no other plausible explanation [that] the alien exemption exists," they argue, because "if Congress believed that the statute did not apply extraterritorially, it would have had no reason to include an exemption for a certain category of individuals employed outside the United States." . . .

***

Respondents resist petitioners' interpretation of the alien exemption provision and assert two alternative raisons d'être for that language. First, they contend that since aliens are included in the statute's definition of employee, and the definition of commerce includes possessions as well as "states," the purpose of the exemption is to provide that employers of aliens in the possessions of the United States are not covered by the statute. Thus the "outside any state" clause means outside any state, but within the control of the United States. . . .

***

. . . While Title VII consistently speaks in terms of "states" and state proceedings, it fails even to mention foreign nations or foreign proceedings.

Similarly, Congress failed to provide any mechanisms for overseas enforcement of Title VII. For instance, the statute's venue provisions are ill-suited for extraterritorial application as they provide for venue only in a judicial district in the state where certain matters related to the employer occurred or were located. And the limited investigative authority provided for the EEOC, permitting the Commission only to issue subpoenas for witnesses and documents from "any place in the United States or any territory or possession thereof," suggests that Congress did not intend for the statute to apply abroad.

It is also reasonable to conclude that had Congress intended Title VII to apply overseas, it would have addressed the subject of conflicts with foreign laws and procedures. In amending the Age Discrimination in Employment Act of 1967 (ADEA) to apply abroad, Congress specifically addressed potential conflicts with foreign law by providing that it is not unlawful for an employer to take any action prohibited by the ADEA "where such practices involve an employee in a workplace in a foreign country, and compliance with [the ADEA] would cause such employer . . . to violate the laws of the country in which such workplace is located." Title VII, by contrast, fails to address conflicts with the laws of other nations.

Decision

Title VII of the Civil Rights Act of 1964 does not apply to United States citizens employed by American employers outside of the United States.

Important note: The U.S. Supreme Court's decision was reversed by Congress when it passed the Civil Rights Act of 1991 and amended 42 U.S.C. 2000e(f) (the Civil Rights Act of 1964) by adding, "Definition of Employee.—With respect to employment in a foreign country, such term includes an individual who is a citizen of the United States."

Questions for Discussion

1. What factors persuaded the Court that the Civil Rights Act did not apply to U.S. citizens working abroad for U.S. companies? What factors were argued by the plaintiffs?
2. After passage of the Civil Rights Act of 1991, who is an "employer" for purposes of the Civil Rights Act? Which employers are exempted from its prohibitions?
3. If a violation of the Civil Rights Act by a U.S. company operating in a foreign country is defended by that company on the grounds that to do otherwise would violate the laws of the foreign country, how likely is it that the courts would make an exception?

RIGHTS OF UNAUTHORIZED ALIENS UNDER DISCRIMINATION LAWS

It is clear that aliens as well as citizens are protected by U.S. immigration-related laws. What is less clear is whether unauthorized or illegal aliens enjoy any rights under U.S. laws. Case for Discussion 12-3 addresses this question.

EEOC Guidelines

In October 1999 the EEOC issued guidelines on claims of discrimination by illegal aliens, recognizing that illegal aliens who have been discriminated against by U.S. employers may sue their employers for job reinstatement, back pay, and other monetary damages. Basically the EEOC stated that unauthorized workers who are subjected to unlawful employment discrimination are entitled to the same relief as other victims of discrimination, subject to certain narrow exceptions. However, this guidance was rescinded in 2002[27].

The Immigration and Nationality Act and Title VII of the Civil Rights Act serve different purposes. The former is aimed at discouraging illegal immigration, whereas the latter seeks to deter discrimination in the workplace. The INS enforces laws regarding illegal immigration by finding and deporting violators. It also penalizes employers that knowingly hire unauthorized workers.

In Case for Discussion 12-3 the U.S. Supreme Court balanced the wrongful action of an employer against the actions of a worker who had no authorization to work in this country. The U.S. Supreme Court denounced the company's violations of the NLRA in interfering with union-organizing activity. However, with respect to Jose Castro, one of the affected workers who had been fired for his organizing activity, the Court did not approve the award of back pay and reinstatement because he had no authorization to work in the United States.

Case for Discussion 12-3

HOFFMAN PLASTIC COMPOUNDS, INC. V. NATIONAL LABOR RELATIONS BOARD, 535 U.S. 137 (2002)[28]

Facts

Petitioner Hoffman Plastic Compounds, Inc. (petitioner or Hoffman), custom-formulates chemical compounds for businesses that manufacture pharmaceutical, construction, and household products. In May 1988 petitioner hired Jose Castro to operate various blending machines. . . . Before being hired for this position, Castro presented documents that appeared to verify his authorization to work in the United States. In December 1988 the . . . AFL-CIO began a union-organizing campaign at petitioner's production plant. Castro and several other employees supported the organizing campaign and distributed authorization cards to coworkers. In January 1989 Hoffman laid off Castro and other employees engaged in these organizing activities.

Three years later, in January 1992, respondent Board found that Hoffman unlawfully selected four employees, including Castro, for layoff "in order to rid itself of known union supporters" in violation of § 8(a)(3) of the National Labor Relations Act (NLRA). To remedy this violation, the Board ordered that Hoffman (1) cease and desist from further violations of the NLRA, (2) post a detailed notice to its employees regarding the remedial order, and (3) offer reinstatement and back pay to the four affected employees. . . .

In June 1993 the parties proceeded to a compliance hearing before an Administrative Law Judge (ALJ) to determine the amount of back pay owed to each discriminatee. On the final day of the hearing, Castro testified that he was born in Mexico and that he had never been legally admitted to, or authorized to work in, the United States. . . . He admitted gaining employment with Hoffman only after tendering a birth certificate belonging to a friend who was born in Texas. . . . Based on this testimony, the ALJ found the Board precluded from awarding Castro back pay or reinstatement as such relief would be . . . in conflict with IRCA, which makes it unlawful for employers knowingly to hire undocumented workers or for employees to use fraudulent documents to establish employment eligibility.

In September 1998, four years after the ALJ's decision, and seven years after Castro was fired, the Board reversed with respect to back pay. . . . [T]he Board determined that "the most effective way to accommodate and further the immigration policies embodied in [IRCA] is to provide the protections and remedies of the [NLRA] to undocumented workers in the same manner as to other employees." The Board thus found that Castro was entitled to $66,951 of back pay, plus interest. . . .

***

Under the IRCA regime, it is impossible for an undocumented alien to obtain employment in the United States without some party directly contravening explicit congressional policies. Either the undocumented alien tenders fraudulent identification, which subverts the cornerstone of IRCA's enforcement mechanism, or the employer knowingly hires the undocumented alien in direct contradiction of its IRCA obligations. The Board asks that we overlook this fact and allow it to award back pay to an illegal alien for years of work not performed, for wages that could not lawfully have been earned, and for a job obtained in the first instance by a criminal fraud. We find, however, that awarding back pay to illegal aliens runs counter to policies underlying IRCA, policies the Board has no authority to enforce or administer. Therefore, as we have consistently held in like circumstances, the award lies beyond the bounds of the Board's remedial discretion.

***

Decision

We therefore conclude that allowing the Board to award back pay to illegal aliens would unduly trench upon explicit statutory prohibitions critical to federal immigration policy, as expressed in IRCA. It would encourage the successful evasion of apprehension by immigration authorities, condone prior violations of the immigration laws, and encourage future violations. However broad the Board's discretion to fashion remedies when dealing only with the NLRA, it is not so unbounded as to authorize this sort of an award.

Lack of authority to award back pay does not mean that the employer gets off scot-free. The Board here has already imposed other significant sanctions against Hoffman—sanctions Hoffman does not challenge. These include orders that Hoffman cease and desist its violations of the NLRA, and that it conspicuously post a notice to employees setting forth their rights under the NLRA and detailing its prior unfair practices. Hoffman will be subject to contempt proceedings should it fail to comply with these orders.

Questions for Discussion

1. What was the Board's rationale for awarding back pay to the four employees?
2. What was the Board's argument for awarding back pay to Castro?
3. What practices would you recommend for employers who operate where there is a large population of legal and illegal aliens? How would you ensure that unauthorized aliens are not hired and at the same time ensure that no discriminatory behavior takes place?
4. What are the penalties for employers who hire unauthorized aliens?

The applicability of antidiscrimination and other employment laws to people who are not U.S. citizens, but who are on U.S. territory, has already been discussed. The following article[29] explores the applicability of U.S. antidiscrimination law to individuals who are not U.S. citizens, are not working within America's physical boundaries, and are working for a U.S. company. In the cited cases the employer is operating abroad through an affiliate company.

A state district court in Texas recently held . . . that a U.S. company may be subject to jurisdiction in the U.S. court system and face liability for actions arising in a foreign country, involving foreign residents, and stemming from the actions of the company's foreign subsidiary. In August 1999 the defendant in *Rodriquez-Olvera vs. Salant Corporation* revealed that the case had settled for US$30 million after the trial court made the unprecedented decision to allow the plaintiffs' case to proceed against the U.S. company. The court's decision and the ultimate settlement of this case, as well as other similar cases, demonstrate the dramatic increase in the exposure of U.S. companies to liability in the United States for actions arising in Mexico.

***

LITIGATING FOREIGN-BASED EMPLOYMENT CLAIMS IN THE UNITED STATES

Although unusual, the *Salant* case is not the first time a U.S. court has permitted a claim to be brought against a U.S. company for the death or injury of employees in Mexico. In *Rodriguez vs. Sierra Western* a sewing machine mechanic at a Mexican subcontracting factory sued a Texas corporation based on allegations that the company was negligent in not providing him with safe transportation to work at the company's operations in Mexico. The plaintiff suffered injuries in a 1996 car accident in which an employee of the U.S. corporation was driving the plaintiff from a plant in Chihuahua, Mexico, to his hometown of Juarez, Mexico. In September 1999 the Texas jury awarded US$632,000 in favor of the injured Mexican worker.

***

In 1994 the *Aguirre vs. American United Global* lawsuit was filed in California. In *Aguirre* a Mexican subsidiary, which was wholly owned by a Los Angeles–based corporation, was allegedly participating in blatant sexual harassment against Mexican employees. A company executive allegedly demanded that female employees perform a "bikini show" for him to videotape at a company picnic. After the officers of the U.S. corporation did not attend the trial in Mexico, the 118 female employees (all residents of Mexico) refiled the action in Los Angeles Superior Court and alleged violations under both American and Mexican law. After the corporation's motion for summary judgment was defeated, the case settled for an undisclosed amount, and the corporation closed down its Mexican operations.

***

IMPACT OF RECENT DECISIONS

These recent court decisions, jury awards, and settlements will undoubtedly encourage more foreign workers to sue U.S. companies with operations in Mexico. Attorneys for potential Mexican plaintiffs are often interested in pursuing their claims in U.S. courts because Mexican laws provide a damage cap for injuries and wrongful death, whereas a jury in the United States has virtually unbridled discretion in awarding such damages. One of the main differences between Mexican and U.S. law in personal injury cases is that Mexican law does not allow for "pain and suffering" damages. The only recoverable damages in Mexico are medical expenses and a limited amount for physical impairment. Moreover, U.S. companies are thought to have "deep pockets."

RECOMMENDATIONS FOR MINIMIZING EXPOSURE TO LIABILITY

. . . The most basic and important recommendation for reducing exposure is to ensure that decisions regarding Mexican operations are made from within the Mexican operation, not in the United States. Another obvious method of decreasing exposure is to reduce practices or activities of the Mexican operations that may result in liability. For example, U.S. companies can limit potential liability by improving employees' working conditions, improving worker safety, increasing awareness of safety precautions, imposing more stringent safety and health policies, and taking other steps to improve the work environment for employees in Mexico.

SIGNIFICANCE

These recent U.S. state court decisions demonstrate a trend toward allowing U.S. courts to hear cases brought by Mexican residents that are based on actions occurring in or arising in Mexico. With the new trend, U.S. companies will face increased exposure to liability in the United States for actions stemming from their operations in Mexico. In response, U.S. companies must make concerted efforts to reduce potential legal exposure in the United States, beginning with a segregation of U.S. and foreign operations.

CONCLUSIONS

In the foregoing paragraphs several topics arising out of immigration law were presented. These represent only the "tip of the iceberg" of the many legal concerns that face employers when dealing with this area of employment law. The Immigration and Naturalization Service is currently undergoing scrutiny stemming from the September 11 tragedy, and efforts are under way to revamp the system and strengthen its ability to screen the flow of individuals into the United States so that those with terrorist intentions are thwarted. To the extent that immigration law will be amended to reflect these concerns and the INS is reorganized or merged with other agencies, employers' responsibilities and obligations may change and expand with them. It is a complex web of regulations and prohibitions for employers, and those who know best how to comply with these laws and utilize the opportunities they present will fare best in the global marketplace.

Summary

National origin discrimination is prohibited not only by the Civil Rights Act of 1964 but also by the Immigration and Nationality Act of 1952 (INA) as amended by the Immigration Reform Control Act of 1986 (IRCA). The INA provides, among other things, that only certain foreign citizens are permitted to enter the United States and work in this country. The IRCA essentially enlists employers to help enforce immigration laws. Because the IRCA was passed after the Civil Rights Act, Congress included provisions to clarify that employers, in carrying out their duties under the IRCA, must remember the prohibitions against national origin discrimination.

Under the IRCA employers must determine whether an alien is authorized to work in this country. To make this decision employers must understand the distinctions among citizens, nationals, aliens, immigrants, nonimmigrants, and permanent residents, as well as other specific terms relating to the categories of individuals immigrating to this country.

Depending on the nature of the employment and the position being filled, legal alien workers come within two categories: those authorized to work anywhere and in any position, and those authorized to work for a specific employer.

U.S. employers must check the documentation of potential employees to verify that they are eligible to work in this country. A Form I-9 must be completed for each hire, and records must be kept up to date and ready for presentation to appropriate authorities. By law, only specified documents are acceptable as evidence of a person's eligibility for employment.

Specialized visas, such as the B-1 and H1-B, are available for employment in particular situations. Employers must choose carefully among the various types of visas when bringing new hires in from other nations, and they must stay abreast of changes in these laws.

National origin discrimination under the Civil Rights Act of 1964 has been defined by the EEOC to include the denial of equal employment opportunity because of an individual's (or his or her ancestor's) place of origin or because an individual has physical, cultural, or linguistic characteristics of a national origin group.

The Civil Rights Act of 1964 also applies to U.S. corporations operating outside U.S. borders. This was codified in the Civil Rights Act of 1991, an amendment to the Civil Rights Act of 1964.

The question of the extent to which the Civil Rights Act protects illegal aliens has been addressed by the EEOC. Such people can sue their employers under the Civil Rights Act and, if successful, can seek job reinstatement, back pay, other monetary damages, and attorney fees.

Questions

1. Kaveh N., a permanent resident alien from Iran, had been working for the Tennessee Valley Authority since 1967 when in 1990 the agency terminated him as part of a reduction in force. He subsequently sought employment

with an agency contractor. When a contractor contacted the agency for approval to hire, the agency denied approval because the complainant was a citizen of Iran, a country not listed by the U.S. Department of State as a friendly and allied country. He was, however, given a temporary position with the agency and then assigned to the agency's Employee Transition Program, which assisted displaced employees in finding new jobs. He was not selected by any of the employers to whom he applied. He filed an action with the EEOC claiming national origin discrimination.

Does Kaveh have a good case? Why or why not?

2. Fernando A., a citizen of the Philippines, worked for a U.S. federal agency in the Philippines. He brought a claim against the agency alleging that the agency discriminated against him on the basis of national origin.

Without any more information, can you make an argument that Fernando cannot win this case?

3. Jenny B. was a maintenance support clerk at a U.S. federal agency in Honolulu, Hawaii. She alleged that the agency harassed her because of her race (Filipino), national origin (Philippines), sex (female), and age. Among her complaints were the following: (a) her supervisor instructed her not to speak on the phone in her native language; (b) management informed her that she would need to swap job assignments with another employee for an indefinite period; (c) she was scolded and yelled at in the presence of co-workers; (d) management and coworkers continually observed her during the performance of her duties; and (e) management burdened her with an unfair distribution of work.

Her manager produced affidavits from several coworkers who complained that she spoke for long periods over the phone in her native language. For this reason, he said, she was asked to limit the length of her calls and that "speaking in her native language for personal business was okay but not for long periods of time." On the issue of swapping jobs, the manager claimed that this was a means of cross-training. On the issue of unfair distribution of workload, it was argued that the division had experienced a reduction of personnel that increased the workload of all employees. Jenny B. was praised as an "excellent and efficient worker" who often had difficulty focusing on higher-priority tasks, which caused her to become overwhelmed.

a. Do the actions of the agency amount to a violation of Title VII?

b. Does the evidence support a claim that the agency has instituted an "English only" rule?

c. Decide the case. What management policies or practices could have been in place to prevent Jenny B. from taking action against the agency?

4. Isabel A., a hearing office clerk for the Social Security Administration, alleges that the agency discriminated against her on the basis of her national origin (Hispanic). She claims that (a) she was harassed and subjected to a hostile work environment when a coworker threatened her with physical violence, a coworker slammed her body into her while in the hallway, her

request for two weeks of administrative leave was denied, and she was subjected to a mock investigation during which a labor relations specialist asked her if she would refrain from speaking Spanish in the Office of Hearings and Appeals; (b) she was harassed and subjected to a hostile work environment when she was told she was not entitled to have union representation at an informal performance discussion, and she was falsely accused of having performance problems and threatened with adverse action; and (c) she was harassed and subjected to a hostile work environment when she was accused of not having requested a travel order for a nonattorney representative for a case she had scheduled.

a. Are these allegations, in and of themselves, sufficient to win the case?

b. In light of this case, what advice would you have for HR managers?

References

1. "President Bush Addresses the Nation on Immigration Reform," May 15, 2006. See www.whitehouse.gov/news/releases/2006/05/20060515-8.html (accessed March 4, 2008).

2. 8 U.S.C. 1401.

3. 8 U.S.C. 1101 (a)(22).

4. 8 U.S.C. 1101(a)(3).

5. 8 U.S.C. 1101(a)(15).

6. Ibid.

7. 8 U.S.C. 1101(a)(20).

8. P. Zulkie, *Immigration Compliance in Employment and Business* (Wilmette, IL: Callaghan & Company), pp 6–7.

9. Ibid. at pp. 91–93.

10. Ibid. at pp. 91–96.

11. See *Immigration Reform and Control Act of 1986 (IRCA) and the I-9 Form,* p. 5 from www.missouri.edu ~hrswww/resources/i9webs~1.doc (accessed September 28, 2006).

12. G. Witte, "Extended Worker Checks Would Use Faulty System,"*The Washington Post,* May 25, 2006, p. A01. See the Washington Post Web site at http://www.washingtonpost.com/wp-dyn/content/article/2006/05/24/AR2006052402400.html (accessed September 28, 2006).

13. U.S. Citizenship and Immigration Services, *Immigration Classifications and Visa Categories.* See http://www.uscis.gov/graphics/services/visas.htm (accessed September 28, 2006).

14. L. Jackson Shultz and P. C. Lebrun, "The H-1B Visa: Requirements and Obligations,"*South Dakota Employment Law Letter* 7, no. 3 (2002).

15. 8 U.S.C. 1184 (2001).

16. M. Ionnides, "Greater Employment Opportunities for Visa Holders' Spouses," *Texas Lawyer* 17, no. 50 (2002), p. 33.

17. "Visa Revalidation Delays Due to 'Condor' Security Checks." See http://www.tindallfoster.com/ExportedSiteImmigrationResources/TravelAdvisories/VisaRevalidationDelays.pdf (accessed September 28, 2006).

18. *Panlilio v. Dallas Independent School District,* 643 F.2d 315 (1981).

19. 29CFR 1606.1. Labor.

20. 29CFR 1606.7. EEOC English-Only Guidelines.

21. The U.S. Equal Employment Opportunity Commission, "EEOC Reaches Landmark 'English-Only' Settlement; Chicago Manufacturer to Pay over $190,000 to Hispanic Workers," September 1, 2000. See www.eeoc.gov/press/9-1-00.html (accessed March 4, 2008).

22. *Fortino v. Quasar Co.,* 950 F.2d 389, Nos. 21-1123, 91-1197, 91-1564, slip op. at 4 (7th Cir. Dec. 3, 1991).

23. *Espinoza v. Farah Manufacturing Co.,* 414 U.S. 86, 6 EPD9844 (1973).

24. EEOC Decision No. 77-26, June 14, 1977.

25. *EEOC v. Switching Systems Division of Rockwell International Corporation,* 783 F.Supp. 369 (1992).

26. *EEOC v. Arabian American Oil Co., et al.,* 499 U.S. 244 (1991).

27. See http://www.eeoc.gov/policy/docs/undoc-rescind.html (accessed September 26, 2006).

28. *Hoffman Plastic Compounds, Inc. v. National Labor Relations Board,* 535 U.S. 137, 122 S. Ct. 1275, 152 L. Ed. 2d 271, (2002).

29. J. W. Cowman and K. F. Rich, "Increased Exposure to Lawsuits in the U.S. Stemming from Operations in Mexico," *The Global Employer—Global Labour Employment and Employee Benefits Bulletin—International Perspectives.* See http://www.shrm.org/global/publications/baker/1299glob/Jan%2000%20docs/ip.htm (accessed September 28, 2006).

Bibliography

Portions of this chapter were printed first in the *Journal of Global Competitiveness* and *Competition Forum.* "Alien Workers, National Origin Discrimination, and Changing Times: A Challenge for Employers," Rosemarie F. Twomey. *Journal of Global Competitiveness,* Vol. 10(2), 2002.

"Extraterritoriality of U.S. Employment Laws," Rosemarie Feuerbach Twomey, *Competition Forum,* Vol. 2, No. 2, 2004.

Age Discrimination

Employers worldwide have been slow to adapt to the aging workforce, believing older workers are more expensive. Instead, they should be viewed as a solution to workforce needs. According to an AARP-commissioned study, "The Business Case for Workers Age 50+," the extra costs per employee range from negligible to 3 percent. These costs are more than offset by reduced costs in hiring and training new workers. Plus, older workers exhibit traits—experience, loyalty, attention to task, and emotional maturity—that take on greater value in today's economy. There is no magic age when someone can no longer work. Many people of "retirement age" have another 10 or 20 or more vigorous years ahead of them. Why waste this human capital?[1]

INTRODUCTION

The Age Discrimination in Employment Act of 1967[2] was enacted to combat increasing incidents of discrimination motivated by age bias, such as mandatory retirement age provisions and age qualifications in hiring. Congress believed that provisions based solely upon age are arbitrary and that chronological age alone is a poor indicator of ability to perform a job. Under the ADEA it is illegal to fire, refuse to hire or promote, or otherwise deprive an employee or potential employee of any term, condition, or privilege of employment—including, but not limited to, hiring, firing, promotion, layoff, compensation, benefits, job assignments, and training—if the reason for the decision is based on the person's age. This law applies to employers with 20 or more employees, including state and local governments, employment agencies, labor organizations, and the federal government.

The ADEA protects employees who are at least 40 years old. The ADEA's general antidiscrimination provision prohibits discrimination "because of such individual's age."[3] Congress stated the following about the statute:

STATEMENT OF FINDINGS AND PURPOSE

SEC. 621. *[Section 2]*

(a) The Congress hereby finds and declares that—
   (1) in the face of rising productivity and affluence, older workers find themselves disadvantaged in their efforts to retain employment, and especially to regain employment when displaced from jobs;
   (2) the setting of arbitrary age limits regardless of potential for job performance has become a common practice, and certain otherwise desirable practices may work to the disadvantage of older persons;
   (3) the incidence of unemployment, especially long-term unemployment with resultant deterioration of skill, morale, and employer acceptability is, relative to the younger ages, high among older workers; their numbers are great and growing; and their employment problems grave;
   (4) the existence in industries affecting commerce, of arbitrary discrimination in employment because of age, burdens commerce and the free flow of goods in commerce.

(b) It is therefore the purpose of this chapter to promote employment of older persons based on their ability rather than age; to prohibit arbitrary age discrimination in employment; to help employers and workers find ways of meeting problems arising from the impact of age on employment.

STATISTICS ON THE U.S. AGING POPULATION

Figure 13.1 graphically presents the increasing numbers of people aged 65 and older in each of the states. Issues of discrimination and intergenerational conflict, as well as the demands that an aging population makes on employee–caregivers, are major concerns for employers.

In 2006, 5.5 million (15.4 percent) of Americans aged 65 and over were in the labor force (working or actively seeking work), including 3.1 million men (20.3 percent) and 2.4 million women (11.7 percent). They constituted 3.6 percent of the U.S. labor force. During the past decade labor force participation of older adults has been gradually rising. This increase is especially noticeable among the population aged 65–69.[4]

Other interesting statistics show that educational levels for the aging population are also increasing—a characteristic that employers can take note of and possibly capitalize on. Between 1970 and 2006 the percentage who had completed high school rose from 28 percent to 77.5 percent. About 19.5 percent in 2006 had a bachelor's degree or more. The percentage who had completed high school varied considerably by race and ethnic origin in 2006: 80.4 percent of whites, 70.1 percent of Asians and Pacific Islanders, 55.1 of African-Americans, and 39.7 percent of Hispanics. The increase in educational levels is also evident within these groups. In 1970 only 30 percent of older whites and 9 percent of older African-Americans were high school graduates.[5]

FIGURE 13.1 **Percentage Increase in Population Aged 65+, 1996–2006**

Source: 1996 and 2006 population estimates from the U.S. Bureau of the Census[6].

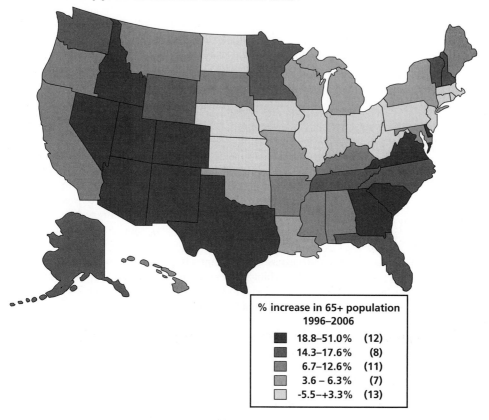

% increase in 65+ population
1996–2006

■ 18.8–51.0%	(12)
■ 14.3–17.6%	(8)
■ 6.7–12.6%	(11)
■ 3.6 – 6.3%	(7)
□ -5.5–+3.3%	(13)

ISSUES THAT ARISE UNDER THE ADEA

A variety of questions arise in age discrimination cases, including the following:

1. If a 40-year-old employee is terminated and replaced by a 45-year-old person, has illegal age discrimination taken place (reverse age discrimination)? Answer: See Case for Discussion 13-1.

2. Can age discrimination ever be justified? For example, can an employer require that all employees over a certain age retire? Answer: See Case for Discussion 13-3 .

3. Can an employer successfully argue that the higher cost of retaining older employees is a legitimate business reason to justify termination in a reduction-in-force measure taken for economic reasons? Answer: Yes.

4. Does an employer violate the ADEA if it terminates an employee just before the vesting of that employee's pension? Answer: See *Hazen Paper Co. v. Biggins*, cited in Case for Discussion 13-1.

5. Under what circumstances will an employer be required to pay double damages for violation of the ADEA? Answer: When a court concludes that the age discrimination was intentional. See Case for Discussion 13-4.

6. Can a successful age discrimination plaintiff receive damages for the emotional distress caused by the employer's violation of the ADEA? Answer: No. ADEA remedies are not the same as those available under other federal antidiscrimination laws. However, if a plaintiff argues under a *state* statute, there may be such a remedy.

7. Can a plaintiff–employee be successful if he or she cannot prove intentional age discrimination? See Case for Discussion 13-5.

Case for Discussion 13-1

Reverse Age Discrimination

In the Supreme Court's opinion here the issue centered on an unusual question—whether it is a violation of the ADEA for an employer to favor older workers over younger workers.

GENERAL DYNAMICS LAND SYSTEMS, INC., V. DENNIS CLINE ET AL., 540 U.S. 581 (2004)[7]

Facts

In 1997 a collective bargaining agreement between petitioner General Dynamics and the United Auto Workers eliminated the company's obligation to provide health benefits to subsequently retired employees, except to then-current workers at least 50 years old. Respondents (collectively, Cline) were then at least 40 and thus protected by the act, . . . but under 50 and so without promise of the benefits. . . .

***

. . . Cline brought this action against General Dynamics, combining claims under the ADEA and state law. The district court called the federal claim one of "reverse age discrimination," upon which, it observed, no court had ever granted relief under the ADEA. . . . It dismissed in reliance on the Seventh Circuit's opinion in *Hamilton v. Caterpillar Inc.,* 966 F.2d 1226 (1992), that "the ADEA 'does not protect . . . the younger *against* the older.'" . . .

[T]he Sixth Circuit reversed, . . . , with the majority reasoning that the prohibition of § 623(a)(1), covering discrimination against "any individual . . .

because of such individual's age," is so clear on its face that if Congress had meant to limit its coverage to protect only the older worker against the younger, it would have said so. . . .

***

Congress chose not to include age within discrimination forbidden by Title VII of the Civil Rights Act of 1964, . . . , being aware that there were legitimate reasons as well as invidious ones for making employment decisions on age. Instead it called for a study of the issue by the Secretary of Labor, who concluded that age discrimination was a serious problem, but one different in kind from discrimination on account of race. The Secretary spoke of disadvantage to older individuals from arbitrary and stereotypical employment distinctions (including then-common policies of age ceilings on hiring), but he examined the problem in light of rational considerations of increased pension cost and, in some cases, legitimate concerns about an older person's ability to do the job. . . . When the Secretary ultimately took the position that arbitrary discrimination against older workers was widespread and persistent enough to call for a federal legislative remedy, . . . he placed his recommendation against the background of common experience that the potential cost of employing someone rises with age, so that the older an employee is, the greater the inducement to prefer a younger substitute. . . .

***

In sum, except on one point, all the findings and statements of objectives are either cast in terms of the effects of age as intensifying over time, or are couched in terms that refer to "older" workers, explicitly or implicitly relative to "younger" ones. The single subject on which the statute speaks less specifically is that of "arbitrary limits" or "arbitrary age discrimination." But these are unmistakable references to the . . . finding that "[a]lmost three out of every five employers covered by [a] 1965 survey have in effect age limitations (most frequently between 45 and 55) on new hires which they apply without consideration of an applicant's other qualifications." . . . The ADEA's ban on "arbitrary limits" thus applies to age caps that exclude older applicants, necessarily to the advantage of younger ones.

***

This same, idiomatic sense of the statutory phrase is confirmed by the statute's restriction of the protected class to those 40 and above. If Congress had been worrying about protecting the younger against the older, it would not likely have ignored everyone under 40. The youthful deficiencies of inexperience and unsteadiness invite stereotypical and discriminatory thinking about those a lot younger than 40, and prejudice suffered by a 40-year-old is not typically owing to youth, as 40-year-olds sadly tend to find out. The enemy of 40 is 30, not 50. . . .

The federal reports are as replete with cases taking this position as they are nearly devoid of decisions like the one reviewed here. To start closest to home, the best example is *Hazen Paper Co. v. Biggins*, 507 U.S. 604, 123 L. Ed. 2d 338, 113 S. Ct. 1701 (1993), in which we held there is no violation of the ADEA in firing an employee because his pension is about to vest, a basis for action that we took to be analytically distinct from age, even though it would never occur without advanced years. . . . We said that "the very essence of age discrimination [is] for an older employee to be fired because the employer believes that productivity and competence decline with old age," . . . , whereas discrimination on the basis of pension status "would not constitute discriminatory treatment on the basis of age [because] the prohibited stereotype [of the faltering worker] would not have figured in this decision, and the attendant stigma would not ensue," . . . . And we have relied on this same reading of the statute in other cases. See, e.g., *O'Connor,* 517 U.S., at 313, 134 L. Ed. 2d 433, 116 S. Ct. 1307 ("Because the ADEA prohibits discrimination on the basis of age . . . the fact that a replacement is substantially younger than the plaintiff is a . . . reliable indicator of age discrimination"). . . .

***

Decision

We see the text, structure, purpose, and history of the ADEA, along with its relationship to other federal statutes, as showing that the statute does not mean to stop an employer from favoring an older employee over a younger one. The judgment of the court of appeals is reversed.

Dissent

Justice Scalia

The Age Discrimination in Employment Act of 1967 (ADEA) . . . makes it unlawful for an employer to "discriminate against any individual with respect to his compensation, terms, conditions, or privileges of employment, because of such individual's age." The question in this case is whether, in the absence of an affirmative defense, the ADEA prohibits an employer from favoring older over younger workers when both are protected by the act, i.e., are 40 years of age or older.

The Equal Employment Opportunity Commission (EEOC) has answered this question in the affirmative. In 1981 the agency adopted a regulation that states, in pertinent part,

> It is unlawful in situations where this Act applies, for an employer to discriminate in hiring or in any other way by giving preference because of age between individuals 40 and over. Thus, if two people apply for the same position, and one is 42 and the other 52, the employer may not lawfully turn down either one on the basis of age, but must make such decision on the basis of some other factor. . . .

This regulation represents the interpretation of the agency tasked by Congress with enforcing the ADEA. See 29 USC § 628.

The Court brushes aside the EEOC's interpretation as "clearly wrong.". . .
I cannot agree with the contention upon which that rejection rests . . .

Questions for Discussion

1. What could General Dynamics have done differently to avoid the lawsuit brought by Cline?

2. Do you agree with the U.S. Supreme Court's interpretation of the ADEA—that it is meant to protect only older workers? Can you think of a situation in which younger workers might be unfairly discriminated against?

3. Justice Scalia felt strongly enough about the majority opinion in this case that he wrote a dissenting opinion in which he referred to a difference of opinion by the EEOC. If Justice Scalia had persuaded the other justices to his way of thinking, what would the outcome of the case have been? What effect would it have had on employers?

4. If an employer favors a 45-year-old worker over a 40-year-old worker, is this legal under the ADEA? How would a court analyze such a case—that is, what factors would persuade the court whether this violates the ADEA?

Cases for Discussion 13-2

The Prima Facie Case and Disparate Treatment

In 1973 the U.S. Supreme Court, in *McDonnell Douglas Corp. v. Green*, established the facts that a plaintiff must assert to establish a prima facie case (which raises a presumption of illegal discrimination). In 1996 the Court revisited the prima facie case for claims of age discrimination brought under the federal statute in *O'Connor vs. Consolidated Coin*. This case clarified what the prima facie should consist of in age-related discrimination cases.

O'CONNOR V. CONSOLIDATED COIN CATERERS CORPORATION, 517 U.S. 308 (1996)[8]

This case presents the question of whether a plaintiff alleging that he was discharged in violation of the Age Discrimination in Employment Act of 1967 (ADEA) must show that he was replaced by someone outside the age group protected by the ADEA to make a prima facie case under the framework established by *McDonnell Douglas Corp. v. Green*, 411 U.S. 792 (1973).

Facts

Petitioner James O'Connor was employed by respondent from 1978 until August 10, 1990, when, at age 56, he was fired and replaced by a 40-year-old man. Claiming that he had been dismissed because of his age in violation of the ADEA, petitioner brought suit in the United States District Court for the Western District of North Carolina. After discovery, the district court granted Consolidated Coin's motion for summary judgment, and O'Connor appealed.

Prima Facie Case for Age Discrimination

The Court of Appeals for the Fourth Circuit stated that petitioner could establish a prima facie case under *McDonnell Douglas* only if he could prove that

(1) he was in the age group protected by the ADEA;

(2) he was discharged or demoted;

(3) at the time of his discharge or demotion, he was performing his job at a level that met his employer's legitimate expectations; and

(4) following his discharge or demotion, he was replaced by someone of comparable qualifications outside the protected class.

Since petitioner's replacement was 40 years old, the court of appeals concluded that the last element of the prima facie case had not been shown. Finding that petitioner's claim could not survive a motion for summary judgment without benefit of the *McDonnell Douglas* presumption (i.e., "under the ordinary standards of proof used in civil cases,") the court of appeals affirmed the judgment of dismissal.

***

As the very name "prima facie case" suggests, there must be at least a logical connection between each element of the prima facie case and the illegal discrimination for which it establishes a "legally mandatory, rebuttable presumption." The element of replacement by someone under 40 fails this requirement. The discrimination prohibited by the ADEA is discrimination "because of [an] individual's age," though the prohibition is "limited to individuals who are at least 40 years of age." This language does not ban discrimination against employees because they are aged 40 or older; it bans discrimination against employees because of their age, but limits the protected class to those who are 40 or older. The fact that one person in the protected class has lost out to another person in the protected class is thus irrelevant, so long as he has lost out because of his age. Or to put the point more concretely, there can be no greater inference of age discrimination (as opposed to "40 or over" discrimination) when a 40-year-old is replaced by a 39-year-old than when a 56-year-old is replaced by a 40-year-old. Because it lacks probative value, the fact that an ADEA plaintiff was replaced by someone outside the protected class is not a proper element of the *McDonnell Douglas* prima facie case.

Decision

The judgment of the Fourth Circuit is reversed, and the case is remanded for proceedings consistent with this opinion.

Questions for Discussion

1. How relevant is it in an age discrimination case that the plaintiff is replaced by someone who is only one year younger?
2. How relevant, in an age discrimination case, is a plaintiff's appearance, health, or demeanor?

AKOS SWIERKIEVICZ V. SOREMA N.A., 534 U.S. 506, 122 S. CT. 992, 152 L. ED. 2D 1 (2002)[9]

In 2002 the U.S. Supreme Court decided an age discrimination case that posed a different but related question: whether a complaint in an employment discrimination lawsuit must contain factual allegations that support an inference of discrimination under the framework set forth by this Court in *McDonnell Douglas Corp. v. Green,* 411 U.S. 792, 36 L. Ed. 2d 668, 93 S. Ct. 1817 (1973). In particular, the question is whether the facts alleged by the plaintiff are sufficient to state a prima facie case. The case is as follows.

Facts

Petitioner Akos Swierkiewicz is a native of Hungary who at the time of his complaint was 53 years old. In April 1989 petitioner began working for respondent Sorema N. A., a reinsurance company headquartered in New York. . . . Petitioner was initially employed in the position of senior vice president and chief underwriting officer (CUO). Nearly six years later, Francois M. Chavel, respondent's chief executive officer, demoted petitioner to a marketing and services position and transferred the bulk of his underwriting responsibilities to Nicholas Papadopoulo, a 32-year-old. . . . About a year later Mr. Chavel stated that he wanted to "energize" the underwriting department and appointed Mr. Papadopoulo as CUO. Petitioner claims that Mr. Papadopoulo had only one year of underwriting experience at the time he was promoted, and therefore was less experienced and less qualified to be CUO than he, since at that point he had 26 years of experience in the insurance industry.

Following his demotion, petitioner contends that he "was isolated by Mr. Chavel . . . excluded from business decisions and meetings and denied the opportunity to reach his true potential at SOREMA." Petitioner unsuccessfully attempted to meet with Mr. Chavel to discuss his discontent. Finally, in April 1997, petitioner sent a memo to Mr. Chavel outlining his grievances and requesting a severance package. Two weeks later, respondent's general counsel presented petitioner with two options: He could either resign without a severance package or be dismissed. Mr. Chavel fired petitioner after he refused to resign.

Petitioner filed a lawsuit alleging that he had been terminated on account of his . . . age in violation of the Age Discrimination in Employment Act of 1967 (ADEA). . . . The United States District Court for the Southern District of New York dismissed petitioner's complaint because it found that he "had not adequately alleged a prima facie case, in that he had not adequately alleged circumstances that support an inference of discrimination." . . . The court of appeals held that petitioner had failed to meet his burden because his allegations were "insufficient as a matter of law to raise an inference of discrimination." . . .

The Prima Facie Case for Age Discrimination

In the court of appeals' view, petitioner was . . . required to allege in his complaint (1) membership in a protected group; (2) qualification for the job in question; (3) an adverse employment action; and (4) circumstances that support an inference of discrimination. . . .

***

This Court has never indicated that the requirements for establishing a prima facie case under *McDonnell Douglas* also apply to the pleading standard that plaintiffs must satisfy in order to survive a motion to dismiss. For instance, we have rejected the argument that a Title VII complaint requires greater "particularity," because this would "too narrowly construct the role of the pleadings." . . . The issue is not whether a plaintiff will ultimately prevail but whether the claimant is entitled to offer evidence to support the claims.

***

Furthermore, imposing the court of appeals' heightened pleading standard in employment discrimination cases conflicts with Federal Rule of Civil Procedure 8(a)(2), which provides that a complaint must include only "a short and plain statement of the claim showing that the pleader is entitled to relief." Such a statement must simply "give the defendant fair notice of what the plaintiff's claim is and the grounds upon which it rests."

***

Applying the relevant standard, petitioner's complaint easily satisfies the requirements of Rule 8(a) because it gives respondent fair notice of the basis for petitioner's claims. Petitioner alleged that he had been terminated on account of his . . . age in violation of the ADEA. His complaint detailed the events leading to his termination, provided relevant dates, and included the ages . . . of at least some of the relevant people involved with his termination. These allegations give respondent fair notice of what petitioner's claims are and the grounds upon which they rest. . . . In addition, they state claims upon which relief could be granted under . . . the ADEA.

***

Decision

For the foregoing reasons, we hold that an employment discrimination plaintiff need not plead a prima facie case of discrimination and that petitioner's complaint is sufficient to survive respondent's motion to dismiss. Accordingly, the judgment of the court of appeals is reversed, and the case is remanded for further proceedings consistent with this opinion.

Questions for Discussion

1. What must a plaintiff put into evidence to have a prima facie case?
2. According to the District Court and the Court of Appeals, what was missing from the plaintiff's complaint?
3. What difference does the Supreme Court's decision make for employers?

THE BONA FIDE OCCUPATIONAL QUALIFICATION AND OTHER EXCEPTIONS OR DEFENSES UNDER THE ADEA

The "bona fide occupational qualification" (BFOQ) defense is available to employers under the ADEA as well as under Title VII claims. When an employer overtly discriminates against any protected group, it must provide a BFOQ defense for such an action. In other words, an employer must be able to show that a specific job or occupation makes such discrimination necessary. For example, to be a candidate for Miss America, a person must be a woman—this is a BFOQ for entrance into the competition. Likewise, the U.S. Supreme Court recognizes a BFOQ defense under the ADEA when an employer requires people to retire at a designated age. The BFOQ must be reasonably necessary to the normal operation of the particular business. The Code of Federal Regulations (CFR) describes the BFOQ for the ADEA as follows:

Bona fide occupational qualifications.

(a) Whether occupational qualifications will be deemed to be "bona fide" to a specific job and "reasonably necessary to the normal operation of the particular business" will be determined on the basis of all the pertinent facts surrounding each particular situation. It is anticipated that this concept of a bona fide occupational qualification will have limited scope and application. Further, as this is an exception to the Act it must be narrowly construed.

(b) An employer asserting a BFOQ defense has the burden of proving that (1) the age limit is reasonably necessary to the essence of the business, and either (2) that all or substantially all individuals excluded from the job involved are in fact disqualified, or (3) that some of the individuals so excluded possess a disqualifying trait that cannot be ascertained except by reference to age. If the employer's objective in asserting a BFOQ is the goal of public safety, the employer must prove that the challenged practice does indeed effectuate that goal and that there is no acceptable alternative which would better advance it or equally advance it with less discriminatory impact.

(c) Many state and local governments have enacted laws or administrative regulations that limit employment opportunities based on age. Unless these laws meet the standards for the establishment of a valid bona fide occupational qualification under section 4(f)(1) of the Act, they will be considered in conflict with and effectively superseded by the ADEA.[10]

A second exception arises when an employment decision is based on reasonable factors other than age. The scope of the exception will be determined case by case[11]. Additionally, if an employer's decision is the result of a bona fide seniority system that clearly was not developed in a discriminatory manner, this would provide a valid defense.

Defenses under the ADEA

Employers can raise three defenses when facing a charge of age discrimination:

- The bona fide occupational qualification defense: that the age requirement is "reasonably necessary to the normal operation of the particular business."
- There is a "reasonable factor other than age" for the employer's decision.
- There is a bona fide seniority system that takes precedence over the age consequences.

Case for Discussion 13-3

The BFOQ Defense

In this case the Supreme Court took on the issue of the BFOQ defense, providing a discussion of its merits and guiding courts dealing with similar situations.

WESTERN AIR LINES, INC. V. CRISWELL, 472 U.S. 400, 105 S. CT. 2743, 86 L. ED. 2D 321 (1985)[12]

Facts

The petitioner, Western Air Lines, Inc., requires that its flight engineers retire at age 60. Although the Age Discrimination in Employment Act of 1967 (ADEA) generally prohibits mandatory retirement before age 70, the Act provides an exception "where age is a bona fide occupational qualification [BFOQ] reasonably necessary to the normal operation of the particular business." A jury concluded that Western's mandatory retirement rule did not qualify as a BFOQ even though it purportedly was adopted for safety reasons. The question here is whether the jury was properly instructed on the elements of the BFOQ defense.

In its commercial airline operations, Western operates a variety of aircraft, including the Boeing 727 and the McDonnell-Douglas DC-10. These aircraft require three crew members in the cockpit: a captain, a first officer, and a flight engineer. "The 'captain' is the pilot and controls the aircraft. He is responsible for all phases of its operation. The 'first officer' is the copilot and assists the captain. The 'flight engineer' usually monitors a side-facing instrument panel. He does not operate the flight controls unless the captain and the first officer become incapacitated." . . .

A regulation of the Federal Aviation Administration (FAA) prohibits any person from serving as a pilot or first officer on a commercial flight "if that person has reached his 60th birthday." . . . The FAA has justified the retention of mandatory retirement for pilots on the theory that "incapacitating medical events" and "adverse psychological, emotional, and physical changes" occur as a consequence of aging. "The inability to detect or predict with precision an individual's risk of sudden or subtle incapacitation, in the face of known age-related risks, counsels against relaxation of the rule." . . .

At the same time, the FAA has refused to establish a mandatory retirement age for flight engineers. "While a flight engineer has important duties which contribute to the safe operation of the airplane, he or she may not assume the responsibilities of the pilot in command." . . . Moreover, available statistics establish that flight engineers have rarely been a contributing cause or factor in commercial aircraft "accidents" or "incidents."

In 1978 respondents Criswell and Starley were captains operating DC-10s for Western. Both men celebrated their 60th birthdays in July 1978. Under the collective bargaining agreement in effect between Western and the union, cockpit crew members could obtain open positions by bidding in order of seniority. In order to avoid mandatory retirement under the FAA's under-age-60 rule for pilots, Criswell and Starley applied for reassignment as flight engineers. Western denied both requests, ostensibly on the ground that both employees were members of the company's retirement plan, which required all crew members to retire at age 60. For the same reason, respondent Ron, a career flight engineer, was also retired in 1978 after his 60th birthday.

Mandatory retirement provisions similar to those contained in Western's pension plan had previously been upheld under the ADEA. . . . As originally enacted in 1967, the Act provided an exception to its general proscription of age discrimination for any actions undertaken "to observe the terms of a . . . bona fide employee benefit plan such as a retirement, pension, or insurance plan, which is not a subterfuge to evade the purposes of this Act." In April 1978, however, Congress amended the statute to prohibit employee benefit plans from requiring the involuntary retirement of any employee because of age.

Criswell, Starley, and Ron brought this action against Western contending that the under-age-60 qualification for the position of flight engineer violated the ADEA. In the district court Western defended, in part, on the theory that the age-60 rule is a BFOQ "reasonably necessary" to the safe operation of the airline. All parties submitted evidence concerning the nature of the flight engineer's tasks, the physiological and psychological traits required to perform them, and the availability of those traits among people over age 60.

As the district court summarized, the evidence at trial established that the flight engineer's "normal duties are less critical to the safety of flight than those of a pilot." . . . The flight engineer, however, does have critical functions in emergency situations and, of course, might cause considerable disruption in the event of his own medical emergency.

***

The jury was instructed that the "BFOQ defense is available only if it is reasonably necessary to the normal operation or essence of defendant's business."

The jury was informed that "the essence of Western's business is the safe transportation of their passengers." The jury was also instructed,

> One method by which defendant Western may establish a BFOQ in this case is to prove:
>
> (1) That in 1978, when these plaintiffs were retired, it was highly impractical for Western to deal with each second officer over age 60 on an individualized basis to determine his particular ability to perform his job safely; and
>
> (2) That some second officers over age 60 possess traits of a physiological, psychological, or other nature which preclude safe and efficient job performance that cannot be ascertained by means other than knowing their age.

***

The jury rendered a verdict for the plaintiffs, and awarded damages. . . .

On appeal, Western made various arguments attacking the verdict and judgment below, but the court of appeals affirmed in all respects. . . .

Throughout the legislative history of the ADEA, one empirical fact is repeatedly emphasized: The process of psychological and physiological degeneration caused by aging varies with each individual. "The basic research in the field of aging has established that there is a wide range of individual physical ability regardless of age." As a result, many older American workers perform at levels equal or superior to their younger colleagues.

In 1965 the Secretary of Labor reported to Congress that despite these well-established medical facts there "is persistent and widespread use of age limits in hiring that in a great many cases can be attributed only to arbitrary discrimination against older workers on the basis of age and regardless of ability." Two years later, the president recommended that Congress enact legislation to abolish arbitrary age limits on hiring. Such limits, the president declared, have a devastating effect on the dignity of the individual and result in a staggering loss of human resources vital to the national economy.

After further study, Congress responded with the enactment of the ADEA. . . . The legislative history of the 1978 amendments to the ADEA makes quite clear that the policies and substantive provisions of the Act apply with especial force in the case of mandatory retirement provisions. The House Committee on Education and Labor reported,

> Increasingly, it is being recognized that mandatory retirement based solely upon age is arbitrary and that chronological age alone is a poor indicator of ability to perform a job. Mandatory retirement does not take into consideration actual differing abilities and capacities. Such forced retirement can cause hardships for older people through loss of roles and loss of income. Those older people who wish to be reemployed have a much more difficult time finding a new job than younger people.
>
> Society, as a whole, suffers from mandatory retirement as well . . . .

***

Every court of appeals that has confronted a BFOQ defense based on safety considerations has analyzed the problem consistently . . . An EEOC regulation embraces the same criteria:

> . . . An employer asserting a BFOQ defense has the burden of proving that (1) the age limit is reasonably necessary to the essence of the business, and either (2) that all or substantially all individuals excluded from the job involved are in fact disqualified, or (3) that some of the individuals so excluded possess a disqualifying trait that cannot be ascertained except by reference to age. If the employer's objective in asserting a BFOQ is the goal of public safety, the employer must prove that the challenged practice does indeed effectuate that goal and that there is no acceptable alternative which would better advance it or equally advance it with less discriminatory impact.

***

. . . Western argues that flight engineers must meet the same stringent qualifications as pilots, and that it was therefore quite logical to extend to flight engineers the FAA's age-60 retirement rule for pilots. Although the FAA's rule for pilots, adopted for safety reasons, is relevant evidence in the airline's BFOQ defense, it is not to be accorded conclusive weight. . . . In this case, the evidence clearly established that the FAA, Western, and other airlines all recognized that the qualifications for a flight engineer were less rigorous than those required for a pilot.

In the absence of persuasive evidence supporting its position, Western nevertheless argues that the jury should have been instructed to defer to "Western's selection of job qualifications for the position of [flight engineer] that are reasonable in light of the safety risks." . . . The BFOQ standard adopted in the statute is one of "reasonable necessity," not reasonableness.

***

Decision

The judgment of the court of appeals is affirmed, holding in favor of the plaintiffs and against Western.

Questions for Discussion

1. In light of this decision, under what circumstances could Western Airlines mandate retirement of all flight officers at the age of 60? What evidence would Western Airlines be required to prove?
2. By what means could Western Airlines determine whether people over a stated age are capable of performing at an acceptable level of safety?
3. What lesson does this case hold for all employers?

REMEDIES AVAILABLE UNDER THE ADEA

The ADEA differs from other workplace discrimination statutes in that it permits double damages for employee–plaintiffs who convince a judge or jury that the actions of the employer were willful. In other respects, the remedies available to a successful ADEA plaintiff are more limited than those under the Civil Rights Act. Punitive damages and compensatory damages for emotional distress, damage to professional reputation, pain and suffering, and similar claims are not awarded under the ADEA. Essentially the damages available under the ADEA consist of the following:

- *Back pay:* Back pay consists of wages, salary, and fringe benefits the employee would have earned had there been no discrimination.
- *Attorney's fees:* A judge may award reasonable attorney fees to the prevailing party.
- *Double damages:* The statute provides that in a finding of a willful violation of the ADEA, the damage award can be doubled.
- *Front pay:* In certain cases a plaintiff could be compensated for anticipated future losses stemming from illegal discrimination.
- *Injunctive relief:* A judge can order reinstatement or other actions to prevent future discrimination.

Case for Discussion 13-4

Willful Age Discrimination

The following federal appellate case illustrates the type of situation in which courts will award double damages for willful violation of the ADEA. It is especially noteworthy that the violation consisted of a failure to provide training in the requirements of the ADEA.

MATHIS V. PHILLIPS CHEVROLET, 269 F.3D 771 (2001)[13]

Facts

Anthony Mathis is a 59-year-old African-American man with over 24 years of experience in car sales . . . [I]n May 1996 Mathis applied for a sales job at Phillips Chevrolet in response to a newspaper ad. No one at Phillips was available to interview him when he applied, so he left his application with the cashier. A few weeks later he returned, not having heard from Phillips, and left a second application with the cashier. The application form asked for the date of his discharge from the military; Mathis indicated that he was discharged in May 1959. Mathis's theory at trial was that this information alerted Phillips to the fact that he was well over 40 years old. Phillips never interviewed Mathis for the sales position; but after he applied, it hired seven new salespeople, all younger than Mathis.

Although Phillips's managers testified that they never received Mathis's application, the jury did not believe them. Furthermore, Mathis presented evidence that suggested the managers were disposed to discriminate on the basis of age. Mathis established at trial that Jamie Pascarella, the general manager of Phillips and the person with ultimate hiring authority at the dealership, often noted the ages of employment applicants by hand on their applications, in a section of the application that he admittedly used to make notes of information he considered relevant to his hiring decision. Pascarella testified that he was not aware that it was illegal to consider age in making hiring decisions. A second Phillips manager, Henry Rhodes, admitted at trial that he looked for applicants who were "bright, young, and aggressive."

. . . Phillips had vigorously denied that it had ever received Mathis's application. Several Phillips managers who were involved in the hiring process testified that if they had seen Mathis's application, they would have interviewed him. Phillips's theory of the case was that either Mathis was lying about having dropped off applications with a Phillips cashier, or, if Mathis was not lying, then the applications had somehow been misplaced before anyone with hiring authority saw them.

It was Phillips's theory that Mathis blamed his misfortunes on a conspiracy among Chicago-area car dealerships and that, as a result, Mathis had set out to harass members of the Chicago Automobile Trade Association by manufacturing false discrimination claims against them. . . .

In order to bolster its theory, Phillips tried to introduce evidence that Mathis had sued at least six other car dealerships for discrimination after they failed to hire him during roughly the same time period as his application to Phillips. According to an offer of proof Phillips made just before the trial began, there were significant irregularities in Mathis's applications at these other dealerships. . . .

In response to Phillips's pretrial offer of proof and Mathis's motion to exclude this evidence, the district court found that Phillips's evidence of the other lawsuits seemed to be merely "an effort to show bad character on the part of the plaintiff." . . . [T]he court held that the evidence would not be admitted to show that Mathis was litigious or that he had a "campaign against car dealerships . . ." . . . After a three-day trial, the jury found for Mathis on his age discrimination claim and awarded $50,000 in compensatory damages. . . . [T]he jury found that Mathis had applied to Phillips and that Phillips's violation of the ADEA was willful.

***

Phillips argues that the jury could not have found that its violation of the ADEA was willful because Mathis could not show which manager at Phillips made the decision not to interview Mathis. As the Court in *Hazen Paper* made clear, however, the jury was free to infer willfulness from the circumstances of the case. Mathis was not required to provide direct evidence of discriminatory intent.

. . . Phillips offers very little reason to suggest that the violation was not willful. Phillips never raised any suggestion that, if it did have a discriminatory policy, the policy was justified because the age requirement was a bona fide occupational qualification or fell under a statutory exception to the ADEA. Phillips's general manager did testify that he was not aware that it was illegal to discriminate on the basis of age, but as this circuit has held, leaving managers with hiring authority in ignorance of the basic features of the discrimination laws is an "extraordinary mistake" for a company to make, and a jury can find that such an extraordinary mistake amounts to reckless indifference. Finally, Phillips notes that its employment applications stated that the ADEA "prohibits discrimination on the basis of age with respect to individuals who are at least 40 years of age" and argues that this boilerplate proves Phillips made a good-faith attempt to comply with the ADEA. However, this evidence appears more harmful to Phillips than helpful, because the jury could easily have concluded that printing this statement on the application but then making no effort to train hiring managers about the ADEA shows that Phillips knew what the law required but was indifferent to whether its managers followed that law.

Decision

For the foregoing reasons, the judgment of the district court is affirmed, holding in favor of the plaintiff and against Phillips.

Questions for Discussion

1. What evidence did Mathis produce to help prove age discrimination against Phillips?
2. What lesson(s) for employers does this case contain?

Case for Discussion 13-5

Disparate Impact Analysis under the ADEA

Just as the courts tend to follow the logic and rationale set by prior Title VII cases of various types (such as sex, race, and religion), so too do the courts tend to follow the reasoning of prior decisions even when a case involves a different antidiscrimination statute. Age discrimination is not a category protected under Title VII but is the subject of an entirely separate federal statute, the ADEA. The fact that disparate impact analysis was recognized by the U.S. Supreme Court in *Griggs* and *Watson* (which involved race discrimination under Title VII) did not require that disparate impact analysis would apply in an ADEA case. In *Smith v. City of Jackson* the Supreme Court in 2005 decided that an ADEA case could be brought with a disparate impact argument.

SMITH V. CITY OF JACKSON, MISSISSIPPI, 544 U.S. 228 (2005)[14]

Facts

Petitioners, police and public safety officers employed by the city of Jackson, Mississippi (hereinafter City), contend that salary increases received in 1999 violated the Age Discrimination in Employment Act of 1967 (ADEA) because they were less generous to officers over the age of 40 than to younger officers. Their suit raises the question of whether the "disparate impact" theory of recovery announced in *Griggs v. Duke Power Co.*, 401 U.S. 424, 28 L. Ed. 2d 158, 91 S. Ct. 849 (1971), for cases brought under Title VII of the Civil Rights Act of 1964, is cognizable under the ADEA. Despite the age of the ADEA, it is a question that we have not yet addressed.

* * *

Petitioners are a group of older officers who filed suit under the ADEA claiming both that the City deliberately discriminated against them because of their age (the "disparate treatment" claim) and that they were "adversely affected" by the plan because of their age (the "disparate impact" claim). The district court granted summary judgment to the City on both claims. The court of appeals held that the ruling on the former claim was premature because petitioners were entitled to further discovery on the issue of intent, but it affirmed the dismissal of the disparate impact claim. . . . Over one judge's dissent, the majority concluded that disparate impact claims are categorically unavailable under the ADEA.

Decision

[We] now hold that the ADEA does authorize recovery in "disparate impact" cases comparable to *Griggs*. Because, however, we conclude that petitioners have not set forth a valid disparate impact claim, we affirm.

* * *

In determining whether the ADEA authorizes disparate impact claims, we begin with the premise that when Congress uses the same language in two statutes having similar purposes, particularly when one is enacted shortly after the other, it is appropriate to presume that Congress intended that text to have the same meaning in both statutes. . . . We have consistently applied that presumption to language in the ADEA. Our unanimous interpretation of Title VII in *Griggs* is therefore a precedent of compelling importance.

Questions for Discussion

Discuss the rationale that the defendants might have utilized in arguing that plaintiffs in an age discrimination case cannot make a disparate impact claim. What was the U.S. Supreme Court's response?

Dealing with older workers is challenging for some managers, especially when a younger manager is hired and an older long-term employee is in the unit. Many cases involving age discrimination reflect this scenario. In light of the statistics presented in this chapter and the evidence of higher levels of education attained by older workers, managers might want to think twice and act differently in trying to retain them. The problem may lie in lingering stereotypical thinking about the abilities of aging employees, and not in actual reality. Both the younger manager and the subordinate older worker might benefit from the advice of Marilee G. Adams in her book titled *Change Your Questions. Change Your Life. Seven Powerful Tools for Life and Work*[15].

Adams offers a useful tool for being more effective in working with people in personal or professional life. A key element of her teaching is learning to recognize when you are operating from a "learner" or a "judger" mind-set. Any time we face a problem encounter, we consciously or unconsciously react as either judgers or learners. That decision point is crucial to our effectiveness in dealing with any issue. When a person operates from a judger mind-set, whether in relation to others or self, learning is stifled.

Adams provides a "Learner/Judger Chart"[16] that lists attributes in two columns—one for the judger mind-set and the other for the learner mind-set. Some of the attributes in the judger column are these: judgmental (of self and/or others); inflexible and rigid; defends assumptions; possibilities seen as limited. Some of the attributes in the learner column are these: accepting (of self and others); values not–knowing; questions assumptions; possibilities seen as unlimited; primary mood is curious.

In relationships the mind-sets are correlated with certain behaviors and dispositions. In the judger column these are win–lose relationships; feels separate from others; fears differences and debates; criticizes; listens for right/wrong and agree/disagree; differences and feedback perceived as rejection; seeks to attack or defend. In the learner column these are win–win relationships; feels connected with others; values differences, dialogues, and critiques; listens for facts, understanding, and commonalities; feedback perceived as worthwhile; seeks to resolve and create.

It is not hard to imagine how these mind-sets might play out in the workplace.

QUESTION FOR DISCUSSION

Analyze the *Swierkievicz v. Sorema N.A.*, *General Dynamics*, and *Western Airlines* cases in light of the Adams Judger/Learner Chart, and consider whether different mind-sets on the part of any of the involved parties could have produced different results.

THE OLDER WORKERS BENEFIT PROTECTION ACT OF 1990 (OWBPA): AN AMENDMENT TO THE ADEA

It became clear to employers after passage of the ADEA that caution had to be exercised to legally dismiss older workers. One method that some employers used was to offer their older workers incentive packages to retire. Although this practice can be favorable for the employee, situations can arise that are ultimately unfair to those employees. For example, an employer might approach an older worker, make a strong recommendation that she retire, and offer an attractive severance package—but give the employee only a brief period to decide. The employee would also be required to sign a waiver that he or she would not file an action under the ADEA for matters arising from the severance agreement. For these and other reasons, the Older Workers Benefit Protection Act of 1990 (OWBPA) was added to the ADEA. The OWBPA limits the right of employers to reduce benefits of older workers, and the act also sets out provisions regarding an agreement to waive ADEA rights.

To execute a valid waiver of ADEA rights, the OWBPA makes the following minimum requirements[17]:

1. It must be in writing and be understandable.
2. It must specifically refer to ADEA rights or claims.
3. The employee may not waive rights or claims that may arise in the future.
4. There must be valuable consideration in exchange for the waiver.
5. The employer must advise the individual in writing to consult an attorney before signing the waiver.
6. The employer must give the individual at least 21 days to consider the agreement and at least 7 days to revoke the agreement after signing it.

Note: If an employer requests an ADEA waiver in connection with an exit incentive program or other employment termination program, the minimum requirements for a valid waiver are more extensive.

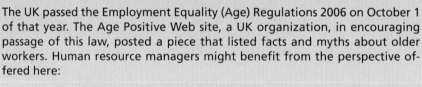

Global **Perspective**

New Law for the United Kingdom

The UK passed the Employment Equality (Age) Regulations 2006 on October 1 of that year. The Age Positive Web site, a UK organization, in encouraging passage of this law, posted a piece that listed facts and myths about older workers. Human resource managers might benefit from the perspective offered here:

Age, Health, and Employability—The Facts, Not the Myths[18]

Are all older workers a health liability?
No. Health is influenced by many factors, particularly lifestyle, activity, and nutrition. Although risk of illness or disease may increase with age, this is not always the case. In fact the good news is that the general health of older adults is improving, suggesting that the risk of certain diseases may be decreasing.

Gray matter declines in direct proportion to the increase of gray hair.
No, it doesn't. Why presume all older workers will experience declines in memory, reasoning, and problem-solving abilities? Both physical and mental capacity does change with age, but evidence demonstrates that any variation in brain functioning in older adults is not decreased function but simply different from younger adults. In fact mental functions can even improve with increased experience.

Surely older workers are less productive?
Don't believe it. There is great individual variation in ability to work at any age. Research indicates that older workers can generally compensate for any decrease in speed by increases in quality and accuracy. Productivity cannot, therefore, be used as an excuse to justify the exclusion of older workers from the workforce. One size does not fit all.

Any change in older workers capability must be bad for business?
No, this isn't the case. There are positive attributes of greater age including increased knowledge, experience, and understanding. In fairness, most of the negative changes are irrelevant in the workplace, with the majority of changes occurring in advanced old age, long after most individuals have left employment.

Aren't older workers more likely to have accidents in the workplace?
No. The fact is that older workers generally show a responsible attitude to health and safety based on life experience, judging the limits of their abilities accurately, and following rules and advice.

Older workers take more time off work sick.
Not necessarily. In fact older workers have lower levels of short-term/noncertified sickness absence than younger workers.

Summary

The Age Discrimination in Employment Act applies to private companies with 15 or more employees and provides protection for people who are at least 40 years of age.

Issues that arise under the ADEA include the following:

Reverse age discrimination: Reverse age discrimination is not a good argument for plaintiffs because the U.S. Supreme Court interprets "age" to mean older workers.

Mandated retirement: Employers can mandate retirement at a specific age only if they can successfully claim a bona fide occupational qualification (BFOQ). For age discrimination, the BFOQ consists of the following:

- The age limit is reasonably necessary to the essence of the business.
- *And* all or substantially all individuals excluded from the job involved are in fact not qualified.
- *Or* some of the individuals excluded possess a disqualifying trait that cannot be ascertained except by reference to age.

Reasonable factors other than age: If an employer's decision is based on factors other than age, there is no violation of the act.

Economic considerations: If a decision is based on economic considerations, such as a necessary reduction in force or the vesting of an employee's pension plan, these constitute factors other than age and are a valid defense to charges of ADEA violations.

Liquidated damages: The statute provides that in instances of willful violations of the ADEA, the plaintiff is entitled to double damages.

Limited remedies under the ADEA: Plaintiffs are not entitled to compensatory damages for pain and suffering, emotional distress, or other such injuries. Remedies are limited to

- Back pay.
- Attorney's fees.
- Liquidated damages.
- Front pay.
- Injunctive relief.

The Older Workers Benefit Protection Act (OWBPA) stipulates the process that must be followed when employers enter a severance agreement with employees and ask that employees waive their rights under the ADEA. If the steps are not followed, the agreement regarding waivers is unenforceable.

Questions

1. George B. was employed by ABC Company for 30 years and performed well enough to be promoted several times and receive numerous salary increases and bonuses. When he reached the age of 55, ABC Company strongly suggested that he retire and offered him an attractive severance package if he retired within two months. If George were to stay for the next three months, his pension would vest.

   a. If George accepts the severance package and retires before his pension vests, would he have a viable claim against the company based on the ADEA? Why or why not?

   b. What advice would you give to ABC Company with regard to this decision?

2. In 1975 Patrick K. took a position as national marketing director for a major nature magazine, then owned by ABC Magazines, Inc. In 1979 he became associate publisher and, two years later, vice president and publisher. In 1986 Dolfi acquired ABC Magazines and the following year sold four of its magazines, including the one Patrick worked on, to Times Mirador. Times Mirador already owned four magazines and hoped the Dolfi publications would complement and thus enhance Times Mirador's sales of advertising space. The parties agreed that once the employees had been evaluated and a reorganization was under way, some employees might be terminated. Dolfi agreed to reimburse Times Mirador for severance

payments to the terminated employees, including Patrick who was 54 at the time. At the time of his termination he was earning a base salary of $150,000 and was eligible for an annual bonus of approximately $45,000.

The events resulting in Patrick's termination began with a restructuring carried out after Times Mirador acquired the Dolfi publications. The concept of the reorganization was that by virtue of combined readership and targeted audience, they would attract more advertising revenue than the individual magazines standing alone.

The inevitable consequence of this restructuring was that the publishers of the Dolfi magazines, who had enjoyed substantial autonomy, suddenly found themselves with greatly diminished responsibility, authority, and staff. Prior to the acquisition, Patrick had been responsible for virtually all of his magazine's business affairs, and, assisted by more junior executives, was essentially on his own to "meet and if possible exceed the budgeted pretax number for the magazine." After the acquisition, he had real authority only over advertising. Patrick chafed at his reduced responsibilities. Indeed, he expressed his dissatisfaction even before the acquisition in a meeting with the president of Times Mirador.

Patrick, along with other candidates, was interviewed for the position of group publisher. In these discussions Patrick stated that the entire group publisher concept was a bad idea and would not work.

Times Mirador thereafter decided to select another executive as group publisher and to discharge Patrick. The group publisher position was given to a person who was 41 years old at a salary of $107,000 per year. Patrick's former downgraded position as publisher was filled by a 35-year-old person at a salary of $85,000.

On May 5, 1988, Patrick commenced the instant action, alleging that these decisions violated the Age Discrimination in Employment Act of 1967 ("ADEA"), 29 U.S.C. § 621 et seq. (1988), and were part of a deliberate effort to replace older, highly compensated employees with younger, less costly employees. Times Mirador replied that its decisions were based on Patrick's resistance to the restructuring program. Times Mirador moved for summary judgment, which, following oral argument, was granted from the bench without opinion, and Patrick appealed.

a. Why would a trial court decide a case before it goes to trial? (Answer: There are no material issues of fact in dispute. The judge need only apply the law to the uncontroverted facts.)

b. What is the issue before the appellate court? (Answer: Whether the trial judge was correct in deciding the case before a trial took place. This is a procedural question and is not related to the question of whether Mirador violated the ADEA.)

c. If you assume that Patrick was a competent and personable employee, should this case be resolved in his favor? Or should Mirador win this case? Explain your decision. What facts support a finding of age discrimination? Do any exceptions apply here?

3. In 1970, at age 48, Ben H. was hired by Minuteman Paper Company (MPC). Ben served as manager of the Corpus Christi division until November 1, 1977, when he was moved to the corporate staff in Houston to serve as corporate director of physical distribution. During that time he routinely received merit raises and performance bonuses. In 1980 Ben received the additional title of vice president. In 1981 Ben was given the additional title of assistant to Kevin P., MPC's president at the time.

While he was director of physical distribution, Ben received most of his assignments from Kevin, who always seemed pleased with Ben's performance. Ben's bonuses at the end of the year were based on his good performance. In 1981 Ben was placed in charge of the completion of an office warehouse building in Dallas, the largest construction project MPC had ever undertaken. Ben successfully completed that project within budget.

In 1981 Ben saw a portion of MPC's long-range plans that indicated that MPC was presently advancing younger people in all levels of management. The employee relations manager of MPC in 1979 testified that from the time he started to work there, he heard repeated references by the division managers to the age of employees on the corporate staff, including Ben.

In October 1981 Kevin became chairman of MPC and brought in a new, 42-year-old president from outside the company, Martin H. When Martin arrived at MPC in November 1981, Ben was still deeply involved in the Dallas construction project; and it was expected that Martin and other top executives would "continue to work very closely together on the completion of the Dallas project." Martin, however, refused to speak to Ben or to "interface" with him. This "silent treatment" was apparently tactical; Martin later told another MPC employee, "If I ever stop talking to you, you're dead." That employee also testified that Daniel L., the president of MPC Global, the parent company, told Martin, "I'm not telling you that you have to fire Ben. I'm telling you that he cannot make any more money."

As soon as the Dallas building project was completed, the effort to get rid of Ben intensified. On March 8, 1982, Daniel asked for Martin's recommendations on how to remove Ben from the MPC organization. On March 9, 1982, Martin responded with his recommendation that Ben be terminated. Daniel then asked the employee relations manager to meet with Ben to convince him to quit.

During the same time frame, Martin was preparing a long-range plan for MPC in which he made numerous references to age and expressed his desire to bring in "new blood" and to develop a "young team." In the meantime, Martin began dismantling Ben's job by removing his responsibilities and assigning them to other employees. He was also seen entering Ben's office after hours and removing files.

Kevin was diagnosed with cancer in February 1982. In March 1982 Ben was hospitalized for orthopedic surgery. Immediately after Kevin's death in June 1982 Ben was given three options: (1) He could take a sales job in Corpus Christi at half his pay; (2) he could be terminated with three months' severance pay; or (3) he could accept a job as warehouse supervisor in the Houston warehouse at the same salary but with a reduction in benefits. The benefits included participation in the management bonus plan, and the loss of the use of a company car, a company club membership, and a company expense account.

Ben accepted the warehouse position, which he thought was the position of warehouse manager. When he reported for duty at the warehouse on August 16, 1982, however, he was placed instead in the position of an entry-level supervisor, a position that required no more than one year's experience in the paper business.

Soon after he went to the warehouse, Ben was subjected to harassment and verbal abuse by his supervisor, who had previously been subordinate to Ben. Finally, Ben was further demeaned when he was placed in charge of housekeeping but was not given any employees to assist him in the housekeeping duties. Ben, the former vice president and assistant to the president, was thus reduced finally to sweeping the floors and cleaning up the employees' cafeteria—duties that occupied 75 percent of his working time.

In the late fall of 1982 Ben began suffering from respiratory problems caused by the dusty conditions in the warehouse and stress from the unrelenting harassment by his employer. Ben consulted a psychiatrist, who diagnosed him as suffering from reactive depression, possibly suicidal, because of on-the-job stress. The psychiatrist also advised that he stay away from work indefinitely. Prior to the difficulties with his employer, Ben had no history of emotional illness.

Ben filed an age discrimination charge with the EEOC in January 1983.

The defendants filed a counterclaim, seeking damages in excess of $10,000 for libel and slander, but later dismissed it.

a. Decide the case. If you find there is a violation of the ADEA, what remedy is Ben entitled to? Is this an example of a willful violation of the law?

b. Are there other legal claims Ben could assert against MPC? If so, what would they be? Be specific and state whether he has a good chance of succeeding.

c. Using Adams' Judger/Learner Chart, review the behaviors of the various parties in the case and observe where they displayed judger mind-sets. What could management have done differently to obtain a win–win outcome?

4. Petitioner Amanda M. worked as a scheduler at a power plant in Louisiana, run by her employer, respondent Entergy Operations, Inc. In 1994 she received a poor performance rating. Amanda's supervisor met with her on January 17, 1995, and gave her the option of either improving her performance during the coming year or accepting a voluntary arrangement for her severance. She received a packet of information about the severance agreement and had 14 days to consider her options, during which she consulted with attorneys. On January 31 Amanda decided to accept. She signed a release in which she "agreed to waive, settle, release, and discharge any and all

claims, demands, damages, actions, or causes of action . . . that I may have against Entergy. . . ." In exchange, she received six installment payments over the next four months, totaling $6,258.

Amanda filed a charge of age discrimination against Entergy in the United States District Court for the Eastern District of Louisiana, alleging constructive discharge on the basis of her age. Amanda did not offer to return the $6,258 to Entergy; nor was it clear she had the means to do so. Entergy moved for summary judgment, claiming Amanda had ratified the defective release by failing to return or offer to return the money she had received. The district court agreed and entered summary judgment for Entergy. The court of appeals affirmed. Amanda appealed.

a. Should Amanda win this lawsuit? Why or why not?

b. Did Entergy comply with the requirements of the OWBPA? Does it matter?

5. Sixty-one former employees of Geronimo, a medical device maker, are charging the company with age discrimination. They were among 721 workers who were terminated under a mass layoff that they claim was aimed at reducing the number of older and higher-paid employees.

They are asking for damages of at least $75,000 per plaintiff. The lawsuit says 450, or 62 percent, of the workers laid off in 2004 were 40 or older. At the time 48.6 percent of Geronimo's workforce of about 12,000 was older than 40, the lawsuit says. The 31-page complaint contains more than 40 anecdotes from plaintiffs alleging discriminatory comments by managers or other evidence of age discrimination. They include a remark by one manager that "people don't grow old at Geronimo" and a comment by another manager that his department had "too many senior level technicians" and needed new hires who were "young and . . . will work for cheap." The lawsuit alleges that in many instances, laid-off older workers were quickly replaced by younger ones.

a. Analyze this ADEA case and predict the outcome. What defenses are available to Geronimo? What evidence supports the workers' case?

b. Using the ADEA cases presented in this chapter, state whether the facts of this case are likely to result in a finding of willful violation of the ADEA.

c. Using Adams' Judger/Learner Chart, create a training program that addresses the behaviors that led to the filing of this case against Geronimo.

References

1. T. C. Nelson, Chief Operating Officer, AARP, News Release, May 31, 2006. From http://www.aarp.org/research/work/employment/employing_older_workers_could_rejuvenate_corporate.html (accessed October 3, 2006).

2. 29 USCS §§ 621 et seq.

3. 29 USCS § 623(a)(1).

4. *Bureau of Labor Statistics, Current Population Survey, Labor Force Statistics.* See http://www.bls.gov/cps/home.htmand and www.aoa.gov/prof/Statistics.asp.

5. *Current Population Survey, Annual Social and Economic Supplement, 2007* and related tables on the Census Bureau Web site. See also www.aoa.gov/prof/Statistics. profile/2007/2007/profile.doc (accessed February 23, 2008).

6. *1996 and 2006 Population Estimates from the U.S. Bureau of the Census.* See also www.aoa.gov/prof/Statistics.profile/2007/2007/profile.doc (accessed February 23, 2008).

7. *General Dynamics Land Systems, Inc. v. Dennis Cline et al.,* 540 U.S. 581, 124 S. Ct. 1236, 157 L. Ed. 2d 1094 (2004).

8. *O'Connor v. Consolidated Coin Caterers Corporation,* 517 U.S. 308 (1996).

9. *Akos Swierkievicz v. Sorema N.A.,* 534 U.S. 506, 122 S. Ct. 992, 152 L. Ed. 2d 1 (2002).

10. See 29 CFR 1625.6, pp. 307–308.

11. See 29 C.F.R. § 1625.7.

12. *Western Air Lines, Inc. v. Criswell,* 472 U.S. 400, 105 S. Ct. 2743, 86 L. Ed. 2d 321 (1985).

13. *Mathis v. Phillips Chevrolet,* 269 F.3d 771; 2001 U.S. App. LEXIS 21879.

14. *Smith v. City of Jackson, Mississippi,* 544 U.S. 228 (2005).

15. M. G. Adams, *Change Your Questions. Change Your Life. Seven Powerful Tools for Life and Work* (San Francisco: Berrett-Koehler, 1998).

16. Ibid. at p. 78.

17. Title II, Sec. 201 of the ADEA. See also the EEOC Web site at http://www.eeoc.gov/abouteeoc/35th/thelaw/owbpa.html (accessed October 3, 2006).

18. Taken from the *Age Positive* Web site at http://www.agepositive.gov.uk/news/age_health_employ.asp (accessed July 26, 2007).

Disability Discrimination

People with disabilities have forged a group identity. We share a common history of oppression and a common bond of resilience. . . . It is absolutely not our job to fit into mainstream society. Rather it is our destiny to demonstrate to mainstream society that it is to their benefit to figure out that we come attached to our wheelchairs; our ventilators; our canes; our hearing aids; etc. and to receive the benefit of our knowledge and experience, mainstream society needs to figure not how we fit in, but how we can be of benefit exactly the way we are.[1]

INTRODUCTION

In 1973 Congress passed the Rehabilitation Act[2] to prohibit discrimination against "handicapped" people. The act applies to three distinct types of employers: the federal government itself (Section 501 of the act), certain federal contractors (Section 503), and employers that receive funding from the federal government (Section 504).

In 1990 Congress extended the ban on disability discrimination to cover private sector employers with 15 or more employees by enacting the Americans with Disabilities Act (ADA)[3]. Congress has indicated that the provisions of the Rehabilitation Act and the Americans with Disabilities Act are to be interpreted harmoniously.

CONGRESSIONAL PURPOSE

Congress stated the following findings in support of its enactment of the Americans with Disabilities Act in 1990:

1. Some 43,000,000 Americans have one or more physical or mental disabilities, and this number is increasing as the population as a whole is growing older.

2. Historically society has tended to isolate and segregate individuals with disabilities, and despite some improvements, such forms of discrimination against individuals with disabilities continue to be a serious and pervasive social problem.

3. Discrimination against individuals with disabilities persists in such critical areas as employment, housing, public accommodations, education, transportation, communication, recreation, institutionalization, health services, voting, and access to public services.

4. Unlike individuals who have experienced discrimination on the basis of race, color, sex, national origin, religion, or age, individuals who have experienced discrimination on the basis of disability have often had no legal recourse to redress such discrimination.

5. Individuals with disabilities continually encounter various forms of discrimination, including outright intentional exclusion; the discriminatory effects of architectural, transportation, and communication barriers; overprotective rules and policies; failure to make modifications to existing facilities and practices; exclusionary qualification standards and criteria; segregation; and relegation to lesser services, programs, activities, benefits, jobs, or other opportunities.

6. Census data, national polls, and other studies have documented that people with disabilities, as a group, occupy an inferior status in our society and are severely disadvantaged socially, vocationally, economically, and educationally.

7. Individuals with disabilities are a discrete and insular minority who have been faced with restrictions and limitations, subjected to a history of purposeful unequal treatment, and relegated to a position of political powerlessness in our society, based on characteristics that are beyond the control of such individuals and resulting from stereotypic assumptions not truly indicative of the ability of such individuals to participate in, and contribute to, society.

8. The nation's proper goals regarding individuals with disabilities are to ensure equality of opportunity, full participation, independent living, and economic self-sufficiency for such individuals.

9. The continuing existence of unfair and unnecessary discrimination and prejudice denies people with disabilities the opportunity to compete on an equal basis and to pursue those opportunities for which our free society is justifiably famous—and costs the United States billions of dollars in unnecessary expenses resulting from dependence and nonproductivity[4].

WHAT IS A DISABILITY UNDER THE ADA?

Statutory language carries great weight when the courts are asked to interpret the numerous provisions of a law. In the Americans with Disabilities Act a number of terms and phrases are specifically stated and defined. Nevertheless, these terms and phrases are subject to further interpretation as courts struggle to apply the law to the facts of particular cases. The phrases *person with a disability, qualified person with a disability, impairment that substantially limits one or more of the major life activities, essential functions of a job,* and *reasonable accommodation* are just a few phrases that have been the focus of court cases arising under the ADA.

Definition of "Person with a Disability"

The first phrase that must be understood is *person with a disability.* The ADA defines such a person as someone who meets one of these criteria:

- Has a physical or mental impairment that substantially limits one or more of the major life activities of the individual.
- Has a record of such an impairment.
- Is regarded as having such an impairment.

In analyzing whether a person has a disability, courts examine the nature and severity of the impairment, the duration or expected duration of the impairment, and whether the effects of the impairment can be mitigated by medication or other means. When determining whether a particular disorder rises to the level of a disability, the courts take into consideration medical information provided by expert witnesses and information found in authoritative sources, such as the *Diagnostic and Statistical Manual IV of the American Psychiatric Association* for mental disabilities. Under the ADA, certain impairments are specifically excluded from the definition of disability. For example, an impairment caused by the current use of illegal drugs would not be a disability for the purposes of this law.

Definition of a "Qualified" Individual with a Disability

Courts seek to determine whether a disabled person is "qualified" to perform the work in question. A finding that a person is not qualified terminates that person's rights under the ADA. Some factors that have emerged as determinants of this qualified status are the following: (1) the inability to perform the essential functions of the job; (2) the disability posing a safety risk to self or others; (3) excessive absenteeism preventing a person from performing the essential functions of a job; or (4) no reasonable accommodation being available to enable a person to perform the essential functions of a job.

Essential Functions of the Job

A "qualified individual with a disability" is one who "with or without reasonable accommodation, can perform the 'essential functions' of the employment position. . . ." For the purposes of this law, "consideration shall be given to the employer's judgment as to what functions of a job are essential, and if an employer has prepared a written description before advertising or interviewing applicants for the job, this description shall be considered evidence of the essential functions of the job"[5].

Reasonable Accommodation

If a court finds that a person is not disabled under the meaning of the ADA, there is no obligation to offer accommodation, and the employer may take whatever action it deems appropriate under the circumstances.

On the other hand, if a disability exists and the individual can do the job if an accommodation is provided, the employer is obligated to provide such an accommodation at the request of the employee unless the employer can show that no reasonable accommodation is available. A reasonable accommodation is one that will not impose an "undue hardship" on the employer. Courts consider a number of contributing factors, such as the resources of the employer, the number of employees, the size of the operation, and so on in deciding whether an accommodation will impose an undue hardship on the employer.

The Undue Hardship Defense

The EEOC guidance on the ADA includes the following information regarding the "undue hardship" defense[6]:

> An employer does not have to provide a reasonable accommodation that would cause an "undue hardship" to the employer. Generalized conclusions will not suffice to support a claim of undue hardship. Instead, undue hardship must be based on an individualized assessment of current circumstances that show that a specific reasonable accommodation would cause significant difficulty or expense. A determination of undue hardship should be based on several factors, including
>
> - The nature and cost of the accommodation needed.
> - The overall financial resources of the facility making the reasonable accommodation.
> - The number of people employed at the facility.
> - The effect on expenses and resources of the facility.
> - The overall financial resources, size, number of employees, and type and location of facilities of the employer (if the facility involved in the reasonable accommodation is part of a larger entity).
> - The type of operation of the employer, including the structure and functions of the workforce, the geographic separateness, and the administrative or fiscal relationship of the facility involved in making the accommodation to the employee.
> - The impact of the accommodation on the operation of the facility.

The Three-Pronged Test to Enforce Disability Rights

For purposes of employment discrimination, a disabled person must pass a three-pronged test to be successful in stating a legal case under the federal law. The following must be established:

- The person is disabled within the meaning of the ADA.
- The person can perform the essential functions of the job either with or without a reasonable accommodation.
- The employer's decision was based on the person's disability.

If all three facts are established, the employer may still have a defense. For example, if the employer maintains that the employee was dismissed because of inappropriate behavior or behavior in violation of the company's rules, a court may find for the employer regardless of the employee's disability status, even if the behavior was linked to the disability. This situation arises frequently in cases involving people with mental disabilities, who argue that their disability is the cause of the inappropriate behavior and therefore the employer must provide an accommodation. In general, those arguments have not been successful, and courts have acknowledged an employer's right to set behavioral standards in the workplace. An exception can occur if an employer knew of an employee's mental illness and did not respond adequately to the employee's need or request for a reasonable accommodation. Employers have also been successful in arguing that a disabled person's condition poses a safety risk in the workplace.

Employer's Decision Based on the Disability

To succeed in a disability discrimination case, a disabled person must prove that a negative decision was based on the disability, not on other factors. Two points are to be considered here. (1) Unless an employer is aware of a person's disability, it is clear that an employment decision could not have been based on the disability. (2) Employers face a dilemma when the reason for a decision is behavior that is subject to discipline, but the behavior is caused by the employee's disability. Most courts recognize the employer's right to maintain a safe and efficient workplace and, therefore, find in favor of the employer in such cases. However, the courts take into consideration such factors as whether the employer knew of the problem and the extent to which it attempted to accommodate the individual, as well as such factors as the severity and degree of the safety risk the disability presents to self and other workers, and the hardship it causes for the employer.

Case for Discusssion 14-1

In the following federal appellate court case several issues are raised, including the meaning of *disability,* the significance of preemployment questions, and the type of damages available to successful plaintiffs claiming disability discrimination under the ADA.

EEOC V. WAL-MART, 202 F.3D 281 (1999)[7]

Facts

The Equal Employment Opportunity Commission ("EEOC") filed this action against Wal-Mart Stores, Inc. ("Wal-Mart"), and alleged Wal-Mart discriminated against John Otero in violation of the Americans with Disabilities Act of 1990 ("ADA"). . . . Otero was injured in an automobile accident in June 1988. As a result of the accident, Otero's right arm below the elbow joint was amputated. Otero applied for the position of night receiving clerk at Wal-Mart and was interviewed by Gloria Reyes, Wal-Mart's personnel manager. Using a prepared interview comment sheet, Reyes asked Otero, "What current or past medical problems might limit your ability to do a job?"

In response to the question, Otero told Reyes about his arm and, according to Reyes, asked her if she knew about the ADA. Until that time, Reyes had been unaware of his prosthesis. Reyes and her immediate supervisor, assistant manager Diane Bingham, ultimately recommended that Otero not be hired. The stated reason for nonemployment was Otero's rudeness, which allegedly occurred after his statements about his physical impairment and the ADA. . . . The EEOC moved for summary judgment on the "improper inquiry" claim, arguing that Wal-Mart's interviewing practices constituted a per se violation of the ADA. . . . The district court . . . granted summary judgment to the EEOC on the issue of liability.

The matter then came in for trial. The district court awarded nominal damages to Otero on the "improper inquiry" claim and submitted the issue of punitive damages to the jury. The jury found that Wal-Mart acted with "reckless indifference to [Otero's] federally protected rights" during the interview and awarded Otero punitive damages in the amount of $100,000.00. The jury likewise found in favor of the EEOC and Otero on the "failure to hire" claim and awarded Otero compensatory damages in the amount of $7,500.00 and punitive damages in the amount of $50,000.00 on that claim.

In a memorandum opinion and order, the district court . . . granted the EEOC's request for injunctive relief. The district court permanently enjoined Wal-Mart at its store in Las Cruces "from failing or refusing to hire a qualified individual with a disability because of his or her disability" and "from making inquiries of job applicants, before a job offer is made, which are likely to elicit information about a disability, unless (a) the question relates to the applicant's ability to perform job-related functions, and (b) the question is not phrased in terms of disability." The district court further ordered Wal-Mart to "conduct ADA compliance training for all supervisory and managerial employees," and upon completion of the training, to provide the EEOC "a summary of the training given and a list of all attendees."

On appeal, Wal-Mart has argued first that the EEOC and Otero failed to present a prima facie case of discrimination in connection with the "failure to hire" claim. Wal-Mart's argument is based on its contention that absent evidence that Otero was replaced by a nondisabled person, this claim should not have been submitted to the jury.

In ADA cases where there is an absence of direct evidence of discrimination, courts generally employ the burden-shifting framework established in *McDonnell Douglas Corp. v. Green* . . . to evaluate a plaintiff's claim. . . . Under *McDonnell Douglas* a plaintiff claiming disability discrimination must first establish a prima facie case by demonstrating by a preponderance of the evidence "(1) that he is 'disabled' within the meaning of the ADA, (2) that he is qualified—with or without reasonable accommodation, and (3) that he was discriminated against because of his disability."

. . . There is no requirement imposed upon a plaintiff alleging a violation of the ADA in this circuit to show replacement by a person outside of the protected class, . . . and Wal-Mart has cited no persuasive authority that holds otherwise. Accordingly, the district court committed no error by denying Wal-Mart's request for judgment as a matter of law to the extent it was based on this argument.

Wal-Mart has also argued that the EEOC and Otero failed to establish that Otero was disabled within the meaning of the ADA. The jury in this case was instructed that "the term 'disability' means, one, a physical impairment that substantially limits one or more of the major life activities of the individual. Or, two, being regarded as having such an impairment."

. . . The jury was further instructed that the phrase "substantially limits" for purposes of the ADA "means, one, unable to perform a major life activity that the average person in the general population can perform. Or, two, significantly restricted as to the condition, manner, or duration under which an individual can perform any major life activity as compared to the condition, manner, or duration under which the average person in the general population can perform that same major life activity."

. . . The jury was also advised to consider the following factors in determining whether Otero was substantially limited in any major life activity. "One, the nature and severity of the impairment. Two, the duration or expected duration of the impairment. And, three, the permanent or long-term impact or the expected permanent or long-term impact resulting from the impairment."

. . . Finally, the jury was instructed that the phrase "major life activity" "means functions such as caring for oneself, performing manual tasks, lifting, walking, seeing, hearing, speaking, breathing, learning, and working."

Decision

Examining the evidence in the light most favorable to the EEOC and Otero, and extending to them the benefit of all reasonable inferences, we find the evidence on this issue does not conclusively favor Wal-Mart and that a reasonable jury could have determined that Otero was disabled within the meaning of the ADA.

The law is clear that an employer is prohibited from making "inquiries of a job applicant as to whether such applicant is an individual with a disability or as to the nature or severity of such disability." The law is equally clear that an employer "may make preemployment inquiries into the ability of an applicant to perform job-related functions."

The parties stipulated that Reyes never explained to Otero the duties and responsibilities of a night receiving clerk or asked Otero to describe or demonstrate how he might perform such duties. The question therefore did not concern Otero's ability to perform specific job-related functions and was prohibited by [the law]. Accordingly, the district court did not err in granting summary judgment on this claim in favor of the EEOC.

Wal-Mart has further challenged the punitive damages awarded by the jury in connection with the "improper inquiry" claim. It has argued that such damages are not supported by the evidence and that the amount awarded is excessive and violates the due process clause of the Fourteenth Amendment to the United States Constitution.

Punitive damages are justified in an ADA case where there is evidence that the employer "engaged in a discriminatory practice . . . with . . . reckless indifference to the federally protected rights of an aggrieved individual." . . . In reviewing the evidence in this case, we conclude that a reasonable jury clearly could have found that Wal-Mart discriminated against Otero "in the face of a perceived risk that its actions [would] . . . violate federal law. . . ."

Questions for Discussion

1. Why is the EEOC the plaintiff in this case, and not Otero? What difference does it make?
2. How does the prima facie case for a disability claim differ from the prima facie case for other discrimination claims, such as race discrimination?
3. What is meant by *injunctive relief?*
4. If the court had ordered Wal-Mart to pay $2 million dollars in punitive damages, would that amount have been upheld in the appellate court? Why or why not?
5. What changes in process would you recommend to a human resource department to prevent suits such as this one?

Case for Discussion 14-2

TOYOTA MOTOR MANUFACTURING V. WILLIAMS, 122 S. CT. 681 (2002)[8]

Facts

In this case the Supreme Court fleshed out to a greater extent than before the meaning of *substantial impairment*. In the *Toyota* case the Court ruled against Williams, an employee who suffered from carpal tunnel syndrome. The evidence showed that Williams "could still brush her teeth, wash her face, bathe, tend her flower garden, fix breakfast, do laundry, and pick up around the house." Williams could not perform all the manual functions required by her job for extended periods and sought an accommodation in which she would do only the work she had performed before the company required employees to do multiple tasks.

Decision

The Court decided that Williams was not substantially impaired under the meaning of the ADA, and therefore she was not entitled to the protection of the act; consequently, Toyota was not required to provide accommodation, and her termination by Toyota was not a violation of the ADA.

Questions for Discussion

1. Compare the Court's interpretation of *substantial impairment* in *EEOC v. Wal-Mart* and the *Toyota* case.
2. How do the two cases differ?

Two other disability cases that were decided by the U.S. Supreme Court added to the body of law interpreting the Americans with Disabilities Act as follows. In *U.S. Airways, Inc. v. Barnett,* 535 U.S. 391 (2002)[9], the Court decided that reasonable accommodation did not require an employer to place a disabled employee in a position for which other employees had seniority rights subject to a bona fide seniority system. In *Board of Trustees of U. of Alabama v. Garrett,* 531 U.S. 356 (2001)[10], the Court held that the Eleventh Amendment to the U.S. Constitution prohibited federal courts from holding states monetarily liable for disability discrimination. The ADA prohibits the states and other employers from discriminating against a qualified individual with a disability because of that disability. However, the trial court granted the state of Alabama summary judgment stating that the ADA exceeds Congress's authority to abrogate the State's Eleventh Amendment immunity. The appellate court reversed, but the U.S. Supreme Court held that suits in federal court by state employees to recover money damages by reason of the state's failure to comply with Title I of the ADA are barred by the Eleventh Amendment.

Although separate from the Civil Rights Act that prohibits discrimination based on race, color, religion, sex, and national origin, the ADA is analyzed under the same principles that govern other discrimination cases. The factors establishing a prima facie case are similar, and plaintiffs can claim discrimination based on disparate treatment or disparate impact. Also, the EEOC enforces the ADA just as it enforces other types of antidiscrimination laws.

Case for Discussion 14-3

In this 2003 U.S. Supreme Court decision the distinction between disparate treatment and disparate impact analysis was at issue in a case involving drug addiction. Note that the plaintiff–employee in this case was precluded from having a trial—the trial court granted summary judgment to the company, and therefore the issue that went to the U.S. Supreme Court was whether summary judgment was proper or whether the case should proceed to trial.

RAYTHEON COMPANY V. JOEL HERNANDEZ, 540 U.S. 44 (2003)[11]

Facts

Joel Hernandez worked for Hughes Missile Systems for 25 years. On July 11, 1991, respondent's appearance and behavior at work suggested that he might be under the influence of drugs or alcohol. Pursuant to company policy, respondent took a drug test, which came back positive for cocaine. Respondent subsequently admitted that he had been up late drinking beer and using cocaine the night before the test. Because respondent's behavior violated petitioner's workplace conduct rules, respondent was forced to resign.

More than two years later, on January 24, 1994, respondent applied to be rehired by petitioner. Respondent stated on his application that he had previously been employed by petitioner. He also attached two reference letters to the application, one from his pastor, stating that respondent was a "faithful and active member" of the church, and the other from an Alcoholics Anonymous counselor, stating that respondent attends Alcoholics Anonymous meetings regularly and is in recovery.

Bockmiller, an employee in the company's Labor Relations Department, reviewed respondent's application. Bockmiller testified in her deposition that because respondent's application disclosed his prior employment with the company, she pulled his personnel file and reviewed his employee separation summary. She then rejected respondent's application. Bockmiller insisted that the company had a policy against rehiring employees who were terminated for workplace misconduct. Thus when she reviewed the employment separation summary and found that respondent had been discharged for violating workplace conduct rules, she rejected respondent's application. She testified, in particular, that she did not know that respondent was a former drug addict when she made the employment decision and did not see anything that would constitute a "record of" addiction.

Respondent subsequently filed a charge with the Equal Employment Opportunity Commission (EEOC). Respondent's charge of discrimination indicated that petitioner did not give him a reason for his nonselection, but that respondent believed he had been discriminated against in violation of the ADA.

Petitioner responded to the charge by submitting a letter to the EEOC, in which the manager of diversity development wrote,

> The ADA specifically exempts from protection individuals currently engaging in the illegal use of drugs when the covered entity acts on the basis of that use. Contrary to complainant's unfounded allegation, his nonselection for rehire is not based on any legitimate disability. Rather, complainant's

application was rejected based on his demonstrated drug use while pre-viously employed and the complete lack of evidence indicating successful drug rehabilitation.

***

Respondent proceeded through discovery on the theory that the company re-jected his application because of his record of drug addiction and/or because he was regarded as being a drug addict. In response to Raytheon's motion for summary judgment, Hernandez for the first time argued in the alternative that if the company really did apply a neutral no-rehire policy in his case, petitioner still violated the ADA because such a policy has a disparate impact. The district court granted Raytheon's motion for summary judgment with re-spect to respondent's disparate treatment claim. However, the district court refused to consider respondent's disparate impact claim because respondent had failed to plead or raise the theory in a timely manner.

***

Under *McDonnell Douglas* a plaintiff must first establish a prima facie case of discrimination. The burden then shifts to the employer to articulate a legit-imate, nondiscriminatory reason for its employment action. If the employer meets this burden, the presumption of intentional discrimination disappears, but the plaintiff can still prove disparate treatment by, for instance, offering evidence demonstrating that the employer's explanation is pretextual. The courts of appeals have consistently utilized this burden-shifting approach when reviewing motions for summary judgment in disparate treatment cases. The court of appeals noted that "it is possible that a drug user may not be 'disabled' under the ADA if his drug use does not rise to the level of an addic-tion which substantially limits one or more of his major life activities." The parties do not dispute that respondent was "disabled" at the time he quit in lieu of discharge and thus a record of the disability exists. We therefore need not decide in this case whether respondent's employment record constitutes a "record of addiction," which triggers the protections of the ADA.

***

The court of appeals concluded that petitioner's application of a neutral no-rehire policy was not a legitimate, nondiscriminatory reason for rejecting respondent's application:

> Maintaining a blanket policy against rehire of all former employees who vio-lated company policy not only screens out people with a record of addiction who have been successfully rehabilitated, but may well result, as [petitioner] contends it did here, in the staff member who makes the employment decision remaining unaware of the "disability" and thus of the fact that she is commit-ting an unlawful act. . . . Additionally, we hold that a policy that serves to bar the reemployment of a drug addict despite his successful rehabilitation violates the ADA.

***

The court of appeals concluded that, as a matter of law, a neutral no-rehire policy was not a legitimate, nondiscriminatory reason sufficient to defeat a prima facie case of discrimination. The court of appeals did not even attempt, in the remainder of its opinion, to treat this claim as one involving only disparate treatment. Instead the court of appeals observed that petitioner's policy "screens out people with a record of addiction," and further noted that the company had not raised a business necessity defense, factors that pertain to disparate impact claims but not disparate treatment claims. By improperly focusing on these factors, the court of appeals ignored the fact that petitioner's no-rehire policy is a quintessential legitimate, nondiscriminatory reason for refusing to rehire an employee who was terminated for violating workplace conduct rules. If petitioner did indeed apply a neutral, generally applicable no-rehire policy in rejecting respondent's application, petitioner's decision not to rehire respondent can in no way be said to have been motivated by respondent's disability.

***

Decision

Once Hernandez had made a prima facie showing of discrimination, the next question for the court of appeals was whether petitioner offered a legitimate, nondiscriminatory reason for its actions so as to demonstrate that its actions were not motivated by respondent's disability. To the extent that the court of appeals strayed from this task by considering not only discriminatory intent but also discriminatory impact, we vacate its judgment and remand the case for further proceedings consistent with this opinion.

Decision of the Federal Appellate Court on Remand

The appellate court concluded that Hernandez presented sufficient evidence from which a reasonable jury could determine that Raytheon refused to rehire him because of his past record of addiction and not because of a company rule barring rehire of previously terminated employees. Therefore, the district court was in error in granting summary judgment to Raytheon. Hernandez can now proceed to trial with his case.

Questions for Discussion

1. In light of the U.S. Supreme Court's decision in this case, discuss the pros and cons of blanket policies such as "no rehire of employees who violated workplace rules."
2. Was the ultimate decision (by the appellate court on remand) decided under a disparate treatment analysis or a disparate impact analysis? Explain your answer.

According to estimates provided by the International Labour Organization (ILO), there are approximately 600 million people, or 10 percent of the world's population, with mental and physical disabilities. Of that number, about 50 percent are of working age. These numbers are rising as life spans increase (the elderly suffer from more impairments), new diseases emerge (HIV/AIDS, stress and alcohol and drug abuse), and the number of disabled children increases, especially in the developing countries, as a result of malnutrition, diseases, child labor, and the violence associated with war.[12]

DILEMMA

There are growing awareness and concern on the part of governments, unions, and other institutions that in an increasingly competitive global marketplace, companies are seeking ways to reduce costs, and this frequently results in termination of disabled individuals who have opted to work rather than rely on disability benefits. An International Research Project on Job Retention and Return to Work Strategies for Disabled Workers was conducted in 1998. Preliminary results suggest "that laws protecting disabled workers may increase the reluctance of private companies to hire them, and existing social insurance system regulations may discourage their return to work." The study covered eight countries: Canada, France, Germany, the Netherlands, New Zealand, Sweden, the United Kingdom, and the United States.[13]

The European Union is working toward implementation of the UN's "standard rules on the equalization of opportunities for people with disabilities," which received the support of all UN member states.[14]

UN DEFINITION OF DISABILITY

The term *disability* summarizes a great number of different functional limitations occurring in any population in any country. People may be disabled by physical, intellectual, or sensory impairment; medical conditions; or mental illness. Such impairments, conditions, or illnesses may be permanent or transitory. The term *handicap* means the loss or limitation of opportunities to take part in the life of the community on an equal level with others. It describes the encounter between the person with a disability and the environment. The purpose of this term is to emphasize the focus on the shortcomings in the environment and in many organized activities in society—for example, information, communication, and education, which prevent people with disabilities from participating on equal terms.[15]

The Republic of Korea (North Korea) has a statute called the Handicapped People Employment Protection Act, which provides that an employer must perform several statutory obligations in order to enhance the welfare of handicapped people, including employing a certain ratio of handicapped people when an employer maintains 300 or more employees.[16]

China enacted a labor law on July 5, 1994, its first code of labor law since 1949, which makes it illegal for employers to dismiss workers (1) who are incapable of work due to occupational disease or industrial accidents or (2) during recovery period for sickness or nonindustrial injuries . . . (Art. 29). The law applies to both the public and the private sectors. The head of the Disabled

Persons Federation is the paralyzed son of China's former leader Deng Ziaoping, who pushed for rights of the disabled[17].

In Japan the law requires private sector employers of more than 63 people to set aside 1.6 percent of jobs for disabled people, and the public sector must set aside 2 percent of jobs. If an employer does not meet the quota, it must pay 50,000 yen ($640) per month for each person short of the quota. In 1995 Takeda Chemical Industries established a new company to employ the physically handicapped to reach the desired objectives. The name of the new firm, LI Takeda, is intended to reflect the idea of a company that loves the working handicapped—the L standing for the English word *labor* and the I for the Japanese homophone for love, *ai*[18].

Case for Discussion 14-4

This federal appellate case addresses the relationship between the Americans with Disabilities Act and comparable state legislation, the nexus between the ADA and workers' compensation law, the granting of attorneys' fees, and personal liability for aiding and abetting a violation of antidiscrimination law.

WILLIAM FAILLA V. CITY OF PASSAIC ET AL., 146 F.3D 149 (1998)[19]

Facts

Failla served as a captain in the Passaic Police Department. In 1989 he suffered a work-related back injury for which he received a partial disability award. In 1990 the chief advised Failla that he wanted to transfer him to the night shift. Failla reminded him of the back pain, and the chief said the night air would "do [him] good." In 1991 the transfer was made. The back pain worsened. Failla claimed that both the night air and the more strenuous duties aggravated his back condition. Expert medical evidence supported his claim. Failla requested reinstatement to day shift. When reinstatement did not occur, Failla filed suit.

The jury decided that Failla was not "disabled" within the meaning of the ADA. However, they determined that he was "handicapped" within the meaning of state law (NJ Law against Discrimination—LAD). The jury also found that the city and the police department were liable for failing to accommodate Failla's handicap, and that the chief was personally liable for engaging in discriminatory conduct within the scope of his employment. Failla was awarded compensatory damages of $143,000 with costs plus attorneys' fees. The defendants appealed on four matters: (1) Failla failed to establish a prima facie case under the LAD, (2) it was wrong to impose a verdict of individual liability against the chief, (3) it was error to admit evidence of a worker's compensation judgment in the trial, and (4) it was error to award attorneys' fees to Failla.

Decision

1. The defendants argued that the jury's determination that Failla was not disabled under ADA precluded a decision that he was handicapped under LAD. The appellate court stated that, in contrast to the ADA, the LAD definition of "handicapped" does not incorporate the requirement that the condition result in a substantial limitation of a major life activity.

2. On the issue of holding the chief personally liable for his actions in this case, the LAD expressly provides that there can be individual liability for aiding and abetting a LAD violation.

3. The defendants argued on appeal that admitting into evidence testimony that Failla received a worker's compensation award for a partial permanent disability was irrelevant and was highly prejudicial. The appellate court found no grounds for reversible error in the district court's admission of evidence relating to worker's compensation judgment.

4. On the matter of awarding attorneys' fees to Failla, the defendants had requested that the trial judge lower the amount because some of the claims were unsuccessful and because the defendant is a public entity that should not be viewed as a "deep pocket." The appellate court stated that the defendant cited no cases to support its contentions and that the mere fact that the city is a public entity does not relieve it of its obligation to pay attorneys' fees when it is found liable for unlawful discrimination. The court found no abuse of discretion on the part of the trial judge.

Questions for Discussion

1. The Court distinguished between state and federal laws regarding the definition of disability, holding in favor of the defendant under the ADA, and in favor of the plaintiff under NJLAD. Explain their decisions.

2. What lessons for managers can be gained from the Failla case?

Management **Perspective**

In disability cases, the disabled employee or applicant is often reluctant to disclose his or her handicap. A culture of openness, honesty, and sharing of information can make it more likely that such an employee will express whatever difficulty or need is present. It is especially important for disabled employees, many of whom are excellent workers, that they, their coworkers, and immediate supervisors are able to effectively discuss work-related matters such as a need for, and feasibility of, accommodations. The research and writings of Argyris and Schon shed some light on how such a culture can be established.

Some management scholars have observed that many organizations operate in a top-down, authoritarian, secretive, low-confrontation mode in which management knows best, information is guarded, "bad news" is suppressed, and mistakes are not acceptable. These scholars theorize that open sharing of information, bottom-up decision making, opportunities to experiment with new ideas and ways of doing things, and honesty and integrity in dealing with one another provide a healthier, more productive working environment. Argyris and Schon write of Model I and Model II behavior[20]. Model I reflects an emphasis on control and seeking to maximize winning, whereas Model II seeks to share valid information, allows free and informed choice, and encourages mutual monitoring of work. They also write about organizations' "theories-in-use" and "espoused theories"—what they do versus what they say they do. When organizations proclaim, "We are an equal employment opportunity employer," that is their espoused theory. What they actually do is their theory-in-use.

A dilemma can arise when an employee has an unseen disability that causes disturbance at work or leads to requests for special consideration. Does the culture of the organization support the type of environment needed for disabled workers to function optimally? What managerial responses are appropriate under such circumstances?

Mentally disabled employees are reluctant to divulge their condition for fear of employer rejection or dismissal. In the event that such an employee's performance unnecessarily suffers, his talents could be lost to the company simply because a minor accommodation was neither sought nor provided. What management practices could be instituted to prevent such a result?

The value of physically disabled workers can easily be overlooked when recruiters *assume* that such people cannot perform the duties of given positions. Recruiters can be trained to operate in a mode of *inquiry* rather than a mode of *knowing*. What other advice can you give to recruiters to enable them to more effectively handle such interviews?

Summary

The rights of people with disabilities were first singled out for protection in 1973 with the enactment of the Rehabilitation Act, a federal statute that prohibited discrimination against handicapped people by federal government agencies, certain government contractors, and organizations funded by the federal government. It was not until 1990 that Congress passed the Americans with Disabilities Act (ADA), extending protective legislation to private companies.

Disabled people must satisfy three criteria to establish a claim under the ADA:

- The person is "disabled" within the meaning of the act.
- The person is qualified—that is, can perform the "essential functions" of the job with or without a "reasonable accommodation."
- The employer's decision was based on the person's disability.

"Disability" is defined in the act to mean one of the following:

- The person has a physical or mental impairment that substantially limits one or more major life activities.
- The person has a record of such an impairment.
- The person is regarded as having such an impairment.

"Essential functions" of the job means what an individual is required to do in the position. This is defined by the employer, and courts are reluctant to second-guess employers' job descriptions.

"Reasonable accommodation" is analyzed case by case. Factors such as the size and resources of the employer are considered in evaluating whether an accommodation is reasonable. An accommodation must not create an undue burden for the employer.

Courts in disability cases often use the term *qualified individual with a disability.* There appears to be no consensus as to what that term signifies. It has been used to mean that a person cannot perform the essential functions of a job, that a person's disability creates a safety risk to self or others, that a person's excessive absenteeism prevents the person from performing the essential functions of the job, or that there is no reasonable accommodation that would enable a person to perform the essential functions of a job.

Class Exercise

Have students list the "essential functions" of their own job or another's (one with which they are reasonably familiar). Distribute job applicant résumés of people with various disabilities. Have students discuss whether these applicants can perform the essential functions of the job and whether a reasonable accommodation would be possible. (The objective of this exercise is to raise awareness of the *abilities* of disabled people and encourage students to think creatively and openly about the prospects of gainful employment for such people.)

Questions

Explore the Web sites www.usdoj.gov/crt/ada/adahom1.htm and www.eeoc.gov to answer Questions 1 and 2.

1. The EEOC made an announcement in May 2002 regarding genetic testing and the ADA. Summarize the EEOC's opinion on this issue.
2. Find the text of the Americans with Disabilities Act. What is the statutory definition of *employer* in the ADA? Which employers are exempted from the act?
3. For the four case scenarios given here, answer the following questions:
   a. What is the likely outcome of each case? What is the rationale for your answer?

b. Compare and contrast the cases. Be specific about the similarities and differences. How do these factors affect the legal outcomes of each case?

c. For each of the cases, what practices or policies would you recommend to management in order to avoid future legal action? How costly would such practices or policies be?

Scenario One

Hank F. was a claims adjuster at National Insurers, Inc., and handled all aspects of an insurance claim. He received numerous pay raises and satisfactory or above-average evaluations. He also suffered from several long-term disabilities, including alcoholism, posttraumatic stress disorder, and depression.

In a particularly stressful year (his mother died and his daughter was diagnosed with a rare and fatal disease), his performance slipped. When his supervisor criticized his job performance and indicated that he would have to be terminated, Hank collapsed in the supervisor's office. Two days later the supervisor threatened to replace him with a much younger employee. Hank then began seeing a psychiatrist. Company workers and managers joked about his mental health, and he was the butt of jokes made by supervisors in front of coworkers. He was called "one of the crazies."

Hank was placed on probation for poor performance and was eventually terminated for allegedly poor performance. He was 47 years old and was replaced by a man in his late 20s. Hank filed suit for disability and age discrimination.

Scenario Two

Mary F. took a civil service test for a food service position at Billings U. The test was a competitive written test required by state law. She failed the test the first time and tried again a year later. She passed two portions but failed the math section. Mary F. had a mental disability and sued the university on the basis of disability discrimination.

Scenario Three

George F. was involved in an accident in which he suffered a broken left tibia and clavicle. Subsequently George maintained that the injury made him unable to work while wearing a tie, and he could only wear loose-fitting clothes on his upper body. He was hired as a computer programmer for a temp agency and was assigned to work for ABC Company. ABC's dress policy required dress shirts and ties, with "business casual" attire on Fridays. George produced a note from his doctor requesting that he be allowed to wear more casual types of shirts in order not to irritate his collarbone fracture. He was excused from wearing a tie. However, he was eventually fired because of inappropriate attire.

Scenario Four

Hannah E. began work as a medical transcriber for the Memorial Hospitals Association (MHA) in 1986. In 1989 she began to have problems getting to work on time because she engaged in obsessive ritualistic activities in preparing herself for work. She would brush her hair over and over, check and recheck papers, and pull out strands of her hair and examine them because she felt as though something was crawling on her scalp. Hannah was given graduated disciplinary warnings regarding her tardiness, and appointments for counseling with the employee assistance program (EAP) were arranged. Hannah had great difficulty showing up for appointments. The diagnosis for her condition was obsessive compulsive disorder, and the doctor said that the primary factor in her tardiness and missed appointments was the OCD. Hannah had an excellent work performance history. She requested that she be able to work from home. Because she was the subject of disciplinary action, company policy dictated that such an arrangement was not to be granted. Eventually Hannah was fired, and she initiated legal action.

References

1. S. E. Brown, "What Is Disability Culture?" Editorial, *Disability Culture—Institute on Independent Living Newsletter,* December 2001.

2. 29 U.S.C. Sec. 701–794.

3. 42 U.S.C. 12101 et seq.

4. Ibid., 42 U.S.C. 12101(a).

5. Ibid., 42 U.S.C. Sec. 12111(8).

6. EEOC *Enforcement Guidance: Reasonable Accommodation and Undue Hardship,* Notice Number 915.002, October 17, 2002. See also the Web site at www.eeoc.gov/policy/docs/accommodation.html (accessed July 25, 2007).

7. *EEOC v. Wal-Mart,* 202 F.3d 281 (1999).

8. *Toyota Motor Manufacturing v. Williams,* 122 S. Ct. 681 (2002).

9. *U.S. Airways, Inc. v. Barnett,* 535 U.S. 391, 122 S. Ct. 1516, 152 L.Ed.2d 589 (2002).

10. *Board of Trustees of U. of Alabama v. Garrett,* 531 U.S. 356, 121 S. Ct. 955, 148 L.Ed.2d 866 (2001).

11. *Raytheon Company v. Joel Hernandez,* 540 U.S. 44 (2003).

12. International Labour Organization Press Release, "Worker Disability Problems Rising in Industrialized Countries: Solutions Sought in Washington, DC, Conference," May 19, 1998.

13. Ibid.

14. Commission of the European Communities, Economic and Social Committee, Section for Social Family Educational Cultural Affairs (86), Wahrolin, Official Journal No. C 066 (March 3, 1997), p. 35.

15. Ibid.

16. *Martindale-Hubbell International Digest,* Republic of Korea, p. 10 (Chicago: R.R. Donnelley & Sons Co., 1997).

17. Ibid., China, p. 40.

18. J. Kee, "Legislation May Help the Disabled in Getting Jobs," *The Straits Times (Singapore),* August 1, 1996, p. 33.

19. *William Failla v. City of Passaic, et al.,* 146 F.3d 149 (1998).

20. C. Argyris and D. A. Schon, *Organizational Learning: A Theory of Action Perspective* (Reading, MA: Addison-Wesley, 1978), p. 137.

Employment Benefits and Family Leave Law

15. The Family and Medical Leave Act, Workers' Compensation, and the ADA

The Family and Medical Leave Act, Workers' Compensation, and the ADA

[T]he ADA is intended to ensure that qualified individuals with disabilities are provided with equal opportunity to work, while the FMLA's purpose is to provide reasonable leave from work for eligible employees.[1]

INTRODUCTION

One purpose of this chapter is to set out the sometimes conflicting provisions of three distinct federal statutes: the Family and Medical Leave Act of 1993 (FMLA), the workers' compensation laws, and the Americans with Disabilities Act of 1990 (ADA). Confusion exists about the guarantees granted under the Family and Medical Leave Act, the benefits provided under workers' compensation laws, and the rights provided under the Americans with Disabilities Act. This chapter explores the distinctions among these laws and how they overlap.

THE FAMILY AND MEDICAL LEAVE ACT OF 1993

The Family and Medical Leave Act of 1993 established an employee's right to take a leave for family reasons—a right that exists not only for women but for men as well. Congress made the following findings to support passage of this law:

- The number of households in which a single parent or both parents work is increasing significantly.

- It is important for the development of children and the family unit that fathers and mothers be able to participate in early child rearing and the care of family members who have serious health conditions.
- A lack of employment policies to accommodate working parents can force individuals to choose between job security and parenting.
- There is inadequate job security for employees who have serious health conditions that prevent them from working for temporary periods.
- Due to the nature of the roles of men and women in our society, the primary responsibility for family caretaking often falls on women, and such responsibility affects the working lives of women more than it affects the working lives of men.
- Employment standards that apply to only one gender have serious potential for encouraging employers to discriminate against employees and applicants for employment who are of that gender[2].

Major Provisions of the FMLA

The major provision of the Family and Medical Leave Act is that an employee who has worked for an employer for at least 12 months for a minimum of 1,250 hours is entitled to 12 weeks of leave in a 12-month period. The employee's reason for such a request must be one of the following: The employee has a serious health condition; seeks to care for a newborn child, a newly adopted child, or a child placed with an employee for foster care; or seeks to care for a child, parent, or spouse who has a serious health condition. Employers of 50 or more employees are subject to this law.

This leave need not be taken in one block of time; it can be taken intermittently. If the statutory criteria are met, an employer must grant the requested leave. There is no requirement that the employee be paid during the leave, but some provisions regarding continued insurance are specified in the law.

In addition to the employee's right to take a leave, the FMLA also guarantees job protection. Employees who take leave pursuant to this statute are entitled to return to the same or an equivalent position and benefits as they had previously. To the extent that the position that was vacated by the employee is still available at the end of the leave, the employee is entitled to reinstatement to that position. If the position is no longer available, the employee is entitled to a similar position with like pay and benefits. Nevertheless, if the employee would have been fired, demoted, or transferred regardless of whether he or she took leave, the FMLA will not prevent the employer from doing so.

Notice Requirements

Employees who wish to take FMLA leave are required to notify their employers. However, courts have sometimes held in favor of employees who did not give notice. For example, the judge in *Lozano v. Kay Mfg. Co.,* Case No. 04 C 2784, U.S. District Court for the Northern District of Illinois[3], denied the employer's motion for summary judgment, in spite of the fact that the employee had not given notice, because the employer was aware the plaintiff had a mental condition, and it was possible a jury could decide that the employer should have figured out that the employee's deteriorating job performance was due to this mental condition[4].

Medical Confirmations

Under the FMLA, an employer may require medical certification of the need for the absence or leave. In a recent case from the Eighth Circuit Court of Appeals, *Thorson v. Gemini, Inc.,* 205 F.3d 370 (8th Cir., 3/3/00), the court of appeals upheld the lower court's decision that the employer had violated the FMLA by terminating an employee for excessive absenteeism. The court determined that the employer may have been allowed to question the employee's need for leave if it had required her to provide medical certification when she took several days off to seek treatment for stomach problems. However, because the employer did not require certification and instead simply accepted her doctor's notes indicating that she could not work, it forfeited its right to challenge whether the employee was covered under the FMLA[5].

FMLA 2008 Update

President Bush signed into law the National Defense Authorization Act for 2008. Among other things, Section 585 of the NDAA amends the Family and Medical Leave Act of 1993 (FMLA) to permit a "spouse, son, daughter, parent, or next of kin" to take up to 26 workweeks of leave to care for a "member of the Armed Forces, including a member of the National Guard or Reserves, who is undergoing medical treatment, recuperation, or therapy, is otherwise in outpatient status, or is otherwise on the temporary disability retired list, for a serious injury or illness." Additional information and a copy of Title I of the FMLA, as amended, are available on the Department of Labor (DOL) Web site[6].

In addition, on February 11, 2008, the DOL issued proposed revisions to the Family and Medical Leave Act that may significantly change current policies and procedures, such as

- The timing of employee notification of the need for FMLA leave.
- Medical certification provisions.
- Employer obligations for providing notice of FMLA rights.
- Call-in procedures for intermittent leave.
- The definition of a serious health condition.

Case for Discussion 15-1

In the *Victorelli* case a federal appellate court explored the meaning of *serious health condition* under the FMLA.

VICTORELLI V. SHADYSIDE HOSPITAL, 128 F.3D 184 (3RD CIRC., 1997)[7]

Facts

Victorelli suffered from peptic ulcer disease, which occasionally flared up and caused her to miss work. She always notified her supervisor of the need to miss work and provided medical documentation of her need for time off, and this occurred several times over the five years she worked at Shadyside Hospital as a technician. Throughout her tenure with the hospital, Victorelli was given high marks in her job evaluations. On July 29, 1994, she called in sick and verified with her doctor that it was a flare-up of the peptic ulcer condition. He recommended that she not work that day.

As a result of Victorelli's July 29 "call-off " from work, Shadyside decided to terminate her employment. Victorelli had a history of tardiness and absences due to sickness, some in excess of her accrued sick time. She had been warned about this on numerous occasions.

Among other things, Victorelli argued that she was entitled to take leave under FMLA and that Shadyside had violated these rights. One of the critical factors discussed in the appellate court's decision was whether Victorelli's condition comes within the meaning of "serious health condition" under the statute. The Department of Labor, which enforces the FMLA, promulgated rules further defining its provisions, and the court expounded on the "interim final rule" that applied here.

"Serious Health Condition"

The interim final rule defines a "serious health condition" as an illness, injury, impairment, or physical or mental condition that involves (1) a period of incapacity requiring inpatient care, (2) a period of incapacity of more than three calendar days, involving continuing treatment by a health care provider, or (3) continuing treatment by (or under the supervision of) a health care provider for a chronic or long-term health condition that is incurable or so serious that, if not treated, would likely result in a period of incapacity of more than three calendar days; or for prenatal care.

Using the interim final rule, the district court found subsection (3) applicable to Victorelli because she was subject to "continuing treatment" by Dr. Adoki. We agree. However, the district court then found that Victorelli could not satisfy any of the requirements of "continuing treatment" of § 825.114(b)(1) or (2) except under what the court considered to be "an expansive reading of the statute." For this reason, the court determined that Victorelli did not have a "serious health condition."

Under the interim final rule, "continuing treatment" is defined as follows:

(b) "Continuing treatment by a health care provider" means one or more of the following:

(1) The employee or family member in question is treated two or more times for the injury or illness by a health care provider. Normally this would require visits to the health care provider or to a nurse or physician's assistant under direct supervision of the health care provider.

(2) The employee or family member is treated for the injury or illness two or more times by a provider of health care services (e.g., a physical therapist) under orders of, or on referral by, a health care provider, or is treated for the injury or illness by a health care provider on at least one occasion which results in a regimen of continuing treatment under the supervision of the health care provider—for example, a course of medication or therapy—to resolve the health condition.

(3) The employee or family member is under the continuing supervision of, but not necessarily being actively treated by, a health care provider due to a serious long-term or chronic condition or disability which cannot be cured. Examples include persons with Alzheimer's, persons who have suffered a severe stroke, or persons in the terminal stages of a disease who may not be receiving active medical treatment.

Decision

The appellate court concluded that Congress did not intend to deny FMLA protection to an employee simply because her doctor was able to mitigate the frequency of her discomfort or incapacity and that the intent of the FMLA is not simply to protect those whose condition causes continual incapacity. The FMLA, the court noted, is also intended to protect those who are occasionally incapacitated by an ongoing medical problem.

Because of the disputed issue of fact concerning the seriousness of Victorelli's health condition, the appellate court stated that the district court erred in granting summary judgment to defendant, Shadyside, and vacated that judgment and remanded the case for further proceedings consistent with its opinion.

Questions for Discussion

1. Discuss the implications of the appellate court's decision.
2. What can an HR manager do to avoid an FMLA charge from employees in medical situations similar to that of Victorelli?

Case for Discussion 15-2

The Meaning of "To Care For"

TELLIS V. ALASKA AIRLINES, INC., 414 F.3D 1045 (9TH CIRC., 2005)[8]

The FMLA states that employees are entitled to take a leave in order "to care for" a family member as specified in the statute. Precisely what the phrase *to care for* means was the subject of this 2005 Ninth Circuit Federal Court of Appeals case, *Tellis v. Alaska Airlines, Inc.*

Facts

Tellis argued that his cross-country trip to retrieve the family vehicle during his wife's late-stage pregnancy difficulties, and his calling her on the phone during the three and a half days he was away, were "to care for" his wife under the FMLA and thus constituted a protected absence from his employment.

Decision

The appellate court concluded as a matter of law that Tellis's trip and phone calls were not "to care for" his wife. Thus his absence from work during that time was not protected by the FMLA.

In explaining its ruling, the court asserted that providing care to a family member under the FMLA requires some actual care, which did not occur here. The Department of Labor's regulations implementing the FMLA explain that the phrase "to care for" a family member encompasses both physical and psychological care. Interpreting this rule, the court had previously stated that caring for a family member with a serious health condition "involves some level of participation in ongoing treatment of that condition," as stated in *Marchisheck v. San Mateo County*, 199 F.3d 1068, 1076 (9th Cir. 1999).

Questions for Discussion

1. In light of the *Tellis* decision, list some activities that would constitute valid absences under FMLA.
2. How detailed should a policy for leaves of absence be? Explain your answer.

THE FMLA, STATE LEAVE LAWS, WORKERS' COMPENSATION, AND THE ADA

As stated earlier, one major problem facing employers with regard to FMLA compliance is the confusion that arises in coordinating benefits and leaves mandated by state and federal laws. Not only do interpretations conflict between federal and state family and medical leave statutes, but also there are workers' compensation and disability laws that involve the right to be absent from work and to collect compensation.

Workers' Compensation

Except for nonmilitary federal employees who are covered by the Federal Employment Compensation Act, workers' compensation statutes are state laws. When employees are injured "in the course of employment," state laws require employers to compensate the injured workers for their injuries as well as to pay them a portion of their salaries during their time off. The laws spell out a specific amount of money that is to be paid for each injury itself, based on the type of injury. One significant effect of the workers' compensation system is

that an injured employee cannot take the employer to court in an attempt to receive more money than the statute provides except in the rare case when it can
be proved that an injury was the result of the employer's willful or gross negligence. Disability benefits can be either short-term or long-term. There is no
guarantee of job protection under workers' compensation laws and no requirement that the employee be granted leave within a specified maximum period.
The workers' compensation laws also provide specified benefits to the depen-
dents of a worker who dies as a result of a work-related accident or disease.

Clearly the provisions of the Family and Medical Leave Act can overlap
with workers' compensation benefits. Because the FMLA is triggered by a serious health condition that requires time off from work, this would include a
serious injury that occurs on the job. The workers' compensation law governs
the amount of money the worker is entitled to, and FMLA governs both the
length of time the employer must allow for any leave needed and the guarantee of job protection when and if the employee returns to work.

The Americans with Disabilities Act

As explained in Chapter 14, the ADA prohibits employers from discriminating
against people with disabilities. The definition of *disability* is not the same for
the ADA, workers' compensation laws, and the FMLA. The ADA protects
people with permanent impairments that substantially limit a major life activity.
For workers' compensation benefits or FMLA protection, the health problems
can be short-term or of limited duration. This is just one distinguishing feature.

There is no requirement under the ADA for an employer to provide leave
for a disabled employee. However, if short periods of time off would make it
possible for a disabled worker to perform the essential functions of her or his
job, a court might require such leave under its mandate of providing reasonable accommodations, assuming that such an accommodation does not create
an undue hardship on the employer.

Consider the Following Medical Conditions

A person has a hearing impairment: Having this disability does not make a
person eligible for FMLA leave. It would constitute a disability under the
ADA if a qualified candidate is not hired based on the hearing impairment.
It would not be a basis for receipt of disability benefits under workers' compensation (unless the hearing loss was a result of an on-the-job occurrence).

A person sustains broken bones in a job-related auto accident: If the injury
prevents the person from working, he is entitled to compensation benefits for the injury (as designated in the statute—for example, for a broken
leg, the statute would specify a stated sum of money) and a portion of
his salary as specified in the law. The broken leg would have to be seen
as a "serious health condition" to trigger mandated FMLA leave. The
person would not be disabled under the definition of the ADA.

A person develops cancer and must undergo chemotherapy treatments: If the
individual is capable of performing the essential functions of her position, she
would not be disabled under the ADA. If intermittent absences are necessary

to undergo the treatments, but she can nevertheless perform the essential functions of the job, and the employer fires her because of the cancer, there is a possibility that a court would consider her to be a person "perceived to have a disability" who has been the object of illegal discrimination and for whom intermittent leave is considered a reasonable accommodation. Assuming the cancer is not related to the nature of her work, workers' compensation does not enter the picture. The FMLA will likely be triggered because the cancer is a serious health condition that may require periods of absence from work.

Advice

In considering the impact of the various laws on employees who may be eligible for the benefits and rights under their provisions, employers are encouraged to do the following:

1. Identify the various laws that govern leave policies.
2. Determine the differences between FMLA and state family leave laws. In particular, review the following in relation to the federal leave law:
   - The purposes for which leave must be granted.
   - The length of leave that must be provided under state law.
   - Benefit continuation requirements under state law.
   - Whether state law mandates salary continuation during leave.
   - Whether state law guarantees job restoration after a leave.
   - Whether state law requires medical verification.

Management **Perspective**   Give Written Notice When FMLA Leave Is Granted

The Department of Labor Web site offers valuable advice on matters that come within its purview such as the Family and Medical Leave Act. The following information comes from the regulations governing the FMLA (see the DOL Web site at www.dol.gov/esa/regs/compliance/whd/1421.htm)[9].

Covered employers must take the following steps to provide information to employees about the FMLA:

Post a notice approved by the Secretary of Labor (WH Publication 1420) explaining rights and responsibilities under the FMLA.

Include information about employee rights and obligations under the FMLA in employee handbooks or other written material, including collective bargaining agreements (CBAs).

If handbooks or other written material do not exist, provide general written guidance about employee rights and obligations under the FMLA whenever an employee requests leave (a copy of Fact Sheet No. 28 will fulfill this requirement).

(Continued)

Provide a written notice designating a leave as FMLA leave and detailing the specific expectations and obligations of an employee who is exercising his or her FMLA entitlements. An employer may use the "Employer Response to Employee Request for Family or Medical Leave" (Optional Form WH-381) to meet this requirement. This employer notice should be provided to the employee within one or two business days after receipt of the employee's notice of need for leave and must include the following:

- That the leave will be counted against the employee's annual FMLA leave entitlement.
- Any requirements for the employee to furnish medical certification and the consequences of failing to do so.
- The employee's right to elect to use accrued paid leave for unpaid FMLA leave and whether the employer will require the use of paid leave, and the conditions related to using paid leave.
- Any requirement for the employee to make co-premium payments for maintaining group health insurance and the arrangement for making such payments.
- Any requirement to present a fitness-for-duty certification before being restored to work.
- Rights of job restoration upon return from leave.
- The employee's potential liability for reimbursement of health insurance premiums paid by the employer during the leave if the employee fails to return to work after taking FMLA leave.
- Whether the employee qualifies as a key employee and the circumstances under which the employee may not be restored to his or her job following leave.

Global **Perspective**

Paid Leave and Paternity Leave

Most countries in the European Union (EU) offer paid paternity leave, from two days in Spain to two weeks in France; Norway (which is outside the EU) tops the list as the most family-friendly country with a full four weeks of paid leave. . . . A newly published ILO study, *Gender Equality and Decent Work: Good Practices at the Workplace,* shows that Norway grants the longest paid paternity leave after the birth of a child, in addition to the mother's 11 months. Norway introduced the four-week paternity quota in 1993. The provision sets aside four weeks of the parental period for the father with the purpose of encouraging more fathers to take an active role in the care of children during their first year. These four weeks cannot be transferred to the mother and are lost if the father does not use them. . . .

In 1978 Norway adopted a Gender Equality Act that prohibits discrimination on the grounds of sex in all areas of society and obliges all public institutions to promote gender equality in all areas of policy, such as labor, education, and health. The Gender Equality Act was reinforced in 2002 and now requires all employers in both the public and private sectors to report annually on women's representation on the staff and in management positions in their organizations.[10]

Case for Discussion 15-3

RAGSDALE ET AL. V. WOLVERINE WORLD WIDE, INC., 535 U.S. 81 (2002)[11]

The following excerpts are from the headnotes in the *U.S. Reporter*.

Facts

An employee with cancer was eligible for seven months of unpaid sick leave under her employer's leave plan. The employee requested and received a one-month leave of absence on February 21, 1996, and asked for a 30-day extension at the end of each of the seven months that followed. The employer granted the first six requests but did not notify her that 12 weeks of the absence would count as her FMLA leave. After the employee had taken 30 weeks of leave, the employer denied a seventh 30-day extension and ultimately terminated the employee when she did not come back to work.

The employee—seeking reinstatement, back pay, and other relief under a remedial provision of the FMLA and other statutory provisions—filed suit in the United States District Court for the Eastern District of Arkansas against the employer. The employee alleged, among other matters, that the federal regulations issued by the Secretary of Labor required the employer to grant her 12 additional weeks of leave for failing to inform her that the 30-week absence would count against her FMLA entitlement. The district court, in granting the employer summary judgment, concluded that the penalty regulation was in conflict with the FMLA and thus invalid as requiring the employer to grant the employee more than 12 weeks of FMLA-compliant leave in one year. The U.S. Court of Appeals for the Eighth Circuit affirmed.

Decision

The U.S. Supreme Court held that the penalty regulation effected an impermissible alteration of the FMLA's statutory framework and was not within the Secretary's power to issue regulations necessary to carry out the FMLA under the regulations because

1. Such a penalty for an employer's failure to provide timely notice of the FMLA designation was unconnected to any prejudice that an employee might have suffered from the employer's lapse.
2. The penalty regulation was incompatible with the FMLA's comprehensive remedial mechanism, which provided no relief unless the employee was prejudiced by a violation of the FMLA.
3. The penalty regulation altered the FMLA's cause of action in a fundamental way, as the remedy created by Congress required a retrospective case-by-case examination.
4. The penalty regulation amended the FMLA's most fundamental substantive guarantee, namely the 12-week leave entitlement, and thus subverted Congress's careful balance of the needs of families and the legitimate interests of employers.
5. The sole notice provision in the FMLA itself merely imposed a $100 fine, enforced by the Secretary, on employers who willfully failed to post a general notice informing employees of their FMLA rights.
6. The penalty regulation's severe and across-the-board penalty could cause employers to discontinue the more generous programs that the FMLA encouraged.

Dissent

Justice O'Connor, joined by Justices Souter, Ginsburg, and Breyer, dissenting, expressed the view that (1) the Secretary's decision to require individualized notice was not arbitrary or capricious; and (2) nothing in the FMLA constrained the Secretary from securing compliance with the individualized notice requirement by providing that leave would not count against the employer's 12-week obligation unless the employer fulfilled this requirement.

Question for Discussion

Would the outcome be the same if Ragsdale claimed that she would have taken intermittent leaves had she known (from a notification) what her options were?

Summary

The Family and Medical Leave Act of 1993 is a federal statute that applies to employers of 50 or more workers. Qualified employees are entitled to 12 weeks of leave in a 12-month period.

The reasons for granting FMLA leave include

- A serious health condition of self.
- To care for a newborn child, a newly adopted child, or a child placed with the employee for foster care.
- To care for a child, parent, or spouse who has a serious health condition.

The FMLA requires employers to reinstate an employee after the leave to the same or an equivalent position and benefits that were enjoyed before the leave.

The FMLA was amended by passage of the National Defense Authorization Act of 2008, which allows up to 26 workweeks of leave to a spouse, son, daughter, parent, or next of kin for the purpose of caring for a member of the armed forces who is undergoing medical treatments or is otherwise ill or injured as specified by the statute.

The provisions of the FMLA, when taken together with state leave laws, the benefits of the workers' compensation laws, and the Americans with Disabilities Act, can cause confusion for HR managers.

Workers' compensation statutes are state laws with which employers must comply. These laws are a form of insurance whereby injuries or illnesses arising in the workplace give rise to automatic compensation for the affected employee. Disability benefits can be short or long-term, and leave may be granted in conjunction with such injuries or illnesses.

The Americans with Disabilities Act (ADA) requires employers to provide reasonable accommodations to disabled workers who can perform the essential functions of a job with or without such accommodations. Granting leave to a disabled individual might be considered a reasonable accommodation that the employer must provide.

A disability under the ADA may or may not be the same as a disability under workers' compensation laws or under state leave laws. HR managers must take into consideration the interactions and overlaps among these various statutes.

Questions

1. Alex D., an employee for a public transit system, suffered from diabetes and was taking medication for his condition. The effect of the drug was temporary uncontrollable bowel movements and diarrhea. Occasionally at work this necessitated bathroom breaks. Eventually his employer began writing him up for failing to return from breaks in a timely manner. Alex then requested FMLA leave to cover these breaks. About a week later Alex was fired.

   a. Is Alex entitled to FMLA leave? Why or why not?

   b. What is necessary to initiate an FMLA request?

2. Julia T., a union employee for the U.S. Postal Service, took FMLA leave without prior notification, and when she announced her return to work, the USPS requested that she be examined by the USPS doctor. Julia refused,

claiming that her own doctor's release to return to work was sufficient documentation. Her refusal to cooperate led to her termination. She argued that this was a violation of FMLA.

a. What are the rights of the employer regarding employees' claims of illness or wellness when dealing with FMLA compliance?

b. Does it matter that Julia is a member of a union? If so, how does it matter?

3. Angelo T. failed to arrive for work one day at Hilton Hospitality Inc. Another employee told hotel officials that Angelo had been hospitalized for a "nervous breakdown." About a week later the hotel received a notice from Angelo's doctor stating that he needed to be off work until April 1. When he did not return to work on April 1, the hotel suspended him. When they told him of the suspension, he allegedly responded, "I quit." The hotel could not deny that it was aware of Angelo's condition because it had sent flowers to him at the hospital. Angelo claims that he was entitled to FMLA leave and that he was constructively discharged.

a. If Angelo takes legal action against Hilton, what will the court decide?

b. What factors are critical to a decision in this case?

4. Kit E. held an outside sales position with ABC Rochester Construction Company. He decided to retire to care for his wife, who had developed an eye disorder. When he announced his retirement decision, he erroneously believed that the Family and Medical Leave Act provided leave only for new parents. After learning that he might be entitled to FMLA leave to care for his wife, Kit decided that he would prefer to take such leave instead of retiring. At some point between announcing his retirement and December 21, Kit orally notified his supervisor Rinker that he wished to take FMLA leave rather than retire. The first step in the process, he was told, was to submit a note from his wife's doctor. Dr. Odom provided a note, dated December 21, 2000, which stated, "Due to decreasing Prednisone the body increases in stress, and decreases the immune system. Therefore a three-month leave would help with the above." The parties characterize this note as a "medical certification," which is a term used in the FMLA. Rinker voiced no specific concerns about the note.

Rinker next told Kit that he would have to complete certain forms. This was eventually done, and the leave was officially approved. On or about February 19, Rinker executed a personnel change notification form indicating that Kit would not be retiring and reinstating him to active employee status, retroactive to his original hire date, so that he would be entitled to take leave pursuant to the FMLA.

The leave was to expire on April 12, 2001. Before the leave expired, Kit called the company and indicated he was ready to return to work. An ABC official informed him that they were in a hiring freeze and that there were no positions available. Kit said that a hiring freeze should not affect someone returning from leave taken pursuant to the Family and Medical Leave

Act. Two weeks later Kit was called and told they had something for him: ABC was willing to reinstate Kit to an outside sales position, but he would have to accept a territory that was "at least 60 miles from his home" and "included areas of the state over 180 miles away from his home that would take over three hours of driving time to reach." Kit was told that he would be expected to spend two to three nights per week on the road, which he never had to do while working in his prior territory.

Kit suggested the possibility of working out a part-time arrangement, but ABC's position was that such an arrangement probably would not work because customers expected salespeople to be available five days per week. Kit was told that someone would call him in a couple of days. No one from ABC contacted him, however, and he subsequently initiated this lawsuit alleging a violation of his rights under the Family and Medical Leave Act. In particular, he claims that ABC violated his rights by failing to restore him to his prior position, or an equivalent one, upon his return from leave.

a. What important facts would Kit have to prove to succeed in his FMLA claim against ABC?

b. What facts would help ABC defend its actions?

c. Does Kit have a strong case against ABC under the FMLA? Why or why not?

References

1. Department of Labor, *Executive Summary of FMLA 2007 Report*, p. x. See www.dol.gov/esa/whd/FMLA2007Report/ExecutiveSummary.pdf.

2. The Family and Medical Leave Act of 1993 as amended, January 28, 2008. See www.dol.gov/esa/whd/fmla/fmlaAmended.htm#SEC_2_FINDINGS_AND_PURPOSES (accessed March 5, 2008).

3. *Lozano v. Kay Mfg. Co.,* Case No. 04 C 2784, U.S. District Court for the Northern District of Illinois.

4. S. H. Adelman, *Labor & Employment Law Newsletter* XIII, no. 3 (June 20, 2006).

5. *Thorson v. Gemini, Inc.,* 205 F.3d 370 (8th Cir., 3/3/00). See also http://www.ppublishers.com/articles/med_cert_fmla.htm (accessed February 13, 2008).

6. DOL Web site at www.dol.gov/esa/whd/fmla/NDAA_fmla.htm. See also www.dol.gov/esa/whd/fmla/index.htm for compliance assistance (accessed March 5, 2008).

7. *Victorelli v. Shadyside Hospital,* 128 F.3d 184 (3rd Circ., 1997).

8. *Tellis v. Alaska Airlines, Inc.,* 414 F.3d 1045 (9th Circ., 2005).

9. DOL Web site at www.dol.gov/esa/regs/compliance/whd/1421.htm (accessed February 25, 2008).

10. "Modern Daddy—Norway's Progressive Policy on Paternity Leave," *World of Work* 54 (August 2005). See also the book *Gender Equality and Decent Work—Good Practices at the Workplace* by the ILO Bureau for Gender Equality.

11. *Ragsdale et al. v. Wolverine World Wide, Inc.,* 535 U.S. 81, 122 S. Ct. 1155; 152 L. Ed. 2d 167 (2002).

Index

Page numbers followed by n indicate material in notes.

A

Accommodation, 256
Action Inquiry (Torbert), 82–83
Adams, Marilee G., 325, 333
Adarand v. Pena, 198
Administrative law
  explanation of, 17
  as source of federal law, 7–8
Affirmative action
  Civil Rights Act and, 174–175
  Constitution and, 170–171, 197
  Executive Order 11246 and, 171
  explanation of, 170
  problems related to, 170
  racial discrimination and, 197–198
  Supreme Court and, 198
Age discrimination. *See also* Elderly individuals
  global perspective on, 326–327
  prima facie cases on, 312–315
  reverse, 309–312
  willful, 321–323
Age Discrimination in Employment Act (ADEA)
  bona fide occupational qualification under, 316–319
  disparate impact analysis under, 323–324
  enforcement of, 31
  filing deadlines for claims under, 43
  function of, 306–307
  issues related to, 308–309
  record retention requirements of, 34–35
  remedies under, 321
  Supreme Court and, 309–315
Agency, law of, 6–7
Aguirre vs. American United Global, 300
Akos Swierkievicz v. Sorema N. A., 314–315, 325
Alcohol testing, 14. *See also* Drug testing
Alexander, P., 224
Alfieri, V., 159
Aliens. *See also* Immigrants; National origin discrimination
  authorized to work for specific employer, 286
  authorized to work with no restrictions, 285–286
  classifications of, 284–287
  documents to verify status of, 287–288
  explanation of, 284
  foreign-based employment claims in U.S. and, 300–301
  legalized, 285
  rights under discrimination laws for, 297–299
  visa categories for, 288–289
Alm, R., 224
Alternative dispute resolution (ADR). *See also* Arbitration; Mediation
  American Arbitration Association and, 60
  explanation of, 30, 52
  function of, 74–75
American Arbitration Association (AAA), 60, 64
American Civil Liberties Union, 140
American Competitiveness in the Twenty-First Century Act, 288
Americans with Disabilities Act (ADA)
  case examples under, 338–344, 347–348
  defining disability under, 335–338
  disability discrimination under, 360
  employee leave under, 360–361
  enforcement of, 31
  explanation of, 11, 334–335
  genetic screening and, 139
  record retention requirements of, 35
Amicus curiae briefs, 211
Antidiscrimination laws. *See also* Discrimination; *specific forms of discrimination*
  employment at will doctrine and, 109
  overview of, 5–6
Appeals, to arbitration, 54
Appellate review, 36–37
Arbitration. *See also* Alternative dispute resolution (ADR)
  characteristics of, 53–55
  explanation of, 52–53
  mediation vs., 69
  Supreme Court and, 53, 56–58
Arbitration clauses, 55
Arbitrators, 54
ARCO v. Akers, 27
Argyris, C., 348–349, 352
Ash et al. Tyson Foods, Inc., 165–167
Asylees, 285
Award, 53

B

Barrier, M., 88
Beck-Dudley, L., 134
Begler, A., 87–88
Bierce, Ambrose, 30, 49
Billings, P., 143n
Bilson, B., 254
Binding arbitration, 53
Blair, Henry W., 225, 254
Board of Trustees of U. of Alabama v. Garrett, 342
Bona fide occupational qualification (FBOQ)
    age discrimination and, 316–322
    explanation of, 164
Bragdon v. Abbot, 144n
Breach of implied contract, 94, 98–99
Breach of implied covenant of good
    faith, 107–108
Brown, H. W., 254
Brown, J. E., 254
Brown, S. E., 352
Brynelson, A., 87
Bullying
    claims regarding, 128–129
    global perspective on, 22–23
Burgess, Heidi, 87
Burlington Industries v. Ellerth, 25, 243–244
Burlington Northern and Santa Fe Railway Company
    (BNSF), 139–140
Bush, R. A. Baruch, 87
Business, legal nature of, 6–7
Business Women's Network (BWN), 176
B-1 visas, 288

C

California Federal Savings & Loan Assn. et al. v. Guerra,
    Director, Department of Fair Employment and
    Housing, et al., 218–220
Camera phones, 139–140
Canada, 230–231
Capacity, 98
Carroll, E., 88
Case law
    common law vs., 14–15
    explanation of, 14–15
    as source of federal law, 7–9
Casellas, Gilbert F. "Gil," 177
Castro, Ida L., 293
Caton D/B/A Caton Sales Company v. Leach Corporation,
    104–109
Caucus, 79
CBOCS West, Inc. v. Humphries, 175–176

Change Your Questions, Change Your Life. Seven Tools for
    Life and Work (Adams), 325
Chiem, L., 204
Children, alien status and, 285
Chimarev v. TD Waterhouse Investor Services, Inc., 141
China
    labor law in, 346–347
    new civil evidence law in, 47–48
Church of Jesus Christ of Latter-Day Saints v. Amos, 266
Circuit City Stores v. Saint Clair Adams, 57
Citizenship, 293–294
City of Richmond v. J. A. Croson Co., 198
Civil Rights Act of 1866, 175–176
Civil Rights Act of 1964
    accommodation of religious beliefs and, 256–257
    employment discrimination and, 5–6, 129
    Equal Pay Act and, 227
    explanation of, 11, 175, 182
    historical background of, 162
    national origin discrimination and, 283–284, 290
    race-related discrimination and, 186–187
    sexual harassment and, 238
    Title VII [*See* Title VII (Civil Rights Act of 1964)]
Civil Rights Act of 1991
    disparate impact cases and, 206–211
    expanded remedies and right to jury trial, 213
    expatriate employees and, 212
    explanation of, 11, 21, 162, 205–206
    Glass Ceiling Act and, 213–216
    mixed motive cases and, 206
Civil servants, 137–138
Civil Service Reform Act, 94
Code of Federal Regulations (CFR), 17
Collective bargaining agreements, 11, 264
Color discrimination. *See also* Discrimination
    explanation of, 185
    facts about, 186–187
    statistics regarding, 182–184
Common law
    case law vs., 14–15
    employment at will doctrine and, 16–17, 90,
        94, 110
    employment cases in, 3
    explanation of, 16
    as source of federal law, 8–9
Communication, action inquiry, 82–83
Community for Creative Nonviolence v. Reid, 150–152
Company policies, 44
Comparable worth theory, 230–231
Compensation, 45
Confidentiality, 71, 84–85
Confidentiality agreements, 147
Congress, U.S., 10, 13
Consideration, 98

Constitution, U.S.
    affirmative action and, 170–171, 197
    explanation of, 15–16
    human resource management and, 15–17
    privacy rights and, 15
    as source of federal law, 78
Constructive discharge, 97
Contract for an indefinite term, 16
Copyright Act of 1976, 152
Copyright law
    explanation of, 149–150
    in Mexico, 154
County of Washington v. Gunther, 228–229
Court-annexed arbitration, 53
Cover-ups, 47
Cowman, J. W., 304
Cox, W. M., 224
Cweklinsky v. Mobil Chem. Co., 120–122

D

Daniels, Charles, 184
Data Protection Directive (European Union), 145–147
Davis v. Manchester Health Ctr., Inc., 115–116
Defamation, 118, 120
Department of Commerce, 145, 147
Department of Justice, 287
Department of Labor, 356
Dependent children, 285
Deportation cases, 285
Depositions, 33
Desantis v. Pacific Telephone and Telegraph Co., Inc., 249
de Villepin, Dominique, 92–93
Diagnostic and Statistical Manual IV (American Psychiatric
    Association), 336
Disability
    Americans with Disabilities Act, definition of, 335–338
    United Nations, definition of, 346–347
Disability discrimination
    under American Disabilities Act, 335–344, 347–348
    global perspective on, 346–347
    legislation related to, 334–335
    management perspective on, 348–349
Discovery
    in arbitration, 54
    explanation of, 32–33, 35
    in mediation, 78
Discrimination. *See also specific forms of discrimination*
    age, 306–327
    based on sexual orientation or gender identity,
        246–247, 249
    color, 182–187
    disability, 334–349

employment, 213–215, 220
    establishing presumption of, 164–165
    global perspective on, 177–178, 186
    legislation to reduce, 162–163, 225–226
    management perspective on, 176–177
    national origin, 283–301
    pregnancy, 216–218
    racial, 185–199
    religious, 256–274
    sex, 213–215, 225–226, 233–235
    training to combat, 244–247
    types of illegal, 163–164
Disparate impact analysis
    under Age Discrimination in Employment Act,
        323–324
    explanation of, 163–164
Disparate impact cases
    defenses for, 164–165
    example of, 167–170, 195–197
    explanation of, 11, 164
    racial discrimination and, 194–197
Disparate treatment cases
    defenses for, 164
    due to religion, 264
    examples of, 165–167, 187–190
    explanation of, 163–164
Diversity
    elderly individuals and, 307
    within firms, 190–191
Diversity Best Practices (DBP), 176–177
Dolph, J. N., 254
Drug testing
    of government employees, 137
    privacy rights and, 15–16
    state laws related to, 14

E

EEOC v. Arabian American Oil Co., et al., 212, 294–297
EEOC v. Target Corp., 33, 37–40
EEOC v. Wal-Mart, 338–341
Elderly individuals. *See also* Age discrimination
    management perspective on, 325
    statistics related to, 307–308
Eleventh Amendment, 342
E-mail, 138–139
Employee Polygraph Protection Act of 1988, 12
Employees
    expatriate, 212
    independent contractors vs., 4–5
    legislation dealing with rights of, 3
    management treatment of, 3
    verification of work eligibility of, 287–288

Employee Termination Act, 14
Employers
    aliens authorized to work in U.S. for specific, 286
    aliens authorized to work in U.S. with no restrictions,
        285–286
    definitions of, 6, 9
    new employee verification of work eligibility for,
        287–288
Employer's Supplemental Tax Guide (Internal Revenue
        Service), 4–5
Employment at will doctrine
    application of, 93
    breach of implied contract and, 94, 98–99
    breach of implied covenant of good faith and, 107–108
    bullying and, 128–129
    common law and, 16–17, 90, 94, 110
    defamation and, 118, 120
    erosion of, 94
    as example of common law, 9
    exceptions to, 94–96
    explanation of, 90
    fraud and, 116
    global perspective and, 92–93, 127–128
    implied covenant of good faith and fair dealing and,
        94, 101–104, 107–108
    intentional infliction of emotional distress and,
        111–114
    intentional interference with contractual relations
        and, 122
    management perspective on, 101
    Model Employment Termination Act and, 125–126
    negligent infliction of emotional distress and, 114
    overview of, 90–91
    public policy exception and, 94–96
    state laws related to, 14, 91–92, 103–104
    tort claims and, 110–111
    tort of wrongful discharge and, 108, 111
    violation of statutory law and, 95, 109–110
Employment discrimination claims
    case example of, 37–40
    litigation of, 30–31
Employment Division v. Smith, 269
Employment law, 3
Employment Nondiscrimination Act (ENDA), 249
English-only rules
    EEOC settlement and, 293
    explanation of, 291–292
Equal Employment Opportunity Commission (EEOC)
    on activities that constitute religious practices,
        256–257
    English-only rules and, 291–293
    Eradicating Racism and Colorism from Employment
        (E-RACE) initiative, 198–199
    explanation of, 31, 40

facts about race and color discrimination and, 186–187
    filing claims with, 31, 175
    genetic testing and, 139–140
    guidance on Americans with Disabilities Act, 337
    mediation and, 74–75
    on national origin discrimination and immigration
        issues, 287–288, 290–298
    pregnancy discrimination and, 216–218
    racial categories defined by, 185
    racial discrimination claims with, 182–184
    on religious discrimination, 257–258, 269–272
    symposium on equal opportunity and corporate
        diversity, 176–177
Equal Employment Opportunity Commission (EEOC)
        litigation
    explanation of, 40, 42
    procedures for initiation of, 43
    statistics for, 41–42
Equal Pay Act of 1963 (EPA)
    explanation of, 226–227
    filing deadlines for claims under, 43
    record retention requirements of, 35
Equal Protection Clause, Fourteenth Amendment, 293
Eradicating Racism and Colorism from Employment
        (E-RACE) initiative (Equal Employment
        Opportunity Commission), 198–199
Espinoza v. Farad Manufacturing Co., 293
Ethical issues, 3
Europe, 177–178
European Union (EU)
    Data Protection Directive, 145–147
    opportunities for people with disabilities in, 346
    paternity leave in, 362
Evaluative mediation, 70
E visas, 289
Executive Order 11246, 34
Executive orders
    explanation of, 17
    as source of federal law, 7–9
Expatriate employees, 212

F

Fair employment practices agency (FEPA), 31
Fair Labor Standards Act (FLSA)
    explanation of, 10–11, 226
    record retention requirements of, 35
Family and Medical Leave Act (FMLA)
    case examples under, 357–359, 363–364
    disabled employees and, 360–361
    function of, 12–14, 216, 354–355
    notice requirements under, 355–356, 361–362
    provisions of, 355–356

2008 update of, 356
  workers' compensation and, 360
Faragher v. City of Boca Raton, 243–244
Federal Arbitration Act of 1925
  background of, 51
  explanation of, 56–57
  Supreme Court and, 56–57
Federal Employment Compensation Act, 359
Federal law, 7–9
Federal Mediation and Conciliation Service, 73–74
Federal Records Retention Chart, 34–35
The Federal Register, 17
Federal statutory laws, 10–12
Felix v. Manquez, 185
Fiancées, 285
First Amendment, 267
Folger, J. P., 69, 87
Fortino v. Quasar Co., 293
Fourteenth Amendment, Equal Protection Clause of, 293
Franklin, Benjamin, 136
Fraser, Edie, 177
Freedom of Information Act, 140
Freeman, J., 254
Fuller, B., 134

G

Gantt v. Sentry Insurance, 97–98
Geller, L. N., 143n
Gender
  glass ceiling and, 213–216, 220–221
  wage gap and, 227
Gender Equality Act (Norway), 363
Gender Equality and Decent Work: Good Practices at the Workplace (International Labor Organization), 362
Gender identity, 246–247
General Dynamics Land Systems, Inc. v. Dennis Cline et al., 309–312, 325
Genetic testing
  myths and facts about, 142–143
  privacy rights and, 139
Glass Ceiling Act of 1991, 213–214, 220–221
Glass Ceiling Commission, 214–215
Global perspective
  on age discrimination, 326–327
  on arbitration, 63
  on copyright law, 154
  on disability discrimination, 346–347
  on discrimination, 177–178, 186
  on employment, 92–93, 127
  on glass ceiling, 220–221
  on litigation, 47–48

on mediators involved in disputes transcending national borders, 84–85
  on paid leave and paternity leave, 362–363
  on privacy rights, 145–147
  on workplace bullying, 22–23
Green Tree Financial Corp. v. Bazzle, 58
Griggs v. Duke Power Co., 167–170, 194, 196, 323–324

H

Hamilton v. Caterpillar Inc., 309
Handicap, 346
Harassment
  bullying as, 22–23
  elements of, 46
  hostile environment, 239, 242–244, 247–249
  quid pro quo, 238
  religion-based, 270
  same-sex, 246–247
  sexual, 238–244, 247–249
  training to prevent, 244–247
Hatcher, C., 28
Hazen Paper Co. v. Biggins, 309, 311
H-1B visas, 288
Health information, 142
Health Insurance Portability and Accountability Act of 1996 (HIPAA), 142
Heilbroner, R. L., 28
Hennessey v. Coastal Eagle Point Oil Company, 14–15, 17
Hewlett-Packard, 140
Hewson, Marillyn A., 177
Hicks v. St. Mary's Honor Center, 194
Hill, Irene, 75
Hoar, Geo. F., 254
Hobbs-Wright, Emily, 50
Hoffman Plastic Compounds, Inc. v. National Labor Relations Board, 298–299
Hord v. Erim, 117–118
Hostile environment
  elements of, 46
  explanation of, 25–26
Hostile environment harassment
  cases on, 242–244, 247–249
  explanation of, 239
Human resource management
  administrative law and, 17
  case law and, 14–15
  changing role of, 18–19
  constitutional law and, 15–17
  executive orders and, 17
  federal statutes applicable to, 10–12
  laws governing, 7–9
  potential problems related to, 19–22

Human resource management—*Cont.*
 state statutory laws and, 13–14
 statutory laws in general and, 9–10
Hymowitz, Carol, 190, 204

I

I-9 Form, 287
Immigrants. *See also* Aliens; National origin
  discrimination
 explanation of, 284
 legislation pertaining to, 283–284
 overview of, 282
 terms related to, 284–287
Immigration and Nationality Act of 1952 (INA), 283, 297
Immigration Reform and Control Act of 1986
  (IRCA), 283
 amendments in 1991 to, 12
 employer requirements under, 287–288
 function of, 283, 290
 record retention requirements of, 35
Implied contract, breach of, 94, 98–99
Implied covenant of good faith and fair dealing, 94,
  101–104, 107–108
Independent contractors, 4–5
In Re Johnny Luna, Relator, 58–60
Intellectual property, 7
Intellectual property law, 149–150
International Center for Dispute Resolution, 60
International Chamber of Commerce (ICC), 63
International Court of Arbitration, 63
International Labor Organization (ILO), 346, 362
International Research Project on Job Retention and Return
  to Work Strategies for Disabled Workers (1998), 346
Internet use, 139
Interrogatories, 33
Ionnides, M., 304
Ireland, 220–221
Irish Business and Employers Confederation (IBEC), 220

J

Japan, 347
Johnson, Lyndon B., 162, 181
Johnson, Michael W., 254
Joint and several liability, 123
Jury trial, 36, 213

K

Kee, J., 352
Kevin A. Moore v. United Parcel Service, Inc., 192–194

Kitchen, P. J., 28
Kmart Corporation v. Ponsock, 101
Kovach, K. A., 254

L

Labor-Management Relations Act, 73
Labor unions, 11
Lamorte Burns & Co., Inc. v. Walters et al., 148–149
Lawrence M. Cleary v. American Airlines, Inc., 101
Lebrun, P. C., 304
Legalized aliens, 285
Legislation. *See also specific legislation*
 employee-rights, 3
 national origin discrimination, 283–284
 to reduce discrimination, 162–163, 225–226
 unintended consequences of, 226
Legislative history, 163
Lemley, G., 159
Litigation
 adversarial nature of, 31–32
 alternatives to, 51–52
 appellate review and, 36–37
 discovery and, 32–33, 35
 EEOC, 40–43
 of employment discrimination claims, 30–31
 federal records retention chart and, 34–35
 global perspective on, 47–48
 jury and, 36
 management errors leading to, 44–47
 public nature of, 36
 rules and procedures governing, 32
Lockheed Martin, 183–184
Lovell v. Western Nat'l Life Ins. Co., 108
L visas, 289

M

Macdonald, J. E., 134
Mackie, K., 88
Management perspective
 on action inquiry communications, 82–83
 on age discrimination, 325
 on antidiscrimination and antiharassment training,
  244–247
 on changing role of human resource management,
  18–19
 on disabled employees, 348–349
 on employee leave under Family and Medical Leave
  Act, 361–362
 on employment at will doctrine, 101, 128
 on English-only rules, 293

on equal opportunity and diversity, 176–177
on eradicating, 198–199
on genetic testing, 142–143
on litigation, 44–47
on religious discrimination, 269–272
on subjective decision making, 211–212
on trust, 61–62
Mandatory arbitration, 53
Mandatory contractual arbitration, 53
Mann v. Frank, U.S. Postal Service, 261–264
Mathis v. Phillips Chevrolet, 321–323
McCarthy, P., 28
McClain, P. D., 204
McClure v. The Salvation Army, 267–268
McDonnell Douglas Corp. v. Green, 164–165, 290,
    312–315, 339
McNamee, Elizabeth J., 33, 50
Mediation
    appeals to, 79
    arbitration vs., 69
    benefits of, 70–71
    in disputes transcending national borders, 84–85
    drawbacks of, 71–72
    employer considerations regarding, 76–79
    Equal Employment Opportunity Commission and,
        74–75
    evaluative, 70
    examples of successful, 72–73
    explanation of, 68–69
    internal, 71, 75
    within legal framework, 81–82
    National Labor Relations Board and, 73–74
    ordinary, 69
    outcomes of, 76–79
    sample ground rules agreement for, 77
    shadow, 70
    transformative, 69–70
Mediators
    action inquiry communication use by, 82–83
    background of, 68
    in disputes transcending national borders, 84–85
    external, 76, 78
    internal, 71, 76–77
    role of, 76
    selection of, 76, 78
Medical testing, 21–22
Meritor Savings Bank v. Vonson, 239–242
Mexico, 154, 300–301
Michaus, M., 160
Millspaugh, P. E., 254
Ministerial exception, 265
Mino v. Clio School District, 119–120
Mitsubishi Motors v. Soler Chrysler, 58
Model Electronic Privacy Act, 140

Model Employment Termination Act (META),
    125–126
Model Uniform Mediation Act (1999), 81–82
Moore, Kenny, 19
Moore v. UPS, 194
Muhl, C. J., 135

N

National Conference of Commissioners on Uniform State
    Laws (NCCUSL), 14, 81, 125
National Defense Authorization Act (NDAA), 356
National Labor Relations Act (NLRA), 10
National Labor Relations Board (NLRB), 73–74
National of the U.S., 284
National origin discrimination. *See also* Aliens;
    Immigrants
    citizenship and, 293–294
    Civil Rights Act of 1964 and, 294–297
    English-only rules and, 291–293
    legislation pertaining to, 283–284
    meaning of, 290–291
    prima facie case of, 289–290
National Workrights Institute, 142
Nelson, T. C., 332
Neuhauser, Maxine, 30, 47n, 49–50
New Lanark Mills, 2
New Zealand, 22–23, 26, 28
Nicosia v. Wakefern Food Corporation, 99–100
Nonbinding arbitration, 53
Noncompete agreements, 147
Nonimmigrants, 284
*Norman-Bloodsaw et al. v. Lawrence Berkeley Laboratory
    et al.,* 144n
North Korea, 346
Norway, 128, 363
NU-Look Design, Inc. v. Commissioner of Internal Revenue,
    12–13

O

Occupational Safety and Health Act, 15
O'Connor, Sandra Day, 205
O'Connor v. Consolidated Coin Caterers Corporation,
    312–315
Older Workers Benefit Protection Act of 1990 (OWBPA),
    325–326
Oncale v. Sundowner Offshore Services, 247–248
Ordinary mediation, 69
Osborn v. University Med. Assocs. of Med. Univ. of S.C.,
    116–117

P

Pacificare Health Systems v. Book, 58
Paid leave, 362–363
Panlilio v. Dallas Independent School District,
    289–290
Parental leave, 13–14
Patents, 149–150
Paternity leave, 362–363
Patriot Act, 141
Patterson v. McLean Credit Union, 166
Performance appraisal systems, 20–21
Performance evaluation, 45–46
Permanent residents, 284–285
Personal development training, 256–257
Pfeffer, J., 135
Polygraph Protection Act, 13
Polygraph tests, 13
Precedent, 14
Pregnancy discrimination
    case dealing with, 218–220
    Equal Employment Opportunity Commission
        and, 218
    legislation related to, 216
    statistics on charges of, 216–217
Pregnancy Discrimination Act of 1978, 11, 162, 216
Price Waterhouse v. Hopkins, 21, 235–237
Prima facie cases
    on age discrimination, 312–315
    explanation of, 164
    of national origin discrimination, 289–290
    of religious discrimination, 264
    of sex discrimination, 234–235
    shifting burdens and, 164–165
Privacy rights
    camera phones and, 139–140
    constitutional law and, 15
    e-mail and, 138–139
    in European Union, 145–147
    genetic testing and, 142–144
    Health Insurance Portability and Accountability Act
        and, 142
    Internet use and, 139
    management issues related to, 140–141
    in public sector vs. private sector, 137–138
Private sector, privacy rights in, 137–138
The Promise of Mediation (Bush & Folger), 69
Promissory estoppel, 17
Public function doctrine, 16
Public policy exception, 94–96
Public sector
    privacy rights in, 137–138
    religious discrimination in, 269
Punitive damages, 55

Q

Quid pro quo, 25, 238
Quid pro quo harassment, 238

R

Race, 184–185
Race Relations Act of 1976, 186
Racial discrimination. *See also* Discrimination
    affirmative action and, 197–198
    disparate impact and, 194–197
    disparate treatment and harassment in cases of,
        191–194
    EEOC facts about, 186–187
    explanation of, 185
    management initiatives to eliminate, 198–199
Racketeer Influenced and Corrupt Organizations Act
    (RICO), 58
Ragsdale et al. v. Wolverine World Wide, Inc.,
    363–364
Raytheon Company v. Joel Hernandez, 343–345
Reasonable accommodation
    for individuals with disabilities, 337
    for religion, 257–258, 265–266, 271
Record keeping
    litigation and, 33
    requirements for, 34–35
Reddam v. Consumer Mortgage Corporation, 79–80
Refugee parolees, 285
Refugees, 285
Rehabilitation Act of 1973
    function of, 11, 334
    genetic screening and, 139
    record retention requirements of, 35
Relevant labor market, 164
Religion
    explanation of, 258
    reasonable accommodation for, 257–258, 265–266, 271
Religious discrimination
    analyzing cases on, 256–257
    cases on, 258–264
    EEOC claims of, 269–270
    global perspective on, 272–274
    management perspective on, 269–272
    ministerial exception and, 266
    personal attire and, 257
    prima facie case of, 264
    public sector, 269
    Workplace Religious Freedom Act and, 265–266
Religious organizations
    case example and, 267–268
    ministerial exception and, 266

Reporters Committee case, 140
Restatements, 149
Restraint of trade, 147–148
Restrictive covenants
    explanation of, 147
    policies against restraint of trade and, 147–148
Rich, K. F., 304
Rodriquez-Olvera vs. Salant Corporation, 300
Rodriquez vs. Sierra Western, 300

S

Safe Harbor program, 145–147
Same-sex harassment, 246–247
Sandnes, Håvard, 135
Santayana, George, 256
Schei, Kristine, 135
Schmidt, P. J., 48n, 50
Schoch v. Info USA, 55–56
Schon, D. A., 349, 352
Schwarz, J. L., 102n
Search and seizure, 137
Self-compelled defamation, 120
Service marks, 149–150
Sex discrimination. *See also* Harassment; Sexual
        harassment
    comparable worth theory and, 230–231
    disparate treatment and disparate impact and,
        233–234
    glass ceiling and, 213–215
    laws prohibiting, 225–226
    prima facie cases and, 234–235
Sexual harassment
    hostile environment, 239, 242–244, 247–249
    overview of, 238
    policies to combat, 184
    quid pro quo, 238
    Supreme Court and, 239–244, 247–249
    training to combat, 244–247
Sexual orientation, 246–247, 249
Shadow mediation, 70
Shaw, Robert Bruce, 61, 62n, 67
Shultz, L. Jackson, 304
Simens v. Ashcroft, 232–233
Simon v. Marvel Characters, 152–153
Singapore, 272–274
Smith, Robert M., 68, 87
Smith v. City of Jackson, Mississippi, 323–324
Snyder v. Medical Service Corporation of E. Wash.,
        114–115
Souder, Mark, 280
Spitzer, Eliot, 265
St. Mary's Honor Center et al. v. Melcin Hicks, 187–190

Staggie v. Idaho Falls Consol. Hosp., Inc., 111
State statutory laws, 13–14
Statute of limitations, 31
Statutory laws
    employment at will doctrine and violation of, 95,
        109–110
    explanation of, 9
    federal, 10–12
    as source of federal law, 7–8, 10
    state, 13–14
Stender v. Lucky Stores, Inc., 245
Stowe, C. R. B., 134
Strict liability, 238
Subchapter S, 13
Subjective decision making, 211–212
Sullivan, A. F., 134
Sullivan, L. L., 134
Summary judgment, 37
Summary jury trials, 36
Superville, D., 204
Supreme Court, U.S. *See also specific cases*
    affirmative action and, 198
    age discrimination and, 309–315
    arbitration and, 53, 56–58
    disability discrimination and, 341–345
    disparate impact and, 195–197, 323
    drug testing and, 137
    expatriate employees and, 212
    harassment and, 239–244, 247–249
    on immigration issues, 297–298
    pregnancy discrimination and, 220
    public function doctrine and, 16
    religious discrimination and, 266, 269
    wage discrimination and, 227
    work for hire principle and, 150

T

Tameny v. Atlantic Richfield Co., 96
Teamsters Local 856 et al. v. Priceless, LLC et al., 140
Technological advances, effects of, 20
Tellis v. Alaska Airlines, Inc., 358–359
Thornton, M., 28
Thorson v. Gemini, Inc., 356
Title VII (Civil Rights Act of 1964)
    affirmative action and, 170–175, 197
    bona fide occupational qualification under, 316–317
    disparate treatment and disparate impact cases and,
        163–170, 191–194
    Equal Pay Act and, 227
    expatriate employees and, 212
    explanation of, 11, 31, 34, 175
    extraterritorial application of, 294

Title VII (Civil Rights Act of 1964)—*Cont.*
   national origin discrimination and, 283–284,
      290, 293, 294, 297
   overview of, 162–163
   race and color discrimination and, 184, 186
Torbert, Bill, 82–83, 88
Tort allegations, 95, 110–111
Tort of wrongful discharge, 108, 111
Torts, 9
Toyota Motor Manufacturing v. Williams, 341–342
Trademarks, 149–150
Training
   antidiscrimination and antiharassment, 244–247
   for managers, 44
   personal development, 256–257
Transformative mediation, 69–70
Trans World Airlines, Inc. v. Hardison et al.,
   258–261
Trial by jury. *See* Jury trial
Trust, in employee-employer relationship, 61–62
Trust in the Balance (Shaw), 61–62
Trust territory residents, 285
Turner v. Texas Instruments, Inc., 290
Twomey, R. F., 28
Twomey, Teresa M., 87

U

Ulrich, David, 17, 25, 28
Ultra vires, 56
Undue hardship, 263, 337
United Kingdom, 326–327
U.S. Airways, Inc. v. Barnett, 342
U.S. citizen, 284
U.S. Patent Office, 155
Universal agreements to mediate (UAM), 75
Unreasonable search and seizure, 15
USA Patriot Act, 141

V

Vest, G. G., 254
Victorelli v. Shadyside Hospital, 357–358
Vietnam-Era Veteran's Readjustment Act of 1974, 35

Visas, 288–289
Voluntary arbitration, 53
Voluntary departure, 285

W

Wal-Mart Stores, Inc. v. Lois A. Canchola, 111–114
Walsh, D. J., 102n
Washington County v. Gunther, 227
Watlow Electric Manufacturing Co., 293
Watson v. Fort Worth Bank & Trust, 195–197, 208, 211–212
Western Air Lines, Inc. v. Criswell, 317–320, 325
Whistleblower protection statutes, 109–110
William Failla v. City of Passaic et al., 347–348
Witte, G., 304
Women, 213–216. *See also* Gender; Sex discrimination
Woolley v. Hoffmann-La Roche, 99–100
Worker Adjustment and Retraining Notification Act of
   1988 (WARN), 12
Workers' compensation, 359–360
Work for hire, 150
Workplace bullying
   claims regarding, 128–129
   global perspective on, 22–23
Workplace Religious Freedom Act, 265–266
Wrongful discharge
   common law and case related to, 16
   management perspective on, 128
   performance appraisal systems and allegations of,
      20–21
   public policy exception and, 95–96
Wrongful Discharge from Employment Act of 1987
   (Montana), 91

Y

Younger, Evelle, 33

Z

Zimmerman v. Direct Federal Credit Union and Breslin,
   122–125
Zulkie, P., 304